COSMIC HEALING

*A Spiritual Journey
with Aaron and John of God*

Barbara Brodsky

*A você a mensagem de amor da casa de
Dom Inácio desejando que os benfeitores
... ... ilumine e ampare.*

João Teixeira de Faria
PRESIDENTE DA CASA DE DOM INÁCIO

North Atlantic Books
Berkeley, California

Published by
North Atlantic Books
P.O. Box 12327
Berkeley, California 94712

Cover photo ©iStockphoto.com/pailoolom
Cover and book design by Suzanne Albertson
Printed in the United States of America

Cosmic Healing: A Spiritual Journey with Aaron and John of God is sponsored by the Society for the Study of Native Arts and Sciences, a nonprofit educational corporation whose goals are to develop an educational and cross-cultural perspective linking various scientific, social, and artistic fields; to nurture a holistic view of arts, sciences, humanities, and healing; and to publish and distribute literature on the relationship of mind, body, and nature.

North Atlantic Books' publications are available through most bookstores. For further information, visit our website at www.northatlanticbooks.com or call 800-733-3000.

Library of Congress Cataloging-in-Publication Data

Brodsky, Barbara.
    Cosmic healing : a spiritual journey with Aaron and John of God / by Barbara Brodsky and Aaron.
        p. cm.
    Summary: "With the onset of sudden profound deafness at the age of 29, Barbara Brodsky set out on a path to understand the nature of illness and healing, examining the interrelationship of mind and body and our capacity to transcend limitation. Asking the questions What is healing? Who and what heals? Why do some people heal while others do not? she discusses karma and free will, our choices not to heal and to hold onto old limits and distortions"—Provided by publisher.
    ISBN 978-1-55643-966-7
    1. Brodsky, Barbara. 2. Spiritual healing and spiritualism. 3. Faria, João Teixeira da, 1942– 4. Spiritual healing and spiritualism—Brazil. I. Aaron (Spirit) II. Title.
    BF1275.F3.B76 2011
    294.3'431—dc22
                                            2010052305

2 3 4 5 6 7 8 9 UNITED 17 16 15 14 13
Printed on recycled paper

Dedicated to:

Aaron and the Entities
of the Casa de Dom Inácio
in Abadiânia, Brazil,
with gratitude for the guidance, healing, and wisdom
that you have brought into my life and into the lives of all
who come into contact with these teachings

to:
João Teixeira de Faria,
in gratitude for his life's work as a medium for Love

and to:
Neem Karoli Baba,
who has always walked by my side

Acknowledgments

NO WORK OF THIS SIZE can come from just one, or even a few, sources. Aaron and I would especially like to thank those whose energy, time, material resources, and love have made this sharing of his work possible.

Forehead to the floor and heart bursting with love, my most heartfelt gratitude and devotion to my guru, Neem Karoli Baba, without whose grace none of this work could have happened.

To Aaron, my soul mate and dearest, forever friend, I offer grateful appreciation for your loving and patient teaching, not just to me; but to all of us. You have taught me the meaning of unconditional love. Whenever I reach out, you are there; but in your wisdom you remind me that you won't do for me what I can do for myself. Your trust of me has taught me to trust myself. You truly lead me beyond a belief in limitations. Thank you, my friend, for your love through so many lifetimes and for being my teacher.

For the book, deep gratitude to Dan Muir and Lalita Doke, who have supported this work from the start and given countless hours to reading and rereading the manuscript. Dan's clear vision is very evident throughout the book. Their editing and suggestions have brought the book from a rough stage to what you now hold in your hands. Aaron and I appreciate both of them for their persistent requests for consistency in phrasings and word choices, and for their willingness to challenge us when text felt unclear. Their skill, sensitivity, and personal knowledge of the Casa were also vital to preparing the final book.

Much gratitude to João Teixeira de Faria for modeling true mediumship, grounded in love, and for his selfless service. Gratitude to the Casa Entities who have so deeply touched my life and the lives of millions of people.

Deep appreciation is given also to Heather Cumming for serving as my initial Casa guide and for sharing her in-depth knowledge of the Casa.

Loving gratitude is sent to Janice Keller for endless volunteer hours of transcribing Aaron's spoken words for almost twenty years; our archives contain thousands of pages that she has lovingly transcribed.

And loving thanks are given to Peg Tappe, who listened and typed while Aaron spoke to me and to her, as he filled in gaps in the material for this book. Appreciation is offered to the numerous readers whose thoughts and sharp eyes helped the book along its way.

Deep thanks to two dear friends and mediums who have helped me deepen in and trust my own mediumship through the years, Carla Rueckert and Judith Coates.

I hold deep gratitude for the time and energy given by Ajahn Thanasanti as we discussed and clarified fine points of karma; and am deeply grateful to Jim Marion for our deep, lengthy, and extraordinarily helpful discussions of consciousness.

A deep bow to all the practitioners of Dharma who have opened the path for me: to my dear friend John Orr, who has encouraged me in the dharma since the day we met over twenty years ago, and who has given me the courage to trust my path; to my loved dharma sisters, Haju Sunim and Aura Glaser, for the monthly dharma we have shared for two decades. Your support has nourished and enriched my life and clarified the Path. I also bow deeply to the many people of our Deep Spring Sangha, fellow teachers and students all, for all that you have taught to me.

Appreciation to all those who have explored healing and consciousness before me; thereby opening the path so that I could find the courage to follow.

Special thanks to my publisher, Richard Grossinger, and to all the people with whom I worked at North Atlantic Books, for believing in this book. And special thanks to my agent, Jenny Arch, who believed in the book and whose hours of work helped bring it into a clear form.

This book exists in part because of the patience and encouragement of my beloved husband of over forty years, Hal Rothbart, who unselfishly lost me to endless hours of work. And thanks to our sons, Michael, Davy, and Peter Rothbart, whose courage to walk their own paths has been a constant inspiration.

I can never repay the debt to my loving parents and brother, from whom I first learned love and kindness in this incarnation. They are the ones who awakened within me the desire to serve others and the curiosity and courage to walk this path.

Thank you to those who shared their healing stories with me and permitted them to be used in the book.

Thanks to the many fellow travelers whose questions and encouragement led me to write the book. I know you will find yourselves here.

Finally, thanks to all of you who have shared this healing journey with me spiritually, physically, or both. I am eternally grateful for the love and support that you have shown to me. You are forever in my heart.

Contents

Foreword

Barbara: Why are you here now?

Aaron: *You are ready. . . .*

B: Where do we start?

A: *You are suffering. Let us start there, to investigate together the causes of this suffering and find the end to it.*

B: Does it ever end?

A: *It does; yes, it certainly does.*

B: With death?

A: *Do you imagine that walking through a doorway will change your experience? No; suffering ends when you know who you are, when you realize the totality of being.*

The above passage, like this book, serves many purposes. Aaron's words are an eloquent and concise statement of the Buddha's four noble truths, a lyrical and profound dharma discourse. We can also find a brief introduction to the state between death and birth that Tibetans refer to as the *bardo*. Aaron's surprising perspective on death offers a measure of comfort about one of the greatest fears of humankind. But first and foremost, Aaron responds to Barbara's needs in the moment, with compassion and profound wisdom.

So begins an extraordinary spiritual friendship, and a remarkable journey of spiritual growth and physical healing. Barbara, a suburban housewife and sculptor, became suddenly and completely deaf shortly after the birth of her first child. Barbara evolved from an isolating pain and anger over her disability to recognition of deafness as a gift. Such a recognition gave her the light and space over the next several decades to reach for more healing, more peace. How can we embrace our pain, and use it as a tool for transforming our lives and the world? Barbara offers her answer, grounded deeply in the joy and difficulty of the human experience. Throughout the book, Barbara repeatedly demonstrates that she is ready to look more deeply, to see more clearly, and to receive greater and greater gifts. Barbara's journey is toward expanded consciousness and greater intimacy with the world. Happily, she takes us with her.

Aaron, who appears on the scene only after this process is well under way, is the loving discarnate spirit that becomes her constant guide and teacher. Although once human, Aaron has evolved beyond the need to incarnate again as a human. What is left is an unlimited being who deeply understands and embraces the human experience, but also fully embodies the complete potential all beings have to embody the divine source. As her spirit guide, Aaron has a unique perspective on Barbara's life. His loving and unlimited spiritual essence never leaves and is never apart from Barbara. Aaron is able to offer the kind word, the reminder, the reproach, or gentle course correction exactly when needed. Barbara has bathed in this love and guidance for decades. But we have been blessed also, because Barbara has kept detailed journals of her interactions with Aaron for all of that time.

Barbara and Aaron are two ends of a pole that connects heaven and Earth. Both ends are essential to the creative endeavor that is this book. Aaron's unlimited perspective, strong presence, and wise and compassionate speech would not be available if it were not for Barbara's clear desire to channel for the good of all. Barbara's life anchors Aaron's teaching in a compelling personal story of growth and healing. Aaron's wise teaching elevates Barbara's biography into something of profound value.

This story is the blossoming of years and lifetimes of sometimes joyful, sometimes challenging spiritual work. Healing through spiritual means is rightly called a miracle, but here the layer of mystery that the word miracle implies is removed, and we are able to see the higher laws that govern the process. Armed with this understanding of what is possible, we begin to believe that we can express into the world the deepest and highest yearnings of our hearts. Barbara's and Aaron's purpose in writing this book is to offer us a way to create within ourselves the conditions that will enable us to reach for a more complete healing, to release ourselves from the constraints of limiting beliefs, and to understand and demonstrate for ourselves what is possible. We can fully manifest the divine creator that is present within each of us. This is our birthright. It is possible for us to do what Barbara has done, and more. There are no limits.

Barbara's method of teaching and learning uses her life as an example. Everything she offers to you as truth, she has lived. She is by no means perfect—none of us are. Anger, fear, and a host of other negatively charged emotions arise again and again. Success and setbacks follow one another. Often the difference between success and setback is simply a shift in perspective or focus. A "success" might mask deeper healing, or conversely, a "setback" might be compassionately offering the lesson needed in that moment. Through it all, she has learned and recorded, and is now offering her experiences for your learning.

Aaron's method of teaching is a bit different. He knows, and more importantly embodies, his Divinity, our Divinity. Aaron is an unlimited being, consciously at one with the Intelligent Essence of the Universe. This Essence is not separate from you. It is intimately familiar with you and your situation right now, and can speak to you through the words in this book, giving you exactly what you need to know. This Intelligent Essence has temporarily adopted a personality, which prefers to be called Aaron, for your ease and convenience. So let Aaron speak to you. It can be an experience to remember.

When Barbara and Aaron teach, their styles knit together nicely. Barbara and her story are an anchor in the physical world, a focus of attention. Aaron plays the role of the wise and compassionate teacher. I can report that both of their methods have served me well. They can serve you as well, if you wish.

Barbara and Aaron offer a beautiful path to spiritual growth that draws from many different traditions. Barbara is a skilled and experienced teacher of Dharma and of Vipassana meditation from the

Theravadin Buddhist tradition. She is also a teacher and practitioner of nondual Pure Awareness. In this book we find that she has a surprisingly close relationship with Jesus and his tradition. She also is the disciple of a prominent Hindu guru, whom we meet several times. And, she drinks from the deep well of Brazilian Spiritism with John of God. All these single traditions are engaged in fully, with powerful results. But we also see how these practices work together synergistically. Corporeal and noncorporeal representatives from all these traditions work together to nurture Barbara's change and growth. The best of all these practices can help create a spiritual vessel to carry the sincere seeking individual through these times of promise and challenge into a higher consciousness and a new way of being.

Barbara's relationship with Aaron takes an extraordinary turn as they begin interacting with the entities of the Casa de Dom Inácio in Abadiânia, Brazil. John of God is a powerful healer, who is surrounded by many saints, angels and other highly evolved, helping spirits. Aaron develops a close working relationship with the Entities there, and explains the work of the Casa to Barbara. Aaron's unique position as Barbara's guide, and Barbara's unique position as a very clear channel for Aaron, allow John of God's mission to be expounded precisely. The result is a profound, yet rational explanation of healing from the spirit world into the human world through Aaron's understanding and voice. So this book can serve as a powerful and inspiring introduction to the Casa and its inner workings, as it chronicles the journey of one extraordinary woman through her own healing process.

When it comes time to teach and comment on Barbara's experience, Aaron and Barbara remain unfettered by ideology and, therefore, cast a wide net. No matter what your background, you likely will find something new. Closed minds, which are set in their beliefs and find no reason to change, may find Barbara's story not to their taste. This book is better read with a deep receptivity and willingness to investigate the witness of a dedicated spiritual seeker. Be assured that Barbara and Aaron's intent here is to help you in your journey.

If you will, allow this book to seep inside of you. Beyond these words, an infinitely loving and caring Presence is attempting to reach you in a deeper way, because it loves you and wants you to learn how to become all that a human being can be. Read this book with an open heart and allow that Presence to transform you. Read also with an open mind because beliefs that cannot change will block your ability to be aware of this unlimited Presence. If you feel nothing happening, do not worry. Know that you are not reading these words by accident, even if that seems to be the case right now. Read Barbara's story as a journey of discovery into an unknown country. Please take away from there what you find to be valuable, and lighten your load by putting down the rest. Perhaps at a later time, you may encounter Barbara and Aaron again, and then you might be ready to take more from them.

Barbara and Aaron are engaged in a fundamentally creative act. They, through their lives and actions, make something new that better reflects the perfection that the Universe wishes us to express. This book is both a record of that creative act, and a creation all its own. A great though indirect part of Barbara's healing is through her writing, and your reading of this book. If one finds healing, all benefit, because we are not separate. Barbara, Aaron, the Entities of the Casa, you, and all others associated with this book have woven themselves into a grand tapestry. Each thread contributes to the whole, yet is distinct. Each thread adds its own color and strength to the final product.

If it hasn't become clear already, let me say that it has been an honor, a deep source of learning, and humbling to be a part of this process. It gives me great joy to see this project come to fruition, and in a small way, to help offer the words and sense of Presence that have nurtured my own spiritual growth for several years now. I am deeply blessed, and my greatest hope is that that blessing will be passed on to you.

Like Aaron's first words to Barbara, this book can be read successfully on many levels. One can read it as an adventure story, or as a gripping spiritual autobiography. It also can be read as spiritual teaching, as one way to find greater spiritual happiness and oneness. It can be read as an introduction to the extraordinary spiritual, emotional, and physical healing that can be found in central Brazil at the Casa de Dom Inácio. Or you might feel the Divine speaking to you directly through these words. Although any one of these levels makes *Cosmic Healing* worth reading, I hope for you that you might find all of these meanings and more. Barbara and Aaron are like servants who have come to bring you spiritual food. They know, as I do, that what they offer is nourishing, but you are free to ingest as much or as little of their banquet as you wish. I would urge you to eat slowly, to chew thoroughly, to enjoy the taste, and to save the leftovers so that you might be nourished again later.

Dan Muir
March 2010

Introduction

IN HER BOOK, *Extraordinary Knowing,*[1] Dr. Elizabeth Lloyd Mayer, a well-respected psychoanalyst, speaks about coming to know something in a nontraditional way and the discomfort she felt when telling others of the experience. When she gathered a group of other professionals to talk about such experiences at a meeting of the American Psychoanalytic Association, it turned out that most of them had had similar events. Despite reporting that their experiences had touched them deeply, they had not spoken to others about their knowing.

She says, "We suffer from an underlying cultural disinclination for publicly acknowledging certain highly subjective, highly personal experiences." Our society debunks such experiences as delusional because they cannot be verified by current science. Yet each reader has had the experience of knowing who was on the other end of the line before picking up the phone, or of thinking of a friend not seen in years just minutes before meeting them on the street.

Mayer goes on to say, "What happens when you have an anomalous experience, but you're afraid to acknowledge it? If you admit to the experience, you run the risk of being disbelieved or thought crazy. It's a profoundly destructive conflict, one that stops us as a society from looking for ways to discover and develop new knowledge. And one that stops us as individuals from embracing our reality."

In 1989 I had just such an experience, the first of many that changed my life. This book tells the story as it unfolded. There are no tools of science to validate my experience. My validation comes from the positive changes in myself, and in those around me, who have participated in this wider reality. When I first opened to these experiences, I shared them with a very close friend who was a psychiatrist and teacher in a large university. He said to me, "Clinically, I'd have to call this a benign schizophrenic experience, but speaking personally, I've never heard you sounding more sane. I hope you'll keep exploring this path."

Medical science has powerful, but still limited tools for healing. What supports our wider healing, and what does "healing" mean? In this book I want to share with you my journey of healing, with the hope that it will open you to the healer, and the profound healing possible, from inside yourself.

Here is as accurate a portrayal as I am able to give, of my experiences during the thirty-seven years following the traumatic loss of my hearing and balance through a severe illness. I can tell this story with a certain sense of immediacy because of the journals I have kept in some detail over the entire time period. Some of the material in this book may seem implausible to the rational mind. Please realize that it seemed so to me, too, as I first experienced meeting my teacher Aaron, a discarnate spirit who once was human; but regardless of rationality, this has been my experience as accurately as I can describe it. Is it real? I can only offer Shakespeare's well-known lines, through Hamlet, "There are more things in heaven and earth, Horatio, than are dreamt of in your philosophy." Throughout the book I refer to Aaron and to other non-physical beings with the simple term, "spirit." We are all spirits; these spirits are simply intelligent beings without physical bodies.

The story told here first took place in my own home, as I experienced the beginnings of healing with Aaron's help. He speaks both to me and through me as I channel him for others. The story continues in Brazil, at the Casa de Dom Inácio, a center for healing run by João Teixeira de Faria, known as John of God.

It seems self-evident that the current Western medical model shapes people's beliefs about wellness and illness, and that these beliefs in turn affect physical healing. One of my goals in this book is to illumine, with Aaron's invaluable help, the deeper and sometimes hidden laws that govern spiritual healing. I also hope to explain a belief system that is both rational and consistent with these broader laws.

However, I do not claim that this belief system is the last word on the realities of spiritual healing. Any belief can only capture a small part of the larger truth that it tries to explain. Belief systems can and must change when new experiences need to be understood and assimilated. It helps to remain as flexible as possible. The belief system that underlies this book, developed over a period of more than thirty years, has facilitated my healing, yet continues to evolve. I present my latest and best thoughts on it to you in the hopes that it will support you in your healing journey. It is also my hope that the experiences in this book can contribute to an expansion and refinement of the current medical model. We must move away from treatment of purely physical disease, and toward a vision of wellness that incorporates the whole person.

A brief word seems warranted, about how more broadly accepted beliefs influence healing. High among the factors that govern health and healing is the relationship of negative thought and illness, and positive thought and health. Traditional Chinese medicine and Ayurvedic medicine have been treating a broad proportion of the world's population for thousands of years. Each has sophisticated and robust theoretical constructs that link thoughts and emotions to both physical well-being and illness. Western medicine and the scientific community also acknowledge the link between physical illness and the mental and emotional realms, albeit in a cruder and more general way. Specific emotions are seen as risk factors that increase the probability of contracting a particular disease.

The most broadly acknowledged link is the concept of stress, a physiological response to any change that increases blood pressure and heart rate, and releases cortisol and other stress hormones into the body, among other changes. Stress combined with negative thoughts or emotions can become negative stress or distress, a toxic physiological state. Negative stress causes or can exacerbate a host of common illnesses ranging from the annoying to the lethal.

Laughter, meditation, and release of identification with negative emotions can trigger the relaxation response, which counteracts the stress response. The relaxation response increases immune system function, normalizes blood pressure, and releases endorphins, the body's natural painkillers. Relaxation also helps one live longer. In short, negative emotions are associated with disease and illness, and positive emotions are associated with health and well-being.

Some final explanations. Occasionally I've changed names or places to preserve a person's privacy. Often I refer to God as male. I now experience God as androgynous, both male and female, having the characteristics of each, but not either specifically. I have left the discrepancy in part out of respect for the person and consciousness I was when I experienced these events, and in part because constantly using "male/female," or alternating between the two is awkward. You are welcome to substitute "she" or "she/he" for "he" whenever necessary or desired. Don't let words get in the way. I have retained the sexes of the discarnate entities I have encountered because this is how they have presented themselves to me.

Throughout the book I use the term "spirit." One could substitute "discarnate entity," but that is an awkward phrasing. When I say, "I was guided by spirit," I am saying there was a sense of the presence of wise and loving discarnate entities who offered direct or indirect guidance. Occasionally I may be speaking of specific entities and use the capitalized "Spirit" to refer to them. We all, human and spirit, have energy patterns. Just as you might feel the energy of a loved one before he/she enters the room, and know that person is about to walk in, so we can experience and know spirit by its energy. Sometimes it is known; sometimes a stranger. One can still feel the love there.

As I lived this story, there was a lessening of identification with my body and mind. I still had to attend to body pain and thoughts, but ceased to think of them so much as mine. The reader will find the journal writing reflects this change, as "my vision improved" changed to "the vision improved," or "my mind was turbulent" became "the mind was turbulent." There is no disassociation here, just an increasingly healthy knowing that I am not the body or mind, though I am still responsible to them.

I have not attempted to organize this book as a completely chronological story. Scattered throughout are excerpts from my journals and from Aaron's words to me through the years. Please do not try to put it in order, or worry about what was said when. Aaron constantly reminds me that all time is simultaneous.

CHAPTER 1

Beginnings

HOT AIR WAFTS conflicting scents of flowers, dust, and cooking oils through the open window of the taxi. We bump down the main street of Abadiânia, a small town in central Brazil, dodging chickens, children flying homemade kites, and a flashy motorbike. It is February 2009. A grey cart horse walks unescorted toward the meadow. Babies play in dirt yards in front of simple brick houses. João Teixeira de Faria, affectionately called John of God, has his primary healing center where the pavement stops on one end of town. We head to the highway and the ninety-minute drive to Brasília, where a plane will take us back to the United States. The town fades into the distance but after six visits to João's center, the Casa de Dom Inácio, my heart carries this town with me everywhere.

Farms and rolling hills slide past. I slip into reflection. What have these trips meant to me? What is healing? My reasons for coming here revolve around my wish to hear again after thirty-seven years of deafness. In my visits here over the past seven years, I've seen miracles, people rising out of wheelchairs to walk, tumors disappearing, body tremors stilled, even a blind man who now can see perfectly in both eyes. My personal history here gives me a great hope for healing, yet I remain deaf in both ears. My journey has not always been easy or predictable. Before my second trip, I faced the terrifying and very real possibility of blindness in addition to my deafness. My vision has improved since then, but it remains weak.

The meaning of the word "healing" has changed for me as my understandings and realizations have grown. My teacher, Aaron, has said that we are perfect right now, just as we are, and that we are always moving toward a greater expression of that perfection in every aspect of our being. That's all well and good from his perspective, but here in this body, I want to experience that perfection now. I want to hear; I want to see well.

My healing journey began in earnest in 1972, six weeks after my first child was born. Over the course of two days, I lost my hearing. I was also violently dizzy with no sense of balance. The world reeled around me, and I couldn't move. Even the slightest turn of my head brought nauseous dizziness almost to the point of unconsciousness.

My doctors said that an unknown cause had constricted blood vessels and cut off the blood supply to the auditory nerves and those in the semicircular canal. The resulting lack of oxygen and nutrients killed the nerves, destroying my hearing and sense of balance. The medical community didn't really understand how or why this had happened, nor could they offer any real treatment. I refused hospitalization. I was nursing my infant son Michael, and didn't want to be separated from him. As I lay in my bed for many weeks, unable to move, unable to hear, unable even to read since my eyes could not focus without increased vertigo, Mike was my firmest contact with life. I needed that contact.

My husband Hal and I lived in Ann Arbor, Michigan, where we both had accepted jobs just after he had completed graduate school. We'd been married for four years and were living far away from our East Coast families and friends. At first my mother and then a nurse came to live with us for those first two months of illness, assisting with our physical needs. Hal found it very hard to accept my deafness and illness. He was already stressed with adjusting to a first child. I felt that with a husband who was torn up by these events and a new infant, the future was up to me. I had no choice but to learn to cope. It was a matter of survival for those I loved, and for myself.

As the dizziness healed, I was finally able to focus my eyes again, to sit up, and to look out a window or read a short note. However, I had no balance. I would have to learn to walk again. First, I had to learn to crawl—to the bathroom, to Mike's room to pick him up and feed him. It was humiliating to find myself traveling on hands and knees and I wasn't yet able to laugh about it. It was painful to feel the roughness of a wood floor against my skin. I learned to lower the side of the crib on hands and knees and lift my baby down to me, to care for him as I sat there on the floor. As I increased my mobility, the nurse left. I was determined to get my life back to the way it had been; there would be nothing except hearing that this illness would prevent me from doing.

I had become sick in early June. By the beginning of August I was crawling, then walking by hanging on to walls and furniture. I lurched awkwardly from one object to another, but determination propelled me onward. I'd been teaching sculpture at the University of Michigan and I had five weeks until the start of the fall semester. I promised myself that I was going to be able to walk into that classroom and teach.

I was able to keep that promise. I was still unsteady, but walked with the aid of a trained hearing dog. When balance felt insecure I could grasp his special collar for support. Mostly, his presence gave me confidence. It terrified me not to be able to hear sounds like approaching footsteps or a car. He was trained to let me know of such noises. My students were wonderful that year, also giving me the priceless gift of self-confidence. I had to change my teaching style because of my deafness, so more individual work took the place of class discussions. Someone brought a typewriter into the classroom to type questions. The class helped me learn how to control my voice level to reach everyone in the room. Returning students from previous semesters assured me that my new approach was better than before.

My husband and I tried to learn American Sign Language (ASL), but found it frustrating. ASL is a beautiful language but has a totally different structure than English, and in this time of trauma and change, we needed a way to use the language we already had. So we learned the fingerspelling alphabet and I learned to lip-read. People began to spell the first letter of each word to me as they spoke. This is the process we still use today.

Working in my studio the first year after the deafness came was very painful. I could no longer entertain myself by listening to records or the radio during long hours of sculpting. I had only silence and my own company, and that company was unbearable to me. While I didn't know what I was running from, or even that I was running, I knew that I didn't want too much time to think and feel. For the first nine months I brought poetry and songbooks into my studio and memorized their contents. I wasn't ready to face my anger.

I had begun to meditate as a teenager when I attended Quaker Meetings, and had kept it up through the years. Slowly the practice had shifted to an awareness of the breath, and to being present with each body sensation and thought as they arose and passed away. Such focus took me to a place of calm and peace in the midst of chaos and confusion. It allowed me to experience the flow of body sensations and thoughts as arising out of conditions* and not as an essential part of the deeper self. It brought me joy. But there was still an element of control in it, holding on to pleasant experiences and avoiding the unpleasant. Now meditation had become difficult; I didn't want to be in the moments that were so painful.

One day a student asked me how I passed the time in my studio when I was polishing bronze sculpture or grinding seams; work that didn't need my full mental attention. I was embarrassed to talk about the poetry and songs, and made a commitment to stop the memo-

---

*Conditions: A basic premise of Buddhist thought is that our everyday world arises out of conditions. If the conditions are present a thing will arise. For example, if there is fertile soil, rain, sun, and a seed, a plant will grow. If any of those conditions are not present, the plant will cease to exist.

rizations and to stay more present. It was an agonizing effort. I feared using the quiet hours in my studio to examine my feelings. How do we open our hearts to our greatest pain? I began by returning my attention to the breath every time it wandered into the myriad stories of "poor me," "it's not fair," or "what will happen to me?"[1]

During the time in my sculpture studio, I watched the boredom that came with tasks like polishing or grinding seams, and noticed how much I wanted escape in those long hours of work. Then I saw that I wasn't bored while walking in the woods or sitting in silence. As I explored boredom, I understood that it was a state that arose because I was separating from myself and my feelings. With intimacy there was no boredom, but I could not remain intimate with the pain and anger.

I saw a therapist for a while. We both agreed that grieving for my hearing was appropriate, and that I was coping well. I convinced myself and those around me that I was happy, and on one level that was true. I had three beautiful children, fulfilling work in my studio, caring friends, and a husband who I knew loved me, despite his outward anger at my deafness. I learned which situations I couldn't handle and adjusted to avoid them. One-on-one communication was okay. Being with a group was hard. No problem; I avoided groups. I was raised in a Jewish home, but I had been a Quaker for many years. I stopped attending Meeting for Worship, and began a daily silent meditation practice at home instead. I found replacement activities for the few physical things I really couldn't do, like riding a bike or ice-skating. People kept telling me how well I was coping. I even took my children to Suzuki music classes and helped teach them to play instruments that I could not hear. I learned to tune their cellos by the vibrational feel, and became the "tuning mom" for their whole class. I simply buried the occasional moment of self-pity. It wasn't useful, I told myself. *Just stop feeling sorry for yourself and get on with what has to be done.*

Yet I felt a growing tightness within me. I snapped at people a lot. My life had lost its spiritual center and meditation had become a sterile routine. Somewhere along the way I gained sixty pounds. While my life continued smoothly on the surface, I had to admit to myself that something was wrong.

In 1986 I was working as an overnight volunteer at Ann Arbor Friends Meeting House, which was hosting a homeless shelter for several weeks. I had spent a few hours walking around the room talking to the men who had come to sleep there, soaking up small bits of their stories and pain that had been written down for me. Finally, the lights were turned out and the men went to sleep on their mattresses. I returned to my sleeping bag in the kitchen, where I tossed restlessly. A feeling of deep inner turmoil puzzled me, so I sat up and began to meditate.

At some point I found myself lifted high above the room, looking down on my body and the sleeping men. I floated and observed, connected to my body by a slender cord of light and yet free to move effortlessly. Everything below and around me, both the men on the mattresses and what I sensed as myself, radiated silvery light. Beneath the shells of bodies and individuated selves, our shared essence permeated everything. I recognized my oneness with everyone in the room. In that moment I knew beyond doubt that nothing is separate and that everything has the same divine core. This realization conflicted sharply with the nightmare of my daily experiences. When I returned to normal consciousness an hour later, I found myself trembling, but very peaceful. I had no idea what had happened. Where had I been? The only drug I'd ever used was marijuana and that only rarely and long ago; I knew I had not hallucinated and it didn't feel like wild imagination. How could anyone imagine that experience? I suppose I should have been frightened, but the insights during the change of consciousness had been so profound that there was no fear.

This experience showed me how I had indulged in the illusion of separation for protection and that while this separateness was real on one level, ultimately there had never been and never could be separation. The illusion was natural, part of the human experience. To refuse to know it as illusion, but rather to take it as ultimate reality was a defense that had become a habit. Perhaps this illusion of separation was no longer necessary. What held it in place? This was the first time I consciously realized that there was a choice.

In the weeks that followed, I began to read everything relevant to that experience that I could find. Where had I been? Soon I stumbled upon information about astral projection, the temporary projection of the conscious mind out of the physical body and into the subtle space known as the astral plane. While the description wasn't identical to what I'd experienced, it was similar enough to allow me to identify this state of consciousness. I felt reassured that I was not losing my mind, but instead gaining a new way of understanding.

Since conversation was still difficult, and classes of any kind seemed impossible, I began to read. For about a year, I read all the basic literature on psychic phenomena, plus volumes on traditional religious paths to a goal that I still couldn't define. I found myself pulled especially to the writings of various Eastern religions. The teachings about reincarnation and karma seemed to contain a key. I had touched on these ideas years before, and knew that they made sense to me, but regarded them with an "I'm busy; come back later" attitude. Suddenly, it was later than I'd realized, and time to start doing some serious work. I was especially drawn to *A Still Forest Pool*,[2] a book about a Thai Buddhist teacher, Achaan Chah. His writing literally fell into my hands from a shelf during a visit to a bookstore. The ideas felt deeply familiar, yet just out of reach.

At the same time, I began to consider deeper spiritual questions, and with a greater understanding than in years past: Why had my deafness occurred? Was God involved? Was it just chance? I had not accepted reincarnation completely yet, but I struggled with the possible implications. If there were past lives, did experiences from those lives affect this one? Was my deafness a result of my own actions and choices in some way; and if so, how? If reincarnation was real and I was just passing through this life, who was I? Why was I here? And what was astral projection? Where had I been while in that out-of-body state? I'd never considered such questions before.

As a child I found joy in solitude, and often sat quietly by a neighborhood pond in the woods, where I experienced deep states of what I did not yet know as meditation. In that quiet space I found myself wrapped in light and with a profound experience of peace. Here I met my guru on an inner plane and found many questions about the human experience were answered wisely. As a preteen girl I had spent hours in his presence. Yet in adult years I'd believed those early memories of spirit-plane friends and of nonordinary consciousness experiences to be childish imagination. The guru, whom I called "the man in the clouds" as a child, and who was the essence of love, was also relegated to the realm of childhood fantasy.

Now my adult experience shouted to me that the Earth plane was only one small part of reality. I began to get a clearer sense of who and what I was. I was on a journey and wanted to go "home," wherever that was. It was the place of love where I had rested in meditation as a child; now it seemed out of reach.

Another transformative experience helped me to grapple with these questions. Traveling alone one late October, about fifteen years after losing my hearing, I had stopped at a state park in Ohio. In the dark and isolated campground, I found myself terrified of wild animals, an old childhood fear. Intellectually I knew that an actual attack was as impossible here as it had been in my suburban childhood neighborhood. I set up my tent, collected a huge pile of wood, built a bonfire, and sat with that blazing light and my own fierce apprehension in the clear, moonlit night. After a while one large cloud appeared, hovered over me, and let loose a torrent of rain that doused the fire, soaked my wood, and passed. By my car's headlights I tried to light my Coleman lantern. I had just gotten the flame going when a second cloud appeared, with another torrent, which soaked the lantern thoroughly. I hurried to my tent for shelter and reached for the flashlight with new batteries. No light.

By this time I suspected I was missing a message. The second storm passed quickly and I had the wisdom to sit at the dark fire pit, meditate, and ask what I needed to know. Almost immediately I saw an image of a Native American woman with an infant, surrounded by a circle of wolves. One tore the child from the woman's arms and began to devour it as the pack turned on the mother. I knew she was part of me. It didn't seem to matter if she was a direct karmic ancestor or a representative of my more general human heritage—of all those who had gone before and suffered terrible trauma. Tears streamed down my face as I sat there in the dark, holding that woman in my heart and offering forgiveness to the wolves. Eventually the scene passed and I opened my eyes to the night sky, now pinpointed with stars. I felt no more need for light. All fear of wild animals was gone, and I experienced the darkness as friendly and lovely. At that point, I really began to accept the possibility that some aspect of this mind/body/spirit had lived before.

Since that day, I have experienced fragments of many past lives. When I encounter a blockage to learning or some habitual unskillful behavior, I always ask what past life might relate to this issue and then begin to meditate. Sometimes the images don't come for a few days, but eventually I see them in the same way I saw the Native American woman. They may come in my daily meditation, in dreams, or through certain kinds of energywork and bodywork. Are they real? I believe so, but the only answer I can give a skeptic is that the images come from somewhere and my work with them is always healing in the end.

I have seen how the unresolved karma, or habitual patterns of a lifetime, is picked up in a later one, just as the unskillful patterns in this present life are repeated and reinforced if we don't pay attention to them. It's like ignoring a leak in the bathroom. Eventually the surrounding wood will rot. Finally a floor or wall may collapse. While several conditions contributed to the collapse, the factor that was in my control—my inattention to the leak—was clearly the root cause. When working with past lives, I can easily see the flow from one situation to another. I can also see a habit arising—the inertia of not attending to something, or of not wanting to blame someone else. If I can skillfully attend to the unwholesome habit in this lifetime, doing so is similar to fixing the leak in the bathroom. Both remove the cause of any further damage.

These unattended patterns from the past, whether in one or many lifetimes, hold us to our unskillful patterns in the present. Eventually they need attention. When they are resolved, we find new freedom. It is sufficient to see these patterns in the present; we don't have to see past lives. But often it is easier to work with the pain and confusion of the karmic ancestor than with our present pain and confusion, because we invariably have a healthy dose of time and distance between their experiences and our own difficulties.

Although I have seen many past lives, a few seemed most relevant to the issues of this lifetime. I have learned that we do not need to go into every lifetime to heal an issue; we just need to investigate the issue and heal it in one lifetime, even this one. That resolves it in all other lives. Throughout this book, there are several past lives that I'll speak of in depth to facilitate the understanding of how healing transpired.

Many other pathways in addition to past-life awareness led to my healing. As meditation deepened, I felt myself opening up and getting more involved with people. Increasingly, I was able to experience brief exclusions from conversations and to know it was just the result of not being able to hear. My mind stopped holding the belief that I was purposely excluded. Tension about deafness gradually began to fade.

I also learned more about my anger at my deafness and at Hal. I thought I had made friends with my own anger and the anger of others. Now I began to realize that I still judged my own anger and other heavy emotions as "bad." *Self-pity won't help you cope,* I'd tell myself. *It's not productive. Get rid of it.* When I couldn't release these emotions, I isolated myself as if fearing that they would poison others. When I wasn't feeling kind and loving I felt bad and separate; unlovable to myself, to others, and to God. The lines of a beloved old song ran through my head, "When you're not feeling holy, your loneliness says that you've sinned."[3] It was exactly like that.

On the other hand, I began to truly understand the gift of my deafness; all that it had taught me, and how it had helped me to grow.

Deafness had given me this illusion of separation as a priceless opportunity, albeit a painful one, to explore difficult emotions and my relationship to them. With these understandings, my fear softened. I fought less against my feelings of separation and became ready to explore them.

This is where I was in 1987 when a friend recommended I read *A Gradual Awakening* by Stephen Levine.[4] Never has a book spoken to me so clearly. It reminded me of things I already knew at profound levels of my being, opening my conscious mind to the wisdom of my soul. The essence of us all is love, yet there was so much self-judgment. I began to ask after these judgments, "Is that so?" *I'm bad* or *I shouldn't* were frequent recipients of this question. I saw how often such an inner voice was just habit and that I didn't have to believe such thoughts just because they entered the mind. My daily meditation practice had shifted through the years, even before the deafness, from devotion and reflection to an intuitive presence with the breath and whatever else was predominant in my experience. I had tried to articulate this practice numerous times to myself and to friends, but without success. This book gave me that articulation and led to more trust of my own inner direction. More importantly, it led me to open my heart somewhat to painful experiences, and to not use meditation to control any experience. It reminded me to do more formal practice of lovingkindness and forgiveness meditation, for myself and for others.

The learning I began was difficult, but very precious to me. I understood my deafness even more deeply as a gift, and no longer felt as tight and afraid. I was discovering a deeper inner peace than I'd ever dreamed existed. And yet my heart was still closed by bitterness at the isolation my deafness seemed to impose. I saw myself as living behind glass walls, in a prison that I didn't know I was creating. The insights of that autumn were not enough to take me past the terrible pain of feeling cut off from human discourse. In fact, these greater insights may have intensified my distress. I felt stuck in anger and confusion.

In January of 1989, I prayed for help. Several weeks earlier, I had started to use a question-and-answer format in my daily journal as a way of deeper communication with myself. As the weeks passed following that prayer, I began to notice that in the question-answer format, the dialogue was beginning to present a new perspective, inviting me to open myself to unfamiliar ideas and ways of thinking.

One snowy evening I sat in the living room with my family, resting on the floor with my journal, writing in front of a blazing fire.

Journal, January 19, 1989

Question: What do I need to talk about? I don't know.

Answer: Stop and meditate for a few minutes or just write what comes.

Q: Let's try that. Intuitive writing. I don't know where to start. ... anger, pain, hope, peace ... can, can't, hate, love, resent, forgive ... I see myself at a balance point. I have hate and love, anger and peace within me. I'm aware enough to know that anger and hate are poisonous, but I don't yet know what to do about them. I don't want to suppress them. I have to be open with myself and accept that these feelings are a part of me, too. Yet dwelling on them only enhances them.

A: Can you express your pain and anger more? Pour it out.

I did this, expressing for several paragraphs my intense anger toward Hal for all the pain of his rage at my deafness. Meanwhile, Hal sat across the room, engaged in a book.

Q: Do I hate Hal or his anger?

A: His anger.

Q: His anger isn't him, any more than mine is me.

A: That's why I'm still with him. I love Hal; I hate his anger.

And then the "answer" writing changed from "I" and "me" to "you." At first I didn't notice the shift. It was not made consciously.

A: You can't control his anger.

Q: I hate that he won't learn.

A: You can't control that either. Can you accept him angry and unlearning? Express the anger and then try to forgive him. How do you feel about all this anger in you?

Q: Surprised that it's there.

A: But your anger is not you.

Q: No, it's one part of me.

A: Your meditation this morning was that love and forgiveness are within you. Your spirit is a vehicle for the love of the universe. This love cannot come through when it's blocked by anger. Accept your anger as a natural part of you, too. It is not bad. It just *is*. But it's not productive to dwell in it. It blocks the light. Recognize it, admit it, allow it, and then release it. Try it.

I spent some time writing angry words, simply venting my anger.

A: That is all from pain about Hal. What about your deafness? Don't you feel anger at that too?

Again, a chain of angry words, this time expressing the rage and isolation that I felt.

A: What do you love about Hal?

Q: He can be gentle and kind. But I'm so afraid of his anger that I can't open to these beautiful qualities any more.

A: Why can't you open?

Q: It makes me vulnerable. It exposes me to his anger.

A: So?

Q: I'm scared. I hate his anger.

A: It's not Hal's anger, but anger itself, and the intensity of your response to it that frightens you so much. The feeling of vulnerability is not only about his anger. His anger mirrors your own; you fear the power in anger and the lack of control when it is expressed. As a child, you were uncomfortable with anger in a room, and learned to close yourself off from your own emotions and those you felt coming from others. Now you have a new tool. When you are aware, without judgment, you have in that awareness a tool to recognize fear as fear, and anger as anger, and not to get caught up in the stories that come with these emotions—stories that someone will be hurt, that someone is bad.

Startled, I realized that was true. Why had I never seen it before? I sat still for some moments, absorbing this insight.

Q: When I talk to him and he's closed and angry, what do I do?

A: Tell him, "It makes me feel hurt when your response is narrow and dogmatic. I want to talk to you. I love you. I am afraid to share with you because I fear the power of your anger. I fear the depth of my own anger that yours awakens in me."

Q: What if he's still angry?

A: Admit your hurt and anger to yourself. Then release it. Forgive him and forgive yourself. Love him and love yourself. You cannot control his reactions, only your own. Understand with compassion that his pain is as deep as yours.

There are words you can use as you practice, to offer him and yourself your deepest kindness. Think of his pain and say silently to him, "May you be happy and have peace." Repeat this, speaking from your heart. After awhile, let go of him and think of your own pain. Say these same words to yourself. "May I be happy; may I have peace."

Now I became aware that the answering and questioning had moved into a dialogue. It confused me momentarily. I let that insight go and came back to the thoughts offered. As I considered these ideas, the way seemed so clear. Why hadn't I thought of this before? After all, I was talking to myself. This must have been inside me all this time. And suddenly, with a pounding heart, I realized that it wasn't coming from me, that there was some external guidance at work.

I experienced some wonder about the idea of another entity, a nonphysical being, communicating with me in a telepathic manner, but felt no fear or doubt. I didn't know what was speaking, but as I opened to its reality, I felt a powerful presence, and an intelligence beyond my own mind. As I accepted this, I felt a great sense of love, both extending out from my own heart and flowing back into me. It was as if a gentle hand reached out and wrapped my chilled body in a warm cloak. I felt tremendous comfort, reassurance, and connection.

I said, "Let's change question and answer to Barbara and guide." With renewed energy and hope, I turned back to the journal.

Barbara: Who are you?

Guide: *My identity is unimportant at the moment. I come as a friend.*

Barbara: What am I supposed to be learning from this? Why am I with Hal and having to deal with his anger in the first place? Why am I deaf and faced with my own rage about that?

Guide: *You've just understood that you are afraid of anger. You experienced that fear first in your youth and now through Hal. Anger becomes the whole world for you. It isn't the world, and you need to learn that. You so deeply aspire to be loving, but anger separates you from the experience of love. You fear your negativity, and your present work of this lifetime is to move beyond that fear. It is not to stop negative thought but to cease to fear it. When the conditions are present, negative emotions will arise. It is only an expression of conditions, just as waves rise in the sea when the wind blows. Until you can accept such heavy emotions in yourself, without fear or hatred, you cannot accept them in others.*

True change comes only from love, never from hatred. You cannot change what you do not accept. Thus, your own fear is a gift to teach you compassion. You are a vehicle for love and forgiveness. But judgment of your experiences of fear and anger blocks the free expression of lovingkindness. You fixate on that judgment with more and yet more anger. The situation can be likened to a window of pure glass that has some dirt. You will wish to wash the window, not to attack it! That loving action will again reveal its natural purity and clarity.

You must learn to open the unlimited vessel of kindness by ceasing to fixate on the judgment. Then you will always be open to love and will feel love, regardless of the external conditions. This is not to say you will not also feel anger at times, but you will no longer judge the anger and fear it. It will just be anger, not a condemned part of you. . . .

As I returned to a more conventional reality, it wasn't the words but the vague image of a figure that created doubts about this experience. Was I just imagining it? I let the doubts surface and opened my heart to the fear surrounding them. Here I was, a middle class housewife from a traditional background sitting in my living room chatting with a spirit. My brain screamed that this was impossible. Or was it? I made a conscious decision to trust. There was no harm here. I was gaining new and valuable insights. Why shut myself off from them? Looking back on what may seem like a naïve degree of trust, I realize how much I needed guidance and answers. They were being offered in an unexpected form, but what I heard made so much sense, and was offered with such kindness and patience, that trust was not difficult. As I looked at the situation, I realized how everything had come together at this time in my life. I remembered a quotation I'd once read: "When the student is ready, the teacher appears."

Eight days later, on January 27, 1989, I met this spirit guide more directly. I saw a figure across the room. He radiated a white light so brilliant that at first I had to look away. It was hard to tell if he shined out of that light or if it radiated from him. His features were clearly visible; piercing blue eyes, high cheekbones and forehead, white hair, and a flowing beard that came to his chest. I trembled in his presence, yet I felt a deep love pouring from him; a love so familiar, but unlike any I had known in this life. There was a calm joy in his presence that washed away all fear.

I'm not going to suggest that I took this casually. I went into the kitchen to get a cup of tea. When I returned, he was still radiantly there. I wondered briefly again if I was hallucinating. But every time I looked, I saw him patiently waiting for me to be ready to move ahead. There was both power and ease in his presence. I wasn't frightened because I felt so much love from him, as well as a gentleness and connection dimly remembered from some unknown past. The white light was also comforting, like a torch in the darkness.

I sat in meditation with this presence for two days before I ventured to talk again. Then I asked him who he was. Very simply he told me he was my teacher.

Barbara: Why are you here now?

Teacher: *You are ready. You are learning to see the responses that build more karma. . . . You can hear these words without ego adding karma. Listen for ego. Don't let it block your openness.*

Barbara: Where do we start?

Teacher: *You are suffering. Let us start there, to investigate together the causes of this suffering and find the end to it.* *

Barbara: Does it ever end?

Teacher: *It does; yes, it certainly does.*

Barbara: With death?

Teacher: *Do you imagine that walking through a doorway will change your experience? No; suffering ends when you know who you are, when you realize the totality of being. Not of "your" being, but of being. Then you will cease to believe in this limited identity, this self, as the whole. I do not deny the existence of this self we call Barbara, but she is not what you think she is. Humans know the self as a collection of form, feelings, thoughts, perceptions, and consciousness.* * *All of these are only the surface. When you take them as your whole identity, then there is a grasping for things to be different in this body, with these thoughts, this consciousness. Then there is suffering.*

Let us not get ahead of ourselves. We have as long as is needed to do this work together. Let us better prepare the foundation before building on the upper floors.

The teacher gave me more information here on what I needed to work on. Then he stepped back and I again experienced that brilliant, all-encompassing light. I was crying again.

---

*Here the teacher has introduced the Four Noble Truths of Buddhism in a very simple and direct way: suffering exists; suffering has a cause; there is an end to suffering; and the path out of suffering. I later learned that these are known in Buddhist teaching as the five aggregates, or *skandhas:* form, feeling, thought, perception and consciousness.

Teacher: *Don't be so solemn. Be joyful.*

I sensed a return to my body. Had I been away? I felt a great joy, although I was still trembling. I opened my eyes and my arms. The sky was intense blue. A large bird soared overhead, wings moving slowly and easily. I felt it was me.

At first my rational mind asked, *Who is this teacher?* Was I imagining his presence? Was he a part of me? Slowly I realized it didn't matter and began to listen with my heart. I was getting information that I needed for growth and to which I had lacked previous access.

I asked for his name. He would not give it at first. He felt it would bring up more doubts, more wondering who he was and why he was with me. It was only after many weeks, as I began to trust his information and my own ability to hear it, that he said I might call him Aaron. His name felt like a gift given as a gracious reward for my work. I had become clearly aware of Aaron's existence as a separate entity. I had learned to trust him and myself. Why "Aaron"? He says it was his name in a former lifetime when he was a wise and loving teacher.

Aaron tells me he is a being who has evolved beyond the need to return to the physical plane. He is from beyond the causal plane, which means he is no longer subject to karma, the laws of cause and effect. He defines himself as a being of light, which he says we all are. He has since told me that in his final human lifetime in the 1500s, he was a meditation master in Thailand. He found liberation in that lifetime, through Buddhist meditation and spiritual practices, but he also had lived in many cultures and practiced many religions. He doesn't limit himself to any one identity, but considers all sincere practices and insights as tools for growth and liberation. I've come to know him as a being of infinite love, compassion, and wisdom. He also has a wonderful warmth and sense of humor. He is a wise teacher.

Our conscious minds are just a small piece of a much larger facility for knowing and understanding. We all have guides beyond our selves and can hear and often see them if we allow it. I have taught many skeptical people to hear their guides. We each have four bodies: physical, emotional, mental, and spirit. If a being leaves the physical and perhaps even the emotional bodies behind, the spirit and mental bodies still retain the ability to communicate with the human mind. We call this the higher self. It is from this aspect of being that our guides communicate with us. Our own higher self may also communicate.

I know now that I have known Aaron in many lifetimes as a friend, teacher, and even as a father. At times he calls me "child" and at times, Barbara. Sometimes he calls other people *son* or *daughter,* sometimes *friend, sister,* or *brother.* A friend remarked to me, "I find great meaning in his terms when he speaks to me. He means something quite different when he says child versus brother, for example, though the tenderness and love remain constant."

I've learned not to take these labels literally; he sees us all as a part of each other, all interconnected. *Child* is not a label used to diminish others or me in any way, but only conveys love and affection. It also reminds me that I can trust his wisdom and that he will never harm me in any way. Sister and brother remind us that he trusts our capacity to be responsible for our own experiences and choices.

While I do experience Aaron as separate from myself, he comes to teach us that nothing is ever separate. That of the divine in Aaron is no different than the divine core within all of us. In this way he mirrors our true nature back to all who speak with him.

Following this initial meeting, every time I sat to meditate Aaron was there, patiently waiting for me to deal with my fears. Each time I sat, I could see him sitting just to one side of me. I could also feel the energy vibration of his presence. It was clear to me that to accept and learn from him meant a deeper level of commitment. I would have to be increasingly honest with myself and more responsible.

I wanted to learn, and especially to move past my suffering, but I was afraid. I wasn't afraid of Aaron, but frightened of the changes that accepting his reality and his teaching could bring to my life. I didn't know if I was ready to give up the old props of blame, anger and fear to which I had clung. I was like a timid and scared little child, wanting but afraid to pat the big dog. It was important to our relationship that there was never any pressure to accept Aaron. He gave me all the time and space that I needed. Slowly I trusted, as I came to understand that I would never be coerced. Each step was always my choice, to be taken only when I was ready.

He also reassured me, although I did not understand it then, that there was nothing to give up. "Just open," he told me, "to the truth of your innate kindness, goodness, and compassion, and these old forms will drop away; there will be nothing remaining to support them." There was such an intense feeling of loving acceptance from him. Everything he said seemed very wise and led me to new insights. I had nothing to lose by trusting and seeing where the experience would take me.

CHAPTER 2

Entering More Deeply

IN THE WINTER and spring of 1989 my work with Aaron began to deepen. He left me to silent meditation in the early mornings. Then I would see my children off to school, and sit down to talk with him. As we worked together, I wrote much of what Aaron told me in my journal, along with my own thoughts and feelings. His guidance was patient and loving, but he made it clear that he expected me to be honest with myself and not to run from issues. He was so nonjudgmental and so patient that I became able to more easily investigate difficult feelings.

Journal, February 7, 1989

A restless meditation; I finally asked, "Aaron, are you there?"

Aaron: *Yes. Come and sit here with me and watch all this restlessness, this wanting to be everywhere in order to escape being here.*

I "sat" with him on a hillside. What I mean is that I saw him sitting there and I saw myself sit down beside him. This is a visualization process I still don't fully understand, but it did not feel like imagination.

Foot itches and wants to be scratched; a little cool; let's get a blanket. Is Peter's cello packed for class? I should go and do it now. Why was Hal distant at dinner last night? What's the time schedule for today? Did I get dinner out of the freezer?

I sat and watched this arising of thoughts and sensations for a while. Aaron asked me to distinguish the difference between the arising thought or sensation and my relationship to it. "Whatever arises is okay. Just watch. If judgment arises, watch that. There is nothing to fix. Whatever has the nature to arise has the nature to cease and is not 'you' or 'yours.' Just watch."

He asked me not to try to stop thoughts or force attention back to the breath, but just to watch thinking itself. I did, for quite a while as thoughts ran rampant and the body was filled with restless urges to move. He reminded me to watch such urges as well. Just another thought; note it as an impulse.

Aaron: *Are you ready for some space now?*

Barbara: Yes.

Aaron: *It looks like a herd of wild animals out there; hundreds of thoughts, sensations, opinions, and preferences. Do you see them rushing around the corral like wild horses desperate to escape? Open four gates, one on each side, and let them all out. See them disappear over the horizon.*

In some part of my mind I could see this scene as I heard his words. I did what he suggested.

Aaron: *Now feel the space.*

I felt a great expanse, like the open feeling of the sea when I sit on the beach at dawn. Suddenly all the noise was quieted, not really gone but shifted to a different dimension. Thoughts still existed but had no more pull. The spacious stillness seemed radiant and wonderful. I sat in this blissful stillness for a while. Then I asked Aaron what I needed to know.

Aaron: *Just sit and listen to the stillness.*

Soon I started to fill it with more noise, more thoughts.

Aaron: *Permit a clearing. Invite the thoughts to move out through the gates again. In other words, do not form a personal relationship with them. Let them be. Allow yourself space. Fill yourself with light.*

Your work is not to stop thoughts and sensations. These will remain, as long as you are in human form. Your work is to learn that this empty space is always here. You have a choice: to become involved in a relationship with the thoughts and sensations, or to just let them be. As you do so, the space will become more apparent and accessible. That which is aware of thought is not thinking. That which is aware of tension is not tense. Rest in that spaciousness.

I did all this, and stillness returned for a few moments; then more noise, more thoughts.

Aaron: *I cannot teach you beyond this level until you allow light and space. The space is there. Where do you choose to place your attention? Stop giving so much energy to the arisings in mind and body. Offer at least equal attention to the real space and stillness that are also present.*

You have seen that this is possible. You must simply practice it. Thoughts and sensations will always arise. There is no need to fixate on them. You are inviting involvement with the noise in order to avoid deeper awareness. Feel the tension that results from grasping after the state of nonthinking. For now, allow the noise and restlessness. You must not suppress them, or judge them, but let them self-dissolve or slip into the background of their own accord. It is not a matter of forcing silence, but allowing it to emerge naturally. Silence and space are expressions of the infinite and therefore do not arise and cease, as do thoughts and sensations that make up everyday life. We call this infinity and its expressions "the Unconditioned." That is, its existence is not dependent upon conditions. Thus, it is always present whenever you allow the experience of it.

As fear that blocks deeper awareness dissolves, you will find that silence and infinite space are always present and have always been there, just as the blue sky is always there beyond the clouds. Just sit now and watch the restlessness. . . .

Thus I learned to stay more present with difficult body sensations, thoughts, and emotions. I was able to see what I had suppressed or blocked by creating distractions—what Aaron called "smoke screens." He spoke of the five aggregates or parts of the everyday self, naming them: first, the body with sensations; second, the mind with thoughts; third, feelings of neutrality, pleasantness, or unpleasantness; fourth, perceptions based on old conditioning or bare perceptions of the moment, free of the influence of old conditioning; and fifth, consciousness itself. He asked me to watch as body sensations and thoughts arise and pass away, and to become aware that there is no need to build a self-identity with them. They arise naturally out of conditions and then pass away. Similarly, there is no need to build a self-identity based on emotional experiences.

This meditation practice allowed me at last to open to the pain of becoming deaf, a pain I had long suppressed. At one point I began to have nighttime dreams of giant surf, of wanting to swim but finding the waves huge and forbidding. Every morning when I sat to meditate, the question would arise of whether I wanted to go down to the beach in my meditation, to a nonphysical but still wild sea. My answer was always *no*. It became harder and harder to meditate. My back began to ache, first just while I was sitting, then in anticipation of meditation. I knew I was running from something, but I still wasn't clear about what it was.

Finally, one February morning during meditation I said *yes*, and felt my inner awareness move to the beach, opening to the experience of the waves while I sat in meditation.

The surf was huge, the waves dark. I understood that I must submerge myself. I had to take a single step into the unknown. A wave crashed down. I stepped into its ebb and saw the next wave tower above me, black belly, white foam. I felt it slap me under, roll me with its power. I was drowning. I could not breathe. Desperately I forced my eyes open. I breathed deeply, gasping breaths of cool air in the safety of my room. I stopped trembling. I closed my eyes. I was back on the same beach. I did the whole thing again, over and over and over. How much time passed? My watch told me later that it had been hours.

I begged for help. Assurance came from Aaron, *You can do it!* Suddenly, in the midst of a terrible wave, Barbara, the strong swimmer, took over. *Don't fight it,* I heard Aaron's voice saying. *Be one with it.* I started to swim with the wave. I gathered momentum; I dove down and came up in the calmer swells beyond. I returned to shore and did it again, and again, until I could enter the water, not without fear, but knowing how to harmonize with this previously overwhelming force. I was complete. Everything I needed to bring to this wave was within me.

Coming out of the sitting, I began to reflect: death is not an end, but just another step. It is the step before birth. I need not fear either. It is all part of the process.

I began to do lovingkindness meditation, repeating the words, *may I be healed; may I find peace; may all beings be healed and find peace. ...*

With this experience I had learned that I could survive that one step into the unknown, and could allow myself to be overwhelmed. But I still didn't know where this was going. I wanted badly to run away from this experience, but knew that I had to see it through.

The next morning I felt like I'd never meditated before. I couldn't sit still. I couldn't quiet my mind from its turmoil. My back, which had continued to hurt through those weeks, ached horribly. My legs were cramped; my forehead itched; I was alternately freezing and sweating. Most of all, I felt totally alone. *Sit with it,* I told myself. *Just watch it. Watch all the pain and anxiety and see where it's going. Watch yourself wanting so desperately for things to be different.* After well over an hour I got up and walked around for a few minutes. The aloneness, the agitation, stayed with me. I sat again.

The feeling of isolation became overwhelming. Searching for something that might help, I reached for the lines of the Twenty-Third Psalm: "Yea, though I walk through the valley of the shadow of death, I will fear no evil. ..." Into the space that I had opened through this small kindness to myself came Aaron's voice: *You are never alone, but this is the isolation into which you have bound yourself. When do you remember feeling like this before? When do you last remember really needing that Psalm?*

And with a rush all the memories came back. I saw those first weeks of my illness. All sound was gone. I couldn't focus my eyes. To turn my head even a tiny bit brought waves of dizziness. I felt helpless and alone. The isolation had felt like dying. I realized that in sixteen years I had never cried for my pain.

Once I understood how I had buried these uncomfortable feelings, I just sat there on the floor and cried and cried. The remembering hurt, but not nearly as badly as burying the pain had hurt. I wept for the loss of my hearing, I wept for the aloneness, I wept for the fear,

I wept for the one in a glass prison, seeing, but totally cut off from the world. All that week I remembered and cried.

I had raged at my deafness but had never allowed the pain into my heart. I had simply buried it, and met any feelings of self-pity with contempt. Now I saw that my deepest separation was from myself.

That night I shared this new awareness with Hal and cried with him, and felt his love. The next day I lay in bed before dawn, in the same bed where I was once so ill, and cried for the frightened young woman who had to cope with this illness. I reached out to my ears, gently searching for the nerves that were oxygen starved and dead. They seemed to ask me for forgiveness for failing me. I touched my ears—that part of me that I had so often cursed—with love. Finally I reached out to myself, to the self I had often criticized for feeling self-pity, for not trying harder. *Barbara, I forgive you; Barbara, I love you.*

Aaron continued the teachings about emptiness. The five aggregates of form, thought, feeling, perception and consciousness are not of the nature of a separate self, but are always forming and reforming as a result of the conditions around them; and those conditions are created by conditions. When the conditions cease, the objects cease. This flow of objects coming into being and passing away is called *samsara*. A seed is planted; sun, rain, and rich soil are present; and a flower grows. If any of the conditions are lacking, the flower will not grow. Our minds and bodies, our feelings and emotions, follow the same law. Mind and body experiences arise from conditions. They do not arise from a solid and separate self.

Journal, July 1989

Barbara: Then what's left, Aaron? If these are not me, what remains?

Aaron: *This is where your meditation must take you. I do not say there is nothing left, only that that which remains is not the aggregates, but beyond them. That which is aware of anger is not angry. What is this awareness?*

The flower dies and decays into the soil. The new flower grows from this rich

earth. Is the growing flower new, or part of the old blossom? Is there any separate
flower? Yet we cannot deny that the flower exists.

Thoughts and physical sensations, and the body itself, arise and pass away
according to conditions. They exist, but have no separate self in which they arise.
You hold your thoughts as "Barbara" and the body as "Barbara." What is this "Bar-
bara" beyond the aggregates? There is great self-identity with the thoughts, but
the thought is just a thought, and need not trigger personal judgments, fear,
anger, or other stories.

Further insight came in the following months. I had been mindlessly
reacting to events according to old habits, creating the same issues
over and over, and burying what was too painful to examine, in the
junk pile of my subconscious mind. When I meditated, all of these
previously suppressed thoughts worked their way out.

With mindfulness I learned to accept what was there and to notice
it without judgment. I also saw how the proliferation of thoughts and
my belief in these thoughts as truth rushed out of control like a brush
fire. Meditation provided a firebreak, so to speak, a cleared space
where there is nothing to burn. I had been so busy running from the
fire, and trying to guess where it would burn next so I could outrun
it, that I had never looked at what was burning. From my new space
of clarity, I had a broader perspective and was no longer trapped by
the brush fire. I had some freedom.

This inner work touched all parts of my life. It wasn't just the pain
of my deafness that I had suppressed, but my pain at Hal's reaction
to it. Hal might say "poor me; I have a deaf wife," or he might be
unwilling to take notes when we were out with people. He would fly
into a rage when I misunderstood a word as I lip-read. I knew that I
was angry at his inability to accept my deafness. I felt that he had
hurt me too badly and that I couldn't forgive his behavior. But I also
felt guilty, because I was the one who had altered our lives by becoming deaf. I believed him to be the victim of my deafness. My mixed
signals of guilt and anger made it even harder for him to move past

his own pain. Aaron addressed this through a focus on forgiveness. He asked me to think of Jeshua's* final words: "Father, forgive them, for they know not what they do." He asked me to relate that to Hal, because he doesn't hurt me intentionally. He acts from his own pain and not from malice. I realized then that I had rarely thought about Hal's pain before; only about his anger.

Aaron then asked me to try a forgiveness meditation. He suggested that I bring Hal into my heart so I could see that Hal has no intention to harm. Just for experiment's sake, could I try to speak to Hal from my heart, acknowledge his pain, and say, "I forgive you"? I felt stuck. Even though I understood what Aaron meant by "no malice," I couldn't get the words out.

Aaron: *Say the words and see if a space can open in your heart. It is not necessary to forgive. Just allow the possibility of forgiveness, child. Forgiveness is a process; it need not be entered into all at once, but gently, as you are ready. It is like entering an icy cold lake on a hot day. Part of you enters joyfully, and part holds back, alarmed by the burning cold. Wade in as far as is possible, and rest there. Use no force. Your own natural inclination to heal will lead you deeper as you are ready.*

Rather than saying "I forgive you," simply extend lovingkindness to him, acknowledging his pain. Try it for Jeshua, who is the Messenger of Forgiveness, and for the Buddha who is the Father of Compassion. Try it for all beings on the Earth who cry out to be forgiven. Just try it as an experiment. . . .

Tentatively I tried it. *Hal, I acknowledge your suffering; I wish you healing from your pain; I wish you peace.* . . . Gradually a space opened. I felt a vast warmth of spaciousness flowing in, thawing the heart, and love flowing out. Then an enormous feeling of grief came,

---

*"Jeshua" is a closer translation of the original Aramaic word into English than "Jesus" so I choose to use this name, "Yeah-shua," with accent on the first syllable and a short, softer *shua* at the close.

and I wept for a long time. The grief seemed to have no object; it was just the breaking open of the logjam of emotions that had been blocking this release in my heart. I felt a great compassion for Hal's pain and I asked his forgiveness, not for my becoming deaf; but for not being able to recognize the depth of his pain.

"Now extend it to yourself," Aaron said. And I felt the beginning of love and compassion for my own pain.

"Extend it to your deafness," suggested Aaron.

Deafness, I forgive you for all the pain. ... As I said this I realized that I must also thank the deafness for the gifts of wisdom and compassion that it has brought me, and for opening a path that has led me to know myself and brought me much closer to God. *Deafness, thank you.* ...

Aaron: *Now reach out to your ears, to the middle ear, to the source of this deafness. Seek out those nerves that starved, that needed oxygen and couldn't get it, that knew as they died that they were failing you. Open to one ear at a time, so that you can focus. Touch them with mercy for their pain. Give them your love.*

I did this, one ear at a time, finding that oxygen-starved part of myself, touching it with love and with healing. I understood that this was a process, not a one-time event. I would need to do this over and over, to grieve and to forgive.

When I opened my eyes the bushes were filled with cardinals—so red on a gray winter morning. I watched for quite a while, empty of thought.

Aaron emphasized that this work of healing the body and the mind must be part of a larger healing of the sense of separation from the divine. The roots of our feelings of unworthiness and our harshness to ourselves and to others lie in the illusion of separation. Just as the flower is not separate from the sun, rain, and earth, so we are not separate from the divine or each other. Intimate knowledge of the nondual, and of our connection with All-That-Is, is the ultimate healing.

Today Aaron asked me if I have any idea where I'm going. "On a journey," I answered, "but I don't understand it." He said that I *did* know and that I must become more conscious of my goal.

Barbara: To find God; to take my soul home. But I no longer know what "God" or "soul" mean. My old definitions no longer work.

Aaron: *Will you know God when you find Him, or will you be like that seeker of the Buddha in the story I related, who didn't know that they had slept in the same shelter and conversed, and therefore set out again the next morning, still on his search? Now, where are you going?*

B: To learn to know God, or what you call divinity.

A: *God is within you as well as without. You will finally come to understand that there is no place to go. When you know the divine within yourself, you will recognize it everywhere, and will know that you have always been "home."*

B: How do I do this?

A: *You must be willing to work very hard; to want this growing awareness enough to give it all of your love. We have spoken of manifesting your energy as purely as possible. You must be mindful of this at all times. You must always be honest with yourself. The way will be hard and painful at times. You will never be asked to do anything that is too difficult for you. Have faith, and trust with an open heart.*

There was much talk of responsibility. I began to see how anger came with denial of responsibility, and also with the taking of another's responsibility from them, and then feeling resentment. For a whole week we had been talking about anger. Aaron said that I needed to have more compassion for Hal, to feel his pain rather than getting so caught up in my own.

Barbara: "Am I my brother's keeper?"
Aaron: *No, you are your brother.*

I thought about this a bit. Aaron asked me to move from reflective thought to meditation. I was feeling very restless. I felt angry with Aaron. I wanted to blame Hal for his anger; I felt that somehow I was right. Aaron told me forgiveness goes beyond right and wrong. I saw that I was caught up in the idea of "righteous anger."

Aaron: *You will find that as compassion deepens, there is nothing left to forgive.*

These words brought even more anger. I felt so far from any true compassion. Finally, Aaron asked me to look at the anger behind the restlessness. He said that I was restless because I didn't want to accept the responsibility for my own anger. I was judging anger as something bad rather than simply acknowledging it as an expression of conditions, and accepting responsibility for ensuring that I did no harm with it. He asked me again to just let it in and look at it. There was no need to suppress it or react to it; just allow it to be there. He reminded me that anger is merely energy and is neither bad nor good. His kindness enabled me to take a closer look.

The next day I exhausted myself wrestling with "righteous anger" and forgiveness. I sat most of the day, feeling overwhelmingly restless. I was trying to do what Aaron suggested and look at the anger behind the restlessness:

Aaron: *You are fighting against this, child, rather than just allowing it to be there. There is a fine line between recognizing the anger and becoming angry. Do you see all the judgment behind the anger?*

Barbara: So there are layers: restlessness—and beneath that, anger; and beneath that, judgment?

A: *And behind the judgment? Go and sit with it again, now.*

The next day brought a series of insights. I realized how directly fixating on anger precludes love and openness. In those few weeks I discovered that when I accept the anger that I'm feeling from my isolation, not judging it to be inappropriate, then I can remain open and loving. As I increasingly experienced this newly opened energy, people sought me out to talk to me. When I was in a group, people would come and sit beside me to write what was being said. In the past, close friends would do this; after this opening, people who were practically strangers would do it. I had been creating this isolation for myself.

With Aaron's help and guidance, I had been looking at the past life of an old woman with deep power and insight. She had assisted her tribe's shaman for decades. When he died, she asked to become the shaman but could not because of her gender. She stubbornly refused to deny her powers or accept any compromises, and was ultimately cast out of her tribe.

Even several months after being sent away, when the chief came to ask her to return as counsel to the new shaman, she refused. She lived totally alone for years, in full view of the tribe, but unseen and unspoken to—treated as a ghost. She was lonely; filled with rage and bitterness, and blamed the others. She would not acknowledge her part in the situation. How does the experience of this ancestor speak to my present anger and isolation? She suffered terribly because of the loneliness, but her self-righteousness made it impossible for her to accept friendship.

That evening, further insight came. I was now able to accept friendship from others with joy, but I still didn't take full responsibility for my isolation. My irresponsibility was caused by the anger about the deafness and the feelings that someone else should fix it somehow. Finally my anger was simply that—anger. I could watch and allow it without guilt or judgment. The choice was mine. I could react, unaware, and do harm, or I could accept this uncomfortable feeling with awareness and mercy and just let it float there.

I saw that my discomfort with the feeling of anger is what made me want to throw it at Hal. The problem wasn't the anger, but my reaction to the anger; my intense dislike of feeling it. Suddenly I understood how the repetition of the story, "He did this; he did that," was solidifying the anger. I understood that behind the judgment was the feeling of unworthiness and behind it *all* was fear.

While I had to learn not to take responsibility for another person's choices, at the same time, I saw the need to accept responsibility for my own choices. When we work hard to learn something, the lesson keeps reappearing.

Journal, March 16, 1989

When Hal left for work he didn't ask Mike or me to move my car from behind his. Instead he tried to drive around my car and got stuck in deep mud. Mike and I tried to push him out. He was really angry. "Why didn't you move your car? It's all your fault!" We told him Mike had planned to move the car but that Mike didn't anticipate that Hal would leave early for work. The wheels spun; Mike and I became totally covered with spraying mud, in our hair, mouths, and clothes. Hal was really upset. "Why didn't you tell me Mike was going to move the car? Now you're covered with mud and that's also your fault," he yelled again.

I'm afraid I wasn't very compassionate, but it was so funny and so wonderful. I had spent months learning about responsibility. This incident followed on the heels of the intensive work of reviewing and going more deeply into the issues that I was confronting. There I stood coated with dripping mud, feeling not at all angry, and all I could think of to say, after the long days and nights of meditation was, "It's not my responsibility to guess what you need to know and to tell you. It's your responsibility to ask."

These teachings are so beautiful. I love this! It doesn't matter whether we're seeking a spiritual understanding or a way out of a mud puddle (And, isn't it the same thing?). The answers are the same. Be present and openhearted with what arises. Be responsible and fearless, but if fear does arise, be openhearted with that too. I enjoyed it all day.

Yet each day seemed to bring something new, and I greeted each new idea with resistance. Finally, Aaron asked me to look at the resistance itself.

Journal, March 18, 1989

Aaron: *What is this fear about, child?*

Barbara: I don't know. There's just so much that's new; it's bewildering. You're taking the foundation out from under my feet. The universe isn't what I always thought it to be.

A: *Can you see how you cling to knowing? What if you allow yourself not to know? Might "not knowing" allow you to come closer to reality than the grasping at knowing that shades all you see through the filters of the self?*

B: What should I do?

A: *I will not tell you what you "should" do, but what you may do. Look at the resistance each time it arises, with no judgment, only a choiceless awareness that says "this is the present experience," regardless of how impossible it may seem to look at it. Ask yourself, what is the fear that lies behind the resistance? What does knowing protect you from? In what way does not knowing make you vulnerable? Slowly you will allow yourself to be vulnerable and the need to control through knowing will fade.*

How do we investigate resistance, fear, and other deeply conditioned emotions and thoughts? Aaron introduced changes into my meditation practice that helped. He called the practice one of choiceless awareness; that is, to bring attention to whatever is predominant in my experience. I was already doing a similar meditation but had introduced a subtle distortion into it. When something became uncomfortable or unpleasant, I shifted attention away from it and returned to the breath. Now Aaron asked me to stay with any discomfort, and also to note the shift from discomfort into a contracted energy of wanting to escape. He asked me to get to know the feeling of wanting to get away, to feel it in the tensions in the body, and in the contracted mind.

Aaron: *When there is body pain, first you feel the strong sensation, then the unpleasant quality of it, and finally the desire to escape it. Each one becomes the predominant object, in turn. The same is true with a difficult emotion. Be with each stage of the process with as open a heart as is possible. You are not attempting to change the experience, only to be aware of it.*

I ask you to extend your practice to twenty-four hours a day, not sitting for all that time of course, but bringing awareness into each moment and remaining in the present as much as is possible. You are a sculptor. Sculpt. You are a mother and a wife; perform the tasks necessary to these roles with as much love and awareness as possible. Clean your house, cook the meals, prepare the garden's soil, walk the dogs, pay the bills. Notice if you awaken with an inhalation or an exhalation. Do all of this with mindful attention to the now. Do it with love, as a service to others and to God.

Stop looking for enlightenment. Indeed, two months ago you had not concerned yourself with the experience of enlightenment. Your grasping takes you further from your path. Even the word "enlightenment" is a problem for you. Watch the ways in which grasping creates suffering.

Focus on your work, on love, on serving others, and on your own mindful awareness of your emotions and ideas. Use your quiet time, in your home or studio, to shine awareness on areas where you were not as mindful as might be desired. But do this without judgment. Mindfulness is a path for learning, not for self-condemnation. Be merciful to yourself. Listen when you feel me close to you. Trust that each moment will bring what is needed.

Slowly, your whole day must become a meditation, so there is little difference between your level of awareness during the time when you are sitting on the cushion and the times when you are active. You will learn to carry that state of nonjudgmental presence into the active times and to observe yourself and others with increasing compassion and acceptance. That which is aware of fear is not afraid; that which is aware of anger is not angry. Rest in awareness. Trust and allow the process to unfold.

I complained of boredom during the long hours of sitting meditation.

Journal, March 31, 1989

Aaron: *Child, you are complaining of boredom. Can you see that your real complaint is of separation from yourself? You know this from your early days of deafness and work with your sculpture.*[1] *When you see "boredom," it is a flashing red warning light that says "separation; fear." Then you must ask yourself what lies beneath the boredom. If boredom was not present, what might you experience? "Judging" is just another mind state that cloaks fear.*

You know that the way to work with fear is not to hate it, but to open your heart to it. You learned this many years ago. Can you begin to open your heart to your fear? What is the fear about?

I understood what Aaron was saying but couldn't answer his question. I did begin to watch both boredom and restlessness with more spaciousness. I found that when I stopped trying to flee from these mind states, they were neither good nor bad, just unpleasant. They were just a gauge of my inner climate. I began to pester Aaron, though, to tell me how to free myself from fear. I didn't feel like I was learning much.

Aaron said that we had worked intensively for two months. Now there were no fireworks, no past lives or explosions of insight, just silence. He said, "You can learn as much from the silence. Just be present with it."

I asked how, when sitting with the silence, I could tell if I was growing, or simply stagnating.

Aaron: When you listen to the silence, child, there is growth. When you are bored with the silence or frightened by it and begin to daydream or just shift uncomfortably, waiting for something to happen, then you must note, "tension." That which is aware of tension is not tense. Rest in awareness and watch the tension as object, not as adversary. As it dissolves, return to your breath; to this "now," and stay with it. Effort is involved—not the effort to grasp or to fix, but the self-discipline and patience to remain aware, to trust the process and to return to the breath, and to awareness, over and over again.

Fear is only a thought. You are not seeking to eradicate fear but to change your relationship with it.

Meditation is not to make anything special happen or to change anything, child, but just to be present with reality without so many filters of attachment and aversion; or at least to be deeply aware of the existence of such filters. Full presence is possible only in this choiceless awareness, which notices the comings and goings of pleasant and unpleasant, like and dislike, without fixation on these movements of the mind. Just notice what is there. You need not strain after the deepest truths but allow them to emerge.

When I awoke one morning a few days later, I had a bad sinus headache. I didn't think I could sit but Aaron urged me to try. Through the first hour I was simply noting the pain, and then my aversion to the pain. I said to Aaron several times that the pain prevented me from focusing. He said no, the pain didn't prevent focus. What prevented it? Suddenly I realized that the pain was just pain, and saw what Aaron meant when he spoke of my relationship to what is. I saw so clearly how my energy and attention were fixed on dislike of the pain and the resulting tension of wanting to get rid of it. Then I tried not to feel angry or wish for the pain to go away; I quickly saw that that was just another fixation, to disown what is. Finally I let go of trying to do anything, just watched the pain and aversion with an increasing spaciousness. The pain didn't go away, nor did the aversion, but a deep peace settled in. The pain and aversion became like clouds in an otherwise clear blue sky. I saw that the clouds were merely part of the sky. They didn't take away the spacious sky. I only lost the sky when I narrowed my focus to the clouds.

Aaron: *Now you are resting in Awareness.*

Think of a mountain stream running out of a pure spring. The water is perfectly pure when it leaves the spring, but picks up particles of pollution as it runs down the mountain. If you wish to drink you must filter out the particles, but the pure water is still there. Where would it go? This is the mix of relative and ultimate reality. In relative reality you must strain the water. In ultimate reality, the innate perfection is never lost.

The clear sky is always present, child. It is the Ground of All Being. By Ground of Being, I mean that which is the essence of you and of All-That-Is. It can never be lost. Where would that spaciousness go? Release your tunnel vision and you will see that you always rest in that infinite expanse, even when clouds are pres-ent. Sometimes there will be clouds, sometimes not. It makes no difference. The clouds are merely an expression of the sky.

Aaron was teaching me many technical terms, and had begun to sug-gest that I learn more about Buddhism, but he still didn't label what he taught me as being of any specific spiritual tradition. It wasn't until many months later that I could identify any of it as related to Theravada* Buddhist teachings. From his perspective there is no need to use labels. I realize now that he wanted me to learn through my experience and not just to gain intellectual understanding. He was also aware that I would have been uncomfortable with the label of "Buddhist" at that time, because I still held myself to a Jewish and Quaker identity. More importantly, if I experience emptiness, what's Buddhist about that? If, at the same depth of meditation I experience a light and energy I choose to call God, what's Christian or Jewish about that?

I didn't understand why Aaron couldn't be more precise, why he wouldn't tell me the concepts behind these practices or let me read about them.

Aaron: *"Concept" is one of the ego's safety devices, child. It gives the ego an illusion of control. Who is in control, and of what? To be present in this moment is not a Buddhist practice, but a human practice. It is the path to maturity.*

"But where is this going?" I asked.

---

*There are numerous Buddhist traditions, just as there are various traditions within Christianity and Judaism. Three predominant Buddhist traditions are Theravada, Zen (part of the Mahayana tradition), and Vajrayana, or Tibetan Buddhism. The Theravadan tradition is primarily found in Southeast Asia and Sri Lanka.

Journal, March 1989

Aaron: *Enlightenment is not something to seek outside of yourself. It is within. It does not come only as a brilliant flash of light, but with growing understanding and the living of that understanding.*

You are in a dark room. You can see nothing. Suddenly the lights are turned on. That is your flash of enlightenment. Yes, there may be such a moment. But it is just a moment. If the lights go off again, how clearly have you been able to see in that moment? Did you truly see what was there, or were you caught up in stories about the light?

If you were present, you then know the shape and texture of the room. You are assured that the room exists, with all its beauty. But your glimpse has taught you little of substance. With that first flash of light you are given a verified faith more than anything else. Then you must work to explore that room, to learn its details; noticing that with each step you take, each moment of mindfulness, there is a bit more natural light that permits you to see more clearly. Do you understand?

Barbara: Yes. What do I do, though? How do I proceed? How do I allow for the first flash?

A: *Do not strive after someone else's enlightenment. It is very simple, really. You know your own path—not just Barbara's path but the path of this higher aspect of your being, the higher self. Live your life remaining faithful to that path, and it will take you where you need to go.*

Each lifetime is but a grain of sand, but each lifetime is precious. Within each incarnation we find the sentient being, with the Ground of Being at its core, manifesting as the aggregates wherein wisdom and compassion may grow.

With every thought and action you must be both Barbara and the Ground of Being. Through Barbara there is consciousness at the six sense doors.* Through the Ground of Being there is the ability to transcend the everyday self and to see through the eyes of awareness. This practice is difficult but necessary. Bring conscious awareness to every step. Before you act, do not ask your highest wisdom,

---

*Buddhist teaching speaks of the six sense doors of eyes, ears, nose, tongue, body, and mind, through which we perceive the world.

but BE your highest wisdom, for in truth you are. Barbara is simply the temporary physical dwelling place for that supreme awareness.

You had a dream that you carelessly parked your bicycle, the Earthly vehicle, and someone stole it away. When you went to claim it, you were told you must never leave the vehicle unattended. The message of the dream is that the aggregates must always be accompanied by awareness.

Even if you are lost, there must be an awareness that observes the being feeling lost, and responds with compassion. This is the only path to integration of the body, mind, and spirit. The body and conscious mind do their work and the wisdom mind observes with an awareness that allows Barbara to transcend this egocentric consciousness.

And later:

It always returns to love. Time after time, in answer to your questions, I tell you, "The key is love . . . love, harmony, and awareness, transcending all form . . ."

In these ways, Aaron helped me to let go of the old ideas of limited self and unworthy self, and to replace them with a knowing of true self. I became more able to watch the process of mind, and to not believe all of its stories.

I began to look more deeply at healing; at what heals, and how? In the fall of 1989, about six months after the above insights, someone who knew of my spiritual work asked me why I was still deaf. I said I had worked hard to learn that I was whole, and that my deafness on the physical plane had nothing to do with my wholeness. She said, "that's true but wholeness is God's will. Manifesting wholeness is an important example."

After she left I realized that I had completely gotten past feeling a lack of wholeness from my deafness. The inner healing was real. It took so much work to learn that I'm whole despite my deafness, and to accept that on a conventional medical level, my hearing cannot be restored. The nerves are dead. I had also moved beyond most suffering from my deafness. There were still painful situations, but I really could accept them and be okay with the pain. I was no longer at war with myself or anyone else. "Being peace, I stop the war." I really felt like I understood that phrase.

Now that I had slowed the karmic cycle around all of the issues that relate to the deafness, I started to learn new lessons. Gaining some hard-won insight into my situation helped me to release attachment to the dream of hearing again. But that same clear seeing also showed me how I was attached to my deafness. I used it as a crutch. I also saw that there's no fundamental reason why I needed to remain deaf. I began this life physically whole and I could return to that wholeness. That thought scared me with its newness and the possibilities it presented. I had stopped looking for a miracle, accepted my deafness, and been genuinely grateful for its lessons; ironically, that shift had created enough space to make further healing possible. Yet still, the prison I knew was more comfortable than the freedom outside.

What was I escaping from through my deafness? How was I using it as a crutch? Why did I fear giving it up? Was this really possible anyhow?

Aaron said it is indeed possible, but that first I had to recognize that my deafness has nothing to do with my wholeness. He said:

Aaron: *In fact you cannot find this type of healing until you first know that you are whole.*

Barbara: Aaron, we're talking about regeneration of nerves here and this is medically impossible. I've finally accepted that and learned that my wholeness doesn't depend on it.

A: *Yes, child. That knowledge is why physical healing becomes possible. If it can be done at all, it is only through love and faith.*

We talked more about this, about love and faith, and about the healing process. I understand that Aaron is saying here that I don't go to a human plane "healer" but to the divine itself.

Aaron: *Deafness has served its purpose. Are you ready to give it up? You see how this prospect terrifies you. What we must first examine is your attachments to it.*

Barbara: Isn't this just more wanting, Aaron? Isn't it just leading me to want to hear and back to suffering because I can't and then there's grasping?

A: *No. If you are longing to hear again, there is still attachment and aversion that must be explored. I am asking you only to look at any attachments to being deaf, and to look further if necessary at attachments to hearing, and finally be ready to let them all go. Then you will have true wholeness, for it won't matter at all whether there is physical healing.*

At this point you will turn to God and hand it to Him. You understand that this is not a puppet master god who heals by whim. But there is a divine plan of which you are a part, and in which you are cocreator. You state your intention to serve the highest good for all beings, through your thoughts, actions, and speech. If the divine plan for you, for the greatest good, is for physical wholeness, then ask the divinity to cocreate that healing with you. If the divine plan is that you continue deaf, that is fine. You accept either with an open heart, with no attachment. Divine will be done. This is not separate from your will, since you say you are a tool of the divine and that your highest intention is to do and live for the highest good.

But first you must look at all the attachments to both hearing and deafness. You have already looked at most of the attachments to hearing.

You cannot "hand it to God" until you have no attachments to the outcome. It must be a totally truthful statement: "if I can serve better healed, help me to manifest that healing. If I can serve better deaf, that's fine." The deeper healing here is that you must move beyond fear of hearing again as you have moved beyond suffering from not hearing. We will start to look at these fears. They relate to the unworthiness we have been working on. This sense of unworthiness must be transcended in any case, as we've discussed. But it becomes crucial to do so in terms of this question about your deafness. Do you understand that?

B: I think so. It will cease to matter if I hear or not only when I am completely healed of these conflicting emotions. If I feel worthy only if I physically heal, I'm not being honest with God or myself and am hoping for one outcome or the other. I see that I can only reach this state of, "which way can I serve you best?" from a space of complete acceptance, and to get there I must get past the unworthiness.

A: *Yes, this is correct. Feelings of unworthiness need not cease completely, but if they arise, awareness knows them simply as old, conditioned thoughts and does not believe the story.*

B: I have one more question. I used to think of God in a subtly dualistic way. Now my meditation brings me to a nondual understanding of God/Goddess as "that which is;" the infinite intelligence and love of the universe; the "unborn, undying, unchanging, uncreated." When I saw God as separate, it was something to which I could turn for help. Now I no longer understand how prayer works. What good does it do to pray?

A: *The divine is within you and everywhere. You have infinite power to manifest what you wish, for good or harm, in the universe. When you clarify the impurities of the expression of divinity you know as self, you manifest with increasing purity, and with increasing intention for the highest good. You align yourself with that energy throughout the universe, and cocreate that which serves the highest good. This is true prayer.*

Think of the strength of a rope of multibraided twine. No single strand can support a heavy weight. No matter how much you wish to save the person who has fallen off the cliff, your thin strand alone cannot hoist them to safety. But when you align yourself with infinite strands of love and compassion, merged with wisdom, your power is unlimited. We use the term God, but you may prefer to phrase it as, "resting in the infinite love and wisdom of the infinite creative force of being." You align yourself through focused intention and purification, and take responsibility for that power, as you trust the ability to use it wisely.

As far as I had already come, I knew then that I had much more work still to do.

CHAPTER 3

Practicing with Fear

NINE MONTHS AFTER meeting Aaron, I began to teach meditation, with Aaron's blessings, and also to channel him for others. Teaching meditation pushed me to speak and think very clearly about my practice. Giving voice to dharma felt natural and comfortable. The channeling was challenging, because I had to be sure my own ego and preferences didn't interfere with Aaron's messages. These practices reinforced each other, deepening my insights and helping me to further investigate the relationship between the ego and the true self.

Shortly after beginning to teach and channel publicly, I met with a man for perhaps the tenth time. I didn't hear much of what Aaron said as I channeled, but I became aware that Aaron was scolding the man for not being honest with himself or with Aaron. I liked this person, felt a friendship with him, and was afraid he would not return, and would dislike me if I channeled Aaron's words. Aaron stopped me and spoke to me silently. He said I must either channel his words, or make the decision to stop serving as a channel for him, but that I could not let my own preferences get in the way of his teaching. I have free will; therefore, I may stop. But my ego must not interfere with his work or we would cause harm to people. He spoke very sternly and fully caught my attention.

I saw clearly how much work there was to do with my desires to be liked, to do good, and not to do harm. I trusted Aaron. He would not do harm. Could I channel him clearly? He said that if I distorted the message, he would stop speaking so that nothing harmful would come through; he said to just be honest with myself and to do the best I can.

In this way, channeling became a powerful practice for observing and responding wholesomely to expressions of the ego. Spiritual practice asks us to move beyond identification with the physical body, mind, and personality. As I observed my thoughts, everything that lay under the surface terrified me. There were hidden agendas, the habits of lifetimes to preserve and advance the self. I was afraid I would act on those agendas. In everyday life I could ignore the ego to some degree, but with channeling, the message would be only as clear as the instrument through which it came. Anything short of clarity would do harm.

Aaron gave me a metaphor of a life jacket. If I am a nonswimmer, it makes sense to put it on before I enter the water. Years later, after I have learned to swim, I may still strap it on out of habit, because I remember how it had kept me from drowning. If I wish to change the habit, I must remember my ability to swim. But if I never address this thinking and behavior, and just continue blindly to don the life jacket, I'll never get to know the strong swimmer, the true self.

The process of channeling also led me to see how much I identified with the personality. When Aaron came through, my personality had to be laid aside. Who was I without that personality? What remained?

One day in the spring of 1990, I had an unusual and telling meditation. I was meditating for about two hours a day at that point, an intensive schedule that Aaron had suggested. I had been restless all week. It was hard to sit. After an hour I gave in and allowed myself to do walking meditation, which was usually easier, for part of the second hour, but on that day the restlessness did not become transparent.

I decided to sit again for the last half hour. A vivid image came to mind. I was being chased by a pack of ferocious, wild dogs. It had the quality of a nightmare, to the point that I wondered if I had dozed off. Upon opening my eyes and closing them again, the image was still there. I was running from them in terror. Teeth were reaching out to me. They were fierce, but there was no hate coming from them; it was just their nature to tear me apart. It didn't feel quite like a past-life image, more like watching a scene that was meant to teach me something.

Returning to the meditation, I watched myself flee. Finally I got a flimsy door closed between us, and just stood and looked at them for a moment, through a thin sheet of plastic. I knew they would break through very quickly. My reaction was to want to run again. Then Aaron said: "No, don't run. Stand there and face them. Send them love. They can't hurt you."

I stood there and observed their sharp fangs, their long claws.

I began to send them love. I felt a deep compassion for their nature, which prompted them to be vicious. There was no personal enmity towards me in their ferocity. As I understood this, my fear dissolved and I continued to send them love.

In two or three minutes they broke through. They were upon me quickly and began to devour me. There was no physical pain. I just sent them love and slowly watched my physical self disappear. What was devoured did not matter. They couldn't touch me, the aspect of myself that was sending them love. I went on sending love to them long after any physical trace of myself remained. They were sniffing the ground, looking for missed shreds. I became aware that I had been crying, hard, but felt very calm and deeply peaceful and loving. I began to talk to Aaron.

Aaron: *Are you aware that the dogs exist on many levels?*
Barbara: Yes.
A: *Tell me what you understand.*
B: They symbolize my fears. I still don't know what I was afraid of that created restlessness, but I've made peace with it.

A: *Fine; keep going.*

B: There is still some fear of losing myself. I know that we are separate, and I see where I end and you begin, but there has been a resistance to channeling these past six weeks; a fear of letting you take over completely. What would be left of me? I know that's my ego speaking, and that the practice is to dissolve that, but the basic fear is still there.

I'm aware of the peace I felt after experiencing the fierce attack; even after being completely devoured, I was still there. This "I" was completely egoless, no self but pure awareness, just sending love and being love. The awareness came from the center of me, not outside of me.

I don't feel that you devour me in that way though. I have no fear of you.

A: *That's not true.*

B: Well, I don't feel you're attacking me or using me out of viciousness but out of love.

A: *And you can't give yourself permission to feel fear or anger at the demands placed on you because you "should" be grateful for this chance to serve. Do you see the trap you're putting yourself into, child, how you are judging the feelings, finding them unacceptable, and denying them? Fear isn't logical. You are suppressing it because you judge it as unworthy, and you are also suppressing the anger you feel at yourself for feeling the fear. You can't move past it by denying it, only by sending love to it.*

I knew Aaron was right. I felt such a churning that I went upstairs and got into an argument with Hal. Anything to escape! I asked, "What happens to Barbara? Where do I go in all of this work?" I had fears, dreams, feelings, and opinions. I knew intellectually that these were not me, but I was so afraid of losing myself. I also had experienced the sweetest peace of egolessness and oneness, and it was wonderful. I didn't really know what I was afraid of. Perhaps just of trusting and completely letting go of control. Aaron agreed, noting that for the past six weeks I had struggled to stay in control. He reminded me to put the situation in God's hands and trust that I would be safe.

Aaron: *You are just playing your part, child. The script belongs to God, that is, to the pure force of love in the universe. Let go of trying to make it come out a certain way. How can you presume to know what needs to happen? When you spoke to a friend about this you became more aware of it in yourself, but you cannot seem to follow through and say "Thy will be done" without a sense of fear. The personal, ego self, wants to take control from the higher self.*

Barbara: I don't think that's true, Aaron.

A: *Child, don't be so defensive. I'm not criticizing you. You are attempting to walk a difficult path. Your, 'Thy will be done' is heartfelt and honest; it is what you want and pray for. Just notice the fear that accompanies it. You can't move through this fear if you continue to deny its existence.*

B: Okay, Aaron. I see the fear. What do I do with it?

A: *If I had hair, child, you'd have me tearing it out! Why do you feel the need to do anything with it? Just allow it. "Feeling fear." Then do whatever it is that needs to be done. As you constantly tell others, have compassion for yourself. Why should you not feel fear, as you place yourself completely at the disposal of something beyond the personal ego? Just notice the fear. Let it flow out of you.*

Once you notice the fear, you do give it to God. You offer the fear to the divine and say, "Thy will be done." Then you must remain open to divine love and compassion. But here is where you shut yourself off. Do you see how you are judging yourself here and building a story of unworthiness? Stop thinking so much! Just notice all this judging. It's just a story of the conditioned mind. Compassion is unlimited; not just for the worthy.

CHAPTER 4

Opening the Heart

IN THE EARLY YEARS of my spiritual practice, I had a fierce determination to learn, but misunderstood my learning as the acquisition of knowledge. Desire for control was still predominant. But another, more wholesome quality had arisen within; I had found a measure of wisdom. Wisdom in the Buddhist scriptures is *pañña*, which combines a right intention toward harmlessness and liberation with a right view of reality just as it is. The Judeo-Christian literature portrays wisdom as a female presence that mediates between God and humanity, extracting from an orderly universe the insights required to lead a long and happy life. The wisdom I had found under Aaron's guidance derived from insight into the absolute, the unchanging divine nature that has no conditions or limits. This wisdom offers a clear perspective on life, knows our deepest interconnection with All-That-Is, and leads naturally to an intention to live honestly from that perspective.

Just as the desire for knowledge can and did lead to an egoic need to control my spiritual path, my surrender to the truth of what is led to wisdom. "Surrender" is a challenging word for us in our Western culture, especially for women, because we think of it as giving ourselves away to a dominating force. But surrender is simply the release of the ego self, and opening to the power of that highest truth of which we are all a part.

As my passion for spiritual awareness began to take root within, I saw that my growing wisdom wasn't enough to support my intentions to dwell with nonharm to all beings, and to live and teach peace at the deepest level. The aspect of spiritual maturation I lacked necessitated learning kindness and compassion toward myself and others, and the qualities of faith and generosity. The fruit of this learning is a joyful, openhearted attitude toward all that we encounter. The open heart holds a profound and unshakable love for self and for others without boundaries or conditions. If we proceed by sheer determination, we carry great tension. Skillful effort is balanced and aspiring, not grasping. There is no forcing in it; the motivation comes from love. Wisdom and the open heart ultimately must become inseparable, and both require surrender to develop.

Many spiritual teachings speak of various sorts of refuge. Going for refuge allows us to practice the art of surrender in complete safety, sheltering and comforting us when the world seems overwhelmingly insane or difficult. In Christianity we have the Trinity and the support we may find in the loving heart of Jesus and the compassion of Mary. Buddhism gives us the support of the Triple Gem of Buddha or awakened nature; dharma, or truth; and sangha, the spiritual community. Hinduism has many great saints to whom we can turn for support. Jews take refuge in the truth of the one God. In all of these spiritual paths we first find something larger than ourselves, then discover that this strength is also a part of us.

Within each of these traditions, the essence of this larger something can be embodied in extraordinary individuals, or gurus. Through a relationship with such individuals, we can discover our divine source. In this way, the guru becomes a refuge for the disciple.

As a young child I knew a connection to a guru. I didn't know his name but called him "the man in the clouds" because of the way he appeared surrounded by light and mist. He came to me often, and left me with feelings of love and hope. He filled and guided my meditations. He even gave me a spiritual name, which guided much of my early life. Then I lost touch with him and tried to find my way through the world alone.

When I began to work with Aaron, there was so much fear of what I might uncover; all the anger, confusion and doubt that I had buried so deeply through the years. Every time I'd get to the level of the quiet that rests beneath thoughts, I would retreat in fear of what I might discover in so much stillness. Aaron kept asking me to trust and to open my heart to it. I kept saying, "How?" His answer was always "love." One particularly difficult morning in April 1989, we had just gone through a dialogue that was getting to be routine.

I was meditating and sat in a space of deep silence. All thoughts were quiet. As the days passed, I had realized that everything is in that stillness. It was I who had pulled away. Aaron said that I feared losing myself in it. When confronted with the silence, he said I must examine and release everything I think I am, or that I identify with as "self." A lot of my experience was uncomfortable to look at, so I turned away. Every time I was on the brink of uniting with the silence, I retreated in fear. That morning, as usual, the silence felt empty and frightening. I heard Aaron's voice. "The silence is full; your heart is closed to that fullness." Feeling a great deal of anguish and frustration, I asked, "How do I open my heart, Aaron?" He answered "Love."

Suddenly I saw a hauntingly familiar old man wrapped in a plaid blanket sitting in front of me, on a platform—alive, moving, talking, laughing. His presence was so well known to me, not the face itself, which had aged, but the beloved presence and energy from my early childhood—the man in the clouds, once loved and then discarded by the logical adolescent. He looked at me after a few moments and our eyes met. I felt my heart open totally, as it had never done before. I felt so much love for him in those few moments. Then I retreated and was confused. I believed I should only feel this much love for God. I asked, "Who is he?" I heard, not from Aaron but from this beloved one's mind, Ramana Maharshi's quote: "God, guru, and self are one."

I felt a total bliss. It felt like time had slowed down. Awareness of the cellular structure of my body deepened; I felt my heartbeat and the flow of blood through my veins. Each breath seemed to last an eternity. A sense of harmony and comfort, of total acceptance from him, led me into total acceptance for myself. I felt a joy I had never felt before; for the first time in this life I knew that everything was just the way it needed to be. It's the first time in my memory that I can say there was absolutely no fear and no wanting to change anything. Instead I felt enfolded in a cloak of loving acceptance. I would follow this being anywhere. There was such total love. I asked Aaron if this love came from God or from this blanket-clad figure. Was he filtering God's love in some way? Aaron said it was not filtering. I don't need an intermediary to feel God's love. The guru focuses the love so I can be more aware of it.

All sense of reason was gone. I'd given in completely to this feeling, responding with my heart. I wanted to sit in this presence forever. I have never known greater joy or greater confusion, but the confusion didn't matter. I was both giddily laughing and crying. Eventually all thought died away, leaving me in an open state of awareness, experiencing intense radiance all around me; deeply aware but with no person who was the aware one. I felt no self, only the spaciousness of his energy and love and my own participation in that spaciousness. *Yes, God, guru and self are one!* I sat there with this presence for about half an hour to an hour. I was not out of my body, nor had body awareness ceased. I was aware that all my physical senses were heightened; yet I ceased to own those sensations. I felt my heartbeat; I smelled the candles burning, and the flowers in the room. I was aware of other spiritual presences and at first this frightened me, but Aaron reassured me.

I felt almost no need to breathe. I wanted to literally touch this loved one, to reach out and hold his feet. He smiled at me and I received the thought, "Read page 33 of Ram Dass's book." This had no meaning for me at the time, but I took this statement, his smile, and acknowledgment of my presence as permission to reach out. It's hard to describe this as of course there was no physical foot; but still I felt the sensation of touching, not the firmness of flesh but the energy presence of that foot, so clearly existent on another plane. I felt love pour into me, and all self melted away. I sat there for a while, holding his foot, totally engulfed by this complete union and love.

Aaron's voice broke through, quietly warning me that it was almost 7:00 a.m., when I would wake my family, make breakfast, and see them off to school. I had to let go of this presence. I wanted to say, "Forget it; I'm just staying here," but before the thought was completed I heard, "Go now and tend to your children. They are also God." The blanket-clad being waved me away and the image and energy faded.

Later that morning my dog alerted me to the doorbell. It was a woman I had not yet met, who brought with her a book. *Miracle of Love* by Ram Dass[1] is a book about Neem Karoli Baba, a Hindu saint lovingly called *Maharaj-ji* by his disciples. She said that she had found it in a bookstore the evening before, at the same time as she had slipped on one of my flyers. Or more correctly, it had found her. When she fell she grabbed at the shelf and the book had fallen down onto her head. Understandably, she felt prompted to bring it to me. On the cover was the picture of the being with whom I had just sat, the being so beloved in my childhood. I turned to page 33.

> ... out of the guru's feet comes the spiritual elixir, the soma, the nectar ... the subtle *pran* or energy that heals and awakens. To touch the feet of such a being is not only to receive his grace, but it is an act of submission, of surrender to God, for that is what the guru represents on this earth.

I was overwhelmed and shaken. My view of reality was constantly being stretched. Later that day, doubt and rationality entered. But my heart knew this had happened. I thought of the lines from the Kabir poem:

> *The arrogance of reason has separated us from that love.*
> *With the word "reason" you already feel miles away.*[2]

In the days following the experience with Maharaj-ji, I found myself looking for him and wanting a repeat of the joy of that experience.

Aaron: You are not meditating to learn bliss, but to learn reality. This includes pain as well as joy. I ask you to simply be with what is, not to try to create what you wish could be. You felt joy in his presence, and now you suffer as you long for his return. No experience lasts more than a moment. He has opened your heart so that you may feel the depths of the moment, be it blissful or painful. The pain is no more lasting than the bliss. Just be aware of each, as you experience them, and try to feel what is beyond them.

We can either live from the ego self or the divine self, but not both. If we live from the divine self, the ego will remain, but it will cease to be in command. For this shift from ordinary consciousness to occur, there must be a readiness to investigate the ego, recognize the ego as part of the conditioned aspect of our being, and then transcend the ego. This investigation had been a major part of my work with Aaron, but I had not been able to surrender the control of ego. Qualities that nurture this process are the sincere intention to do no harm, the humility to acknowledge the harm we have done—whether intentional or unintentional—an aspiration to release and balance karma, and the passionate desire to see all beings liberated from the cycle of death and rebirth.

Other masters beside Maharaj-ji offer me their support, presence, and love. Jesus of Nazareth, or Jeshua ben Joseph as he has asked me to call him, is one of these great teachers. My first deep, direct encounter with Jeshua came in 1989. Most of the teachings I have related thus far, as well as my experience with Maharaj-ji, have been from that intense and transformative period. Jeshua had offered me baptism and I was unable to accept. My meditations and reflections on righteous anger had created profound inner turmoil, rendering my ego unable to surrender to any power higher than itself.

For several days I had been feeling lost, scared, and alone. All my meditations were restless. I sat for long periods but could not get past the chatter in my mind. When I did succeed in letting the noise slip past, there were disturbing visual images. I could not focus my mind. Aaron, there beside me as always, was saying, "Will not, child; not cannot." I asked him, "Aaron, what am I doing wrong?"

Aaron: *You tell me, Barbara.*

Barbara: I guess I'm running from my fears and feelings; not looking at them. But I don't understand what I'm running from.

A: *Try to answer this for yourself. What are you seeing?*

B: Just chaos and confusion. I'm scared. My faith isn't deep enough. It's so very, very dark and I don't know the way.

A: *Child, you are already there. Why are you so afraid to open your eyes, your ears, and your heart? Today you pleaded for help. Maharaj-ji came. You said he was just the memory of your past meeting and closed your heart to him. You refused to look into his eyes. You knew in your heart that if your eyes met, you could not deny his reality. And you fled in terror from where that reality leads you, which is into your own heart, and into an honest understanding of your own karma and responsibilities.*

Then you begged for help again. In your meditation you sat with your hands in the running water and felt Jeshua's presence. You opened so briefly to His love. He asked you to accompany Him to the beach. You went with Him but when He asked you to submerge yourself in the sea, you retreated. Your "noise" began again.

Do you understand that He, Jeshua Himself, offered you baptism, offered to touch you with His love? All He asked in return was your faith and love, your total commitment to "Thy will be done." Yet you retreated. Why?

B: I don't know. I don't even know what baptism means. To me it's just a ceremony performed by some Christian churches. I didn't retreat consciously. I felt that both Maharaj-ji and Jeshua faded away.

A: *You are not being mindful or honest. We have spoken of this before. The eternal is always with you. It is you who retreat. You have acknowledged this with your mind but not your heart. And in your heart you do know what this offering of baptism means. What are you afraid of?*

B: I don't know.

A: You do know. It is not easy. Try to be honest.

B: The unknown; losing myself: what will be asked of me if I take that step? Losing control and giving myself over to God.

Some portions of the same question still existed for me years later, even as I knew that God is not separate from me, as some external force, but is the deepest core of all of us. Looking back, I remember the difficulty of each bit of letting go of control, and how afraid I was. I said I was afraid of "what would be asked." I know that each surrender of self is the greatest gift. This is what I have most sought for myself. It is what my path asks; and yet, always we walk blindly. Do we follow the divine plan or do we follow ego's desire for comfort and safety? Is it ego that believes it can affect the world's suffering, or is it truth? What if we really do have the power to touch suffering and change it? It took me many years to trust the answers to these questions.

In those early years, Aaron suggested that I was not being fully honest as I prayed, "not my will but Thine be done." He said I didn't really want it that way, that I accepted divine will only if it was what I wanted. He told me then:

You must be honest. You say "the images fade." You refuse to acknowledge that you are the one who has chosen not to trust. It is your choice. But be aware that fear and love cannot coexist as seemingly separate entities. You must choose to follow one or the other. You need not get rid of fear but must draw it into the heart of love and allow that love to transform fear.

Reading that old journal, I see the changes in those years. I understand now that divine will for me is always consistent with my own deepest will for myself. There may be a desire to be safe, happy, and so forth, but the highest aspiration that I know is to grow in clarity, and to express love more fully in my life. Trust is no longer a matter of faith but of experience. God will not ask me to do the impossible.

I asked Aaron, "Where do I find that faith? How do I let go of self, not knowing what will be there to replace it?"

Simply be aware of all your fears and doubts. Recognize them for what they are. As they appear, note them, name them, and release them. After some time you will start to know them when they first appear. They will simply be as those clouds passing by, and you'll be able to greet them with, "Hello; you again." Then you will not identify with them so strongly.

Try to invite the opening of your heart. I have told you the silence is not empty, but filled with love. There are no opposites. Emptiness and fullness are the same. Look for the love in the silence, as Maharaj-ji has shown it to you.

Let faith become a conscious thing. Pray for it; think of it. Examine all the ways your faith has been confirmed. Realize when arms are opened to you in love that the choice is yours. At that moment call on your faith, with all your physical and spiritual strength. Open your heart to God with no holding back and God will be there.

Do you understand that faith is what you must learn here? You can go no further on this journey until you open your heart. The choice is yours. Will you follow God, knowing divine self, or will you follow ego self? You cannot be one with Him and truly experience Him, unless you are willing to give yourself completely to His service with joy and gratitude for His love. This does not mean that you cannot serve Him with less than total surrender, but any less than total giving creates great suffering for you. Any separation from God enhances ego, and it is from the dominant ego that your pain arises. The only end to suffering is the total offering of self; not to a force outside of the self but to that which is All— within and without.

You have never been promised that there would be no pain. You have faced great pain and embraced it for all that it taught you. All along you have stated that you are led with love. Allow love to continue to lead you. You have trusted when I've said you will never be asked to do anything that is too hard for you; but that does not mean it may not be very hard, only that it will not be too hard. Suddenly you are afraid it will be too hard, so you cease trusting and withdraw. Love cannot reach you through this wall of self-protection. It is the same wall that your anger and fear about your deafness created in the past. You created it then to protect yourself from real pain, and because you were too frightened to examine the pain.

Now you build it to protect yourself from imagined pain and from the unknown. Please try to trust us, child. You are dearly loved, as is every being. If you can trust to follow this path you will not be harmed by the journey. Love will give you the strength to deal with any pain you meet.

I asked him, how do I do this? I do look at fear and doubt but they trip me up before I start.

Be mindful, child. Just be aware. Try to keep open the channel to your Higher Self at all times. Try to maintain that triple level of awareness: the mundane mind and body, the Higher Self observing the mundane, and the watcher—the Christ or Buddha consciousness, watching it all with pure, nonjudgmental awareness. Just put one foot ahead of the other on this path, child. You know that the first step is the hardest.

In late April of 1989, I was still searching for the route to opening the heart. That month, I had offered to meet and talk with a man regarding a difficult issue that was causing pain for many people. The issue involved his righteous anger. I knew that speaking with him was a perfect learning experience for me, an opportunity to release and balance old karma. Yet I saw the judgment that I carried about his speech and actions, and doubted myself and my ability to speak from an unbiased place of love.

Aaron asked me to examine the fear; why I was so armored, and why I held my heart so closed. Aaron suggested I simply offer my fear to God; acknowledge that I was afraid of bringing in ego and doing harm, and ask for divine help. We talked in depth about my aspiration to offer love and do no harm; and of my feelings of ignorance and of inability to do so. After talking, I meditated for a while then felt strong energy around me and started to get up. Suddenly I heard Aaron say, "Sit again, now, and focus all of your attention."

I did, of course, and felt a vital flow of love surround me. A very beautiful, radiant being was in front of me, what I have come to know as the Christ energy, or simply as Jeshua. The loving compassion that flowed from Him was reflected in His eyes. He held out both hands to me and raised me to stand in front of Him. He began to sing and perform a beautiful Sufi prayer and dance, *"May the blessings of God rest upon you; may His peace abide with you. ..."* Slowly I joined in, matching my voice and hand motions to His. As He sang, *"May His presence illuminate your heart...."* and touched my heart, I felt overwhelming joy and felt the divine presence within me.

We went through the song twice more, singing together as I looked deeply into His eyes. I've never seen eyes like those, bottomless and full of love. He truly touched my heart. As we stood there after the third time, I heard a deeper voice, almost echoing so it seemed to come from everywhere and from nowhere but within my heart.

Somehow there was a wordless thought, *"I am pleased with you, daughter; you are learning to trust my love."* A glow seemed to fill the sky and surround us. Only once before, as a child, have I experienced such brilliant light. I know that I stood in the presence of God. I also know that the words were not to enhance ego or to single me out, but just a statement of fact. I am learning to trust! After a few minutes the light dimmed a little, we sang this song one more time, and then Jeshua's energy dissolved. I just sat there filled with tears and joy.

That afternoon I met with the man, along with a friend who signed for me. He talked about his "righteous anger" with a situation in which he felt accused by people. He felt he had to say no to their accusations by attacking them. I really opened my heart to him, talking about my experiences in the South with violence and with love. I told him things I've never shared with anyone. In so doing, it seemed all my own righteous anger dissolved. I kept returning to love, a necessary ingredient we both agreed on. It was the only point of agreement. There was just no opening. He would not listen to any new thought that threatened his carefully built structure of anger and blame. He seemed to be able to twist everything I said to make me appear wrong. It didn't upset or anger me; I just couldn't find any way to get past the intellectual and emotional barriers and reach his heart.

The whole three hours was calm, even pleasant. I felt a great deal of love for him. But I also felt a sadness that he was so locked in to bitterness, rage, and misunderstanding. He kept saying he wasn't angry but that the wrongs done to him had to be righted. I kept talking about starting from now to work toward healing and forgiveness. He insisted there was nothing to forgive, that his actions against others were merely necessary to right the wrong.

That night about 1:30 a.m. I awakened with a start, feeling a sense of deep negativity. Something powerful was pushing at my mind, distorting my dreams and thoughts. I came fully awake hearing Aaron say, "You are safe. Speak to this negativity as I have taught you."

I tried to say the Lord's Prayer and couldn't remember it. The words came out all wrong. I tried the Twenty-Third Psalm. Same problem. I felt myself as if in a dense, dark cloud, awakening terror and confusion.

"Go to the Bible, " Aaron suggested. I did, and read and reread the Twenty-Third Psalm aloud until I felt my mind quiet and I regained centeredness. Then I went to sit on my meditation cushion in the living room. The fear slowly dissolved. There was only the image of the man to whom I had spoken.

I simply talked about love. "Love is the strongest power in the universe. Nothing can harm me while I hold fast to my faith in His love. ..." For about twenty minutes I spoke like this, repeating some of what I'd said that afternoon. I invited him to put his righteous anger aside and join me in a forgiveness meditation. I sent him my love, as clearly as I could.

Slowly, eye contact was made. I repeated, "Love is the strongest force in the universe. Its supports are forgiveness and compassion. Anger and hatred cannot touch it. I do not fear you and I will not be brought to your way of thinking. God has touched my heart with His love. That love is also available to you. The choice is yours." I was able to say this with deep love for him and with no fear. Then his image faded. I glanced at the clock and it was 3:00 a.m. I began to talk with Aaron.

After a period of talk, I began to end the meditation when I became aware of dawning, brilliant light and of another presence. It was Jeshua again. And again I felt all the love and compassion that He brings with Him.

With great gentleness He reached for my hands. He asked me again to do what I could not do earlier that month, when He came repeatedly to where I stood on a wave washed shore, and asked me to walk with Him into the sea. Each time my fear was profound and I withdrew; and the image simply faded. Now He asked again, *"Will you come to the water?"* That night the water was quiet. At least there would not be surf to contend with. There was a full moon and it gave off bright light. The living room was there and no less real, but this image of the sea overshadowed all else.

He held both my hands and looked at me with great lovingkindness shining in his eyes. I looked for a moment and then turned away. He walked backwards, supporting me. I had fled from this experience so many times. Could I really trust to submerge myself? I felt a sudden and familiar sense of terror. A voice from deep within my heart commanded me, "trust." At the same moment I was impelled to look into His eyes, and they were filled with such love, such compassion that I was able to take the next steps. I did this knowing full well where they led, and that there would be no turning back—not then, not ever. This was an irreversible vow, to not be caught in the stories of the ego and put myself first, but truly, "To love thy neighbor as thy self" and, to "Do no harm; do only good." Perhaps that knowledge is what made it so difficult. It wasn't the promise itself that was hard, but my fear that it might be the ego that was making the promise, and that I would not be able to live up to it. I saw that this had been the constant background fear; to take a vow and betray it felt more harmful than not taking the vow at all. Can we do what we promise and intend? All my life I have held to the moral code, "Do no harm; do only good for all beings." It is a lovely concept, but now He was asking me to love enough to truly commit to it, regardless of the personal consequences.

Journal, April 1989

At chest depth we stopped. The water was warm. I felt comforted by His love and totally protected by my love for Him. He told me, as I submerged myself, to trust in my love for Him and I would have no difficulty in breathing, even beneath the sea. Then we knelt and the water closed over us.

All was still. I could breathe. I heard His voice, somehow. He told me that He would let go of my hands and to not be afraid. He let go and I was afraid and suddenly I could not breathe. He took my hands again, and breath returned. He asked again, *"Trust me;"* and released my hands. This time breath continued.

He asked me if I understood what baptism meant. I said no. He said that baptism is a confirmation of my love of God and of my willingness to follow Him wherever He asks that I go; and to follow with gladness, and no holding back. Placing His hands ever so gently upon my head, He said, *"I baptize you, Barbara, in the name of Abba, our Father, in the name of the Son who I was, and of the Holy Spirit that I am."* Then He gently took my hands, raised me onto my feet and walked back to the beach with me.

What we talked about is etched deeply into my memory and recorded in my journal. We talked of love and of following that love, not just when it's convenient, but always.

He said He was a brother to all mankind, and we talked about the eternal Father/Mother and His/Her love. If we harm or kill another, we harm the essence of the eternal in ourselves.

He talked about humility, about serving God, and praying for the grace to serve. He asked me to remember that this baptism was a sign of His and God's love and a symbol of my commitment to God. I must always trust God and His love and follow it, no matter how difficult that is. It must always be, "Thy will be done," and I must never oppose my will to His but listen joyfully and answer with a resounding, "Yes!"

He explained that this does not contradict free will. His will for me is always what I most need, although I may not see it clearly at the time. When in doubt I must ask, and listen, and the answer will always be in my heart.

He reminded me that God does not protect me; my protection is in my love and trust of God. With that faith, although my body can be destroyed, my essence cannot be harmed.

God never opposes our free will. When I do not trust, I create the conditions out of which the future arises. When I trust, I invite a different future.

I must continue to concentrate all my thoughts on both aspects of *ahimsa* or dynamic compassion. "Do not harm others," is basic, but nonharm to every living thing is not enough. The element of dynamic compassion must be there. Not just nonharm, but to do good for others; serve others. If I withhold, through fear, that is a type of harm. Here is where I must keep myself as clear as is possible, learn to listen, and trust. Do only good.

I asked how I could know. He said if I'm honest with myself and listen to the voice within I would always know.

At the deepest level there is no good or evil, as Aaron has already explained. All beings are perfect in their essence, immaculate and unlimited. It is this aspect of us that dwells in the eternal and through which is found "the deathless," or eternal life.

All being is illusion, as is all nonbeing. All that is, is the eternal; all else is illusion. But even here there are no opposites, no duality, since even the illusion is an expression of the eternal.

Know that nothing matters, even though I must act as if it does matter. No suffering must be allowed without trying to heal it; and yet there is no healer and no suffering. I must live on both planes simultaneously.

He reminded me of the rose garden I had seen several months ago. What I wrote about that experience is below:

Journal, February 25, 1989

As I meditated, I discovered that my rose was not the only one, that it is part of a garden with so many rosebuds, all touched by frost, all closed tightly. The sight of all those rosebuds touches my deepest compassion. I understand now what is meant by not just "my pain," but "our pain," the pain of humanity, the isolation of us all. I am able to step beyond my own pain, to ask the sun to touch us all, to allow us all to unfold. My isolation is diminished daily as I watch my own bud, and the entire garden, blossom into the light.

Jeshua also told me that compassion must be at the heart of all I do, compassion and forgiveness. When I have found true compassion there will be no need for forgiveness. There will be nothing to forgive.

He told me if I *"keep open a heart of compassion and forgiveness,"* I would always know what I should do. He reminded me that help is always available. I must not be too proud, or afraid, to ask. And when I hear God's voice, to always answer "Yes," with joy and gratitude.

There are only two emotions: love and fear. If I keep my heart open to love, I'll walk the true path. Fear seems the opposite of love but it is only a distortion of love. In the end, there is only love.

Finally, we rose and did the Sufi dance again on the beach, *"May the blessings of God rest upon you. May God's peace abide with you. May God's presence illuminate your heart now and forever more."* Each step has an accompanying hand motion. With the last step, each participant places a hand over the other's heart. I felt so much love as He touched my heart; saw the deep compassion as I looked into His eyes. I understood this love did not come to me because I was any more worthy than another, but simply because I had opened my heart to it. It is the birthright of us all, if we could but learn to open to it.

The moonlit sky was brilliant and I could feel God's presence once again.

The music ended. He turned to Aaron and said *"I entrust her to you,"* as he placed my hands in Aaron's and His image and energy dissolved.

It is impossible to explain this but Aaron gently held me for a few minutes while I cried. In an indefinable way, I literally felt the support of his presence. Finally I stopped crying and we sat to talk. We were still on the beach. This is what I experienced. He suggested we return to the living room.

He asked me to breathe deeply and to focus on my breath. I did, and slowly the surroundings changed. I became more aware that I was in the living room but everything else was the same. It was simply a matter of which scene was superimposed on the other, sea or living room. This was not a distant dream that snaps to a close but vivid, tangible experience.

Aaron simply assured me, "Yes, it was real, as real as I am. Everything you just experienced happened, just as you experienced it."

Finally Aaron and I began to talk, and I asked him many questions.

I asked him about the Buddha. I love Jeshua but am coming to love the Buddha too. Is this wrong? My heart answered, *no*. Aaron explained again what I already knew, made clearer by hearing it from him. There is one eternal. There is one law. The Buddha nature within yourself is no different than the Christ consciousness within yourself. The name does not matter. It is the part of each of us wherein dwells the eternal. It is that "still, small voice within," which I have known so well.

"I go for refuge to the Buddha," means just this; I go for refuge to the eternal, which is manifest in you and in me. We are all Buddha; we are all Christ. The essence is there. We have only to allow ourselves to more fully become this, to realize and express our true natures.

We talked of my purposes in this life and in all my lives. Aaron emphasized that I've agreed to teach, allowing him to speak through me. While I had agreed to this while still on the spirit plane before this incarnation, I have free will and may choose to stop at any time. If I wish to serve Him, it is one way that is offered.

He reminded me that there is no being that is teaching, and no being that is learning. I am simply a channel through whom the dharma can flow. As soon as there is self in this, the dharma is distorted. I must do this as purely as possible, watching constantly for signs of the ego's grasping, which will cause distortion. He reminds me, however, not to fear ego. "You cannot transcend ego until you accept ego. Ego is also an illusion. It is a mist that you may watch arise and then dissolve again. It is not ego's arising that creates distortion, but taking it as real and fixating on whether to act it out or to destroy it."

He reminded me that I am a servant, not a master. I'm here to serve God and all beings. My work is not to gain for myself but to give all that I can. Sometimes the choice to offer service illuminates an inner conflict and fear. When it does, I can also offer myself the deepest service, which is to create the setting in which my own growth may flourish.

And yet, there is no separate being that serves and none that is served, just service, just being, offered as purely and unselfishly as possible.

I asked Aaron why Jeshua, rather than the Buddha, had appeared to me. He said because it is more meaningful to me at this time. He reminded me that I have been Christian, Buddhist, Jewish, and of other religions. I have been teachers, monks, or nuns of all different traditions, in so many lifetimes. In this lifetime I'm bringing much of it together.

He also said, "The Christ is formless and unlimited. While Jeshua and Gautama Buddha are separate and unique as they lived their lives on Earth, they are also one and the same. There is no duality, certainly not in the deepest essences. How could the Buddha be anything but the Holy Spirit of lovingkindness and compassion? How could the Christ be other than pure awareness itself?"

I understood that I must be mindful at all times. I must learn to see through my preferences. One is as another. There is a Buddhist sutra or scripture Aaron had been teaching me, the *Heart Sutra*.[3] One of the lines is, "Form is emptiness and emptiness is form." These lines reminded me that everything is empty of a separate self; all things are interconnected. The sun and rain are in the flowers; the cloud is in the flowers. None has a separate identity, unrelated to the whole. In the same way, the blissful states of meditation and the most painful emotions are not separate. The heavenly realms exist; yet the thoughts and material forms of our relative reality are real and must be met with lovingkindness. I must stay in the middle, preferring neither the form nor the emptiness, but knowing that they are the same. Neither is solid or real. The only path is the middle way, avoiding both the promise of heavenly bliss and fear of the abyss; mindfully keeping my attention fixed only on the eternal and how I may serve the divine.

In alignment with those words, there is neither birth nor death, good nor evil, being nor nonbeing. Birth and death follow each other and each is necessary to the other. Sometimes there is material form; sometimes there is no material form. Yet also, "form is form and emptiness is emptiness," as he, Aaron, had taught me. I knew I must not get lost in the seeming paradoxes or in intellectual debate. Simply honor what is, which is the eternal.

Aaron returned to my purposes in this lifetime. There is a second purpose besides service to the light. I must seek out each life that has karmic ties to the present and resolve all that remains unresolved. All traces of lingering karma must be eradicated. He reminded me that forgiveness and love end karma, but the forgiveness and love must come from my own heart. As long as the karma is not attended to, it will return again. It must be resolved, and then balanced through action in the present.

I saw then how my willingness to teach is a way of balancing the old karma of ego-centeredness and fear, but only if it is done from a clear, centered, and loving place. He reminded me it doesn't have to be perfect, and that to grasp at perfection is also a voice of ego. Just hold the intention to love.

He promised me that there would be an opportunity to explore each life that has karmic ties to the present, and that is happening. He has helped me as much as he was able, but he can do nothing but show me and guide me. The forgiveness and love must come from my own heart. All debts must be paid. I must be totally responsible.

If even one seed is left, it may take new root.

I have learned that each new action and choice in the future must be made with great care, with awareness and love, always with the honesty and courage to confront new karma as it starts, and to correct it then. Only in this way can the wheel of birth and death be stopped. When I was confirmed in the synagogue at age sixteen, I received a Bible that had the words inscribed on the inner cover, "Think of the end and you will never do amiss." Those words have guided me for so many years and continue to do so; they are no different than "Do no harm; do only good."

I must extend forgiveness to all who brought harm to each being that I was. I cannot be free as long as there is another being who needs my forgiveness for his own freedom. "All beings, one body, I vow to liberate," are the opening words to the vow of the Bodhisattva, the one who wishes to live in service to all beings. What I do for others is for me, and what I do for myself is for all. Yet I must know that in the end there is nothing to do (or not do); nowhere to go; nothing but being. To believe that there is something to do, and a doer, is to solidify both the karma and the ego-self. I must balance both, the relative act of forgiveness and the ultimate in which nothing was ever done. I already knew this truth; Aaron told me I will be given the opportunity to learn more about it in the coming months. Each moment is new; there is nothing but that moment. There is never a need to be anywhere else but in that moment, as open-heartedly and fully as possible.

We talked a bit more about karma. He told me that I must be totally honest and look fearlessly at all that is there. The beings who have done whatever harm has been done are not me, yet I am all that remains of them. I must act to bring them peace and to balance the damage done by their unskillful choices, in whatever ways that I can. I must ask the forgiveness of all who have been harmed. I must allow space for total healing. Only then is the root cut. I must find all the seeds within myself and remove them, always with love, mercy, and forgiveness.

As we ended, Aaron cautioned me, "Do not cling even to the wonder and beauty of this memory of baptism and your conversation with Him. Know that it was real, but it is just a memory. Be with now, not the past or the future. It is not the memory which sustains you but the living presence of the eternal, which is always in your heart." He asked me to reflect upon this night with gratitude, to know the enormity of the gift I have been given, of having spent time with the one I know as Jeshua, and to have directly received His blessing. The entire experience lasted over four hours. Somehow my body had sat motionless for all of that time.

Much of what Aaron and Jeshua discussed with me that night revealed itself further in the years to come. The presence of these divine beings has been a great gift. But I've also learned that it's not necessary to have a direct encounter with these beings to experience their blessings. They are always here with us. Each of us has our own guides and teachers. The real gift of meeting Maharaj-ji and Jeshua has been to begin to know the divine level of self that each awakened in me. We will all have an opportunity to take that step, each in our own ways.

The practice with Maharaj-ji was devotion. There are many forms of devotional meditation. Just to sit in the divine presence is powerful. Many people like to chant and find it a heart-opening practice. The practice with Jeshua was surrender and faith; releasing fear into the fullest trust of the divine. Other paths lead us through the practices of compassion, gratitude, and generosity. One beautiful form of generosity is *seva,* a Sanskrit word that means service in all its many forms. In the Hindu tradition, "karma yoga" means to work in service to others. It is a way of helping the heart to remain open, and a path to balancing of karma. Any and all of these practices help to bring balance, and to keep the spiritual path connected, both to the world and to the divine, avoiding the narrowness of ego-centeredness.

INTERVAL I

Compassion *(Karuna)* and Lovingkindness *(Metta)*

A Guided Meditation

To be read to yourself or shared aloud with a friend. Please pause frequently.

Traditionally, lovingkindness meditation begins with the self. In our culture it is very difficult for many people to offer loving wishes to themselves, and so we begin with one to whom it is easier to offer such thoughts and then come around to the self later. In the traditional practice, one also offers loving wishes to a neutral person before the more difficult one. Here this step is left out to make the practice shorter. Please include it if you wish.

Compassion goes beyond lovingkindness in that it sees deeply into the suffering of others. It is not forgiveness, which is a further step. Rather, compassion opens the heart to the pain of all beings and wishes them well.

There is no right or wrong way to do this practice. If resistance arises, simply note it and reenter the meditation in whichever way you are able. You are not requested to dive all the way in, but only to enter as deeply as is comfortable for you.

As you work with this practice, please feel free to modify it and make it your own.

Find a comfortable position, body relaxed, back erect, eyes closed softly.

Bring to the heart and mind the image of one for whom there is loving respect. This person may be a dear friend, parent, teacher, or any being with whom the primary relationship is one in which you have been nurtured.

We often take such a person for granted. We see what is offered to us, but fail to see deeply into that being's situation. Look deeply at that being; deeper than you ever have before, and see that he or she has suffered. He has felt pain of the body or the heart. She has known grief, loss, and fear. He has felt loneliness and disconnection. She has been lost and confused. Along with the joy, see the ways in which this dear one has suffered.

Speaking silently from the heart, note this one's pain, offering first the person's name.
> You have suffered.
> You have felt alone or afraid.
> You have known pain in your body and your mind.
> You have known grief and loss.
> You have felt alienation, and the constriction of the closed heart.
> Your life has not always brought you what you might have wished.
> You have not been able to hold on to what you loved, or to be free of what brought pain.
> You have suffered.

What loving thoughts can you offer to this dear one? Let the thoughts come with the breath, arising and moving out.
> May you be free of suffering.
> May you find the healing that you seek.
> May you love, and be loved.
> May your heart open and flower.
> May you know your true nature.
> May you be happy.
> May you find peace.

Please continue silently, repeating these or alternate phrases for several minutes. Go slowly. Allow your heart to connect with this dear one, to open to his or her pain and to offer these wishes, prompted by your own most loving heart.

Now, let this loved one move aside, and into his or her place invite your own self. It is sometimes hard to open our hearts to ourselves. What blocks this love? For the sake of experiment, please try to follow the practice and see how it feels, even if it is difficult; always proceed gently, and without force.

Look deeply at the self and observe that (just as with the loved one), you have suffered. Speaking to yourself, say:

I have suffered.

I have felt pain in the body and the mind.

I have known grief, loss, and fear.

I have felt loneliness and disconnection, felt lost and confused.

I have not been able to hold on to what I loved, nor to keep myself safe from that which threatened me.

I have suffered.

See the ways in which you have suffered. Without engaging in self-pity, simply observe the wounds you have borne.

Speaking silently from the heart, this time to your own self, say your name.

What do you wish for yourself?

May I be free of suffering.

May I find the healing that I seek.

May I love and be loved.

May my heart open and flower.

May I know my deepest connection with All-That-Is.

May I be happy.

May I find peace.

Please continue silently, repeating these or alternate phrases for several minutes. Go slowly. Allow your heart to connect with your deepest self, to open to your pain and longing, and to offer wishes guided by an intuitive sense of what you most need.

Now let the self move aside, and in its place invite in one with whom there have been hard feelings. It is best not to choose the most challenging relationship at first, but to allow yourself to practice with a less difficult relationship, and then to move slowly to those relationships that bring up heavier emotions. Letting go, we invite the open heart. If it is difficult, use no force. Note any resistance.

For the sake of experiment, you might follow this practice just to see how it feels. Please express your own pain too, as you speak to this one. Can you feel the space where your pain and that person's pain are one? Say this one's name. Speak from your heart.

> You have hurt me, through your words, your acts, even your thoughts.
> Through what came from you I have experienced pain.
> When I look deeply, I see that you have suffered.
> You have felt alone and afraid.
> You have known pain in your body and your mind.
> You have felt loss and grief, have felt alienated; you have felt your heart closed.
> Your life has not always brought you what you might have wished.
> May you be free of suffering.
> May you find the healing that you seek.
> May your heart open and flower.
> May you love and be loved.
> May you come to know your true nature.
> May you be happy.
> May you find peace.

Please continue silently for several minutes, repeating these or alternate phrases. Go slowly. Allow your heart to connect with this person, to open to his or her pain, and to offer wishes prompted by the loving heart.

Throughout the world, beings suffer. Not just humans, but plants, insects, animals, even the Earth herself.

> May all beings everywhere be free of suffering.
> May all beings be happy.
> May all love and be loved.
> May all find the healing that they seek.
> May all beings everywhere find perfect peace.

CHAPTER 5

The Path of Healing

My work with Aaron over almost two decades has shown me that my deafness—like all illnesses of body and mind—has many, often subtle, causes. Environmental and genetic causes may be beyond our ability to amend. However, we can change the damaging tensions we unknowingly hold in the body, because these tensions originate in our thinking and perceptions. Think an angry thought and see where the tension occurs in your body. Perhaps your face gets red, your jaw tightens, or you start to cry. Your pulse and blood pressure may increase. At other times, perhaps an unpleasant fluttering sensation arises in your abdomen, or a headache develops. If the anger then dissipates and compassion arises, new physical experiences such as relaxation or a sense of ease might become predominant. We can think of the body as the mirror of the mind, because even subtle and transient mind states will reliably manifest in the body. If we are unable or unwilling to acknowledge and release these mind states as they arise and dissipate, the body will faithfully store its responses to tensions, thoughts, and emotions for years, even lifetimes.

Our beliefs of unworthiness, self-limiting thoughts, and fears can also damage the body. It is vital that we not scold ourselves for our habits. But it's also imperative to take responsibility for learning to make more skillful choices, and for learning what blocks us in choosing wisely. If we can develop an attitude of kindness toward our bodies and our minds, both in illness and while healthy, a space is created wherein we can find greater potential for healing.

The ailment can become the teacher, using our body to lead us to profound self-discovery. This newfound wisdom can bring the light and space that often leads to physical healing. The result comes as a gentle correction that happens naturally and lovingly. This is in stark contrast to the results obtained by my first approach, which followed a now-familiar pattern of trying to control and "fix" the problem.

I learned this lesson deeply about five years after I first met Aaron. A bowel obstruction resulted in a hernia that eventually required surgical repair. With meditation and Aaron's guidance, it became clear to me how much tension I held in the belly. Whenever I was angry or controlling, the intestine poked through; a very painful reminder of these tension-inducing mind states.

Journal, November 12, 1994

I have never lived in my body, but tolerated it—even caring for it reasonably— as a tool. I've always maintained a distance. I went home after my hospitalization for the bowel obstruction with a tear in my abdominal wall. I have to keep my bowels soft or the intestine protrudes through the wall, creating a painful hernia. "Stay put," I command. On an almost daily basis I feel the enraged panther begin to pace and snarl. I lie down on my back and literally push this seething mass back inside. I am at war with my body and it is at war with me. This morning Aaron asked me, "What is this war you perpetuate? Peace never comes with hatred, but only with love. Can you learn to love this body just as it is, in this moment?"

I spent the summer of 1995 in a cabin in the forest. There I was graced to live for eight weeks, in a "tree house" on a steep hill. I came to the wilderness with a program to mend what was broken. I would do intense meditation and some exercise, try a set diet, and work with specific body energy practices; all of which sounded reasonable to my brain. I began this healing regimen, but no surprise; there was no change in the hernia or pain.

In the hospital the previous year, I had reflected on the Greek myth of Sisyphus, who was condemned for eternity to push a boulder up the hill and watch it roll back down again. "Sisyphus couldn't make the boulder stay at the top of the hill," I observed. "Suffering results from his belief that he could." Yet here I was, like Sisyphus, still trying to make my body and mind follow certain rules. I needed to watch and listen deeply to see what was actually there, and to hear what healing was desired.

All summer I read from the Buddhist sutras. "If the body is cultivated, then the mind can be cultivated." To cultivate my garden is to reach my hands deeply into the soil. I saw how I had been refusing to dirty my hands with the body, but striving to stay apart from it, untouched by its pains.

Slowly I stopped trying to control and fix, stopped trying to tell my body what to do; and began to listen to both body and heart at deeper levels. I put diet aside. I ate small amounts of food, and then meditated to discover which foods my body could not tolerate. Nurturing "don't know," instead of dictating terms, I asked and listened. I got a deeper sense of the karmic imbalances I'd carried, not just for a year, but also for lifetimes.

I learned to watch these myriad contractions that filled my days. I offered the mental note, "contracted, contracted;" allowed the deep experience of that contraction; and noted any holding or opposition to it as just further contraction. There was no need to attack the contraction or otherwise perpetuate it. I found it very powerful to watch the whole movement and see how it eventually dissolved. The more I worked with it, the more spaciousness I experienced. There is nothing separate from the divine; nothing that I needed to cling to or fight against.

Journal, October 3, 1995

I sit at a rolling desk chair in my cellar office, under high slits of window where a gray predawn morning peeks through the spruces beyond the glass. On the altar the candles are still lit. The counter behind my back holds the inevitable piles of mail, class notes, and phone messages awaiting attention before I leave town to lead a retreat. My appointment book announces a day of meetings and a promised evening of folk dancing with my family. My belly speaks a warning, "tension, tension," and I bring gentle awareness to the tight place. "Breathing. . . ." Tension is just tension. No need to let it go further.

Yesterday afternoon the intestines pushed through the hernia as they had not done for several weeks. Bean sprouts; another food I cannot eat. For the first time there was no Sisyphus attempting to hold the rock at the top of the mountain, just a soft awareness that touched this tender spot with mercy. I went to lie down, embracing the belly and the pain. A shrug. If it's going to be out, it will be out. 7:00 p.m. and twenty-four people are waiting for me to begin the class; belly still out. I lifted myself from my bed, walked out to the meditation hall, briefly sat and told the class why I would lead the meditation lying down. "We must be honest with our bodies. . . ." Lying there in the warm glow of candlelight, surrounded by the loving energy of these students, I observed the tension releasing completely. No secondary contraction and no denial; just there with pain and aversion to pain; noting it all arising and then passing on.

Finally the doctors agreed that it was time to operate. I began to look more closely at the tension about surgery. Clearly I was not about to die. While it was major surgery, the question was whether it would hold, would work; not whether I would survive. So what was the fear? I began to see the multiple meanings of "live" and "die." If the body is to survive, what must die?

The thought of someone cutting open the belly brought an awareness of letting down my defenses. I saw fear's unwillingness to allow the heart to really be touched. I could see the armor, however thin, that I've always carried. Yet armor can become a prison. I viewed the operation as a crossroads where my life's path offered a clear choice to "live or die." To "die" means to remain imprisoned in the armor. The words of a favorite old poem ran through my mind:

> I have heard the key
> Turn in the door once and turn once only
> We think of the key, each in his prison
> Thinking of the key, each confirms a prison.[1]

To die is to live in the ego, to continue a belief in one's limits.

To live is to dissolve the armor, transcend the prison; to invite the death of the ego and to rest in the vast spaciousness that remains. How do we do that? By allowing oneself to be touched utterly, completely; by allowing the heart to be broken open to its natural state.

The actual surgery was simple, so much so that they decided to send me home that day. The anticipated internal patch was not needed. The tissue was healthy. The process of the surgery was profound for me. As they strapped my arms to either side before the anesthetic was given, I thought of Jeshua on the cross and was able to surrender all fear, and to offer the body and the tender belly with love.

The learning was not just related to the physical body but was also about emotions and the emotional body. The emotion of anger first brings contraction; sometimes, a further contraction follows, based upon aversion to the anger. I learned that I couldn't just push away anger, or my reaction to it. I could see the damaging effects and, with kindness, choose not to hold on to difficult emotions.

One day when the children were young, I was angry because the truck delivering the new refrigerator was hours late, and so I was late picking up one of the boys for a music lesson. I had told the men that I was angry when they came. Driving into town twenty minutes later, I was still fuming. Aaron finally asked me "Are you enjoying your anger, child?" I saw how I was misusing it to blame others and feel powerful. His question made me notice how bad the anger felt: stomach tied in knots, shoulders tight, a headache. I could see exactly where I was holding the anger in the body. Then Aaron said, "Let it go. This is not a judgment on anger, but you can see that you don't need it. Just let it go." And just like that, I was able to make the decision, and to let go. I was truly not suppressing the anger, or feeling an aversion to being angry, just letting go. I could look at myself experiencing anger and smile at myself for getting so caught up in it. The energy of the anger had simply exhausted itself, and now I had ceased to feed it any more fuel.

I asked Aaron if this wasn't choosing a pleasant experience over an unpleasant one, instead of treating it all equally with his "choiceless awareness?" Choiceless awareness means to bring awareness to whatever is predominant in this moment, but now I was not letting go of an experience that was blissful, but of an experience that was painful. This seemed contradictory to what he had been teaching me.

Aaron: When there is a blissful experience you also cannot hold on to it. You must just know it, and then let it go. If you continued to hold on to it, I'd tell you the same thing: examine your attachment to it, and then let it go. This is no different than your attachment to anger. Attachment to anything needs to be explored, and then let go. There is no judgment of good or bad, just recognition that there is an attachment. The recognition itself is usually enough to diminish the attachment. If it is not, then you may remind yourself to let it go, or ask yourself what would support that release, which cannot be forced. That which is aware of the attachment is not attached. Rest in that awareness. Attachment slips to the background and releases itself in time.

There is another issue. When your energy is directed in an unskillful manner that creates suffering, then you may choose to redirect the energy. You must use care here not to judge the feeling. You are not judging the anger, but noting that it is creating suffering. Why hold on to it? It is more skillful, and more compassionate to yourself and others, to let it go. As you better understand the nature of your desires and aversions, you will find that increasingly you have this choice: to redirect your energy, to choose the more harmonious path.

Letting go can never be a grasping to let go; rather, it is something that you allow. You have learned to be aware of and label each mind moment and sensation. Can you see the beginnings of letting go in that labeling? As you say "feeling anger," in a very real sense you have already begun to let go of anger. This is because of the pattern you have established through your meditation, which is to observe, but not to be carried off by an experience. Each time you became aware of the mind wandering you labeled what was being experienced and, as its intensity waned, let go of it as part of the process of returning to your breath. That practice created the foundation.

Now when you feel a strong desire, emotion, or physical sensation and label it, you move again into that more skillful pattern. You see the anger, label it, and allow the return to the breath. You are aware of the physical remnants of the anger in the body, but the intensity of the pain is already lessening. In this way you allow a letting go.

Yes, the mind is still following a pattern; there is not total freedom. But with mindfulness, there will develop an awareness of this pattern and even more choice. For now, can you merely accept that the pattern of nonattachment carries less suffering than the pattern of attachment?

I found that I could follow this new and more practical pattern of response with increasing ease. When a thought or feeling was creating tension, I could see "through" it, to the place where it no longer was. I became aware of it as just something passing by, and was no longer caught up in it. When I did get caught in the story—the anger, fear, or worry—there was no longer a self-judgment, just the experience of the emotion and the awareness of getting caught.

I'm thinking of a time when I had lunch with several friends who took me out for my birthday. At the table they were all talking about a movie I had not seen and the old feelings of rejection arose. That kind of reaction had not happened in a long time. But that day was my birthday; I felt that the day should be different, that I should be included. I saw the anger coming up, the old story of, "It's not fair," and felt a hatred of the deafness. Aaron reminded me, "There are two things happening; one is that friends are talking while ears can't hear.

The other is that there is anger at this non-hearing, then anger at the self; a judgment of the first anger. Open your heart to yourself, child. The anger is just anger. Allow yourself to feel the anger, and to feel compassion for this human who suffers."

I shifted my focus to my breath: "Breathing in, I am aware of the anger. Breathing out, I smile to the anger." I allowed myself to feel the heat and tension of it, and also to feel that which was cool and spacious right there with anger. The anger stopped being the entire experience and was just a part of it. As it opened up, I began to relax and follow the energy of the conversation, to enjoy the animated looks and feel the love of my friends. In a few minutes I was totally at ease again, and enjoyed the lunch and the people.

Through the years, many people have offered ideas for healing the deafness and related balance problems: perhaps this energy practice or that herbal formula, this healer or that ritual. I was willing to try some of what people offered, but I also knew that it all would unfold in its own time and way, and that nothing presented thus far felt right. The deafness was a result; and its multiple causes needed to be dealt with first. I was healing in deeper ways, opening my heart to my own pain and that of the world, and living with less fear. I had addressed physical causes as much as possible with traditional and alternative medicine. But unwholesome mind states needed to be addressed through meditation and inner work before the deafness could be addressed more fully.

Balance was a major concern in my life as the dead nerves of the middle ear deprived me of normal balance. For over twenty years, just standing upright had been a literal struggle. During a personal retreat in the woods, walking in the dark was difficult without balance. Aaron asked me, "What does it feel like to allow imbalance? Mind is clinging; tight. Experiment literally with balance. Do you see how you fight for balance, or rather, fight to avoid imbalance? See in detail what occurs when balance is lost. What maintains balance, fear or love?"

At Aaron's suggestion, I went out early one morning, in the moon-light, and allowed myself to lose balance, literally to fall over in the snow as I stood in the dark woods. First there was fear, then falling. Falling was easy. It was hard to watch the fear. I quickly saw the metaphor of physical balance to the concept of being upright in terms of being good. There was a hard moment, watching myself grasp to remain upright. I did it about ten times, watching tension and allow-ing myself to fall. I was able to see the myth of uprightness, being in control so that I would do no wrong.

Aaron told me, "You work so hard not to fall, as you worked to fight the belly, as you have striven to fight anger and other negative thoughts. Yet, within you there is an innate perfection that you dis-regard in your fight to control negativity. When you trust this inherent radiant strength and goodness, the war will end."

After Aaron spoke, I saw that I wasn't finished, so I went back out to the woods. Snow was falling hard, big white flakes. Using walking sticks for support, I walked to a clearing by the stream, where there was a small waterfall. Snow was soft and deep all around. I closed my eyes, let myself lose balance and fell; feeling the loss of balance, then fear, then immediate contraction into an effort to rebalance. "Bring attention to the fear. Just watch it," said Aaron. I watched myself fall and felt the big tension of I *must stay balanced*. Again the falling was easy. Being present with I *must stay balanced* and all the ancient habits wrapped up in that myth was very hard. Balance equals certainty; control equals safety.

I fell into the deep snow again and again. Tears began to come fast, as I allowed myself to fall, to not have to be upright in all the meanings of that word.

There was a memory of how hard I worked to cope with my deaf-ness to protect Hal and infant Mike, how much of my experience I needed to deny. I thought I had resolved this issue years earlier. Here was another layer. Let it arise. Letting go of craving for certainty, craving for control, grasping at staying upright, to be the good one, the one who takes the responsibility on herself, to "do no harm," to be impeccable, clear. Knowing these all as thought, just conditioned thought; the energy of them dissolved as I fell and fell. Allowing falling, I let go of belief in the old stories of mind, of someone wrong, unworthy, or incomplete. Eventually the thoughts and tension ceased, leaving just Barbara, sitting in utter peace in the snow, tears still flowing, but the need to be upright in all its connotations was released. I had fallen and no harm resulted. I do not need to be perfect! I felt Aaron's energetic hug and his joy for me.

Now I became mindful of the experience of deafness and the ways I had used deafness as both shield and sword. Aaron asked the question, "What might this deafness protect you from?" I had to admit to myself that deafness had its uses. It was a shield. I didn't want to hear the enormous pain of the world and face my seeming helplessness to change the suffering. In a more personal way, I saw how deafness allowed avoidance of boring or unpleasant conversations, permitting retreat into my own world. Deafness was also a sword. It's so useful and hurtful, when someone is yelling at you, to be able to say, "I missed that; please repeat it." That's certainly having the last word in an argument. It gave me a sense of control. I wasn't a mean person. I just acted out my fears as most of us do. My meditation practice helped me to acknowledge this dynamic and take responsibility for it. Aaron asked me:

Journal, December 20, 1995

What does it mean to be a peacemaker? Certainly one thinks twice about attacking one who has a sword. But sword bearing does not lay the groundwork for peace. It only means that you must always carry your sword. There is nothing wrong with carrying a sword. I personally carried swords in many lifetimes with no desire to use them. But the sword does no good unless there is an intention to use it if one feels such use to be necessary.

And again:

Journal, November 1996

What is the sword that you carry? How long are you going to wear it? I'm not condemning the warrior with his sword. I'm not judging the frightened person who wants to be safe, or the habit energies of so many lifetimes.

Get a clearer understanding of the nature of the sword that you presently aspire to lay down; a clearer understanding of what would support that movement.

We do not condemn the negative behaviors; we simply note, "This habit is unskillful," such as self-blame, self-judgment, or judgment of others. "This is unskillful. It is only a habit to pick up my sword to protect myself." You know what would help the move to lay it down: your deep intention to do no harm to yourself or any being. What nurtures that intention? Certainly not more judgment or armoring. And you must also ask yourself, "What resistance is there? If I know that seeking out and nurturing the intention to kindness will help me to lay down the sword and I don't do it, it's because there is some fear." You spoke of relief at laying down the sword but failed to acknowledge the fear that would come up once you stood without the sword. That relief is genuine but also, there you are, naked. You're vulnerable, because you carried the sword with belief in its protective power.

Once this foundation of nonreactive awareness was in place, I could better cease to use deafness as a sword or a shield, and simply be present with kindness in whatever situation arose. Each of us carries the karma of many lifetimes into this one, and as we balance and resolve that karma, we find the healing that was our plan before we moved into the body. We don't need to see past lives or even believe that they occurred. What most needs to be healed shows itself very plainly in this life. What's hard for us? Is there selfishness, impatience, feelings of unworthiness, a quick temper? Meditation is one path for resolving karma, because we are able to become mindful of these difficult places. This new presence with challenging situations, with kindness, releases old karma and is the healing for which I took birth. I had looked at my hatred of deafness, and feelings of loneliness and despair. I was healing my sense of separation from my self, from other people, and from divinity. That healing allowed me to be kinder to my self and to others.

After many years of such explorations and practice, I felt I could clearly say that I no longer have any use for the deafness. I had learned what I could from the deafness, and had at least partially balanced the karma surrounding it. I no longer needed it as a defense or a way to avoid the pain of feeling rejection. I no longer used it as a weapon against others or myself. I felt ready for the next step, unknowing of what it was; only that it had not yet appeared.

CHAPTER 6

A Door Opens

IN 2001, I received a very personal e-mail from a stranger named Jan whose mailing list I had crept onto through a computer glitch. In it she told her friends about her healing journey to the Casa de Dom Inácio (House of St. Ignatius of Loyola), in Abadiânia, Brazil; and about João Teixeira de Faria, affectionately known as João de Deus (John of God), who heads the Casa. He is the medium for very loving, discarnate healing spirits known collectively as the Casa Entities. An entity is simply a discarnate spirit, complete with his/her mental qualities, skills, and personality. In contrast, the soul is a deeper level of the spirit, that which is beyond most of the attributes of mind and personality.

I had made peace with my deafness, and had not been consciously looking for such healing. Yet the information in this e-mail resonated deeply. Now that the mental and emotional consequences of my deafness were healed, I had often wondered, could the body heal also? I opened various websites to read about John of God. When I saw João's photograph, I felt a profound sense of familiarity and connection, and knew that this was a path that I might take. Once I had decided to go, it took another year to make plans, earn money for the trip, get immunizations and a visa, find a guide, and convince my husband that it was a safe journey. It took months to even find the small village of Abadiânia on a map. Now, fortunately, it is much easier to get there.

I needed that year for inward preparation too. I had learned to trust my intuition. There have not been many times when I have felt very called to something, but each time, the prospect has arisen seemingly out of nowhere. When I have followed the call, it has always led to wonderful results. It had been many years since this little voice inside had spoken in this way; a whisper more than a shout. I read everything about João and the Casa on several websites, but more importantly, I began to meditate with this possibility. I had no precise idea what the connected feeling was about. I just trusted it. My hearing might be restored but that was not the primary issue. If it happened, wonderful; if not, that would be okay too. I felt I just needed to go.

When I first read about João, I initiated a correspondence with Jan. In that six-month interval, three other people mentioned João to me. Jan had been there for three months. In her words:

"You asked why I stayed for three months—I had to because of how ill I was at the time. I have had a relationship with systemic lupus for almost thirty years. It has damaged my heart, lungs, and kidneys. This past August the disease went into my brain and I had acute cerebritis. I was certainly not long for this world. I had lost my motor skills and my speech was deteriorating very quickly. The doctors put me on extremely high doses of steroids and chemotherapy once again. Within two days, four people told me about John of God, and the miracles began immediately.

"I managed to get to Brazil with great difficulty. I was in a wheelchair when I arrived and it was seven weeks before I was strong enough to walk on my own. I had over twenty surgeries. It took me a long time to get this way, and it took me three months to turn it around.

"I went from twelve medications to one. I have twelve days left of prednisone, then I will be 100 percent off of all of my medications for the first time in probably thirty years."

Her story certainly was dramatic and inspirational, but three months was much longer than what I could contemplate, and her situation was more dire than my own. I wanted to give myself three weeks or a month there, time to live very quietly in this rural village, do a lot of meditation, walk in the countryside, talk some to people who live there, and attend deeply to spirit.

By February 2003, I had deeply explored both aversion to deafness and attachments to it, seeing the way I might hide in it or misuse it. I was very much at peace with deafness, but there was certainly a preference to hear. Such hearing would not simply drop into my lap, but would be a result of my sustained intention and effort. I had always felt that I needed to follow up on possibilities. This is part of the process of manifestation, to take the responsibility to invite that which we seek into our lives. Without will and intention, nothing can happen. But how does one invite without grasping?

Is such an invitation consistent with letting go and with, "Thy will be done?" This is what confused me and was something I had to investigate. The question of how to invite this healing into my being without grasping at it was a hard one for me. Through considering it, I began to learn more about manifestation in all areas of life.

To manifest is to cocreate what we desire. We might manifest a good relationship, or job, or better health. When it is for the highest good, we have broad support for such manifestation as we work in harmony with others. Two people together can cocreate a loving relationship. One cannot do it alone. As a world, we can cocreate a healthful environment. It does take intentional effort.

While we envision and hold intention for what we want, we simultaneously know that we cannot control the outcome, only invite, and the invitation is made with joy and spaciousness, not with fear and grasping. This seemed a paradox to me at first. How could I desire and envision without grasping? How could I reconcile effort toward hearing and "Thy will be done?" Through the years I had developed friendships with several other mediums and the entities they channel. One important such friendship is with Judith Coates[1] and Jeshua, an expression of Jesus (I described some of my own meditation encounters with Jeshua, earlier). Jeshua's words through Judi were very helpful to me as I pondered the relationship of healing, intention, and fear.

I said to Jeshua, "I'm planning to go to Brazil next January, inviting hearing and healing. I find myself with the question, how does one seek and invite without grasping? I do see the grasping as it is, just grasping, and am able to not get caught in it. Is the invitation to healing consistent with 'Thy will be done?' I no longer suffer from the deafness, yet there is still pain from this loss. I'm afraid to try to go beyond it. I don't know how to do this, or even if I should try.

"Jeshua, I think of you on the cross; of the fear and the pain you must have experienced. Yet you said, 'Thy will be done.' Did you choose to go beyond fear and pain, and if so, how?" Jeshua replied, speaking through Judith:

Jeshua: *"It was a choice to rise above the pain on the cross. I had experienced many opportunities for pain and fear of pain when studying with masters prior to the beginning of my 'ministry' and I knew human emotion. I knew fear. I knew its effect on the body; I knew contraction of bodily functions and the emotional reaction of hatred of fear. I also knew the skill, a learned skill, of expanded consciousness through the breath—allowing space, as Aaron has put it, for the fear, and then choosing to focus on the space around and beyond fear; breathing (not only physical, but a soul-spiritual breathing) to remember the divinity of man, which even allows the creation of fear. What I did, you can do also, and even greater things will you do. Have you not this saying in your Holy Scriptures? So, you see, I did not choose to do something that is beyond your human ability to do, but I modeled a choice, a very important choice, and yet an easy choice when one remembers who and what they are, Holy and Beloved Child of the Father— which is you."*

Through Jeshua's words, I began to understand that I could choose without grasping and could hold the clear image of that which was desired, without denial of the present experience.

There was still so much to understand. What confused me most was that if there is true equanimity, I wondered how we move toward anything. What supports effort?

I began to reflect on nonattachment around deafness/hearing. That nonattachment was genuine. I did trust that I experienced what was needed. I was able to watch feelings of desire to hear and to see that such desire could be free of contracted grasping. I could see the loss and sadness without aversion. I was also able to appreciate the depth of silence in which I lived, and not grasp. And I could see the potential loss of this seclusion in which I live, without aversion. There was equanimity.

Finally I understood that this equanimity is not incompatible with the joyous embracing of ultimate perfection. Jeshua spoke of choice. One can, and must, choose, but without grasping. This is not only possible, but is a necessary next step.

At the highest level this body is perfect. There is no deafness (or any other distortion). On another level there is distortion. To invite the re-expression of the Ever-Perfect on the physical level, there must be a conscious choosing. I choose to hear. There is still equanimity: a deep knowing that if there is no hearing, that's okay. The choice of hearing doesn't entail a grasping energy. But there must also be acknowledgment of the readiness to hear everything, all the laughter and all the cries, and a joyful embracing of that possibility. There must be the statement, "I want this, if it serves all beings," not the old "either is okay."

The intention to service, the intention to evolve, and the intention toward love and healing are choices. If my "YES, I want to hear again," does not serve beings best, I can let it go, but if it is harmonious with the needs of beings, I choose this! The energetic thrust of an active reaching out to manifest healing is necessary to the healing. Invitation and grasping are very different. There must be invitation/intention.

There is a fine line between grasping and appreciation. Lacking the trust in ourselves not to grasp and thereby suffer, we often don't allow ourselves to appreciate that toward which we aspire. Lacking appreciation, there can be no reaching out with an intention to re-express wholeness; therefore, one remains caught in one's seeming limitations. Then one replays those limitations. True equanimity and resignation are completely different experiences.

I also struggled with the ideas of limitation and innate perfection. I explored the word "distortion" and how that word relates to the word "limitation." Aaron uses the word distortion in a very specific way, using the example of a light that seems to bend as it enters the water. The water is a heavier density; therefore, the density shift affects the light ray. Distortion isn't bad or good, just an apparent bend.

It is true on one level that there is no distortion; everything is perfect. However, the perfection of this moment may be based upon an intention to learn something, and an assumed need to create limitation in order to invite that learning. Perhaps I want to get from point A to point B via a straight trail, but I also want to climb a hill so that I can see the entire landscape. The climbing detour seems to distort the direct path from A to B. Seen from another perspective, however, the longer route is perfect, because I wanted to see the view. Hiking the straight trail then seems to become the distorted action.

I am limited when I get stuck in the belief that I must always get from A to B by climbing up the hill. Then there is no freedom. Or I am limited if I get stuck in thinking that it's bad to climb up the hill and, therefore, that I must avoid it. Belief in any limitation of the mind or body contracts the energy and locks us into that pattern of thought. Then we create the future based on those limiting beliefs.

The pain of my deafness, a distortion, had served its purpose. Belief in the need to continue that pain is a limitation based in fear. When we can see where we wish to go and, paradoxically, that we are already there, then there is no going or coming. Then distortions become possibilities, and we can play with the various possibilities

without holding them fixed in such a way that they become limitations. On the one level there is a deaf Barbara. On another level there
never was, nor will there be, a deaf Barbara.

I had learned in meditation and through Aaron's guidance the the-
ory and practice of how to move beyond limiting beliefs. I respond
to the human level on which I experience this illusion of limitation
as if it were a temporary climb up the hill to see the view, so to speak.
Then I am able to release the need for that arduous climb when it is
no longer necessary. After releasing, I invite in the innate perfection,
which has always been there. Then I am no longer stuck in the illusion
of limitation that has manifested itself so convincingly.

I asked myself, somewhat audaciously, "What prevents me from
using this process with deafness?" I had been seeing it as an either/or
situation; I was either deaf and caught in the deafness, or hearing and
free of the pain of not hearing. I had not realized the simultaneity of
both. But after much learning and practice, I no longer identified with
the limitation. There was no "should," such as "I should embrace
this," or "I should get past this." These had passed. Instead, I had a
genuine gratitude for the illusion of limitation and all that it has
brought forth, as well as gratitude for the innate perfection and beautiful gift of human sensory experiences. I saw no fundamental problem with my intention to heal my deafness. Not only was it possible,
it seemed practical. I saw the beginnings of the path.

Remembering to express our innate wholeness is part of our
work as humans. We are not here just to become enlightened and
move on, but are also here to express the fullness, the joy, and the
love of this wonderful realm that we have been given; a realm which
contains opportunities for both suffering and joy. We need to choose
consciously.

Insight deepened as the months passed. Below is part of a letter to my
guide for the journey to Brazil, Heather Cumming.[2] I had connected
with Heather on the Internet. She's one of a select group designated
by the Entities as Daughters and Sons of the Casa. She was raised in

Brazil but presently lives in the U.S. and speaks Portuguese and English fluently. She takes groups to the Casa numerous times a year. Since João and the Entities speak Portuguese, a translator is helpful. There are volunteers at the Casa who translate into many languages, but my travel companions and I decided to obtain the services of a personal guide for this trip.

August 2003

Dear Heather,

... João came to my attention at a time when I was looking deeply into questions of manifestation and karma. I understood the karma behind the deafness, had seen the various past lives that contributed to that karma, and understood it energetically also. I had not yet understood that along with equanimity and intention to service there needs to be a more compassionate response to myself. There is no more grasping to hear, nor hatred of the lack of balance. But there is still a choice to hear and to not have to struggle in order to stand up. To invite hearing and balance as a facet of wholeness is very different from grasping at them.

Wholeness is already present. But there is also a distortion. What invites healing? I have seen that my work is to release anything that blocks my healing. Whether further physical healing can happen is yet to be seen. My work is not to worry about that, just to clear the way for the possibility, to make the clear statement of invitation to that possibility, to bring myself to the Casa where that healing is most possible, and then to let go.

So that's why I'm going to Abadiânia. The most important insight gained this year was how to invite without grasping, even seeing that this is possible. We allow the flow of karma as part of learning, seeing the results we invite through our conditioning. We understand how we have invited unpleasant results. We learn, and then release the teacher. This is what I have recently begun to understand.

My understandings would grow dramatically in the coming months and years.

CHAPTER 7

Casa de Dom Inácio

I LEFT FOR BRAZIL in January of 2004, accompanied by three people. Kate, a longtime student, came to help me, as well as to heal her own vision, and for personal spiritual reasons. My son Davy came to heal his psoriasis, and to do a documentary for National Public Radio. A new friend named Mel decided to travel with us. She had visited the Casa in November 2003, seeking help for her deafness.

We flew to Brazil on Sunday, January 13, 2004. The flight was smooth; all three legs were as comfortable as twenty-four hours of travel can be. A highlight was flying over a chain of Caribbean islands at a time when the sky was clear. They were lit by full moonlight, and looked like jewels in the sea. The stars were brilliant and seemed to be just outside the window. Mesmerizing. Unfortunately, when flying over the Amazon rainforest, we were in deep clouds. I hoped the flight home would allow a glimpse of this natural wonder.

The promised taxi, a large station wagon, met us at the airport in Brasilia, the driver waiting with a sign that read, "Barbara." Since he spoke no English, we got no further than introductions. We were all too tired to care, and fell asleep during the ninety-minute drive out of the city and into an increasingly rural Brazilian countryside of farmlands, woods, and rolling hills. I kept waking to lovely vistas, then falling back to sleep.

Our *pousada*—Portuguese for hotel—was a clean two-story stucco building with about twenty rooms. Each room had beds for one to three people, and a private bath with toilet, sink, and shower. This pousada also included one central room, an outdoor courtyard, and a kitchen. I've found that this is typical. The food, served cafeteria style, was delicious and simple. Breakfast was typically plain rolls, cheese, and fruit. Cereal and eggs might be available. Lunch and dinner were usually fresh salad and fruit, rice and potatoes, beans, several cooked vegetables, meat, and the best free-range chicken I've ever tasted. Occasionally there was a dessert in addition to the fruit.

Abadiânia, the village that holds the Casa, is small and rural. Children play soccer in the field across the road from the hotel, and fly kites. Toddlers play in the dirt with small toys, while mothers or older siblings watch and talk. Men sit at tables in front yards and play cards in the evening coolness. Life seems to be lived in these front yards. Small lanes have stucco houses with outer courtyards that face the street. Some are polished-looking and with fresh and bright paint; some are very poor. Overall, there is a sense of bright color, between a rainbow of paint hues and a huge variety of flowers growing everywhere. Chickens roam the streets, dashing out from underfoot as one approaches. Horses and cattle also walk freely, sometimes eating from the raised trash stands in front of houses, although I noticed two goats tied to a post. The road carries a mix of pedestrians, cars, bikes, motorcycles, and horse-drawn carts. The shops in this part of the town include an Internet café; a few restaurants including a pizzeria; several gift shops selling clothing, jewelry, and items like soap, towels, and flip-flops; and one small bookstore. Signs of new construction are evident also. The Casa itself is a sprawling cluster of buildings within walking distance of most pousadas. Across a two-lane highway is another section of Abadiânia with a more commercial area, which includes hardware and feed stores, a larger market and pharmacy, an auto repair shop, and more restaurants.

We arrived In Abadiânia on a Monday, and met with our guide, Heather, at the Casa on Tuesday morning. João, or Medium João, as he is often called, incorporates the Entities Wednesday through Friday of each week. On Saturday through Tuesday, João is not there and the Casa is very quiet. The Entities are still present and there is a real benefit to going there and meditating in the outer room or gardens. Heather took us on a tour, and explained to us the process that takes place at the Casa.

There are several rooms in the main building. The largest outer room has one side open to the air, a high ceiling of corrugated metal that is supported by wood-framed trusses, and a stage-like platform on the wall opposite the open end. The floor is tile, the lower walls are light blue up to about three feet and the upper walls are white. Big exhaust fans attempt to keep the room temperature tolerable, but it still gets very hot.* Benches line the walls and fill the center area. The room feels serene.

Heather said, "This is what I refer to as the Great Hall. This is our place of worship, our temple. If you want to ask me questions, I can answer them here at the doorway, but inside we need to hold the silence, just the same as if we went into a church. You can have a lot of work going on in there before you even see the Entities."

Next is the Mediums' Current Room. People sit there in meditation while the Entities work in the next room; the energy is powerful. Heather described the experience: "I liken sitting in this room to a spiritual bath where you are washed in divine light. I also think of it as unburdening yourself of what keeps you separate from your divinity, so that you may better receive the healing light and energies that are already being poured upon you." This room has the same blue and white walls and tile floor, but its ceiling is wooden. There are rows of comfortable upholstered benches.

The Entities' Current Room is where João sits while the Entity is incorporated. By that term, I mean that João moves out of his body, similar to the way I astral traveled to visit Maharaj-ji and Jeshua years

---

*Structural work in 2006 added ventilation that makes the rooms much cooler, including air conditioning in the Current Rooms.

earlier. The Entity then moves in to the body or "incorporates." It takes enormous love and faith to offer the body in that way.

This room looks like the first Current Room except that part of the space is allocated to a chair for João, an immense crystal that offers out high energy, an altar, and a wider aisle that allows people to move through the room. The distinctive energy generated and channeled in the Current Rooms is found throughout the Casa and the town, although it's of lesser intensity. If someone leaves the room, they don't lose the opportunity to experience the energy of the Current, since that energy is everywhere.

Much of the energy in both Current Rooms flows through people designated by the Entities as mediums. We are all mediums; a medium is simply the material through which something flows. Some people have a more conscious understanding of this ability to hold and transmit energy and to support a high vibration. People with such ability will be invited by the Entities to sit in one or another of the Current Rooms and support the work in useful ways. In the Mediums' and Entities' Current Rooms that usually means holding the high energy vibration that supports João's and the Entities' work. Some people who live in Brazil come regularly to serve as mediums. Others are invited to join these Currents after seeing the Entities.

The word "Current" is very specific. Aaron told me:

The Casa Current energy is analogous to an electrical current. It is a chain of energy, passing from one person to the next as long as it is unimpeded. Such energy must have a source. For the Casa Current, the source is the divine itself. As with an electrical circuit, the source can be constantly drained or it can be supported with new input. In your outer world, that new input might take the form of power gained from the sun or wind, which are expressions of the source. At the Casa the crystals, the Entities' high vibrations, and the loving intention of those who sit in the Current offering their energy; all provide support for an ongoing source of power that cannot be drained. The Entities draw on that Current for the high vibration and energy that is so necessary to their work. Those who sit in the Current do not merely give but also receive the fruits of cocreation of that high vibration. Giving and receiving are nondual; it must be reciprocal.

Heather explained the etiquette in the Current Rooms: "To honor the Entities we sit in silence in the Current Rooms. Close your eyes. Don't cross your arms and legs. The word "current" in Portuguese is *corrente*, like electrical current, but it also means a chain. So we are really like a chain of light, the creative life force that created us all. And the Entities of Light can work on us. If you cross your arms and legs, you are keeping it all to yourself and breaking that chain.

"Even when we're standing outside the rooms and not sitting in the Current, your guides and the Entities are with you so you want to not cross your arms. I'll always be reminding you; I do it myself. So we are forming a chain of love and light and healing for our highest good and the highest good for all. The Entities will start working on you when you're focused, making that divine connection, and have closed your eyes. Keeping the eyes closed helps protect you from negative entities, and from any discordant energy in the room. So, rule of thumb is, eyes closed, focused and concentrating in a place of connectedness to our divine light, inward light, our divinity, our higher selves; then the Entities can work on us. If we're making a shopping list, then we're not available for the Entities."

The fourth room is the surgery room, which is similar in appearance to the other rooms, except there are several hospital tables covered with clean sheets, lined up against the walls. The Entities invite people who have very serious conditions to lie here each day throughout the Current sessions. The final room is a surgery recovery room. This room is very simple and serene, very clean, with ten beds, all of sturdy wood painted white, and white sheets with the Casa emblem printed in the center. There are blue walls and a wood ceiling, and the room is somewhat dim and cool. A cabinet contains basic medical supplies such as gauze and bandages. There are several pictures, of Jesus, of St. Ignatius Loyola, and a few others. There are two crystal lamps. At one end is a small bathroom.

Beyond these rooms are offices, and an open-sided dining area where the daily spiritual soup is served. This is a huge pot of delicious vegetable soup lovingly prepared by volunteers and staff and served on the Casa days, Wednesday through Friday. Offered freely, the soup is blessed by the spirits and considered an important part of the healing process. Often served with a hunk of bread, this becomes the midday meal for people who come with little money. On Tuesday morning, volunteers can be found chopping the soup vegetables. I asked them how they know how much to make and was told that there's always just enough, not too much or too little. When I asked Aaron about this, he said the Entities advise about the expected number of guests.

The Casa is truly an ecumenical temple. The walls throughout the Casa are adorned with photographs, statements of gratitude, and religious paintings and icons, including drawings of many of the Casa Entities. Many of these adornments are Catholic, with many pictures of Jesus. But in the Great Hall there's a very large framed offering from the Dalai Lama with a statement of his blessings to João and to this work. I also noticed a framed object with pictures of many Hindu saints and other teachers, including Maharaj-ji. I felt great joy to see him on that wall, a confirmation that I had chosen wisely when I made the decision to come here. On the doorway into the Mediums' Current Room is a mezuzah, an important symbol of the Jewish faith. The altar beside João has a Christ figure, several statues of Mother Mary, and many flowers.

Behind the outdoor dining area is a lovely garden filled with many kinds of trees and flowering plants gathered from all over Brazil; there are winding pathways and hand-carved wooden benches. A bust of the founding saint, Dom Inácio, is at the front of the garden. We know him as Saint Ignatius of Loyola. Heather explained that the Entities prefer we not use the word "saint" because in their eyes, we are all equal, though some may be more mature. *Dom* is an honorific-like sir, a statement of respect. It is not unusual to see people sitting in prayer by this statue. People also often leave loving tokens here, such as flowers and prayer beads.

Also in the Casa complex, there is a small store where people can buy gifts, books, crystals, and water. The Entities suggest that you drink water charged with Casa energy. They raise it to a very high vibration. It's about the same price as the bottled drinking water one would otherwise buy in the market. Each morning they bring many bottles into the Entities' Current Room for blessings. Later, Aaron discussed the significance of the Casa's charged water:

Aaron: *The content of the cells in your body is largely water. That water is of a diminished vibration, even at birth, for the fetus picks up the mother's vibration. The cells in the average human body have a sluggish frequency that replicates the frequency of the earth around it. The cells contain water that contains impurities and toxins that have built up throughout the lifetime. The causes of the toxins are many, but primary among them are negative energies such as anger and fear, which draw a very low and distorted vibration into the body; and the lower frequency of our present-day Earth with its environmental damage. Even pure water from a fresh spring does not carry the light it might carry if it were able to express its full potential. The best you seem able to do then, at the human level, is to constantly fight disease rather than being able to live the wholeness that is your birthright. Imagine your teeth, which have the capacity to last through the lifetime if kept clean; yet decay when they are not kept clean. On your ideal Earth, the body also would not decay into the diseases caused by lowered vibrations. Even those who are careful about what they eat and drink still breathe polluted air and are constantly conditioned by the low frequency of the Earth itself.*

The books about the gardens of Findhorn[1] describe what happens when the lower vibration is deeply endowed with light. At Findhorn in Scotland, the gardeners attempted conscious cocreation with the plants, and worked with the plant devas,* rather than taking authority over them. When the devas are respected and the plants are cherished, the vegetables grown in such a situation have a higher frequency. They are healthy in themselves and promote higher frequency in those who eat of them. This is the Eden you were promised. It is not God's job to create it, but yours, through the manifestation of your own highest consciousness, your own divinity. It is what you volunteered for, and you have come again and again, working toward it.

---

*Deva is the Sanskrit word for deity.

The Entities remind you that a high vibration is your human birthright; but that this vibration has been forgotten. Everything at the Casa is of a higher vibration. The Entities' work brings a much higher vibration to the water in the cells. People are urged to drink a lot of the very pure, high vibrational Casa water, and to bring some of that water home. This replaces the lower quality water in the cells. Sitting in Current helps to support this shift. As the water quality of the cells raises in vibration, the cellular tissue becomes increasingly able to support the deeper changes the Entities are inviting the body to express. It is a continual process, and is supported everywhere at the Casa. The Earth energy is charged from the crystal bed beneath the Casa. The waterfall soaks the body with this high vibration. The kindness you feel around you supports this higher vibration.

There is a pharmacy. The Entity incorporated in Medium João's body writes out energetic prescriptions, if appropriate, as part of the treatment. In the pharmacy, humans and Entities work together to fill each unique prescription. Physically each capsule is filled with the same simple herb, but every capsule is charged with energy specific to each person's needs. The usual prescription ranges between four and six bottles, but may be more or less; about forty to seventy days of herbs.

Heather told us more about the herbs and prescriptions, "There are different energetic dots that the Entities put on the prescriptions, little signatures of energy. This communicates what is to be given at the pharmacy. Entities like us to fill the prescriptions the day we receive them so that the impression is fresh.

"The herbs are *Passiflora,* or passion fruit. Passion fruit juice is given to children here. It helps people to sleep. There are no contraindications, but it's not really the physical content of the capsule that's important. What's important is that the Entities imbue those capsules with energy uniquely for you. Your pills are not going to help me. You'll find that you're given herbs here, in the beginning perhaps, to prepare you for surgery. And then you get post-surgery herbs. Then you get herbs at the end, so you won't run out, the Entity says. After surgery herbs are done, you take the latest nonsurgery prescription first, and then work your way backwards. We keep taking the herbs because in that way, the Entities, who are of course formless beings who are part of the universe, can be with us wherever we are. So that if you're going through a particularly hard time, you can hold your herbs and know that the Entities can amp up that energy and work through it. So please honor your herbs."

The last building we toured houses the crystal beds. These are devices designed by the Entities with seven crystals. Each has a color base that relates to the seven primary chakras,* or energy centers, that lie within the physical body. The crystal beds help open and align your energy so that the Entities can work on you more deeply. You lie on a bed and the crystals are aligned over the body. Then you rest there for twenty minutes while the lights move in a preset pattern, energizing and opening the chakras, and balancing and supporting the energy field. The entire Casa rests on an immense underground layer of crystal with very high, clear energy. This underground layer also helps to energize the crystal beds.

When I arrived at the Casa for the first visit, Heather requested that I have a session on the crystal bed. I was resistant, skeptical of the seeming magic of a set of lights and crystals having power, but went as asked. I lay face up on the table and the attendant adjusted the crystal lights over the chakras, and then covered my eyes with a cloth. At first I wasn't aware of much, just a slight vibration from the machine. There is music, but I couldn't hear it. After about five minutes I began to feel energy pulsing gently through my body in a rhythmic pattern. It was a pleasant sensation, but not a strong one. When the attendant returned and lifted the eye covering, I felt relaxed, but

---

*Chakras are energy centers that run from the base of your spine out the top, or crown, of your head. The word *chakra* is a Sanskrit word, meaning wheel or disc. There are seven major chakras, each a circular wheel of light spinning in the energetic system, associated with certain body parts, a color, stone, element, and function. By learning to tune into the energy of your chakras, you can begin to embrace the fullness of who you truly are.

knew I'd feel that way after any twenty-minute rest with closed eyes. The experience of energy didn't really take hold until I went outside. As I exited the building, I felt a profound connection to everything around me, and could see the truly visible energy fields of the people, trees, and buildings. I experienced an energetic linkage with these living and nonliving objects. I was curious, and turned to Heather for more information about the crystal beds. She said:

"The crystal bed is the array of crystals that starts at the bottom, red, orange, yellow, green, blue, indigo, and violet. They're specially cut and shaped by the Entities, who put energy through these crystals. The energy flows through to realign our chakras and restore the flow of energy in our bodies. I wouldn't get too caught up on why and how. We know it works. It's another way for the Entities to break up the blocked energy within us. It's contracted energy; it's energy that's not flowing. If you have a blockage, think of the light flowing in until the energy can flow through again.

"But also the Entities come to us in the crystal bed rooms. Some people feel they sleep, some people smell a certain fragrance, some people feel family members coming back to them. But if you don't feel any of that, don't feel nothing has happened; the crystal bed is still working."

As we walked through the Casa, Heather talked more about what to expect on the following day in each of the different rooms. People begin to come after 7:00 a.m., to sit in the Current Rooms. At 7:45 a.m., people are gathered in the Great Hall. Around 9:30, people will begin to move past the Entities for healing. The morning session usually ends around 11:30, and then soup is served. Those who are staying in the village usually go back to their pousadas for lunch. For the afternoon session, those whom the Entities have instructed to sit in a Current Room enter the rooms by 1:45; the others return to the Great Hall by 2:00. This afternoon session ends about 4:00 or 5:00, sometimes later. The Entities will continue until everyone is seen.

After our tour, Heather sat with us in the garden and spoke more about the workings of the Casa. She is a highly experienced Casa guide, so I want to share this in her words, which were recorded and transcribed, since they were very helpful to me.

"We come on a pilgrimage. The intention of pilgrimage powers your healing work. We come to this place that is divinely blessed. Here we have the energy from Medium João's devotion to helping humanity and creating this sacred sanctuary, from everybody's prayers, focus and concentration, and from spirit. This is a place where the spirit touches very, very gently and compassionately. We are able to really mingle with the spirits in a very profound way. They give us this opportunity to be a family. And incredible changes happen. I've seen people who wondered if they'd even have the strength to come regain such vitality. This is literally where heaven meets Earth, right here.

"The first week can be difficult. People ask, 'Am I doing this right? Am I going to get everything done?' On Friday there's a big sigh of relief. 'Wow, we did it!' Then you have the weekend. I really urge you to take it easy over the weekend, to sleep a lot, to rest. Don't get into a lot of social activities. You do that at home. This is a place of retreat. Yes, have meals with everybody, take a short walk, but stay quiet.

"We're here to go inward. What opportunity do we give ourselves to spend several weeks in solitude, in a place where we can go to our rooms and quietly meditate? The Entities come to you in your rooms, so again, close your eyes, invite them in, and open your heart to receive the healing for your highest good, whatever that may be. The Entities help us with our finances, our jobs, our relationships, and our well-being, physically, emotionally, mentally, and spiritually. So, just be open to that. Have some lunch and retire to your rooms and pray. While you're here, raise your vibration by reading spiritual books or prayers or uplifting books of a spiritual nature instead of bestsellers.

"What is important here are our faith and our willingness to open our hearts and be healed. We can then better help others with our compassion, with a kind word. The Entities often say that to help others you don't have to give up your life. Helping others means a kind word: 'Can I help you today? Can I get you a bowl of soup? How are you doing today?' It's sort of like a twelve-step program, coming here. We come here ill or emotionally distraught; we realize there is a higher power; and then we can give up the ego and ask for help.

"So the work is about us opening up our hearts. Many times I've heard people say, 'What can I do to better help?' The Entity usually answers, 'Love yourself.' While here, you need to give yourself the gift of being really gentle and loving and compassionate to yourself and allowing yourself to be vulnerable while here. When you more fully love yourself, then you can love your neighbor. This container of spirit will help you. The first few times I came here I cried and cried. I cry every time I come and I cry every time I leave, even if I'm only going home for three weeks!

"The other thing is to hold the vision. The shaman holds the vision for the community, for rain to come, or that the community will be healed. There's the law of attraction, a universal law that has been practiced since the beginning of time. We invite healing by knowing the healing. If we focus only on the issue that brought us here, some people keep repeating their wounds, what Carolyn Myss calls 'woundology'; there is no awareness of what is whole. That is like tuning to a radio station. If I want to hear rock music, I'm going to go to a rock station. I'm not going to go to a classical music station. I'm going to change the frequency to what I want to hear. While you are here, try to change the frequency of your thoughts, your emotions, and your being to the result you most deeply desire, to wholeness.

"If we're coming here for help and keep repeating that a particular malady is the issue, then we are attracting more problems associated with that issue. And here things work very fast because the frequency is very fast. You want your focus to be on acknowledging the issue that brought you here, but also your willingness to let the problem go. You want to hold the vision of yourself dancing and singing and laughing and being healthy and well and helping others, and telling your story.

"Similarly, people might say that they have an obsessing spirit, and they keep returning again and again to the Entity for help. The Entity says, 'I'll clear it,' and then they go back and ask, 'Has it gone?' They still think the earthbound spirit is with them. This is attracting the vibrations of other earthbound spirits. The Entities can seal up where that being has been, but if we keep the same habits of thought, we call in that same fear vibration, and similar problems will reappear. The Entity will always say, 'Give it no more thought. Give it no more thought.'

"When people come to the Entity, it's not really the diagnosis that the Entity is interested in, because he sees your entire being. By the time you are in front of the Entity, he's already on to the next person because he's seen you as a being of light, seen you in totality, as you came through the line. He knows your needs. If I were to get a ball of mud or snow and throw it on the car, I'd need to use the wipers to clear it, right? The same way, the Entities are able to clear off those blotches or distortions of the light. So don't get too focused on your diagnosis, get focused on the root cause of your issue to be healed; so that you can really feel and focus on, enjoy, and experience wellness, health, vitality, joy, peace, love, and exhilaration. As we change ourselves, so our outside world changes around us.

"When we want world peace we do not go to an anti-war rally, we'd go to a pro-peace rally. So let's focus on peace within ourselves; then peace around us begins to happen, and peace spreads into the further community all around. So hold the vision of your wellness, and let go of the diagnosis.

"Sometimes you think that you've been blown off by the Entities and feel sad or angry. Perhaps they're blowing us off to get to that wounded part within us so that we'll deal with that. They're not ignoring us; they're pressing our buttons. Where does something need to come up? So sometimes by not giving us special attention or looking in our eyes, the Entity brings up past experiences. Then we work through that, and the next time, they give you a big smile. Know that we're getting everything taken care of, in the right order, in the right time, better than we know. So that if you come to the Casa and insist that your knees be healed, well, perhaps there's some karma that needs to be healed first. Or perhaps there's a more important root physical cause that needs to be healed, that we don't even know about. It's about letting go, being able to say, 'you know what I need better than I do.' If you can stand there before the Entity, and say, 'I'm willing to follow what you think I need,' then you can really go places.

"In the Current here and then in our inner questioning, we see where we need to change a little bit. Maybe we have no self-confidence, or maybe we're too egotistical, or withdrawn, or depressed. Here's an opportunity for us to look at those inner issues. We can gently and with much compassion and love, begin to change and become more open. Be able to ask the group for help, or come to me, so that these issues come to light.

"The last thing the Entity says to remember is that it takes many years for a physical issue to happen. There is no magic when resolving these issues. Medium João says that he does not do the work; it is God that does the work. By the time we come here, the physical issue could have been brewing for many, many years. Please don't come here expecting a one-hour cure. When the solution they seek is not immediately forthcoming, people sometimes say, 'Oh, that didn't work. I'm not going back again.' Allow the healing process to work gradually within you. Return here to the Casa until the Entity says, 'Your work is complete. Now you come to visit.'"

I needed some time to reflect on what Heather had said. Just beyond the garden is a covered deck overlooking miles of rolling hills fading into purple haze in the distance. The sky is huge and often holds stormy clouds in this rainy season, and then rainbows come forth. The view is of emerald green fields, darker green woods, rolling foreground with a herd of horses, and a winding red brown ribbon of a road that weaves in and out of sight as it flows over the hills. There's always a breeze, even on the hottest day. I went there with my doubts, fears, and questions.

Heather had done an excellent job of introducing the Casa, but, predictably, I found myself confused. The work here went so much beyond any reality I had ever considered previously. Already I had met a man with stage-four cancer who had been told by his California physicians to "go home and prepare to die," and who was now cancer-free; and a woman who had spent years in a wheelchair with MS, who walked with ease and grace. They both spoke matter-of-factly of their healing. They had come seeking help and it was given. My brain struggled to understand that which is the province of the heart. But uncertainty, held with love, can lead to greater faith, a joyful opening and surrender to God. If these qualities facilitate wholeness, as Heather had suggested, my inner healing had already begun.

The next day was intense and full of Casa activity. I wrote in my journal of my first impressions and experiences.

Journal, January 15, 2004

There is an atmosphere of sacred expectation. Everyone is here for healing of some kind or another; almost everyone I've talked with understands that body, mind, and spirit are connected. People are open and sharing of themselves, and they listen deeply. There is a warmth and kinship that transcends language barriers.

Very early Wednesday morning I was amazed to see over a hundred people dressed in white, walking down the road or rolling in wheelchairs. I was told the Entities request white clothing so they can better see our energy fields. I had brought white clothes, but didn't expect to see it everywhere. While it's optional, most people comply.

At the Casa, people settled quietly on the benches. While there's some talking, there's a sense of prayer and reverence too. People with no meditation training sit in silent meditation for four hours at a stretch. Even children sit quietly. For me, four hours was hard, although at times I meditate for that long a period. The first two hours were comfortable, the third a little restless, and by the fourth hour, a lot of restlessness and pain, but the people around me were mostly still. There is a sense of sacredness and hope, many people centered in prayer and devotion.

On my first Wednesday there were about 600 people (a guess), Thursday maybe 450. The people are from Brazil, other South American countries, the U.S., Canada, Europe, Asia, Australia, Africa—all over. The age span is from babies to octogenarians and beyond. Heather has a woman in her nineties coming from the U.S. in the next week.

We gathered in the Great Hall at about 8:00 a.m. The room was packed, all seats occupied and many people were standing. There was an excited and expectant energy, yet many people were also praying and meditating. At the opening, Heather and a man who spoke Portuguese stood on the stage and led prayers and gave instructions, first in Portuguese and then in English. Then people began to file into the Current Room and pass in front of the Entity. First in line were all the people having surgery this morning, second were people who have been through the line at least once before, and lastly were first-timers like me. This order of events apparently changes daily. I had a long wait, probably three hours, and I chose to meditate.

Finally it was our turn. Heather walked though the line with us. I was nervous, wondering what the Entity would say and do. When I finally stood before him, he smiled, said a few words to Heather, handed me an herbal prescription, and waved his hand indicating where I was to sit. It was clear that it was another being in João's body, a very different facial expression and eyes than the man I had seen in the pictures of João. The eyes looked deep, far away, and filled with compassion. The face was very serene. The smile lit the room. After seeing the Entity and receiving instructions we each went our own way. I sat in the Current Room João was in, to join the Entities' Current. The others were sent to the Mediums' Current Room. Because of the long initial wait, I only sat in Current for about an hour that morning, but was back there for four hours in the afternoon. You are asked to keep your eyes closed while sitting in the Current Rooms. If you need to leave to use the restroom, or otherwise require assistance, you raise your hand and a volunteer will come to help you. Several times in that last hour I almost raised my hand to ask to leave because my body felt so cramped, painful, and restless. Each time it seemed too uncomfortable for me to continue, I reset my intention to hold loving space for myself and others, and asked for help with fulfilling that intention. As I did this, I immediately felt more ease and my mind moved back into stillness and focus.

After the session I went to the pharmacy to fill my prescription for herbs. They come with specific instructions: not to eat pepper(s) of any kind (except bell peppers) or pork while taking them, and not to drink alcoholic beverages. I understood the cautions against pepper and alcohol but wondered why no pork. It was explained to me that pigs have no lymphatic system to carry poisons and toxins out of their bodies; therefore, those harmful substances go into the pig's muscles, tissues, and internal organs. In our culture in the U.S., pigs are not fed as much refuse and the meat is more wholesome, but in many countries of the world the meat can be tainted.

With the Entities' permission, that afternoon we traveled about a mile from the Casa to the sacred waterfall that complements the Casa healing process. The water there is highly charged by the Entities and runs over an extensive underground bed of rock crystal that adds to its healing power. It is an exquisite place, with a feeling of sacred energy like that of a beautiful, ancient cathedral. Specific rules exist to maintain the integrity and high vibrational energy of the waterfall, thereby ensuring the optimal spiritual environment for each being who enters. All who go to these falls must first have permission of the Entities. Males and females are asked to visit separately. Only one group is permitted at a time, but for safety reasons, that group must consist of two or more people. Each group waits patiently until the prior group leaves the area. Photographs, picture-taking devices, soap, candles, electronic devices, and nudity are not permitted.

At the top of the trail to the waterfall the magic was already present, with small lizards, singing birds, and butterflies in abundance. An open-sided shelter offered protection from the rain and scorching sun, for those who wait their turn. The trail from there is steep in parts, but there's a handrail, and the walkway is paved. We climbed down through a thickening forest, finally opening to a glade where the water was first heard and seen. Crossing a bridge, we paused by a tree that is said to be the guardian of the falls, and offered thanks to the healing spirits who provide us this place of beauty and grace. Here I am always led to reflect for a short time on the interconnectedness of All-That-Is; everything comes from God and returns to God. I offered a prayer: May all beings be healed through my healing. May all beings be blessed by the blessings I now receive.

We continued down the hill and over a second bridge to the falls. The trees are sometimes alive with small monkeys playing, bathing, and drinking the water. Butterflies filled the air. An orchid was blooming. The water drops down only about fifteen feet, but powerfully, and then runs out over rocks in a series of smaller falls, over the water-carved rock bed, and down into the valley.

As we arrived at the waterfall we paused, joined hands, and prayed. Then one person at a time moved under the main waterfall. When my turn came, I moved carefully over rocks slippery with moss to reach the falls. I took my time to receive the fullness of the experience, as did others, but did not loiter, aware of those who waited above for their turns. I always wish I could stay longer, but also know that I can return. The cold water felt fresh and alive, and the energy penetrated deeply. I found myself crying with no thoughts about the source of these tears, just alive, whole, joyful, and shedding tears of release. Afterwards, while others stood under the falls, I climbed down onto some smooth rocks, watched the monkeys play, and experienced a deep sense of joy and peace. When our small group was finished, we climbed up out of this deep glen, pausing again at the guardian tree to offer thanks before heading back to the pousada.

That night I asked Aaron to tell me more about the Current Rooms, their purposes and differences. Aaron used my question to start educating me; his concepts were consistent with and expanded on Heather's talk. However, his explanations created more questions than they answered about the deeper processes that were happening inside of me and inside of other Casa visitors. I felt that same uncertainty and desire to control through understanding that I felt after Heather's talk. Many of the topics that Aaron brought up this night would be expanded upon in the weeks, months, and years ahead.

What follows is not vocally channeled, just what I heard from Aaron as he spoke to me. There is a request that we do not serve as a direct medium for spirit for others (what I have called channeling, with Aaron) while at the Casa; and that we not do any kind of energy work, such as Reiki or other hands-on energy healing. This is not a judgment of the skill of the energy work, only that it can disrupt the energy work that the Entities are doing with us. It would be like going to a doctor with an infection, receiving and taking a prescribed antibiotic, and then seeing another doctor to get a different antibiotic. Either alone may help, but together they could cause an adverse reaction. Thus, when at the Casa, I don't move into a trance and channel Aaron directly, but listen to his thoughts and write them out for myself. This is how I have always worked with him personally, for if I'm in a trance state, I cannot hear what is said.

The other reason for my not channeling for others when at the Casa is that one focus of the Casa work is for each person to connect to their own guidance, to remind each that we are all mediums, and to encourage the practice of skillful mediumship. These skills are taught indirectly; while here, people have a higher energy vibration that makes connection to their guidance easier. Mediumship is taught more directly to some of the more experienced Casa mediums.

Aaron told me the Entities have created the two Current Rooms. The Current in the rooms is shaped moment-to-moment by all of those sitting in meditation, by the Entities working in the rooms, and by the divine in all of its manifestations. People may experience them somewhat differently depending on whether they pass through the room in the line or sit within the room. For the one who sits in Current, there is both giving and receiving: the giving of one's own energy, love, and highest intention to support the healing of all beings; and the receiving of care from the Entities.

The one who passes through the line begins in the Great Hall and then enters the Mediums' Current Room. This room has the function of releasing what is extraneous. When the person comes into the first room he or she brings with him or her the four bodies: the three heavier bodies, which are physical, emotional, and mental; and the spirit body. Each of the heavier bodies includes four levels. These four levels are the form, energetic, etheric, and karmic levels. Therefore, there may be a physical body-form level, a physical body-energetic level, a physical body-etheric level, and a physical body-karmic level. The same schematic holds true for the emotional and mental bodies.

There may be negatively polarized energy attached to the bodies at any of these various levels. Aaron said:

In the Mediums' Current, some of this heavier energy is released. When a human enters the Mediums' Current room, its energetic Current greets the energy field of the seeker. Everything that is contracted, distorted, and unsettled appears almost as larger streaks and bits of gritty dirt blown against clear glass. The streaks, metaphorically, are those deeper issues that will be carried into the direct presence of the supervising Entities of the day in the Entities' Current Room. The random grit is metaphorically swept away in the Mediums' Current room. Certainly what I am calling "supervising Entities of the day" could easily remove the grit also, when the seeker reaches the incorporated Entity. From the Entities' perspective, any work that they do is a timeless procedure. But the human who is passing through is on linear time, our time of conventional reality, and the Entities respect that difference. In the human's linear process, he needs first to release that which is more secondary to the situation, the so-called "grit," so as to be able to center himself in his own deepest prayer and to bring forth in himself the deepest intention for clarification and healing, by the time he finds himself in front of the incorporated Entity.

Aaron explained, for example, that a human passing through the line might be suffering from cancer. He has been told that he will die and that there is no possible cure through conventional medical means. The metaphorical streaks that are brought to the Entity will be: (1) the physical body distortion such as the tumor in the physical body; (2) the emotional body distortions of great fear, anger, and grief that are a result of the physical condition, and which further impact the physical condition; (3) the mental states such as doubt and despair; and (4) the karma involved. These are the major areas needing attention and healing and are what Aaron metaphorically refers to as "streaks."

The emotions of the moment are also a part of what our hypothetical patient brings into the Mediums' Current Room. In this example, his feelings of doubt about whether this will work, which are based more on the skepticism of others than on his own beliefs; his anger at his doctor back in California; his annoyance that he didn't get scrambled eggs for breakfast; the thoughts flickering through his mind that this trip cost a lot of money and had better bear fruit—these are all a part of the grit that is blown away and released, so that he may more easily become centered and refocused on his major intentions, which are to heal the body, to release negativity, and to heal and balance his karma. The doubts and opinions may return, but he moves into the Entities' Current Room relieved of them for the most part.

By the time the seeker reaches the Incorporated Entity, that Entity has received a full report on the seeker's condition from various assisting Entities and needs only to give the instructions for the seeker's care. So although only one Entity is incorporated in João's body, many Entities have supported the healing as the seeker passes through the line.

The other value of the first room is that the Current raises the frequency vibrations of all the bodies within the seeker. The more that this seeker can center in awareness, or in what some might call Christ or Buddha consciousness; that is, can center in his own divine being, the more easily the grit will fly away. As Aaron reminds us, that which is aware of anger is not angry. That which is aware of fear is not afraid. When we center in that awareness, it does not mean the anger or the fear goes away, but that the self-identification with them goes. Then one can watch any movement of the mind or body with a sense of peacefulness and compassion, and can attend to it when appropriate, but without the fear-contraction which gives rise to the need to fix it. Heather spoke of "woundology," the over-focus on one's woundedness that causes wounds to reappear over and over again. With release of self-identification, one comes to know and focus instead on one's innate wholeness.

When the seeker approaches the Entities in an uncontracted state, the Entities' work can be more direct. Aaron offered a second metaphor, similar to the gritty window he used to describe the Mediums' Current Room. "If you have a large bed sheet that is tied in hundreds of knots, you need to untie the knots before you can smooth it. Since the human line flows past the Entity in linear time, and there is only a brief time for direct and immediate contact with each human, it is very practical for as many knots to be untied as possible before the arrival at the ironing board. If the Entities are presented with a terribly wrinkled but completely unknotted sheet, they can lay it out and press the whole thing smooth. But perhaps there are several very tight knots; then they iron what they can, begin to loosen the tension of the knots that remain and then suggest further treatment. The Casa energy and especially the water and crystal beds loosen the knots. Sitting in the Current Room will open the knots. Surgery, sometimes called intervention, will open the knots. So the more open, centered, and uncontracted the human is upon arrival before the incorporated Entity, the more quickly the Entity can assist him in bringing back balance and resolution."

What of the human who is very uncentered, who comes into the Entities' Current Room with the knots still very tight, and the grit not completely blown away because there was so much of it? He will be lovingly attended to, but the first step will be to help to release the grit. Surgery will not be offered at this stage unless it is life-critical, but sitting in the current, use of the crystal beds, visiting the sacred waterfall, and even the herbs can each bring more release.

Aaron added:

These knots may be of physical, mental, or emotional nature, on the form, energetic, karmic, and etheric levels. Each treatment addresses specific circumstances. Sometimes tight knots can be dried in the sun and then invited to open. You have worked enough with knotted cord to know that sometimes you need to cut through the knots; if they are very old and decayed into each other, you need to cut them away and splice the strong ends together. This seems to me to be a part of what surgery does. Surgery also literally cuts out distortions such as malignant tissue.

The physical, emotional, and mental bodies each have a karmic level. Thus, karma is inherent in the physical condition, in the emotional response to the condition, and in the mental formations, as various thoughts, beliefs, and judgments. The Entities help the seeker to understand, release, and balance the karma. They do not release it for the seeker, but will offer loving assistance so that he or she gains insight into the long-held patterns that have directed the mental and physical expressions. These patterns are then more easily released.

You have asked in what order healing occurs. There is no one order. Imagine you own a field of many acres that has lain fallow for several decades, so that many kinds of weeds and even weed trees have grown upon the land. Now you wish to plant a vegetable garden, so as to feed yourself and your loved ones. Where will you start? If you give all the effort to the massive task of clearing the land, you will have no crops. But you cannot ignore the weeds completely or your crops won't grow.

You may choose to clear some areas of the field, plant some sturdy crops and nurture them while you continue, at a slower pace, to attend to the weeds. You will probably leave the densest thickets for last, and begin the clearing where the weeds are thin. But if there is one particularly virulent weed that produces a huge number of seeds and spreads itself quickly, you may decide it is necessary to start there, even if it is a thick tangle of thorns and brush. As the seasons pass, your cultivated land will expand, and there will be fewer weeds that remain to fertilize each other and to serve as sources for future weeds.

The work with healing is the same. We cannot say we always start with karma, or with the mind or emotions. It may be necessary to "prune out" a severe body distortion so that the body can continue to live. Then the attention can be turned to the mind and emotions, and to karma. Or, as an example, in a situation where there have been several recurrences of cancer, then remission, then a new recur-

rence, it may be more useful to attend to the conditions that cause the cancer, before or while it is also being removed.

We had talked for a long time. I agreed this was enough for now and asked that he continue on another day. I especially wanted to know more about surgery, but Aaron asked me to save those questions also. I could see that I was nervous while asking questions, and that I wanted some control and assurance as we walked into the unknown. There was so much that was unknown, despite my years of acceptance of other planes of being. I had previously understood healing as linear, and was suddenly awakened to the fact that nothing is linear. As Aaron said to me, "The clear sky and the clouds exist at the same time. The blue sky can be known if you don't become lost in the clouds. Yet clouds may still exist and, therefore, must be acknowledged."

I would spend the next months and years attempting to understand what happens at the Casa, even as I changed and grew and healed under the loving care of Medium João and the Entities.

CHAPTER 8

Medium João and the Entities

I WAS EAGER to know more about the workings of the Casa and about Medium João and the Entities. What I have learned has supported my own healing process; therefore I gladly share it with you, the reader. Since I had no direct access to João to ask questions about his life, most of what I learned about it is anecdotal, drawn from various books and websites. However, I was fortunate that my guide to the Casa, Heather Cumming, knows João personally; therefore, she was able to give me a more specific picture than that contained in the general stories. Heather and Karen Leffler have written a fascinating biography of João, accompanied by photographs taken by Karen. For more detailed information, I recommend their book, *John of God.*[1] There is also much detailed information about João and the Entities, and Spiritism, on my website, www.vipassanahealing.com, including some dialogue with Aaron.

Many of the stories about João are common knowledge that has been passed on by word of mouth, although I cannot verify that they are factual. João Teixeira de Faria, or John of God as he is affectionately called, was born in a small village in central Brazil in the early 1940s, the youngest of six children. He was raised in a town about 105 miles from Abadiânia. His father was a tailor and ran a laundry service; his mother ran a small hotel. The family income was meager, so João as a boy of six started learning his father's trade. At the age of eight, after two years of primary school, he was forced by his family's poverty to begin working, a common happening in Brazil before the social reforms of the 1960s.

At the age of nine, while on a trip to visit family, João predicted with some urgency that a storm would come through the region. He pointed to specific houses that would be flattened. His mother had faith in young João's prediction and they sought shelter. The storm came as foretold, and 40 out of about 150 homes were badly damaged or destroyed. This incident was the first demonstration of João's unusual gifts. João was forced by poverty to move from town to town, searching for work as a manual laborer and a tailor. At sixteen he had the experience that would start his healing mission. He was looking for work and decided to pause under a bridge at a stream to bathe. There he met what appeared to be a beautiful woman who engaged him in spiritual conversation. She suggested that he go to the Redemptor Spiritual Center in Campo Grande where people would be waiting for him. When he arrived at the door, the director of the center asked if he was João Teixeira de Faria. He was surprised to be recognized, but entered the building as invited.

Almost immediately upon entry, João lost conscious awareness. When he awoke he felt ashamed, believing that his hunger had caused him to faint. He was told by the group that the spirit of King Solomon had entered into him and that he had healed many people. He protested, saying that his fainting was surely due to his hunger and exhaustion. Finally the many witnesses persuaded João that he really had incorporated King Solomon, and had healed the people. The director of the center took João to his home, fed him and gave him a comfortable bed for the night. The next day they returned to the center where King Solomon again incorporated, and did more healing work. This is how João began his mission as a healing medium in service to God and humanity. He often says, "I never healed any one; it is God who heals." Over the next few months, the Entities themselves instructed João in mediumship. Word of his abilities got around, and until about the age of twenty-two, he traveled all over Brazil, and was known as João Curador, or John the Healer. Repeatedly arrested and jailed for practicing medicine illegally, João Curador was also persecuted by the religious clergy who felt threatened by his work.

In 1964, he became a full time military tailor, making army uniforms. His healing work continued, and he gained the friendship and protection of the military people with whom he worked. For the next nine years, he was able to continue his mission without persecution.

In 1973, João was directed to Abadiânia by a loving Entity. There he did his healing work, in a one-room hut without electricity. Since that time, the Casa has steadily grown into a much larger operation. João now has over thirty employees at the Casa and many volunteers, serving hundreds, sometimes thousands of seekers per week. The Casa gladly accepts donations, but the donations do not begin to cover the costs of running the Casa. João funds the difference. In addition, he runs a soup kitchen at the south end of the town; and provides many people with the funds for an education. He has improved the lives of the residents of Abadiânia, even as its population has grown and new businesses have sprouted to support visitors to the Casa.

His early life of poverty taught João the importance of money and honed his business and entrepreneurial skills. He owns or has owned two cattle ranches, and several mines. João uses the proceeds from his business ventures to run the Casa and other service projects all over Brazil. Medium João also travels to different centers in Brazil, which have been specifically set up to serve the local Brazilian populations, because many Brazilians cannot afford to travel. Apart from travels within Brazil, Medium João has also traveled to Bolivia, the United States, Argentina, Portugal, Germany, New Zealand, and Peru. In Peru, it was necessary to rent a sports stadium to accommodate the large crowds. During fifteen days there, over twenty thousand people were helped, including the President of Peru, Alberto

Fujimori, and his son. Medium João was awarded a Medal of Honor for his work.[2]

João suffered a stroke in 1987, which left him quite weak and atrophied on one side of his body. When the Entities incorporated, however, his body seemed healthy and vibrant. Eventually, one of the Entities performed visible surgery on João while incorporated, making an incision on João's left front torso. In other words, the Entity incorporated in João did surgery on the body in which he was incorporated. A photograph of this surgery is available for viewing. João made a complete recovery, and remains in good health.

João is married and lives modestly in Anápolis, about twenty miles away from the Casa. Heather Cumming's excellent book[3] gives far more detail about these stages of João's life, his early wanderings and persecution, and the founding of the Casa.

This is the bare-bones version of the biographical details for John of God. But in his words, he is finally only an Earthly container for the Entities that incorporate into him and heal through him. João repeatedly says that "only God heals," and this is a profound truth. The Entities at the Casa form a smoothly functioning and enormously complex web that ultimately includes thousands of discarnate beings in addition to the thirty-plus Entities that incorporate into João. The interactions of these Entities with visitors to the Casa, before, during, and after their visits, weave a vast tapestry of healing that can only be partially explained or understood.

One significant modern attempt to understand these sorts of interactions between spirit and the material human world was Spiritualism, a movement prominent in the nineteenth century, and generally linked to the writings of Emanuel Swedenborg. Spiritism, based on the writings of the French author Allan Kardec in the mid to late 1800s, is an offshoot of Spiritualism. Spiritism has an essentially Christian moral and philosophical edifice, and assumes that reincarnation is for the purposes of spiritual evolution. The dead, who reside in a spiritual world that overlaps our own, can communicate with the living through mediums. These spirits, like humans, are evolving toward greater union with God, and in appropriate circumstances, can offer help and guidance on various matters. Spiritism is not separate from other religions, although it does look to Jesus as a great master. It is based on the premise that spirits exist and are a part of our reality, and it has a willingness to work with spirit. The reader who wishes to know more can find helpful information on a Kardec website.[4]

This philosophy found fertile soil in Brazil, which is about 80 percent Catholic, but also has a strong indigenous tradition of contacting spirits for help and guidance. Medium João was raised as both a Catholic and a Spiritist. Today, many Brazilians will use the services of Spiritist centers at some point in their lifetime.[5] Yet Spiritism is not a separate religion. Spiritists often are more focused on providing services like spiritual healing to the community. Bragdon cites a center in San Paulo that provides "healing, child care, kindergarten, free soup, a library, lectures, artistic and musical productions, parenting classes, sewing and knitting, and consultations with doctors, homeopaths, dentists, or financial planners."[6]

Yet the more traditional religious, medical, and political authorities do not look favorably upon this movement, and often harass its practitioners, as they harassed João in his early career. The Catholic Church no longer accepts the Doctrine of Reincarnation, and looks dimly upon exorcism or communicating with the Holy Spirit without the services of a priest. The medical community does not accept spiritual healing, and considers it to be a form of superstition practiced by the uneducated. The political authorities argue that Spiritist healers practice medicine and perform surgery without a license. Still, many medical doctors now come to the Casa to observe the work and learn from João and the Entities.

João and his work at the Casa fit firmly within the Spiritist tradition, and João has had lasting friendships with several prominent Spiritist mediums, including Chico Xavier. In like manner, many of the most prominent Casa Entities had former lifetimes as Catholic saints. Despite these close ties, however, the Casa intentionally eschews formal affiliation with Spiritism, Catholicism, or any other particular institution or religion. All paths to the divine are instead venerated, and all who come for treatment are attended to without regard to their beliefs. This broad ecumenism and inclusiveness is evident—objects of worship and pictures of saints from Buddhist, Christian, Hindu, and other major religions are amply displayed in the Casa Current Rooms. It was comforting to me on my first trip to find a photograph of Neem Karoli Baba in the Great Hall. That reassured me that I was where I needed to be.

The Entities are discarnate spirits who choose to serve God and humanity through their work at the Casa. The spiritual hierarchy that governs the Casa begins and ends with God. All workers at the Casa, human and discarnate, have their places and roles, but all act in harmony with divine will. In this context, the clearest answer to the question of the Entities' identities is similar to the explanation that Aaron gives me now as I ask him the question of his own identity: "I am a being of love and light who has finished my development as a human and has no need to incarnate further. As such, I have no separate identity from the divine source, except that which I choose to assume for the comfort and ease of the humans I assist. I am here as an agent of divinity and my sole purpose is to lovingly help other beings in their spiritual development." That said, there are over thirty Entities who incorporate, one at a time, into João's body. Thousands of other Entities are present without incorporation. Many of the Entities have personalities that they choose to display as they work; often based in part on one of their well-known previous human lifetimes.

Saint Ignatius of Loyola is one of the Casa's most prominent Entities, the one from whom the Casa takes its name, Casa de Dom Inácio. He was born in 1491 as Iñago de Oñaz y Loyola, the thirteenth son of a Basque nobleman. He was stubborn and easily angered as a young man. While in the Spanish army, in 1521, his leg was badly broken in a fierce battle, which left him with a permanent limp. During a long and painful recovery, he read the lives of Christ and the Saints. This led to a spiritual awakening, an austere new lifestyle, and a period of intense education. In 1540, he founded the Society of Jesus, also known as the Jesuits. Until his death in 1556, he educated others and ministered to the spiritual and material needs of the poor. *The Spiritual Exercises of Saint Ignatius* remains a classic Catholic manual for spiritual growth through meditation, prayer, and confession. According to Dr. Augusto, another of the Entities, Dom Inácio is the light that oversees and protects everything at the Casa. Other Entities with previous lifetimes as well-known religious figures include St. Francis Xavier and King Solomon.

St. Rita is the lovely woman under the bridge, who first directed the young man João to his calling. He later understood her to be the spirit of Saint Rita of Cascia[7] who was born in the village of Roccaporena in central Italy in 1381 and died May 22, 1457. She is known as the Saint of the Impossible. Those who bear heavy burdens, especially women, worship her as the patron saint of desperate cases.

The symbol most often associated with St. Rita is the rose. One source[8] tells how she would regularly bring food to the poor, which her husband prohibited her from doing. One day, her husband confronted her as she was leaving to bring bread to the poor. The bread was concealed in Rita's robes; when she uncovered the bread as her husband demanded, the bread became roses and Rita was spared her husband's wrath.

At the end of her life, when Rita was bedridden in a convent, a visiting friend asked if there was anything Rita wanted. Rita replied that she would like a rose from the garden of her parents' home. It was January, and this seemed like an impossible request but the friend went to look, and discovered a single brightly colored blossom on the bush just as Rita had described. She brought the rose back to Rita at the convent. The rose is thought to represent God's love for St. Rita and her ability to intercede on behalf of lost causes or impossible cases. St. Rita is often depicted holding roses or with roses nearby. On her feast day, churches and shrines of St. Rita provide their congregations with roses that are blessed by priests during the mass.

Interestingly, during my first visit to the Casa, I often smelled roses as I sat in meditation with my eyes closed. Many people have reported this phenomenon. I had not heard this story or anything of St. Rita at the time I first smelled the roses, and wondered where the scent was coming from. There were many other flowers in the room, but no roses. Now, whenever I experience St. Rita's energy, there is a mix of strength and gentleness, and the smell of roses. I often feel moved to address her as Mother. Since Medium João does not incorporate female Entities, St. Rita works in the background.

The first time she clearly appeared and spoke to me in meditation, Dr. Augusto was doing very deep work on my eyes and energy field. Within that session, I was aware of very painful past life karma related to the eyes. I was crying and didn't know if I could do what was asked—to look deeply into the situation and forgive. Suddenly there was a loving, supportive energy in my meditation, holding my head, and carrying with her the intense smell of roses and quiet reassurances that she would help me. Her love allowed me to go on.

Now she comes to me often, just lending her loving presence when I'm doing challenging spiritual work. She rarely speaks to me; her greatest power for me is just the love she brings. When she does speak, I experience her thoughts more as images than words. The image usually invites me to see the larger picture that I have resisted, and supports my opening to that picture and its implications.

Some of the Entities who do incorporate have a past history as medical doctors in a recent past life. An example is Dr. Oswaldo Cruz, who lived from 1872–1917. Graduating at nineteen from medical school, he quickly went on to become a brilliant bacteriologist at the Pasteur Institute, producing vaccines for smallpox, the bubonic plague, and other diseases. At the Casa, Dr. Cruz rarely announces himself, but his identity can be deduced from his mannerisms, an interest in communicable diseases, and a concern about wristwatches, which disturb his current. He can be quite direct in his communications. He powerfully radiates love and compassion, and kindly cares for all Casa visitors. Dr. Cruz is also the Entity who later directed me to the specific tones of tuning forks that would support my relearning to hear, and is the one who has coached me in their use. I have been deeply moved by his patience.

Another familiar medical figure is Dr. Augusto de Almeida, one of the most frequently incorporated Entities at the Casa. Dr. Augusto worked in the military in one previous lifetime and as a rubber tapper in another. In his last incarnation, he worked as a gold miner. In addition, he was a physician and surgeon before the development of anesthesia and, therefore, saw much suffering. Although he appears to have a serious and authoritarian manner, which both gives and elicits respect, people at the Casa respond to his kind and deeply loving energy with their own love and affection. I am told that he has mellowed through the years into a less stern personality.

Many Entities who incorporate choose not to divulge their names or details of their personalities at all, and others give little beyond their names. Dr. Jose Valdivino is one of the Entities about whom little is known. He is very gentle and loving, with an energy that is especially suited for healing paraplegics. Perhaps a judge in a former life, Dr. Valdivino only says when asked, that he was a "protector of families."

Dr. Augusto has been the Entity who has directed the healing of my ears and eyes. I've come to think of him as the specialist. Dr. Valdivino, on the other hand, has been what I think of as my primary care physician. When I meditate at home, away from the Casa, Dr. Valdivino will work with me to help to open the energy field. This opening is vital before bringing very high energy into a specific part of the body. Once the field is open, Dr. Augusto will come in and work with intense energy to the eyes and ears. My entire body shakes with the force of this energy.

For several years, up to the writing of this book, I have felt Dr. Valdivino's energy with me almost daily in meditation. He comes to support and direct the energy work that is needed in the body. His support has also been very present as I have worked with karma. His help has been profound. Much of it has been related to helping me to feel which chakras are closed, and then to open to and heal the issues involved therein.

Dr. Valdivino is not there constantly, as Aaron is. But when I request his help, either he comes immediately or another of the Entities comes to tell me that Dr. Valdivino has been detained, but he or she has come in his place. Once just a few days after I had left the Casa to return to the U.S., Dr. Valdivino was incorporated and said to Heather, "I am helping your deaf friend. Tell her I am helping her."

Most of these Entities have worked through João for many years. Occasionally new Entities do incorporate. One newer Entity whom I have found very loving is Jose Penteado. I am told that Jose Penteado is especially willing to explain what is being done, which many people find very helpful.

In addition to the Entities who incorporate into Medium João, there are literally thousands of mostly anonymous spirits that assist with the various material and non-physical services at the Casa. These Entities do not incorporate in João's body, but are present nonetheless. People tell of experiencing an Entity in their pousada rooms, where deep energy awakens them at night. An incomplete list of the services performed by these helping spirits would include energizing the holy water, soup, and herbs; removing stitches after surgery, which happens wherever in the world we happen to be; and assisting with various tasks in the Current Rooms, infirmary, and crystal beds. These beings move outward over the entire Earth to support the care and healing of the Casa visitors, both before and after their Casa visits. Most people who decide to visit the Casa begin to experience their energy weeks and even months before the visit. This should not be surprising. We all have spirit plane guides who are present with us all the time, though most of us are unaware of that presence. The Casa Entities and our personal guides work together to provide for our needs in very loving ways.

CHAPTER 9

Surgery at the Casa

SURGERY AT THE Casa intrigued and mystified me. Things that happened routinely here have not happened anywhere else in my experience, or in the experience of anyone I know. A neighbor in my pousada awakened in the morning with a very clear, small incision on her breast and a growth removed. She had not yet been through the line to see the Entity about this worrisome growth. At first I was resistant, looking for some fakery. I quickly saw how strong my habit was to understand through the left brain, and to reject that which the brain could not fully comprehend. I thought back to the first months of conscious awareness of Aaron, when I had wanted to dismiss that which was beyond the rational mind, and yet I could not deny my experiences. At the Casa, I understood that this observation of the seemingly impossible was another opportunity to relax into a new way of understanding our multi-faceted universe.

I needed a very open mind to comprehend the visible surgery I witnessed at the Casa. Many times, the Entity incorporated into João will insert an eight-inch surgical instrument, known as a Kelly clamp, far into the nose of a patient and twist it, without any apparent discomfort to the patient. Incisions made into the body hardly bleed. The Entity will sometimes scrape what appears to be a paring knife across the eyeball of a patient. You can see the eye pushed inward by the pressure, again without apparent discomfort. All these procedures are done without conventional anesthetics, yet few if any complain of pain. Traditional sterilization techniques and antibiotics are never used, but infections are unknown. How are these things possible?

If you refuse to open your heart and mind to what happens at the Casa, the answer is simple. Some believe that John of God is a charlatan, and that the people whom he has helped over the years have been tricked; therefore, they are either not being healed, or are healing themselves through a complex placebo effect. A forceful proponent of this view is James Randi, a generally recognized skeptic of the paranormal who was brought in by ABC News when they reported on John of God in 2005.[1] Randi expressed the opinion that the surgeries are carnival tricks without real benefit to the patient. He believes that the lack of need for an anesthetic is the result of an adrenaline rush. This skepticism, taken to the extreme, can become a self-fulfilling prophecy. Those who are overly skeptical will not allow for the existence of any possibilities that the mind cannot readily comprehend.

The skeptic's view is important to mention because some level of disbelief is a normal, even healthy response to witnessing something that the logical human mind has previously deemed to be impossible. I knew that part of my work at the Casa was to open my heart and mind in ways that supported the healing that I sought, not to hide in conventional views of limitations or denial. If I believe the medical doctors who have said for almost forty years that I will never hear again, then I become closed to the possibility of hearing. The mind leads and the body follows.

Yet this is not just about blind faith. The good news is that the gifts and possibilities that the Casa offers do not require a suspension of the intellect. The laws that govern quantum mechanics sometimes appear to contradict Newtonian mechanics. Yet upon very careful examination, both sets of laws are consistent. In the same way, the laws operating at the Casa are consistent with and expand upon the laws that seem to operate in conventional Western medicine.

Almost all the physical healing work accomplished at the Casa is based on the high vibration of matter. This work takes several forms. When the Entity uses his fingers or a knife for surgery, the heavy density matter is charged to such a high vibration that it becomes light. Such radiance is one expression of energy. It is a very high vibrational energy; so high that bacteria, for example, cannot live within its field. Thus there is no need for further sterilization.

Surgery at the Casa, often called an "intervention," can be either visible or invisible. Sometimes the phrasing used with "surgery" is "real" or "energetic." I choose to say visible or invisible because it's all real, and all energetic. Most people for whom surgery is recommended receive invisible surgery. This surgery happens while the person sits and prays, or holds the healing intention in the mind and heart. No one touches you, yet the needed intervention is accomplished. A man told me of his invisible abdominal surgery and how the physical X-rays taken by his doctors when he got back to the U.S. showed the cuts and stitches in the bowel where the malignant tumor had been removed. Yet there was no external sign of an incision or scar. So visible or invisible, the surgery performed at the Casa is real. Visible or invisible, it all involves energy. All Casa surgery is just that, surgery; and, therefore, must be respected as such. Surgery, as with any intervention by the Casa Entities, is never forced upon anyone. The Entities may recommend, but the final choice is always ours.

Aaron began his explanation of surgery at the Casa by discussing the different options that are available:

Physical healing through surgery occurs with two inseparable tools, material intervention and energetic intervention. Material intervention means either visible or invisible surgery. In both there is a direct manipulation of the cellular body structure. With visible surgery there is use of an actual tool, often a knife, which carries the energy. With invisible surgery, similar energy movement occurs, but without a visible, external tool. The choice of invisible or visible surgery is up to the human. There is always respect for one's free will. You may think that the human lacks the necessary facts on which to base this decision but at some level she understands. If there is severely distorted tissue such as a malignancy, it can be removed directly when visible surgery is chosen. If invisible surgery is chosen, diseased tissue can also be cut away. The tissue's complete release from the body with invisible surgery can be immediate, as it is with visible surgery, or more gradual. Such direct intervention on the physical body, be it visible or invisible, is one method of facilitating healing. It is often the method of choice if there is a damaged organ to repair, such as a leaky valve in the heart or the intestinal system, or damaged tissue such as a bone distortion.

The second healing practice is the bringing of energy as light into the body. Light can be infused through the incision, through the eye, through the nose using the Kelly clamp, through the hands of the Entity incorporated in João's body, or through other means. The light supports the growth of healthy new tissue, and also supports the transformation of unhealthy tissue into healthy tissue. Visible surgery is rarely done only to draw in light, but sometimes this method is chosen. Visible surgery is usually done to remove or repair, and since the wound is open, the healing power of light is brought directly into the distorted area. The insertion of light through the eye or nose uses an opening that is already present in the body. So the Entities use light and energy to support the healing of all the bodies—physical, emotional, mental, and spiritual—and on all levels.

Visible surgeries are done with a scalpel or knife, often a simple kitchen knife, without conventional antiseptic or sterile techniques, yet almost no one has ever had an infection or complications from this work. Energetic anesthesia replaces traditional gas or chemical anesthesia, and is highly effective and quite safe. It is startling to observe the Entity cut a deep incision into the body of a person who is standing before him with his eyes open, alert and able to converse. "Is there pain?" the Entity asks. "No" is the usual answer. If there is pain, the Entity will usually increase the intensity of the energetic anesthetic.

A woman named Beatrice said this to me about her surgery:

"We sat together in the operation room, maybe fifty people. They asked if any one wanted to have a physical operation. My hand went up—it was not me—my hand got up and my feet walked to the front. We stood in the Entities' current room, about five people, in a line. João came and walked around us. I was so scared that the translator, said, 'You must leave.' I said, 'No! I can't! I must do this.' It was so strong. Then the Entity came and put his hand on my head. It was like an anesthetic, normal anesthesia. I was completely out of it, but I could hear. There was no more fear; I was very peaceful. I could feel touch but no pain. This operation opened my inner heart. He just cut flesh near the heart and sewed it up. Then they moved me into the recovery room. It healed very fast, about six or seven days."

The Entities are aware of the concerns that brought the person to the Casa, and more. Sometimes the Entity will open a hole with the knife and insert a gloveless finger into the opening or insert a forceps with which he may withdraw tissue. I spoke to two different people who were each encouraged to have the material tested when they returned home. In both cases, it was found to be malignant, although there was no previously known malignancy.

On Thursday afternoon of our first week, the Entity recommended that the four of us have surgery the next morning. We had a choice of visible or invisible surgery. We spent an hour discussing the two possibilities, the reasons for or against each, and which choices we would make. Mel chose visible surgery, which would give her a more direct contact with the Entities, through João. Kate, Davy, and I were uncertain.

I asked Aaron for guidance. He reminded me that it makes no great difference whether we elect visible or invisible surgery. Both are real. If internal work is needed, there will be internal stitches in either case. But with invisible surgery there will be no incision on the surface, which then takes time to heal.

If we cannot believe that healing can happen unless we have this direct experience of visible surgery, then we need to choose it. The only other consideration is the one expressed by Kate, to have phys-ical surgery just to be a witness to it, and to be able to share the expe-rience with others such as family members who are physicians.

I felt pulled to the visible, but also afraid of it. In the end I had no choice since anyone over age fifty-three may not have visible surgery. It is simply not offered as an option.

We went to bed, but not quickly to sleep, each of us nervous about what the next day would hold. I had a dream of resting in a brilliant radiance. I felt surrounded by loving energy, but was still afraid because I could not move my head. There was a pressure in my ears that made me a bit dizzy and abdominal pressure, too. A voice in the dream asked me to relax. Then the discomfort and the dream ended, and I slept peacefully until morning.

The next morning we gathered at the Casa at 8:00 a.m. and were led into the surgery room, along with about twenty-five other people. Those who chose physical surgery then went to the Entities' Current Room. Davy and I had invisible surgery. Kate and Mel elected visible surgery, but the Entity sent Mel back to have invisible surgery. The incision would have resulted in a scar on her face in front of her ears so invisible surgery was preferred.

Those of us who chose invisible surgery remained seated in the surgery room, and were asked to close our eyes and place our hands over the area where surgery was needed, or over our hearts if there were multiple areas or if the surgery was related to spiritual or emo-tional issues. I felt very high energy that increased in intensity for about twenty minutes as we sat there. At one point I felt a slight burn-ing sensation in my ears, followed by a lot of heat in my face. I also felt what seemed like very light touches on many parts of my body, though no human was touching me. Aaron kept reassuring me that it was fine, and that the touch was energy from the many discarnate Entities that work in the surgery room. Mostly, I attempted to med-itate and pray, asking for hearing and stating my highest purpose of healing for the greatest good of all beings and myself.

The Entities strongly suggest that after surgery you return to your room by taxi, not on foot, and go to bed. I dutifully came back to my room at 9:30 a.m. and slept five hours, even after a good sleep last night. Although I wasn't physically touched, I found myself with chipmunk cheeks just in front of my ears, and my ear lobes were red and swollen. None of it felt painful, only full and warm.

Kate chose visible surgery for her extremely poor vision. She was taken into the Entities' Current Room and asked to stand. When the Entity touched her shoulder, she moved into a deeply peaceful state. She said he could have done anything, with no pain or resistance on her part. He apparently came toward her with an eight-inch Kelly clamp that she had previously hoped he would not use because it frightened her. But he stopped with it just inches from her face, and just held her head. She felt a very powerful touch but no pain. She swooned, was caught and moved into a wheelchair, and carried into the infirmary where she slept. She returned to the pousada at noon and fell asleep again. Her eyelids were puffy just like the front of my ears where they touched the cheeks.

None of us had an instant cure, but something certainly happened. We were told that the Entities would continue to work on us throughout the week. We were to stay in the hotel, either in our rooms or in the garden, for a few days, and to remain very quiet. One week after surgery, the Entities would come to our rooms as we slept, to remove internal stitches. The following Friday we would go back through the line, past the incorporated Entity, for a post-surgery review and to learn what should happen next—more sitting in the Current, more herbs, more surgery, or something else.

There is one question that we all had after the surgeries. Only one Entity at a time is incorporated into João's body, yet that single being could not perform all the surgeries done in the surgery room in any one session. During our surgery, there were at least twenty-five people in the room with us. We realized that much of the work came through the other Entities that were not incorporated. "What was the incorporated Entity's role?" I asked Aaron.

He explained that visible surgery seems to come through the Entity incorporated in João's body. The actual work is a result of the merging energies of both João and Entity, with great support from other Entities. The incorporated Entity is drawing on João's energy as well as that of the current and the deep crystal beds that lie under the Casa. The effect is powerful. João's body serves as a focusing mechanism. This is possible because João does the work to allow himself to hold that high vibration as service. Thus his whole body becomes a tool through which the Entity's energy may move.

While one Entity is incorporated into João's body, many others are present to assist. The incorporated one may make an incision, for example, while other Entities support the surgery in many other ways, including holding the anesthetic, helping to extract a tumor and supporting the life force of the patient. This is no different than what we find in a traditional operating room where there is one surgeon and a large support staff. The process is much the same with the invisible surgery except that there is no visible incision.

Aaron said:

João himself is a powerful healer with a high vibrational body, yet is grounded in the Earth plane. The fact that his energy combines with the Entity's energy seems to be the greatest benefit to the visible-surgery route, though perhaps João would deny this. His ability to move into full trance, release the body, and allow this body that is grounded in Earthly vibrations to serve as a bridge-vehicle, to carry the high spirit vibrations into form, is vital. João's body serves as a link so that the full power of spirit can act upon the lower vibrational, physical body of the patient. Without João as that bridge, the Entity would only be able to use a portion of its energy for the healing work, in order not to overwhelm the human body that is receiving the energy. In this situation, for example, when the Entities are working at a distance without João's direct assistance, the healing work can be done, but the process will take longer.

In the surgery room, those who elect invisible surgery are attended to by literally hundreds of Entities. These Entities do not have the advantage of that powerful focus through João's body. They are still able to do their work, however, because the current supports them. When João is not directly present, several Entities will work together. At other times one of the Entities might work directly through one of the other Casa mediums.

After our surgeries we were filled with questions about our own treatments and about the surgeries we had witnessed earlier in the week. I learned that surgery and healing take several forms.

After talking to many people I realized that most people who have been here a while (several weeks, or on a return trip) have experienced healing; that some have experienced complete healing; and that most of it has been gradual, not immediate. Aaron said that the nerves of my ears were not being regenerated but replaced. As a general rule with severe nerve damage, even including spinal cord damage, the Entities seem to prefer to gradually grow a new network of nerves in order to restore the lost nerve function. If damage is minimal, the Entities will build on what's there and make a short link to connect the working ends. While I am still not sure exactly what they did for me that day, I do know that this first intervention began a long and complex process of healing on many levels that will literally take a book to describe.

The operation that I saw* João and the Entities perform with the hemostat or long forceps is simply impossible according to the logical, rational mind. Anyone who has ever had a nosebleed can attest to the delicate nature of the nose's interior. Traditionally, inserting a hemostat that far up into the nose, then wrenching it around would almost inevitably create a dramatically bloody outpouring that would be difficult to control. A medical authority has told me that conventional nasal surgery requires an endotracheal tube and other controls, which protect the anesthetized airway from potentially deadly complications. Yet the Entity pushes the hemostat far up into the nose,

---

*We are asked to keep eyes closed in the Current Room, but sometimes the Entity also does visible surgery in the Great Hall, in front of the gathered crowd who may watch.

and there is almost no bleeding. Then he twists it within the nose so that the handles are up and the end is tipped downward toward the throat. There are several small cavities in the skull, but none large enough to accommodate such an object and no wide, open passage to such cavities. A medical professional who observed the procedure said that if a doctor in traditional surgery generated such downward twisting force with a hemostat, that it would break the bone and surrounding structures, and that a fracture of the hard palate would result. In effect, this would manufacture a cleft palate, a very disfiguring deformity. Yet none of this happens. It is as if the bones and anatomical structures that would ordinarily block the hemostat's movement, or the hemostat itself, temporarily cease to exist.

I watched another "impossible" procedure: The Entity cut with a knife into a man's shoulder while the man stood with a totally serene expression on his face. The man was able to follow instructions easily and move his arm as the Entity requested. There was little bleeding. Each time the Entity asked if there was pain, the man said no. At the end, the Entity simply waved his hands together and the large wound closed itself and was sealed with two stitches. When I asked Aaron about all of this, he noted that everything that I saw would be rational if I were to release old beliefs about the solidity of matter.

The week passed differently for each of us. I was exhausted and slept a lot. Others were restless. Some had minor pain. Kate spent most of the week with a cloth soaked in Casa water over her closed eyes. At the end of a week, the Entities came to our rooms during the night to remove the stitches. Following the suggested guidelines, we each went to bed early—with a glass of the blessed water that we were to drink upon awakening—on our nightstands. It felt like waiting for Santa Claus. Again, I had to move beyond old beliefs and make room for a new paradigm. I believe I was aware of the Entity's visit, and a feeling of high energy and some pressure on the face near the ears, but I can't be certain if it was real or just imagined. People who have had visible surgery and obvious stitches often do report that the stitches disappear during the night.

The next morning was the scheduled surgery review. The Entities look to make sure that all stitches have been removed, to see how effective the work was, and to decide which steps to take next. We were all told to come back into the current rooms for the next week. It felt a little anticlimactic; I understood that healing would be gradual but had hoped for some physical sign of progress in at least one of us. It was good to be able to talk with Aaron.

Aaron: So, what is happening when the Entities work? What I say here is a mix of what I have seen, what I understand from past observations of similar work in other times and places, and what the Entities have explained to me.

I will use the word "he" here but please understand there is no gender restriction. Such entities are all androgynous just as I am. They appear in a masculine or feminine guise to give you humans someone with whom to relate. Just as I am not Aaron with the form in which Barbara knows me, but am energy and light, so these Entities are also energy and light. Like me they chose a lifetime in which their work was related to what they do now, and one with which humans can feel comfortable. Like all beings, St. Ignatius of Loyola, St. Francis Xavier, Dr. Oswaldo Cruz, Dr. Augusto de Almeida—I am offering just a few examples—have each lived in many incarnations. They were healers in many incarnations. Here is one in which they are known. But their soul force is far greater than simply the single being whose name they currently bear for your human comfort. So we use the word "he" or "she" as related to the outer expression, understanding that this soul is neither masculine nor feminine, and that we are assigning this label just as a convenience.

When the Entity picks up the knife, in the moment before contact it is still a knife of Earth density, although a frequently used tool will carry a higher vibration even when not in the Entity's hands. When the Entity, which knows itself to be nothing more than infinite love and intelligence expressing as light, lifts the knife, he literally charges the knife with Energy. Just as the Entity gives its energetic force to the water you drink here to bring it to a higher vibration, so does the Entity bring the knife to a higher vibration. The knife is made up of molecules that are simply a different expression of light. When the knife's vibrational frequency is raised, all that is held is a shaft of light. To human eyes, the knife still looks like a knife, although in the glimpse that Barbara got of it, she saw something a bit different. Barbara saw the simple knife's transformation into a crystal of light superimposed over the form of the Earthly knife. The implement the Entity holds is now both the crystal of light and the metal knife; there is no duality between them.

What cuts the skin is not the knife blade. That is why it can be very dull. What cuts the skin is energy expressing as light. There is no need of a sharp scalpel. There is no need for sterilization of the tool. The power of its high vibrational frequency would not destroy, but would simply release anything harmful, like shaking dust off a blanket. The Entity could have used something other than metal but only certain material could sustain that vibration; softer material would explode with the super charge, The best tool to hold the vibration is something like metal or crystal, any substance that won't disintegrate quickly. But he could just as easily have used a spoon. However, it would be harder for people who truly believe that he is cutting with a knife to accept the spoon.

When a body cell suffers trauma there is seepage of fluid. If you cut into many cells and their blood vessels, you can have severe bleeding. In traditional surgery the surgeon cuts with a knife and disrupts the integrity of the individual cells. The Entities have a very different approach. The knife is not used as a sharp implement but as an energetic tool. Through the knife, the Entity brings a high energy that gently pushes between the cells. Picture a dense cluster of balloons. If you wish to move through, you can hack your way with a knife, breaking balloons, or you can gently sweep them to either side with your hands. The latter illustrates how the Entities cut into body tissue. The cells are invited to move aside and very few are traumatized so there is little bleeding. Even most blood vessels are energetically redirected to create an opening. Blood flow is redirected. When the work is finished the cells are invited to come back together and the blood flow is released into the normal channels. The wounds heal quickly.

When the Entity inserts a finger into the incision, the finger retains a semi-solidity, yielding when required, firm where necessary in order to grasp. The Entity can very easily shift that finger from a primarily material form to a more light-based form. This surgery has some small kinship to your much more primitive laser surgery. The finger is light and light projects from it. It can easily cut away, for example, malignant tissue. This cutting process is also similar to what Barbara does to restore a photograph on her computer. She enlarges the picture enough to see the individual pixels. If the eye has a bit of red from the flash bulb, she is able to remove the color red and change it to the brown of the eye, or the white. She is able to be very precise. If there is a stray single hair over the face, she can pick up the color of the adjacent pixel, delete the brown of hair and paste in the appropriate flesh color, thus removing the hair from the picture.

The Entities can work this way using the body as their palette, clearly perceiving the difference between benign and malignant cells. Just as Barbara would not disturb the pixels of the surrounding photograph to correct that single troublesome pixel, so the Entity can follow any thread-like path of malignancy with no damage to the surrounding tissues. The high intensity light cuts away the cancerous thread. Then it reaches in, almost like cutting the hemline of a skirt where there is a very tight stitch, and releases one thread at a time. When the entire malignancy is released, it can be withdrawn whole and intact, or piece by piece.

When I say "cut away," this is never by force. The malignant cells are cut away, but the Entity also communicates to the distorted tissue, giving clarity, explaining that in that malignant cell's effort to protect the body it is doing harm. There is no force; free will is observed even at the cellular level.

The healthy cell contains very pure water with a high vibration. The malignant or otherwise distorted cell has water with a low vibration. Light touches deep within, helping to purify the water content of all the remaining cells. This higher vibration is supported by the intake of high frequency water, and by the high energy of the Current.

When the Entity feels that that which needed to be treated has either been physically removed through surgery or successfully invited to transform into healthy tissue, he will then use the same light that was used to make the incision to heal the incision. The healing is swift for two reasons. First, there has been very little trauma to the tissues. Second, the Entities energetically invite the reconnection of the tissues. Think of two slabs of clay. If you bring their raw ends together, they meet, but may not stick. If you apply water to both raw ends so that a light film of water and clay exists on each side, and you then bring them together gently, they will unite. The molecules will bind. The healing of the incision is similar but energy is used in place of water. Before they close the incision they energize the cells so that there is high vibration and movement, and then invite their edges to meet.

When closing the incision we are dealing with the water content of the cells, but more so with the radiant energy within each cell. Light draws the tissue together. There is only a thin seam remaining. This is true of both the deeper layers and the surface layer. If the human could be kept from moving for about two hours, and if the Entity were able to reinforce its light healing of the seam within the hour, no stitches at all would be necessary. But the human being will move and there are not enough Entities involved in this work for one to attend to one human for the ideal length of time. The compromise they have developed, however, is quite satisfactory; it will heal very quickly, leaving only the barest trace of a scar or none at all.

Visible and invisible surgeries are equally effective in most situations. It is my understanding that in the case of a distortion such as a malignancy, the visible surgery may allow a quicker removal of the distortion through the incision, but ultimately, either means will give the same results.

The second style of visible surgery that you asked to have explained may be used to heal any portion of the body or mind, but does not require a skin incision. Instead, the Kelly clamp enters the nostril, a convenient entry point, so that no cutting is necessary. I watched the Entity access the body in this way in order to repair a foot injury. The nostril also leads into an area that we could call the seat of the soul, the third eye. From there it is easy to access the major chakras.

In the process of placing the clamp into the nostril, when that clamp penetrates into the body the solidity of the clamp dissolves; it is just light. The body structure around it also temporarily dissolves into a semi-material form, much more light than solid. Perhaps you have watched your own face in a mirror for a long period of time and seen how other aspects of the self come forward into the face, even past beings. If you have not thusly observed the face, you may wish to try it, just looking easily at your face in a mirror for about twenty minutes. Look in the eyes. How dramatically the face seems to change. Perhaps you have seen this in deep meditation when looking into another's face. The facial features are just molecules held together temporarily in this form. The form opens up. So when working with the Kelly clamp, there is not a hard metal tool being forced through the nasal bones, sinuses and into the skull. Immediately, all is light. The Kelly clamp is used, I believe, because as uncomfortable as it may seem, it is a bit more comfortable for people to view than to watch the Entity *push Medium João's finger far up the nostril. I mean no disrespect here. It is a culturally conditioned form that a finger does not go there. I am uncertain whether the metal material of the clamp has an advantage over the flesh of the finger, but certainly the use of the tool is easier on Medium João. These tools have been brought to a high vibration before surgery. They are consecrated to this work. Certainly a new tool could be used but the Entity would need time to bring it up to the necessary vibration.*

Another visible surgery is the scraping of the eyeball. Again the knife is light and what appears to be only a scraping away, is also the bringing of light into wherever it is most needed. People observe what seems to be pressure on the eye, which is the effect of the light. The matter that results from the scraping is the result of karma and distortion that have been burned away and released.

Several days later I was given the opportunity to observe more surgery. We are asked to keep our eyes closed in the Current Rooms, so one does not usually witness surgery directly. Surgery is occasionally performed in the large room where everyone can watch, as I had experienced during the first week. Perhaps the Entity does this because he knows people are curious. Special permission to watch surgery in the Entities' Current Room may be requested and granted. Now I was in the Entities' Current Room, much closer to the action. I asked Aaron to speak to me about what I might see, and about how I personally could best support the process happening before me, without getting in its way. My concern grew out of my greater sensitivity to the energies around me, and the need to be as supportive as possible.*

Aaron: *The greatest help you can be tomorrow as you observe surgery while sitting in the Current, is to be a pole connecting Earth and heaven. The work you do in the pole meditation supports the work that the Entities do. You are in*

---

*The process Aaron delineates below was his specific guidance at that time for my personal use. A longer, more generally applicable version of the Pole Meditation is available in Interval II, following this chapter.

alignment with their highest purpose. This allows their work to penetrate the physical body more deeply, promoting extensive healing.

Envision a pole rooted deep in the Earth. This pole comes out of the Earth and ascends through the atmosphere into space where there's nothing to block the sun's light. It is very light above. The air has a high vibration. Deep in the bowels of the Earth it is quite dark. At the Earth's core we find gas and fire, layers of rock, earth, and water. The rock and earth have a lower frequency vibration. The water has a somewhat higher vibration but may be pulled down by the lower vibration of earth. Above are the heavens, filled with light and space.

Hold the image of a stringed musical instrument; the lowest string is not lesser than the higher string, it simply has a lower vibration. For harmony, you need all the strings tuned together, not discordant. For example, think of what types of beings or levels of vibrations you may consider to be just above the hell realms; beings that are consumed by fear and anger, or imagine a dark place with low vibrational frequency. Just bring them to mind. Next, consider angels, with a high vibrational frequency of love, light, and laughter, as you occasionally find in meditation.

I request that you very carefully center yourself and invite in not only me but also Jeshua and other high beings for protection. Now, as much as possible, imagine the darkness, the horror, the very low vibration of that place of deepest darkness and despair.

I did this for perhaps sixty seconds and found myself crying, not with fear but with compassion and with sadness for the depth of darkness that is possible. It was a more dense darkness than I've previously entered. Just as I felt I couldn't tolerate it any more, I heard Aaron's voice asking me to feel the highest frequency vibration, to literally be with him, Jeshua and divine beings and ascend with them to the highest light realms for a minute or so. It was an experience of ecstatic bliss, but I could not stay there long as the intensity of the vibration felt like it was pulling me apart.

Now I ask you to be that pole, feet grounded in the Earth, head in the heavens. Can you allow both extremes simultaneously? On the highest level, there is only light, and in the hell realms, there is extreme darkness. Be the pole that joins them together. If you have heat in one room and the air is frigid in the next, you can open a conduit to conduct heat to the icy realms, or to release the cold air. I ask you to be such a conduit to release darkness, and to bring light into the dark spaces.

I tried this and faltered at first, shifting from darkness to light, back and forth, unstable. Aaron spoke to my fear and gently reminded me that I was safe.

Don't be in either place, be all of it, feet on the Earth, not hell realms, but know the Earth vibrations and these lower ones, and hold the head in the heavens. Feel both and join them. Sambhogakaya.* You have been thusly trained and understand this work. This is the non-bridge, nonduality.

With this instruction, I got it. I was able to hold both spaces at the same time, knowing them as nondual, light and darkness, terror and love, aloneness and unity. There was a feeling of great joy and transcendence, yet I still had the ability to witness, and to not separate myself from pain and darkness. I practiced for some time until Aaron spoke again.

Where you experience any tension as you watch the surgery, hold that tension in a container of light, as you have been trained. Become the pole. I believe you will not have any difficulty with what you will see. You know that a cut may yield blood and you are not squeamish around blood. It is helpful that you will feel the enormous compassion around the doing of this work.

To some notable degree you will see and feel the Entities. Be respectful of

---

*Sambhogakaya: This relates to the Buddhist teaching of three *kayas*, or bodies. Dharmakaya is the truth body, the highest level of expression, the expression of our true divine nature. Nirmanakaya is the form body, the relative expressions of physical, mental, and emotional form. Sambhogakaya is the transition body, which holds both dharmakaya and nirmanakaya and knows them as nondual.

them. Do not ask them questions or interject thoughts while they are working. I will answer your questions.

Aaron's words returned me to the meditative experiences of nonduality. Everything is connected. It is important not to lose myself in either extreme, thereby losing touch with the whole.

During the surgeries I practiced as Aaron had directed. They were fairly routine (for the Casa), an incision to remove a growth from a man's back, and another of the Kelly clamp procedures on a young woman. I was very aware of how calm both people were as the Entity worked on each. At first I tensed as the Entity began to cut, then remembered the practice and relaxed into it. It felt important to be able to contribute to that calm, and to support the high and loving vibrations that filled the room. I more fully realized how Aaron's pole meditation in many ways describes the core of the Entities' work at the Casa. By lifting the Earth heavenward and drawing down heaven to Earth, while knowing that both states are a fundamental unity, the Entities are able to support healing. The Casa is a portal for light, with no denial of the heavy realms of suffering.

I watched a surgery where the Entity scraped the eyeball with a knife. I was able to speak to the person, Ann, a week later.

"I went in front of the Entity, a year ago, to ask if he could help me to have more insight and to have better physical vision too. I returned here this year. Last week, as I passed through the line, the Entity asked me, "Do you want to have an operation now?" I said yes. The Entity asked me if I would like to have a visible or invisible one. And "visible" came out of my mouth! He said, "Good!" and had me sit in a chair. I was so scared, but I knew I would not wish to get up or change anything in the situation. Then he asked me to hold my right hand on my right eye and he opened my left eye very wide and came with the knife, and he scratched the eye. I saw a lot of light. I felt something, but there was no pain. It was over fast and they took me away.

"Afterward, I had to be careful. My eye was not painful but sensitive. I put the blessed water on it. After this operation, it helped me to trust myself. I gave speeches (about the Casa) after this operation and I never would have stood up in front of so many people before. In my energy work, I could more easily see where my clients were and I could even see past lives sometimes. And my physical vision improved. So the operation really changed something."

I had the opportunity to speak later with a man on whom the Kelly clamp was used. In his words:

"My name is Leonard. I am a fifty-two-year-old veterinary surgeon from the UK. For over thirty years I have suffered from a blocked nose, and have been unable to sleep without oral breathing all night. I somehow felt called to come to the Casa to see if Medium João could help improve my breathing. I also felt called to have a physical healing (not realizing that there was an age limit of fifty-three for physical surgery, so I came to Brazil with only a month to spare).

"Over the years, I've had steroid nasal sprays, allergy tests, and cameras up my nose under local anesthetic, all to no avail.

"My eyes were shut, as I stood before several hundred people in meditation. Medium João proceeded to insert forceps up my right nostril. I had anticipated feeling a lot of pain, and was surprised to find very little, but probably more shock at the speed of the procedure. There was very little bleeding, no post-operative pain, no swelling or bruising.

"Imagine my great delight and surprise that night to find that I could sleep all night, in any position with my mouth shut. I felt great, almost on cloud nine.

"I shall be eternally grateful that somehow I was guided to find my way to Abadiânia and to the caring hands of Medium João and everyone at the Casa."

I heard this over and over: the immense gratitude for this work that has saved lives and alleviated suffering.

INTERVAL II
Chakras and the Pole Meditation

Our bodies contain innumerable channels through which energy flows, fulfilling the basic energy needs of the body just as our arteries and veins carry our blood. A chakra, or energy center, is where two or more of these channels cross. Our bodies have many chakras, some with more connections than others. There are seven core chakras down the midline of the body where a great number of these channels meet, plus one floating in space above the crown. Each has a specific function, color, and primary musical tone. In summary, the core chakras just in front of the spine are:

Location	Chakra	Color	Function	Tone
Base of Spine	Root	Red	Life force, survival, and sexuality	C
Navel (1 inch below)	Sacral	Orange	Personal relationships with ourselves and with others	D
Diaphragm	Solar Plexus	Yellow	Relationships in the world, such as work and family	E
Breast Bone	Heart	Green	The connection of human and spiritual forces	F
Indentation at Neck	Throat	Blue	Speaking one's deepest truth (Speaking truth to power)	G
Forehead between eyes	Third Eye	Indigo	Spiritual vision	A
Top of Head	Crown	Violet	Connecting to the Divine	B
Above the Head	Light	White	The Unconditioned	C

There is also a back chakra system, with those chakras located approximately in between the front ones, vertically.

Each chakra has a closed position and a released position, almost like a water faucet. If it's turned off, the water cannot flow. The contraction of fear tends to close the chakras.

The lower chakras relate to the heavier, more physical aspects of being, and the upper chakras relate more to the spiritual realm. The lower chakras are of the physical plane, while the upper chakras are of the astral plane. Each of us is a pole, grounded in the Earth plane and carrying the very highest energy of the crown chakra. Sometimes we prefer to be more in the body and avoid the spirit plane, or more in the spirit plane and avoid the world and the body.

There are many different material and nonmaterial planes. Some have a very heavy density, and a very low vibration, and some have a much higher vibration. The emotional and physical bodies and the Earth plane do have a lower frequency vibration than the spirit realm. Our human effort brings body and spirit together, thereby helping to raise the heavy vibration of body and Earth. Don't think of heavy vibrations as bad and high vibrations as good. Think of the strings of a cello; there are low strings and high strings. One is not better than the other, but they each offer a different energy. As we work to clear discordance among the lowest vibrations, we are clarifying and raising the vibrational frequency of the body. This raised vibration allows us to live in the world with more freedom, less suffering, and more kindness to others and ourselves.

When the chakras are open, each tunes to the one next to it. This is the same process as tuning our example's violin, by holding your finger on the string as you play it, and then tuning the next string until it vibrates to the harmonious tone. An open chakra's resonance enhances the vibration of the others until the whole collection of the chakras, the entire meridian running from the first to eighth chakra, is open and radiant. Each chakra still has its own vibrational frequency, but they are all in tune with one another.

Open chakras spin. When the physical or energetic bodies contract, that contraction to some degree shuts down the harmonic energy movement between the chakras. The energy becomes discordant because the chakras are not open and have stopped spinning. If you stub your toe, it hurts. If you sit down and hold the foot in your hands, massage it, and offer loving energy to it, then the vibration of your kindness changes the nature of the experience of pain. If, instead, you curse at the pain, you can feel how the whole body further contracts. The chakras close; the whole body moves into a lower vibrational frequency and becomes increasingly discordant. The discordance is really the result of the closed chakras, which have closed due to the unbalanced contraction.

The more discordant the energy becomes, the more your habit energy leads you to react to that discordance by closing down even further. We can learn to feel this spin, and to feel the openness or contraction of the chakras. I personally feel it as though my body was closing in and shutting down; my breath becomes rigid and shorter; and my muscles contract. When the chakras are spinning, my breath is easier and my mind is more peaceful. I feel in harmony with myself. There will be an opportunity to explore these sensations in the guided meditation below.

Most of us have come into this incarnation with the intention to hold peace and love in the face of difficult experiences. Because we have forgotten the deeper truth of our being, we try to enact this intention through only the lower chakras. Or, having remembered that truth of our being, but finding the Earth plane situation unpleasant, we prefer to abandon the lower chakras altogether. These are habits we need to release.

We have come to this heavy-density Earth to shine light into the darkness. When we hold all of the chakras open, it helps to bring a higher vibration into this Earthly environment; it brings light to the places where there is darkness, pain, and fear. So through our courageous work, we raise the vibrational frequency of the entire Earth plane, thereby making this plane a much more vital force for love and light.

I want to offer you a guided meditation, which uses the chakras as its basic structure. We start by opening the chakras.

Breathing in through the crown of the head, bring red light down to the base chakra. Exhale, and with each exhalation, allow that light to expand within the center to which it has been invited. Continue to breathe in the red light until the base chakra can hold no more of it. Let it rest in the base chakra, which you can now feel spinning.

(Pause.)

Inhale, bringing orange light down to the sacral chakra at the navel. Exhale. Again, allow that light to expand within the center to which it has been invited until it can hold no more.

(Pause.)

Breathe in yellow light through the crown and bring it down to the solar plexus. Exhale. Allow it to expand.

(Pause.)

Breathe in green light to the heart. Exhale. Expand.

(Pause.)

Breathing in through the crown of your head, bring blue light down to the throat, and release it there. Expand.

(Pause.)

Breathing in through the crown, hold indigo light at the third eye and release. Expand.

(Pause.)

Breathe in violet light at the crown, and release it there. Expand.

(Pause.)

And then above the head, see a very white light, somewhere between six and eighteen inches above the crown chakra. Let it expand there.

(Pause.)

(Short pauses are not further noted, but follow between most steps.)

As much as possible, feel yourself centered in these spinning chakras. Hold the back erect to maintain openness to the flow of the energy.

Feel yourself centered so that the energy rests equally in the lower and the upper chakras. Bring one hand to the heart center. Feel it as the fulcrum, the balance point. Relax. If there is tension, notice where that tension resides. If it is in the second or third chakras, bring the other hand gently to the abdominal area. On one level, offer the release of tension; on another level, know that which is already free of tension, and rest in that space.

(Pause.)

Now I am going to ask you to think of something painful, something that has brought you sadness, fear or anger. Hold the heart open to this difficult emotion. As you first bring it to your attention, you may feel a closing in one or several of the three lower chakras. It will feel tight, the way it feels when you clench your fists. Simply bring kind attention to that feeling of closure. Breathe more of the appropriate color into the chakra; or several colors, if several chakras are involved.

Observe how you can hold the memory of that painful experience and simultaneously know that the lower chakras can be opened and that you can invite such opening. They may not be perfectly open, but when there is not much self-identification with their closing, you can rest in the spacious awareness that sees them closing, in the same way that you can watch yourself zip a jacket. It closes; however that closure is not the self. Awareness watches, even as "self" zips. The habit energy may be strong and the lower chakras may seem to close, but rest in that which is always open, while watching the illusory closure in relative reality.

Breathing in. And breathing out. Breathe deeply into the belly, all the way down to the base chakra until you feel stable. If something is still closed on the relative plane, note it. Without denial of the closure, rest in that which is open.

(Pause.)

Now I ask you to experience the body as a pole, able to be with the lower vibration and closure that were triggered by fear, sadness, pain or other heavy emotions. At the upper end of the pole, there is a space of clarity and love, which is uncontracted and free. That highest, non-material energy cannot descend into the lowest vibration of the Earth plane. We, divine beings who are in the physical body, are able to ground into the heavy Earth plane as well as open into the heavenly realms. Spirit can't do that; we can.

Let us do this meditation together.

Bring into your mind a place where others are suffering greatly. Hold the vision of those whose bodies, even right now, are being exploded by bombs or bullets; those who are burning in a fire or drowning in a sea. Our usual conditioning is to run fast in the other direction when we see such pain, but here we allow ourselves to deeply touch it.

Breathing in, breathing out. Be aware of the enormity of suffering that exists on the Earth, among sentient beings. One of the challenges and gifts of our international news today is that we can literally turn on the television and see people dying. This is a nightmare, and yet it is also a teacher of compassion. You may wish to hold such a scene in your mind as we practice.

(Pause.)

Realize how easy it would be to become ensnared in that low vibration and have the chakras close. The closing of the energy field is the conditioned way to create a safe place for yourself, like the turtle withdrawing into its shell. Watch the impulse, if there is one, of wanting to withdraw. Instead, stay as present as possible.

(Pause.)

Without letting go of that place of suffering, move the attention up into the heart center, touching the heart area with a gentle pressure. Breathe into the pressure and release. Continue to move up into the throat, then into the third eye and crown chakras.

Touch the core of being at the crown chakra, and then breathe the high vibration of that Unconditioned essence through the body and down into the base chakra. When you do this, you are raising yourself into the highest vibrational frequency of which this body and mind are capable.

Draw in the suffering through the lower chakras. Now breathe it up through the heart. Do not try to release the low vibration. Just let the tension rest there until it releases. What remains is the highest expression of being.

Breathe that highest energy in. Bring it down through the chakras. Hold the memory again of that place of horror, of pain. Offer this higher energy to it. Breathe in that pain, up through the chakras, and hold it in the light. Rest in the crown chakra, third eye, and throat. Breathe that light and love in and down through the chakras again. Feel it all the way at the base. You may be experiencing the horror that injured, maimed, and dying beings feel, but experience also the potential for love, for the open heart, right there amidst the horror. Breathe in that pain. Bring it up to the higher realm again.

You might want to take several breaths with each step rather than one, to spend more time at either end of the pole. Never forget that you hold the entire pole. That trauma is your trauma also; certainly at some time you have experienced pain, loss, fear, hatred, and greed. And that love is your love, the highest love of which the greater self is capable.

The highest energy is that of the Unconditioned or Ever-Perfect. You may lose sight of it but you cannot lose it because it can't go anywhere. The vibration of fear is conditioned. The Unconditioned cannot be stained, so you carry this high energy down and into the lower chakras. You carry the pain up but it cannot distort or stain the higher chakras.

Allow yourself to experience the brilliant radiance of that light at the upper level. Use the imagination to envision the brutality of which beings are capable. See the enormity of suffering, the nightmares of natural disasters. Do not dwell in stories but rather direct your awareness to human anguish, human pain, and to the highest love and light. Feel yourself as the pole that can hold it all together.

Aaron tells of a lifetime long ago in which there were terrible rains that brought mudslides. The mud filled up the well from which the village drew its water. This was water from a pure underground spring, but now mud buried the source. People began to dig. As they got several feet down, it was necessary to climb into the well and scoop the mud into buckets that were lifted up from outside. They dug their way down through thick black mud until finally the last was removed and the fresh spring remained there at the bottom.

They scooped out the first muddy water, and the spring kept replenishing with water that was progressively clearer. They continued to scoop until finally they had reclaimed the bottom of their well, and the spring had filled the well with pure sweet water. This is what we are doing in a very real sense.

As you do this pole meditation, you must remember that the pure energy, light, and love are not just at the upper chakras, but that the lower chakras also can resonate with pure energy. A lower vibration as tone is natural to those chakras, but it is pure. The lower chakras are not grounded in fear; the same love and light animates all the chakras. However, any one of them can become ensnared in the distortion of fear.

As we do this meditation again, breathe the light and love through the open chakras and into whatever horror you have seen, much like the spring bubbling through the mud and purifying the well. Breathe into that horror, lift it up and release it. As you purify that place of darkness and sweep out its layers of dirt, the natural light that was hidden can come forth.

(Long pause to practice.)

Now let us pick a place to practice. Northern Japan had terrible earthquakes in the past. Fortunately, there was not too much loss of life, nor too many injuries; however, people were without food, without water, and without the homes that were destroyed. Many people lost all that they had worked hard to create in their lives. People were suffering.

Hold the image in your mind of the rocks and buildings tumbling, people caught under the debris, needing to be dug out: people in pain and afraid.* Try to touch that pain from the most open place of the

---

*At the time this material was being reviewed, the devastating earthquakes in Haiti and Chile had just occurred. Aaron suggested we work with any place in the world that has known such destruction.

heart. Then go into the lower chakras. Be the pole reaching all the way down into that pain through your own intimate knowledge of your own pain, fear, and loss. Breathing in, allow that pain to come through you into the heart, and further into your body. Just let the pain float, until it disperses. Breathe in the love and light of the heavens, spaciousness, kindness, and freedom. Draw it all the way through the heart and down into the base chakra. Bring love and light to the pain and darkness.

Again, breathe in that pain, fear, and darkness. Let it come up through the chakras, drawing it up, just allowing space for it. The pain is just pain. The fear is just fear. No contraction around it. Breathe in light. Breathe in spaciousness and love. Feel the body as a pole connecting to that light and love and drawing it back down and into the Earth. Reach out again for the image of the earthquake and its victims, and of the stressed Earth itself, for the Earth is also the victim of the earthquake. Breathe in that pain and darkness and raise it up into the light. Breathe in the light and carry it down through you into the realm of darkness.

(Pause.)

Just as you can do this with a natural disaster, such as the earthquake or tsunami; or with places that are embattled, as in Iraq or Afghanistan; so then can you do it within the self. See the places that have pain and the places that have light; then come to the nondual awareness of the simultaneity of light and pain. Rest, uncontracted, around that human pain, offering it light and love.

CHAPTER 10

"How Do They Do That?"

WHEN DAVY, KATE, MEL, and I returned home to Michigan, we gathered to ask Aaron some remaining questions about surgery. We wanted more information about how the higher vibration at the Casa in surgery and in the current rooms supports healing.

Aaron: *The knife used in the surgery is an ordinary kitchen paring knife but it has been worked with to the point that, in itself, it has a very high vibrational frequency. The hand wielding the knife has a far higher frequency and that is conveyed through the knife. Because the knife and energy-wielding hand have such a high frequency vibration, it simultaneously opens the skin and invites the flesh into that higher vibration. The knife cut is not so traumatic to the flesh. The flesh is not receiving low vibrational energy but high. So even while the flesh molecules are parted, this higher vibration gifts the flesh.*

I am told that the forceps surgery elevates the chakras to the purest possible frequency. When the forceps are inserted into the nostril, the Entities are activating the pineal gland near the third eye. The third eye brings forth the reality of innate perfection, which allows the other chakras to open more completely, spin faster, and vibrate at a higher frequency. Any chakra's vibration always corresponds to its specific note in any octave, but when fully open the chakras collectively shift upward into a higher octave. The pure, high vibration of the chakras acts as a model for the whole body. In effect, the Entities are re-tuning the whole body through tuning the chakras.

Just as an old musical instrument string cannot hold its tuning and goes flat very quickly, so the body with a habitually low frequency cannot hold a high vibration. The current rooms have the effect of replacing the strings, let us say, creating the possibility in the strings to hold the tune. The charged water does the same, as do the crystal beds.

When beings leave the Casa, the strings will fall flat again to some degree. The absorption of this very high vibrational frequency in current and in the Casa environment will help to reinforce the higher frequency until the body shifts far enough into that higher vibration to maintain stability and hold that vibration even while away from the Casa. Think of the singer who at first can hold a tone only when there is musical support, but eventually learns to hear that pure tone within and to reproduce it anywhere. That is why some people feel pulled to stay at the Casa as a shift is happening. The physical healing will come later, after the body can better hold the higher vibrations of those purified cells. Most beings who come to the Casa are consciously or subconsciously working to help raise the frequency of the Earth, beginning with their own physical, emotional, mental, and spiritual bodies. They come not only for their own healing, but are drawn to service as beings of light.

What of those who are unaware of—or less concerned with—the need for the Earth's healing and rising to higher frequency, and more concerned with their own physical healing? When beings are in pain and experiencing the sharp limitations of a semi-functioning body, it is merciful to heal. The healing will raise the vibrational frequency of the body at least temporarily. Hopefully those beings will do their work on the mental and emotional levels, and resolve karma, so as to keep that frequency high. Some will; some will not. As the personal frequency elevates, it brings its surroundings along with it. But some are called here who are already quite awake. I am enjoying how many beings we talk with, who don't have a specific physical ailment or emotional depression, simply feel called here by the high frequency.

I asked Aaron about Medium João's involvement. I had seen the Entity insert Medium João's finger into an incision and seem to wiggle it around inside the body. I feel that Medium João is a part of this effort in a more direct way, not just as the vehicle for the Entity. I asked him to speak about that.

This is not the human João's finger inserted into an incision. Rather it is a light probe that is simply using the form of João's finger. The finger has nerves and muscles; it is sensitive. And because it carries the vibration of the Entities so easily, it is easier to charge it than to charge a surgical tool.

Here is where I suspect Medium João as human comes into it. His deep compassion is part of the charging of this light tool. The Entities have compassion but it is important to bring human compassion into it too. This is a cooperative effort.

K, you experienced being touched at the start of your physical surgery, and simply melting into that touch, feeling no resistance or fear. What touched you was this very high vibrational frequency. It literally stunned all the tissues of your body, and raised the frequency in an instant to a very different vibration.

If you think of a conduit for water, if it has any surface texture there will be friction. The friction will affect both the conduit and the water. If you can imagine the Ever-Perfect conduit, completely smooth, there is no friction. Friction equates with contraction. Frictionlessness equates with release and spaciousness. With a touch, the friction in all the bodies that express as K dissolved itself, and there was nothing there but God, nothing but light. God's will was expressed through the Entity that knows itself as servant of God, and was also your will. I don't want to make God into a kind of person. I am not speaking of an Entity when I say "God," but All-That-Is. God's will is the highest will of all beings, for the highest good, but only "God" can see that composite highest good. It is infinite love and intelligence. You found yourself able to surrender completely to that in large part because the touch released all friction and allowed the bodies to be raised to a very high vibration.

I understand the Casa is built on top of a deep bed of crystal. What effect does this have on the work of the Casa? Was the Casa site chosen specifically because the crystals are there?

The Casa site was chosen specifically because of the high energy of the crystals that lie underground. The energy of the Casa and especially of the Current nurtures and supports the crystalline energy, just as the crystalline energy nurtures and supports the Current. The energetic power of the Entity/Medium João/Current connection is such that the Entities can work quite effectively far away from the Casa for a limited period of time. However, the Current must be supported in the place where they are working, through the intention of loving beings, physical and non-physical, who also hold that high energy vibration.

Do these same crystals energize the waterfall?

The crystals do indeed energize the waterfall, and also purify it. The ground water that emerges to form the stream that flows into the waterfall comes from deep down upon the crystal beds. Rain runoff also fills the stream. The Entities help to purify that runoff and to bring it to a high vibration.

Is there some reciprocity between the waterfall, the crystals below, and the current energy above?

They are all in a reciprocal relationship. It begins with the intention of service for the highest good of all beings. The crystals follow this intention and draw to them those who would thusly serve. The crystal energy supports the high vibration of the waterfall and of the Current. The Current energy, human and Entity energy alike, also supports the high vibration of the water, and of the crystals. Because of the power of that Current the crystal energy is constantly replenished. So it is a constant process of giving and receiving for crystals, waterfall, Entities, and humans. It is always this way; giving and receiving are nondual. One who would give must be willing to receive. One who would receive must keep that gift cycling, giving it back out. It all comes from God and returns to God.

If the Current energy did not give back to replenish the crystal energy, would the crystal bed beneath the Casa eventually lose its power?

I cannot say for certain. Nothing can give constantly without restoration. The crystals are teachers. They teach the art of letting go and of giving. If for some reason the Entities all departed the Casa, yet people still came and grasped at the crystal energy, certainly it would fade in time. In part this response would be offered as teaching of the truth that you cannot receive without giving. But since the Entities have no intention of departing the Casa and are highly positively polarized beings, they see that the balance is kept in such a way that all is nourished.

Yet it sometimes seems to me that one can receive without giving.

No. It is not always clear what one gives. A newborn infant seems to receive constantly but it gives much love. We look at a quadriplegic who needs constant care. What does such a person give? She gives the opportunity to the caretaker to practice giving. Look at this water bottle. It can receive for a certain length of time. When it is full it cannot receive anymore until some is spilled out. So it is with humans.

It would seem that for the healing we find at the Casa, we must be in that location with crystals, waterfall, and Entities. Can healing continue at home, and if so, how is it supported?

Once you have worked with the Entities, in person or through pictures and prayers, they continue that connection as long as you wish it. The energy of the Casa is further available to you through the prescribed herbs, in the blessed water you may carry home, and also through the crystals you may purchase and take home, which are imbued with high energy. But the most significant aspect of that high vibration is your own prayer and meditation. When you meditate you open to your own highest aspect of being, your deepest divinity that always carries a high and pure vibration. This is the ever healed, and serves as a mirror, reflecting that innate perfection back to the lower bodies.

What is the relationship between our free will and healing?

The Entities cannot create something against the will of the human. On a conscious level the human may wish to heal, but the human may also be attached to the status quo. Illness is a result of many conditions. Often it relates to old karma that is not fully resolved. An illness may become a hiding place, offering a veil so that the human does not have to see deeper issues. If the human is deeply willing, the Entities will support the balance and release of old karma. The high vibration of the Casa is a supportive environment for this work to happen.

You have noted that surgery can be done away from the Casa and wondered why people have needed to come to Brazil. For the human with highest intention to healing, ready to look honestly at issues that have enhanced distortion, the work can be done from afar. That human must also take responsibility for meditation and other practices that maintain a high enough energy to support the healing work. At the Casa it is easier. The environment itself provides that high vibration.

I had several crystal bed sessions and felt very intense energy during the sessions. I was light-headed afterward. How do the crystal beds work? I know crystal beds exist outside of the Casa. Is there a relationship between crystal beds and the underground crystal?

The crystal bed is an apparatus that contains lights, crystals, and colored filters in the colors related to the seven chakras that are within the physical body. A person lies on a literal bed with this apparatus suspended above. The lights are adjusted to shine at each chakra in sequence. One lies there for a set period of time, perhaps twenty or forty minutes, as prescribed by an Entity. The process helps to open and energize the chakras. This energizing helps to raise the vibrational frequency of the entire body, thus supporting healing. The Entities cannot work on a person's body, bringing in the high energy of surgery to one small part of the body for example, unless the whole body energy field is somewhat open. To attempt that would be to blow a fuse so to speak. So the body energy must flow openly before intense energy may be brought to any one part of the body.

The crystal beds at the Casa participate in the same energy flow as does everything else at the Casa. They are supported by the underground crystals and by the Current energy, and thusly they receive. They offer energy to those who are served by them. Energy is fluid, moving, and is constantly being recycled. Some things may be hoarded; energy can never be hoarded.

Crystal beds have been brought to all parts of the world. These do not have the advantage of the high-energy vibration that is in the Casa area. However, numerous Entities support each crystal bed and maintain a useful level of energy. The crystal beds outside of the Casa area are not quite as powerful as those of the Casa but are quite sufficient. The one who maintains the crystal bed must "feed" it with love.

I watched the extraction of wisdom teeth. The woman whose teeth were removed said the next day that she had almost no pain and her jaw wasn't swollen. I asked Aaron to explain.

With the removal of teeth, the Entity uses the knife or finger to sever the root cells, using care not to traumatize gum tissue, in the method I have previously described. They break down the tooth roots and gently lift out the now rootless tooth. There is no need to sterilize other than this high vibration. No bacteria can exist within it. The high vibration continues for several days, thus making the cells less susceptible to infection that might come from a new contaminated source. Still, in the case of a body incision, the wound should be bandaged and kept clean, as one would treat any incision.

I was curious about the anesthesia at the Casa and how it worked to block pain.

What is pain? There are many nerve endings throughout the body. Certain sensations such as extreme heat or cold, or penetration by something sharp, are felt as uncomfortable or unpleasant. There is a very fast movement through the neural pathways from the site of injury to the brain. The mind perceives this sensation as pain; therefore, the habitual reaction to pain arises. The Entity energetically blocks the perception of pain moving to the brain. Sensation is still experienced, perhaps as heat or pressure but the brain does not register that perception as pain.

Could you explain further how the Entity blocks the perception of pain?

There are two parts to this answer. For the first, the closest metaphor I can offer is a heat shield. If an object is radiating heat and you place a shield between you and that object, the heat remains, but you do not feel it. Energy has many forms. It can be active as in the type of energy used to create an incision; it can be passive, or even receptive. Essentially the Entity inserts an energy catcher at the point where the nerve connects to the brain. This energy is receptive; it acts like a blotter absorbing the pain impulse.

To understand the second part you must understand perception. Only rarely is bare perception experienced, uninfluenced by old conditioning. Jumping into a cold lake may feel pleasant or unpleasant regardless of water temperature. Much of what is perceived is based upon prior conditioning. If you expect the sensation to be unpleasant, you contract before it is experienced. This first contraction influences the next experience. The Entities help bring the perception faculty to a centered place of bare perception. Thus there may be a feeling of heat or pressure, but the body does not jump in alarm and contract with the anticipation of pain. When the body stays soft, the sensation is just sensation. Most pain is largely a result of contraction around sensation. So there is this mix in anesthesia. There is blockage of the strongest sensation and the assistance to stay centered and not contract.

While at the Casa, we were told the Entities would come at night a week after the surgery to remove the stitches, even for people who had gone home. We all experienced this visitation to some degree one week after surgery. A neighbor in my hallway awakened to find the physical stitches removed. I awoke from a sound sleep to the experience of small flashes of light in my room, and a sensation of pressure on my face. It would have frightened me if I had not been expecting their visit. We had many questions for Aaron. We wondered how they find us, especially those of us who had left the Casa and were thousands of miles away?

Each human has a different energy pattern. The Entities are able to "see" that pattern and go to where they are needed. This is no more difficult for us than it would be for you to notice your friend's car in the market parking lot and know that he or she is inside the store.

Why one week later, and why are we asked to follow a specific protocol, to wear white and to have a glass of Casa water by the bed to drink upon arising?

They return in one week because that is the average time it takes for the healing work to settle. The drink of Casa water has two functions. It helps bring the body to a higher energy. It also alerts the Entity to the fact that the patient has awakened. An Entity will come almost immediately as you drink the water to observe the place where the stitches were removed and to be certain that all is well. Your prayer of gratitude as you drink that water serves the same two pur-poses. The white nightwear is requested for the same reason white is requested in the Casa. The Entities can see the energy field better when there is no busy pat-tern or dark color blocking their view.

If one has returned home and there is someone else in the bed or a pet lying on the bed, is that a problem?

Each being has a distinct energy field. Besides, your partner or your pets do not have stitches to be removed. Remember that one is asked to refrain from sex-ual activity for a period of forty days following a first surgery or eight days fol-lowing subsequent surgeries. One reason for this request is that during sexual activity energy fields merge. This merging would make it much more difficult for the Entities to isolate the body upon which they must work.

You said that is one reason for the limitation on sexual activity. What are the others, and why a longer period of time, forty days, following the first surgery, and only eight days of abstinence from sexual activ-ity following subsequent surgeries?

The limitation is not a statement of wrongness of sexual intimacy or self-gratification. The primary reason for the limitation is that you have just had sur-gery, sometimes major surgery. You are asked to refrain from any lifting or activity that could tear open an incision that has not yet healed or could tear internal stitches. A second important reason is that much of the healing is ener-getic. The high expression of energy during sexual activity reduces the amount of energy available for healing. The same is true of sexual energy released in self-gratification.

The forty-day request for first time surgery is because that person is usually newer to the Casa and the Entities and has not had the benefit of ongoing work. The person receiving a second surgery usually begins with a higher overall vibra-tional frequency.

Through intimacy one does share energy. After surgery, your energy field is very open and vulnerable. Sexual intimacy further opens the energy field. This doubled openness makes the person more vulnerable to negative distortion.

Although only eight days abstinence is requested in the case of surgeries beyond the first, sometimes the Entity will suggest a longer abstinence period when there are deep internal stitches.

In visible surgery I'm told that the site of the incision is not always the place where the Entities have worked. I spoke to someone who had the nasal procedure for colitis. Why and how would they have entered the body in one place to work on another place?

There are several reasons. First the site of the apparent distortion and the site of the source of distortion are often different. The Entities attend to the apparent distortion but are even more concerned with healing the source. For example, while the scraping of the eye may relate to a distortion in the eyes or the vision, equally often this operation is a way of releasing karma. That karma may have nothing to do with eyes or vision. As another example, I observed an Entity doing invisible surgery on a person's sacroiliac joint to release knee pain. The distortion in the sacroiliac joint was the true cause of the knee pain. Once that distortion was attended to, the knee could heal.

When doing visible surgery the Entities will elect not to create an opening in the skin if they can avoid such. However non-traumatic, it is still an opening in the skin. Thus they will go in through an available opening such as the nostril, whenever possible. I have seen them operate on abdominal tumors and hernias through the nostril and even on a malady of the foot. In that latter case, a visible operation on the foot itself would have meant the patient would have been unable to walk or tend to her wheelchair-bound husband for a week or more.

The town of Abadiânia is growing, with new pousadas and other services for all who come. Many people decide to stay. The owners of our pousada first came from the United States for healing, and were so moved by their experience that they made the decision to remain here. A pousada was available and they bought it. We heard of many such co-incidences. Certainly there needs to be support services for João's and the Entities' work. Is there a karmic connection between those who move to Abadiânia and the Entities? Do the Entities support these projects in a direct energetic way?

The Entities support healing in all its forms. Someone who has lived a self-

centered life may come to the Casa and feel drawn to service there. Such service is part of their healing. Another being may see a means to earn money and choose to open a pousada largely for reasons of profit. In the first situation the Entities will certainly support any endeavor. In the second situation the Entities may still support that step if they feel there is a good possibility of a shift into more self-lessness and generosity as the person runs the pousada. If that person were to continue in selfishness, I think the Entity would first speak to that person and if there was no shift in the behavior pattern, the Entities would withdraw support. In short, the Entities support every path toward healing of the self and service to others. If they see a path leading into further distortion they may seem to with-hold support. They are not ceasing to support growth and healing, they are ceasing to support distortion. The Entities are experts at avoiding enabling behavior.

I want to know why these specific Entities are working through João. Is there a karmic connection?

In the early days of João's ministry there were several Entities with whom there was a karmic connection and the pre-incarnation agreement to do such work. João worked hard to become a clear medium, to work with love, humility and honesty, and with the highest intention of service. Because of the deep love within him, he was not highly vulnerable to negativity and thus not highly vulnerable to distortion. Other Entities with whom there was no prior karmic bond, and who had a high intention to service, observed the value of this work and joined in. More and more Entities choose to participate in the work in this way.

The human mind is so filled with questions. Aaron asked us to pause our questions here and observe how our intellects were trying to figure all this out so as to feel some control over what seemed bewildering. Can we let go and open to a place of faith that sees good things happening and trusts, even without full understanding?

CHAPTER 11

Questions about Healing

PEOPLE COME AS we did, willing to experience what the Casa has to offer, but often with no understanding of what happens here at a deeper level. It seems like magic, or a miracle, when healing happens; but there may be confusion or anger when there's not a visible, physical healing. People may wonder if they are not worthy, or what went wrong. Each of us is at a different place in our understanding, and attitudes can range from fear to deep trust. Many people are more goal-oriented and impatient. Others with whom I've been able to speak seem to have a more wide-open faith and patience with the entire process of healing.

Some people also seem to come with more of a sense of shame about their illnesses. We do have a part in creating our illnesses, but only a part. Personal, genetic, and environmental factors each play a role. We need to remember that while illness is partially shaped by karma and our habit energies, the recognition, release, and balancing of these patterns are among the very reasons we came into these bodies. We incarnate with the intent to heal the distortions that may contribute to illness, and also to become more compassionate and skillful in our lives. We need to be very careful not to blame ourselves for illness, just to ask, "Where is healing to be found?" We're not failures if the body does not heal.

After my weeks at the Casa drew to a close, several questions about healing were forwarded to me from new Casa friends and guides who have seen many people experience the Casa, some with physical healing and some with no apparent outer healing. Other questions came from those who had traveled with me. After our return home, Aaron spoke directly to a Casa Guide's question, "What of a situation where one person is cured of cancer and another is not? The latter sometimes feels that she is a bad person."

Beings have free will, which must be respected. Beings have different inten-tions. The Casa Entities and your own spirit guides work to support the whole-some intention. Why didn't Barbara come down here five years ago? Her highest intention was not to heal the deafness but the causes of the deafness. The deaf-ness is an unpleasantness, an inconvenience. Yes it brings sadness, but it is toler-able. Deafness is not life threatening. It is a teacher. In some ways not hearing is the perfect teaching distortion in that it doesn't present limitations such as a life-ending malady or terrible physical pain. Deafness not only allows, but also invites, her work in the world. Her highest intention was to resolve the causes, or karma, associated with the deafness, with a long-term intention of moving toward lib-eration. But now that the karma is largely resolved, there is an intention to heal the deafness because there is no longer a reason to carry it, and it does impede her work in some ways. Hearing would also be highly joyful, and would help her to more deeply experience this Earth plane on which she resides.

Some beings do not have the option of choosing to resolve the karma before physical healing occurs. Take the example of cancer that you gave. The body would die. So the cancer is a wake-up call. Other beings may come to the situ-ation with the clear intent to resolve the karma first even if the body deteriorates and dies. In that case, the healing of the body is experienced as secondary to the healing of the karma. This may not be a consciously held intention, though some-times it is a conscious one.

Some beings have the mistaken idea that if they resolve the cancer first, they will not have the impetus to deal with what caused the cancer. There is a fear of the mood of "forget about it; let's go play on the beach." Spiritual laziness is a natural human tendency, because beings seek comfort, and tend to move away from discomfort; learning often involves facing discomfort. People are aware of this tendency, but they also seek growth. So instead of observing the dilemma on the inner level, and outwardly giving themselves permission to do what needs to be done to improve their physical health and growth, they retreat. Then there is the dilemma of choice: choosing that which may initially look like the path of comfort and ease, although it carries some level of stagnation; or directly facing uncomfortable challenges. People often retreat from making this choice. Harboring a sense of helplessness is one expression of such a retreat. Another is holding some level of shame. This may arise from feeling that they should be able to meet the choices with a more open heart, from seeing their evasion and judging it, or from feeling that they should be able to resolve the distortions on the physical level. Also, there may be a sense of shame in seeing spiritual laziness, and as a result of that, they judge self as not being deserving of physical healing. Or there could be a sense of shame because they have not yet been able to resolve the karma, and therefore have not earned the right to the physical healing. These are just a few examples of the ways in which belief systems can negatively affect the body's ability to accept healing energies.

I think the most important thing here is to ask people to reflect on whether they hold any belief systems that may hinder healing on the karmic or physical levels.

His reply drew forth the next question, "How do I guide them to that learning?"

My answer here is to all beings who would support another's learning. I teach Vipassana meditation; it is drawn from the Buddhist tradition but is accessible to anyone of any faith as it requires no special beliefs, just a willingness to investigate the present moment. The word passana means seeing; vipassana means a deeper, clearer seeing. I teach this for two reasons. First, through this practice, the physical being who I was in the final human lifetime found liberation from karma and from the cycle of death and rebirth. It is a viable path, and deeply healing. It is a path that anyone, regardless of religious orientation, can follow. The second reason is that it can lead people directly into the question, "What, within my belief system, blocks the fullest expression of my innate perfection in the physical, emotional and mental bodies?"

We train people to become observers, watching the arising of a thought without believing in the thought. The thought of unworthiness or shame may arise as "I don't deserve this." It may arise as a strong thought or just a subtle contraction. We train people to see the full-blown thought and even the small contraction. We train them to rest in awareness; being aware of the thought without becoming caught in the story line of the thought. "I am unworthy," is a thought. That which is aware of the thought knows it is not unworthy. It is important to see both.

There are many kinds of practices that teach people to replace "I am unworthy" with "I am worthy." As long as there is an assumed need for, "I am worthy," that thought must be repeated again and again. However, there is still the stalking demon of unworthiness, from which the "I am worthy" is supposed to protect one. Awareness sees the whole picture. It knows that there is no such thing as worthy or unworthy; it can only smile at that distorted belief. We teach people to find this innate spaciousness of being that need not buy into beliefs. The karma may not be fully released, but they are at least ready to proceed with the healing work on the physical level, because they have a tool to relate skillfully and lovingly to the thoughts and emotions that arise.

How can we respond when one person heals of cancer or another ailment, while another does not? With the person who has healed, you will want to guide him to look at any karma related to that previous ailment, and to encourage him to do the work to resolve the karma. It is important that he sees the ailment as an expression of the karma. It is also important to not say this in ways that create fear, but to say it from a loving place that reminds him that the immediate threat to life has been resolved. Now he has a chance to give back to spirit, to support the welfare of all beings, and to support light and love itself, by resolving any residual areas of darkness and contraction in the self. He has been given a gift and now has an opportunity to give back a gift, for himself and for all beings. He may choose, as he will.

For those who do not heal, it may be helpful to ask them if they are aware of any beliefs that they are not fully worthy of this healing. Perhaps they believe, for example, that they must first resolve the karma, become perfect, and express perfection in their lives before they are suitable to receive the gift of physical healing. These suggestions may start people on more helpful paths towards full healing.

Our culture has so many sensitivities—worthiness, surrender, free will, and faith are among them. A friend asked, "In the Current Room, the question came up of whether I could accept not being healed with equanimity. Could I surrender? I said, 'Thy will be done.' But I came home and all my issues came up around not feeling worthy. How can I accept not being cured with equanimity and with faith in the will of the spirits?" Aaron replied:

This is a very important question for all of you. It brings us right back to, "What is healing?" First let me address your words, "the will of the spirits." The Entities have no will other than to serve for the good of all, and to alleviate suffering and support healing. However, they will not oppose your free will nor override it. Thus, you must be certain that you are ready to embrace healing before they can fully support your healing path.

What is healing? What is intention? Imagine the baby not quite mobile, just barely creeping on its hands and knees. It sees the adults in the room running back and forth, and thinks, "Oh, I want to do that." But it needs to develop balance and train its muscles first. It begins this process by pulling itself up to an upright posture. It stands up, plops down; and it stands up and plops down a thousand times. It takes several steps and falls over. It walks. Finally it can aspire to run. It must cover each intermediary step before it can run.

The physical body is the heaviest and the slowest of the four bodies to respond to healing energies. In some cases there may seem to be a "miraculous" physical healing. This can happen either when the karma is already resolved so that no work remains except to heal at the physical level; or it can happen[1] when the primary concern is healing at the physical level before attending to the karma. But always, when there is a fast physical healing, we would say that the "baby" has "learned to stand upright and walk" and is now ready to learn to run.

If there is an intention to balance and resolve old karma, and an intention for spiritual growth, at some level the soul acknowledges the physical catalyst as the teacher. Let's use the assumption that someone has tumbled and sprained an ankle, and badly cut the bottom of the foot. The pain of the cut reminds them, "Oh, don't put full weight on it yet." The ankle might not be throbbing but it's not yet strong enough to hold the full weight of the body. The pain in the sole of the foot is helpful because it reminds you, "I must do my exercises and strengthen my ankle." By the time that you've finished the series of exercises, the sole of the foot will have healed.

So it's very important to bring forth the intention for physical healing, and to know that as part of that intention you hold open a space for the healing of your entire being on all different levels. For healing of the physical voice or eyes to be true and complete, change must also happen in the emotional and mental bodies. You must be willing to do the needed work on every level. It's very hard for the human to be patient. Your lifetimes are as this (snaps fingers); so brief. It seems to you endless—sixty, eighty, one hundred years, but it's the blink of an eye, in the universe. You've been working on some of these issues for many, many lifetimes. It is time to bring forth the full healing that is possible, now.

There are two different issues here that must be considered as you invite healing. One is the willingness to simultaneously hold the intention for healing on all levels including the physical. The other is to see deeply into the healing that does happen, to not be dismayed when the whole thing doesn't come together at once, but to be willing to take it step-by-step as the baby does. None of you would ever learn to walk if you looked at the adults running around, tried it, fell flat on your face and said, "That's it. I can't do it. I'm unworthy of walking." You must have the same initiative as the baby, willing to keep going and going and going, knowing that in its own time, it will come together.

Each of you has long held a belief in your limitedness, in your imperfection. This thought first came into being as play; to try different modalities of being, to see what was pleasant and what was unpleasant, what was skillful and what was not, what gave power, what gave weakness, what gave safety, what gave way to danger. Now you are interested in learning love. But those old belief systems of unwholeness and limitation are still intact in the karmic field, and are expressed as habit. The work now is to deconstruct this old paradigm and invite a new paradigm that does not just believe in, but knows your wholeness. This knowing will allow you to immediately release each self-limiting thought that arises.

Each time the self-limiting thought arises: "I am helpless, I am limited, I am unworthy," you note, "Ah, a story. I am no longer going to play that recording." There is no denial of the existence of the thought, just the recognition, "This is just the old story."

Barbara has been working with visualizing the higher self and knowing the higher self as hearing: as fully unlimited. She then makes the statement, "I am that." Instead of saying, "I want to hear," she says, "I hear." This is different from an affirmation. It's not an affirmation of, "I will hear;" it's the statement, "I do hear." Hearing has not yet moved into full expression, but the hearing is there. It is like crawling through a long tunnel and saying, "There is light at the end. There is light." You know that there's light at the end of the tunnel; there has got to be. You are not saying, "I will get to the light." Of course you will get to the light. The light exists. It is a distance off, yet already it lights your way. Just keep going. Eventually there it is in its fullness. Hold that space open. You must see yourself already whole, even as you strengthen the parts that will allow the fullest expression of wholeness.

But you must also be careful because if you ask for physical healing, regardless of the consequences, truly you may get it. Do you want the physical healing at the cost of neglecting the deeper healing? I don't think so. I cannot say that this is true for everybody but it is true for many people. You entered this incarnation with the highest intention to learn to love, not an intention to live a life of comfort in a perfect physical body.

You do not have to be a master of love before the physical healing happens, but you also don't want to focus merely on the physical healing and put aside the deeper learning. If you do that, another catalyst will come along to take you back to another physical distortion, because dealing with and transcending these issues is the work that you planned to do before you came into the incarnation. Suddenly you fall and you're paralyzed. I got my vision back, I got my voice back, and now I'm paralyzed. Why is this happening to me? It may be because you haven't truly learned to love the self. I'm not predicting this; this is a hypothetical example. As long as you think of yourself as limited, knowingly or unknowingly you will inevitably continue to create limits.

I, Barbara, would like to add to Aaron's comments. After a lifetime of unwitting practice, I feel I am a master at creating limits for myself. Even with Aaron's wise guidance, at times my emotions loomed large on that first trip, when those limits began to crumble around me. I felt like a failure, had bouts of anger and fear, and cried sometimes. It took two weeks before I began to look past the hearing into what else needed to be healed. I then saw the old habits of self-criticism, and of keeping myself small. It was a familiar pattern. I read from a journal of a decade earlier:

Journal, January 1994

I keep coming back to the question, "what does deafness protect me from?" I see the unlimited aspect of self, including that wholeness that Aaron and I continually talk about; and then I feel less than whole because I can't manifest it. As long as I believe in limitation, I express that limitation. What prevents me from knowing and expressing the fullness of my being? When people are angry and desire their own way, and then feel shame about such feelings, Aaron sometimes asks them, "What if you really were that powerful?" There is still negativity present on some level and I still identify with it. I'm afraid that I may misuse my capability and use power to do harm. In meditation I can rest in a deep place that watches negative thoughts with no self-identification, but in the active life, I'm afraid of these negative tendencies that are not yet resolved.

Now I knew that I was moving past this issue, yet I still felt stuck. I remember asking the Entity incorporated in João during my first visit for help with the karma as well as with the physical healing. The Entity said, very tenderly, "I am helping you with the karma." That afternoon I sat at the overlook, crying.

I had felt so abandoned as I saw the real healing around me. Was I not worthy of this? As tears subsided and quiet came, I moved into deep meditation.

I felt like a boulder in a raging stream, a rock encrusted with eons of debris. I saw an immense wall of water approaching and terror arose at the thought that its power would destroy me, but there was no place to go. "Allow it to come," invited Aaron. I wanted to scream for help, but before I could give voice to my terror, the water was upon me. The ground shook beneath my feet. And then there was the mighty power of the water, but the boulder rested firmly, washed but not displaced. The water cut deeply, eroding away all that I had thought of as self; layer upon layer of old stories that I thought had dissolved decades before, were now washing away. I saw stories of limitation, of fear, of childhood hurt and shame. These beliefs and habitual thoughts were not the essence of myself, but the clothing I had chosen to wear, a burden I had allowed myself to carry in this and past lives. As each layer flaked off, a new one emerged and was similarly washed clean. After this beginning, I relaxed into the process, and the fear gave way to wonder and joy. Finally, all that remained was a glistening crystal, radiating light. I am that! It was one of millions of brilliant crystals on the stream-bed, separate yet all were expressions of the One. The mind wasn't creating a new story, just experiencing the true self from the deepest nondual layer of consciousness, and was able to see all the surface appearances as unnecessary accumulation. The water subsided and there was nothing but these radiant crystals lying on the calm streambed.

When I opened my eyes that day at the overlook, I felt a deep sense of peace, a certainty that the healing was happening just as was needed. It is a precious memory.

Another important question relates to those who continue to sicken or die in the body. Physical death raises a deep reflection on what healing is.

Aaron: *Healing happens at all levels. Once I lived by an orchard that was overcome by a brush fire. Many trees burned. We worked to save what we could. One tree by the edge of the orchard appeared healthy on the outside and even bore some fruit that summer. However, within three winters it had rotted and died. Another tree that was at the center of the conflagration had only a few leaves left after the fire. Much bark was burned away so others thought it should be cut down and removed, but I asked them to let it be. The outer surface was scarred, but as summer passed there were a few new leaves, though no fruit. Through the winter the tree looked dead, blackened and bare. The next spring this blackened hulk filled with buds and rich fruit ripened on its black limbs through that and many summers.*

What heals? There is nothing to point to with the assurance, "That is healing." We each show the fruit of healing in our own unique ways. At one level the body

is the Ever-Healed. By that I mean there is a level of the physical, emotional, men-
tal, and spirit bodies that is beyond any distortion. So distortion does exist and
also the Ever-Healed. The body may fail, yet deep healing may happen. Who are
we to judge what is healed and what remains to heal? And consider that the one
who has found the Ever-Healed may no longer need the body, may be ready to
release it, though in the conscious mind there may still remain some attachment.

Is there ever a complete lack of healing?

I have never lived in such an incarnation nor known any incarnate human that
did not find some healing in any particular lifetime. I knew a man who was known
by all as heartless and vicious. He was a ruthless murderer and a thief. He and his
three companions, all armed and on horseback, were surrounded by an angry
mob. He had one chance to escape, when a baby boy toddled from an adjacent
dwelling right into the path of the outlaws' mounts. The crowd pulled back to
avoid harming the child and the outlaw might have driven through on his horse,
right over the boy. What is one child, one life, to one who has killed so many? He
saw the baby and froze, then dismounted and lifted him to the side as his com-
panions drove through to fight and flee to freedom. He carried the baby to the
mother as everyone watched, then dropped his weapons and accepted the fatal
attack to his body.

Another story, this of a woman with leprosy. Her rotting body gave her phys-
ical and mental anguish, and she was filled with anger and despair. She refused
to dwell in that despair. Each time it deepened, she went out from her dwelling
to find another who was even sicker, and cared for them with tenderness and
love. In her short life she cared for many other lepers and was known by all as an
angel of mercy. Who could doubt the depth of her healing?

Many people find physical healing. Others do not. Yet most people
find deep value in the time spent at the Casa. The Entities support us
to manifest what we most wish if our desire will not harm others and
ourselves. I didn't come for physical healing alone, but healing of
both the physical and the deeper areas of karma and distortion. Even
while there was disappointment at the lack of physical healing, the
healing of karma was equally important.

Aaron speaks of our four bodies—physical, emotional, mental, and spiritual—and says that healing happens on all these levels.

If there is healing only on the physical and emotional body levels, but no healing beyond that, it will not be stable but will shift again into distortion. The mind creates the template for the expressions of the emotional and physical bodies. If the mind is released from distortion, then the physical and emotional expressions have the possibility to become free of distortion. If these denser bodies do not clarify, the healing is no less. Think of poor soil in which seeds will not grow. When the soil is fertilized, and other necessary conditions are present, the seeds will finally sprout. They will sprout when the soil is ready.

How do we clarify the mind? Firm grounding into the present moment is the path of clarity for the mind, for presence leads to knowing the true self, nondual with All-That-Is. This doesn't mean the personal self is nonexistent, but that the personality and physical bodies are temporary expressions. Do not mistake them for the true self.

Come to know the true self through meditation. Watch the mind and see how fast it leaps into stories of limitation and into old beliefs. Know these tales for what they are, products of old conditioning. Ask, "Is that so?" when the mind says, "I can't," or "I am unworthy," or raises judgments of others. Find the awareness that rests beyond the everyday consciousness and learn to rest in that awareness even as the everyday mind mouths its old tales.

So again, tackling that question, "What is healing?" It is the resolution of distortion so that the form bodies can get a direct message from the Ever-Perfect or Ever-Healed. If they are not able to enact that message, the healing may still be great. You are told not to judge the book by the cover. Do not judge the healing by the outer envelope. Instead, appreciate all healing wherever you find it.

I, Barbara, still cannot say for certain what healing is, but as the years pass, I have a greater understanding of the process through which we heal and a deep trust of our ability to open to the healing that we seek. The mind stops playing with old beliefs, or at least is increasingly aware that they are present and creating an influence.

CHAPTER 12

On Karma and
Human Evolution

I HAVE BEEN talking quite a bit about karma—my karma, the laws of karma, and wholesome and unwholesome responses to the karma that we experience. I would like to talk a bit more explicitly about some issues related to karma in this chapter. Understanding the basics of karma is just the beginning. Aaron's perspective on the workings of karma opens into a broader view of human spiritual evolution. A clear understanding will give us a firm foundation for exploring the deepest questions of who we are, and what purpose our existence serves. I hope that concrete examples and analogies will help to keep the discussion grounded.

One English translation of the Sanskrit word *karma* is simply "consequences." Every thought, word, or action has a corresponding effect. In the same way that a billiard ball, when struck by another ball, will travel in a predictable direction, so will wholesome or unwholesome actions lead to either happy or unhappy results, respectively. Unlike billiards, however, with karma several balls may impact each other at once, pushing in many directions.

Imagine a gentle rain over a lake, with a multitude of raindrops. As it hits the water, each individual raindrop creates concentric circles of expanding waves in an easily understood pattern. Each of those expanding waves moves at a particular speed, with a particular shape. Basic physics teaches us that the shape and size of the wave at any one point on the surface of the lake is the sum of all the waves from all the raindrops that are passing that point at that moment. Even though the wave emanating from any particular raindrop is predictable and the rules governing the water's shape and size at any one point are relatively simple to understand, the surface of a lake during a rainstorm appears chaotic and random. Simple events governed by simple rules multiplied many times over make for a hopelessly complex puzzle. Karma operates similarly—the laws can be expressed simply but the effects are not predictable. If every action has consequences, then the results of many actions combined make the moving parts of any situation at any particular time so complex that it seems to be random and chaotic.

Compounding the issue, any particular action's result may take hours, days, years, or even lifetimes to come to fruition. Like a seed waiting for the proper combination of soil, moisture, temperature, and sunlight in order to sprout, the consequences of our actions may lie dormant until several conditions come together to facilitate karmic ripening. As the effects of any particular action manifest, the energy behind the karma dissipates, and the manifestation eventually ceases. A toy I once owned illustrates this process: five balls hung by strings from a frame. If you pulled ball one backward and released it, it hit ball two. The energy moved through all the balls, causing ball five to swing out. As it fell back, it hit ball four. The energy traveled back through all the balls and ball one swung out again, but not as far as the first time. With each back and forth movement of the balls, the thrust diminished until all the balls lay quiet. However, if I were to react and pull at the balls again, I would create a new thrust. In the same way, if we again react to a manifestation, we create new karma, which in turn must also ripen. This process of continuous action and reaction both creates the world we inhabit, and keeps the wheel of death and rebirth turning endlessly.

Understanding this process allows us to recognize and work skillfully with the karma that we inherit in this and other lifetimes. Many years ago Aaron spoke these words about karma. He talked about how to work wholesomely with karma, and offered a broader perspective about karma with respect to human evolution:[1]

There are two ways in which karma is addressed: as release, and as balancing. To release karma is to cease to be ensnared by the old forces, which still may arise but no longer carry any weight. For example, someone's assault of you with words of judgment may still bring up anger and a thought to defend yourself, but as you see that emotion and intention arise, it is noted as the result of old conditioning. I have said, "That which is aware of anger is not angry." The anger is there, but will resolve; the wanting to defend arises but will resolve. Kindness watches the whole movement. One does not get caught in these things. We can say that the karma around any reaction to being judged and a subsequent need to defend has been released.

Balancing takes many forms. To balance the karma is to see deeply into the harm that has been done through the playing out of such habit energy, and to give recompense for it. Using the above example, you may see how you have harmed others through years of defending the self and blaming others. You no longer do that, but the old karma must be balanced. That payment need not be direct. If you have harmed someone through your anger, a means of balancing that harm is to teach another how to make space for anger, for example, or simply to be kind and spacious with someone who is caught in anger. Ultimately, both release and balancing must occur for full liberation; however, graduating from the human experience requires only a certain amount of karmic release.

Human beings generally are made up of four bodies: the physical, emotional, mental, and spirit bodies. The physical is obviously the present material manifestation. When you are no longer in this body, what remains are the other three, located together in what we call the astral level. Over many lifetimes, people continue to move in and out of material form, all the while working to clarify the shadows in the heavier bodies.

You are not working to end thought and emotion here on Earth. You can never be entirely free of thought or emotion for any sustained period while in human form. Rather, you are working toward what we would call equanimity with emotions, where the rising of an emotion no longer leads to reactivity and contraction. As karmic release and balancing continue, fewer heavy emotions arise.

On the astral plane between human lifetimes, you communicate telepathically, yet you still broadcast emotions. Heavy emotions can feel uncomfortable whether experienced as a human or on the astral plane. Beings often believe that their emotional broadcasting causes discomfort for the other, higher density spirits, although this is not true. The one who broadcasts heavy emotion on the astral plane between lifetimes is like the young child who is aware that the elders smile at his antics in loving tolerance; he soon returns to his friends where he can more fully be himself. He will have the opportunity to be an adult in later years; there is no need for him to perfect adult skills as a child.

As the being evolves, there is increasing equanimity with emotions, and there is karmic release and balancing so that fewer heavy emotions arise; the ripples subside and cease. This process continues on both the physical and astral planes. Because you forget the truth of who you are, it is more challenging to find equanimity on the physical plane. That is why the human experience is a profound learning one. Eventually the being transcends the astral plane. Emotions have ceased and only the mental and spirit bodies remain.

So you keep returning to the physical plane, practicing kindness, faith, and love, and learning to move beyond reactivity to the emotional body. In third density, the emotional body is still experienced strongly in the conscious self and is often in control. When you accept the arising of emotions within the self nonjudgmentally, only then are you ready to learn the lessons related to being nonjudgmental towards others. This readiness is the gateway to fourth density where emotions no longer rule.

Let me explain the term density here. Those of you who are evolving fully through the Earth plane have taken rebirth over and over, in one form or another. Your first lives on the Earth plane were first density, in the form of mineral, which includes water. The lesson at that level of density is awareness. The spark moved into awareness at the moment of experiencing the illusion of separation. With this first move into personal expression, there is the beginning of the experience of a pull to the light, not yet with self-awareness, but always reaching for the light.

When the lessons of first density are sufficiently mastered, the being moves into second density. The forms that density takes on Earth are plant and then animal. The main lesson of second density is growth into self-awareness. The rock begins to have awareness and then is ready to move into the simplest forms of plant life. Increasingly aware through many incarnations, the being first experiences group self-awareness and finally individual self-awareness. The ant or bee is aware on a group level. The pet dog or cat moves into personal self-awareness. Those animals that are your pets are often in the final stages of second density.

The third density is human. Your primary lessons on this plane are faith and love. These are not the only lessons, but the primary ones.

When you move beyond the need to incarnate in human form, you are still learning. There is simply no longer any need for materialization as an aid to that learning. The karma that pulls you into the heavier vibration of materiality has been resolved. The primary fourth-density lesson is compassion, and the fifth is wisdom. Again, this does not mean you learn no wisdom and compassion as a human, but in higher densities you further develop those qualities.

There is an overlap between the lessons of wisdom and compassion. One cannot be learned entirely without the other. To aid this learning, fourth density beings dwell in groups where sharing is at a more intimate level, and then move from there into fifth density to find deeper wisdom.

When you enter fourth density, you find yourself capable of full telepathic sharing and are beyond the dictates of the emotional body that would lead you to feel shame or pride. Thus, all sharing is honest, and you no longer need to experience something yourself to understand and learn fully. As you share in this way with your beloved companions, you enter loosely into a group energy, where beings are free to come and go as feels appropriate. You always have free will. When the time is right, a being will begin to move away from that group to better understand and find deep wisdom in its own being. When it is useful for its own learning or to teach others, the being will return to a group, moving back and forth. Finally, the being will break free of the group and emerge as a full fifth-density being. As such, it may serve as a guide to fourth-density groups, or work more on its own, deepening in compassion and wisdom.

The sixth density is a learning of love and light, a coming to know your true being. Essentially, the end of sixth density is a movement to total knowledge and acceptance that you have never been separate, a movement back into such total unity with the One that, by the end of sixth density, you are ready to allow the dissolution of all memory and individual identity. This does not mean that you cannot put on a cloak of consciousness, cannot regrasp those memories if needed. That is what I do. I am a high, sixth-density being. In order to teach, I need personality and memory, so I resume these past attributes. The difference is that there is no attachment to them, nor any delusion that this "Aaron" is who I am.

The seventh density has been described as a gateway. It is beyond my experience. I assume the experience of the seventh-density gateway to be similar to the gateway of enlightenment experience in third density, of realization of the true self, and release of self-identity with the body and ego, but in a far more profound way. To move into seventh density is to release individuation fully, not just to release self-identification and attachment to individuality, but to release individuated experience totally. Many beings hold themselves at high sixth density, not crossing that gateway, in order to continue to have access to individuated thought and expression so as to allow teaching. Please remember that seventh-density beings do not cease to exist. They only cease to maintain individuation. The energy continues and serves all beings as it enhances love and light. It is the Ground out of which all expresses. Seventh density is a gateway to the eighth density, and that I cannot describe to you at all. It is the drop of water fully returned to the sea. Let us simply label it as mystery. It is God.

There is a wide range within each density. They do not have fixed borders; movement from one to another is a process of gradual transition. It is also important to remember that you are not forced into these densities. This is an open-classroom school. But as the third grader will feel a bit bewildered when he sits down and listens to the teaching in a sixth-grade classroom and will eventually choose to return to a more appropriate class, so you tend to stay in the appropriate class because that is where learning occurs. Remember that there is no competition to move faster than another or to outdo another. You are most content to be where you learn.

Some of you disagree with that statement, feeling a pull to graduate from this density. Yes, and that is appropriate for your present level of learning. Does the able student about to finish her grade in the spring not look forward eagerly to the next grade? Does the spring bulb not send out shoots that seek the sun?

You know that movement beyond the veil of third density will give you fuller exposure to the light for which you so yearn.

We are entering a time of transition to a fourth-density Earth. There is an urgency to prepare beings for the transition, to teach the skills needed, and to support the needed release of karma so that third density humans are ready for this shift for which many of you hold such high intention. A core of your work here is to speak love to fear; it is this practice that leads you further into positive polarity; the work is not to destroy fear, but to be able to send it love.

There are then these two aspects to karmic cleansing: release and balancing. There are beings that have the ability to help cleanse karma, to allow people to more quickly reach that level of readiness for transition. Some great masters can do this. The Entities do some of this. They literally take away the karma. The karma is released and its effects on the physical body are released. Healing becomes more possible.

Aaron's words clarify karma and its workings, but it is also important to be aware of what karma is not. In preparation for this first trip, I began to look more deeply into the old myths related to karma—myths which at some level I still carried. Karma, even unwholesome karma that leads to suffering, is never punishment. Karma is likewise never a reward for virtue. Karma is just the natural result of the seeds that we have planted, consciously or unconsciously. A mix of wholesome and unwholesome karma conditions every life. Conditioning and misinformation is so strong in our culture that I ask the reader to reread the following two sentences out loud before moving on. *Karma is neither punishment nor reward. Karma is just the natural result of the seeds that we have planted, consciously or unconsciously.*

When we can be present with difficult experiences, while showing kindness to others and to ourselves, we plant a very different karmic seed than we do when we fight with the discomforts of such experiences. Kindness and forgiveness release karma.

Karma is not mainly about past lives in exotic places, but about right now. Some people search out past lives—many have the ability to see such lives—but most of what we need to know shows itself to us right here in each moment. Our karma is displayed in each of our actions, words and thoughts. It is in this present moment that we can balance and release unwholesome karma, and establish more wholesome habits. These habits create wholesome karmic seeds, which help to create conditions conducive to further spiritual growth and ever-greater freedom from karma and its effects.

As a simple example of karma and conditioned reaction, when one feels pushed, what is the habit energy that comes forth? In meditation classes, I introduce the following as an illustration. I ask people to form pairs. One person closes the eyes; the other pushes firmly, but not so hard as to overwhelm. What happens when one is pushed? First there is a consciousness of touch and pressure. With that first push, the body may contract. That's natural. If one has been trained to watch that contraction, the mind simply notes "contracting" and watches the body hold and then release the contraction.

If one hasn't learned this approach, the usual human pattern is to further contract around the first contraction. The result is like a whirlpool, sucking one into wherever the habit energy takes us; to body tension, anger, old stories of helplessness, or a need to control. Several of these results and more may occur. The body holds the karma in the cells, quite literally. The mental aspect of this habitual energy response deepens. These patterns may reappear with not just a push, but also with the traffic jam, words from an angry boss, an overdue bill, or an illness. We can learn to simply watch the push, then the arising thoughts and body energies. When I recognize a story, it helps me to catch the patterns of contraction before the physical and mental movement solidifies as karma.*

---

*The Buddhist teaching of the Chain of Dependent Arising speaks of a progression: contact of sense organ to object; consciousness of the contact; perceptions; feelings of pleasant, unpleasant, or neutral; and arising mental formations based on those feelings. Each segment arises based on the karma and conditioning that preceded it.

Real-life experiences can help to make these processes more clear. If through the years we have developed the habit of always thinking of ourselves first, then experiences of selfless giving can slowly shift that habit and begin to resolve the karma. The conscious decision to think of others instead of ourselves begins the process of karmic release. The new, more wholesome habit of selfless giving begins to karmically balance the legacy of the old unskillful habit. Karmic resolution requires both these steps: first, releasing, or in this case making the wholesome decision; and second, balancing, or living that decision. I'm reminded of a friend who was terrified of spiders and always smashed them with a shoe. Then she made the commitment not to kill, so when she saw a spider and fear arose, she had to make space for the fear in order to honor her commitment. Finally, she learned that she wasn't as afraid of the actual spider as of the idea of them, and that she was just reacting to an old habit. She didn't learn to love spiders but to tolerate them, and to tolerate her own reaction of fear to their presence. Here is a major change in karma that will translate far beyond spiders, into everything that she was afraid of in the world.

In a different example, if we've developed the habit of feeling ashamed to acknowledge our own needs, then we might feel that we must care for others regardless of the consequences to ourselves. A moment of deep compassion for ourselves can start a karmic shift in this old habit. One friend spoke about being the caretaker in his family and of the intense pain that he felt when he could not rescue dysfunctional family members with addictive habits. The more his brother drank, the more he blamed himself and the harder he tried to save his brother. The harder he tried, the more his brother drank. Years of therapy helped him to see the early childhood conditioning. Outwardly, he stopped trying to rescue the family, but the pain of self-blame remained. In his meditations he began to see the patterns, and that everything arose out of conditions. The family's dysfunction and the brother's alcoholism had arisen from several conditions; he did not need to blame himself. Finally, at one retreat, he broke down crying, expressing deep compassion for himself, his birth family, and the patterning that had continued for so long. He saw that he didn't need to save anyone, or to blame himself; he only needed to love. With this realization he was able to acknowledge and to some extent release the karmic patterns he carried. Balancing could then begin as the next step on his journey toward healing. At that point he also became able to deal much more skillfully with his family's dysfunctions.

When habit energy is very deeply ingrained, patterns can extend beyond interwoven thoughts, emotions, and behaviors, and into the physical body itself. If I tense my jaw every time anger moves through, I'll eventually experience ongoing jaw pain. The cells of the jaw may become imbued with the message that the jaw tension in some way protects the self or protects others from this anger. Even surgery will not bring release, because the habit of holding anger as jaw tension runs so deep. Or I may just transfer the holding else-where, thereby starting a new stressed area in the body. But when I'm able to note the whole process—anger; fear or shame about the anger; jaw clenching to hold the anger; tension or pain that diverts me from anger—then I'm able to place attention on the basic cause of the pain. This is usually a combination of both the arising emotion of anger and a fear of or discomfort with it. When I'm able to be present with the anger, with kindness, the jaw will no longer need to hold that tension. Then the pain may dissolve, or at least be more open to medical treatment. In contrast, the old habit of reacting in a mostly uncon-scious way to anger, then focusing on the painful result, just perpet-uates unpleasant outcomes. Instead, with mindfulness, I can heal the body and transform anger into compassion. This, then, is the release and balancing of karma.

Often these physical patterns can manifest as disease. For example, a student who was abused as a child talked about being forbidden to be angry. If she expressed anger at the abuse, she was hurt further. She learned quickly to turn the anger onto herself, as many of us do, and thereby, experienced severe feelings of shame, unworthiness, and severe depression. I describe this as the "smoke screen," wherein we divert our attention to a different pain, in order to escape the one that feels even more difficult to acknowledge.

She also suffered from chronic back pain so debilitating that at times she could hardly walk. Medical tests could find nothing wrong besides tendonitis. As we worked together, her meditation opened her to memories of the abuse and an associated anger. With these recovered memories, her back pain increased.

I asked her to try to sit with that back pain at a retreat. She felt that she couldn't sit still. When someone is in so much physical distress, I often suggest that they get up and move around, or lie down; but in this case I asked her to try to stay with the pain. I sat near her and at times she held my hand. Through the long sittings she sobbed, and her body rocked back and forth, but eventually stilled. When we talked at our meetings, she spoke of being beaten across the back with a strap when she was not immediately compliant with her mother's wishes.

She was able to see the step-by-step experiences she had co-created. It wasn't safe to feel angry with her mother so she had redirected the anger onto herself. She used the pain of the strap as a focus and took it inward. Her back pain equated with feelings of unworthiness. If she stayed with the pain she could dismiss the anger. If she dismissed the anger, she could avoid the feelings of overwhelming fear and helplessness of the young child who felt so unsafe, so unloved.

I asked her to consider that the child did the best she could, and not to blame the child but to honor her for surviving such a difficult relationship. She began to do the practice of compassion (described in Interval I) with the child she had been, seeing her pain and wishing her well. In time she was even able to do this practice with her mother, seeing her as the product of her own conditioning, perhaps also of brutal childhood or life experiences. The process took about two years, but slowly she was able to release the karma that had resided in her body. The back pain healed gradually, and so did the feelings of shame, unworthiness, and depression. She said to me towards the end of that period, "I see that it was all karma, not just of this but of many lifetimes. How long I've carried that concept of badness! I don't need to do it anymore." She seemed to have fully acknowledged and released the karma associated with that relationship. The process of balancing could then begin. She is a very compassionate mother and has recently begun to visit her own mother who is now very ill and in a nursing home.

Karma is a deeper and more fundamental process than the psychological processes that the above examples might suggest. If we remain diligent in our spiritual investigations, eventually we will uncover the root habit that most of us have, which is to think in terms of a fundamental separation between self and others. Here is where most karma is created. This may show up as experiencing our personal selves as separate from all the other beings in our lives, or it may show through believing the personal self to be separate from the divine. In meditation, we begin to see this alienation as a created concept. Then we discover that we don't have to act and think in this dualistic manner. We can choose to free ourselves of the loneliness and alienation that are the natural result of this illusion of separation.

We can then begin to know our connection with All-That-Is. Here we can begin to acknowledge and release the most fundamental karmic process that attaches us to the human experience, the illusion of the separate self. We begin to understand that this idea of separation was created for our protection; a way to bind ourselves in and keep the source of pain outside the "walls." We have done this without recognizing the price that we have paid. Now we can begin to lower the walls behind which we have barricaded ourselves.

Separation takes many forms. In 1998 I had a cellulitis infection in the left leg; I was very sick, and hospitalized for over two weeks. It didn't heal even with the strong antibiotics the medical doctors tried. I have previously mentioned that looking at past lives has often helped me to resolve areas of confusion and conflict. Lying in bed in pain, I looked again at a past life, which I had seen before. This karmic ancestor from the 1600s was a Catholic nun who didn't believe that we needed to go through priests in order to speak to God. For these beliefs, she was labeled a heretic. She was captured and forced to walk for many days while wearing a leg iron on the left leg. At the end of the walk, she knew she would be raped and tortured before her trial, then burned at the stake. One night she obtained a sharp stone, put a tourniquet around her left thigh, and sawed her leg off above the ankle. As you can imagine, this was not a quick blow, but a slow and excruciating cutting through flesh and bone. She crept into the underbrush with the intention to untie the tourniquet, meditate, and let herself bleed to death. They found her, retied the tourniquet, took her to prison, and she died a horrible death.

While in the hospital I saw how she had abandoned her leg and foot as she amputated it. Through this very deliberate act, she had deepened the very human habit of separating from what is painful.

Lying in the hospital, I saw the need to bring this leg back into my heart and to simultaneously bring everything that I had separated from, into myself. I meditated with the situation for a few days. The leg was grossly swollen and very painful. The infection spread, antibiotics were unsuccessful, and it was coming close to the point of possible amputation. I felt helpless. This was not unwholesome karma as punishment, but instead the results of many conditions come to fruition. The karma from that incident long ago had to be acknowledged and released or I would most likely lose my leg in this lifetime. Here in the inflamed leg was the opportunity for the deeper healing for which I had taken birth.

One night an old woman was brought into the next bed, with a newly amputated leg. I sat up in bed and began to meditate as the doctors worked on her. Watching her pain and their compassionate work, my heart burst open to the immensity of suffering in the world. With what seemed more than imagination, I envisioned one person lying in a ditch with his leg blown off; I saw another person with a leg crushed by a building collapsed in an earthquake. I saw thousands of us with this experience, right in this moment. I had one leg to heal for us all. How could I not embrace it?

That moment of opening completely released all the karma manifesting as an infection in my leg. I sat up in my bed all night doing lovingkindness meditation. By the next morning the infection had started to diminish. I had no intention of losing my leg, but an intention to learn to open my heart to everything and not separate from painful objects. Perhaps if I had not understood the karma I would have invited the learning in another way and the infection would still have responded to antibiotics. My intention was to learn. We don't need to experience pain in order to learn; we only need to pay attention. However, extreme pain is one certain way of drawing that attention.

Karma explains how conditions affect our experience; every action creates something new. Consider a wooden table; it contains the sun, the rain, the tree, the seed of the tree, a carpenter, the cow who provided him with milk as a growing child, the hill where the ore was mined that became the carpenter's saw blade—this list could swell until literally the entire world is included. The sum of these expressions—or conditions—all may result in a table. The creation of this particular table is dependent upon these conditions. If any of the conditions are not present, that specific table cannot come into being, or continue to exist. Without the ore, the saw no longer exists. Without the tree, the table ceases to be.

Consider also an emotion like anger, which is likewise conditioned by current issues, by past beliefs, and by any number of other things. If you can see deeply into the other person's situation with compassion, the anger is no longer supported and it may cease. This whole external world is conditioned just like my two examples. All mundane expressions arise out of conditions and cease when the conditions cease. Therefore, when we blindly draw in a new experience based on old conditioning, we keep this wheel of unwholesome karma turning. We don't have to see into past lives to resolve karma, just to see our predominant conditioning in that moment and have the courage to say no to our old, unwholesome patterns. Then the karma is released, and the space can be found for balancing and eventual karmic resolution. To become aware of and release that conditioning is a great challenge.

Buddhist teaching also speaks of that which is beyond conditions. The Unconditioned has many names—God, The Ever-Perfect, and more. It is free of conditions. That is, it requires no conditions for its existence: it simply is. The Buddha described this Unconditioned when he said, "There is an Unborn, Undying, Unchanging, Uncreated." The nature of the Unconditioned is to give rise to the conditioned, just as the sun gives rise to heat and light. This metaphor is useful but ultimately incomplete because the sun is a conditioned thing. When we feel the sun's warmth, we say, "the sun feels good on my back," although, of course, what we actually feel is an expression of the sun. When we feel lovingkindness, we are experiencing an expression of the divine.

Sometimes the conditioned realm is pleasant; sometimes it's unpleasant. We need to take it as it is. Even the unpleasant is a manifestation of the divine. We learn to relate to these distortions—including physical ones—with a mind and heart that do not hate difficult expressions but rather learn to open to their teachings. If what is expressing is unwholesome, we attend to it so that it is released. This is what I was able to do with the infected leg, to hold it with kind attention.

The Vipassana practice I introduce in Interval III is a practical method of working with karma, in part by becoming aware and accepting of both the Unconditioned and conditioned in our experience. We can see the origin and end of karmic knots. On the ultimate level, there is no karma; there is no knot; there is no mind or body distortion. The knot exists and the Ever-Perfect level exists before and beyond the knot. But we can't go to the Ever-Perfect and pretend the knot isn't there, as that would involve a subtle denial, another contraction that expresses a karmic result.

Contraction can be compared to having a tense muscle. By being aware of it, one can relax into it. One knows both the tense muscle and the possibility of relaxation. But both are present simultaneously, not only one or the other. If we attempt to remove the energetic or muscular knot without realizing the lack of contraction available in the Ever-Perfect, we might succeed temporarily. But we would realize no deeper healing because we're caught in an "it's broken/fix it" pattern. This habit brings more contraction, which further tightens the original knot.

I continued to ask which karmic patterns blocked healing, and to apply what I understood of karma to my present situation. One large obstacle was that while I conceptually understood the distinction I make above, of the simultaneity of relative and ultimate, I could not yet live it. This segment from a journal may provide further illustration:

Journal, January 17, 2004

There are several questions I've been looking at for the past few years. One is that while I have deep equanimity, not just about my ears but about most things, something has also felt flat for a while. I see the relationship of my deafness, low-functioning thyroid, and retention of body fat, to a subtle sense of separation from the world, a subtle protecting. I see this like a dirty window. When it's filthy I just shrug and don't expect much light. Then there is resignation that poses as equanimity. For me, not hearing sometimes takes on this "sour grapes" quality, not true equanimity that has no need to hear but a shrugging off of the experience with an attitude of, "It doesn't matter." Then I can move into a protected space and ignore what's happening around me. This is avoidance of intimacy with myself and the world; an escape from helplessness. It doesn't happen often anymore, but I see that the old pattern is still present and shows itself occasionally.

When the window is very clean, the few streaks really stand out and make me yearn for the streaks and the window itself to be gone. Here lies the other face of the coin: grasping at connection. There's a yearning to more fully touch both the mundane world and the divine. In other words, a yearning to heal the obstacles to full intimacy at all levels. This can be a powerful force for growth when it is genuine and in balance; but when there's grasping, this force can lead to harsh judgment of the remaining streaks on the window, a grasping at perfection. There has been contentment these past ten years but not as much joy and delight. Where did it go? What am I trying to avoid? I offer the intention to hear everything, both joy and sadness, to know my capacity to embrace it all.

There must be a willingness to let go of control, to be in the moment, and to embrace it just as it is. Through the years I had tried so hard to cope with deafness, and to stay in control of my life with the deafness. Meditation takes me into an emptiness that is full of light and love. It is a safe resting place. However, as long as I cling to some place of safety, I never surrender to the fullness of being. Having come so far, I felt like I had settled into a safe space, a safe enlightenment. I know that the enormous suffering that sometimes catalyzes growth isn't necessary. But there must be a release of identification with the personal self in order to realize the greater self, and that release does involve suffering if I'm attached to an idea of this body and mind as "me." It also involves suffering if I deny this body and mind as "me."

Aaron pointed out my lack of balance. He reminded me that the divine self is real, but no more real than its expressions of body and mind. He said, "The personality self still exists; the body still exits; mind still exists. One ceases to think in limited self-identity, but rather, cherishes these radiant expressions of the divine. You must arrive at the place wherein you can hold both essence and expressions and see them as the same. It is only in that place that neither the manifest bodies nor the essence can be used as escape."

In the decade before I came to the Casa I had believed that I needed to seek only healing of the karma, and to accept the deafness. I knew that this deafness had served many people as I taught and channeled, and had served me in that it led me to Aaron. So I felt I should be able to say, "Thy will be done," and let go. When I first came to the Casa, I asked for help to heal the ears, for I saw that the karma and outer manifestation heal together. One must ask for what one seeks, set the intention to healing, and also trust the process, not knowing how that healing happens and what it will look like. But fear led me to try to control the path of healing. Many years ago Aaron asked me if I could sit in the back seat of the vehicle, state my destination, and leave the driving to God. Now I see how much I had been a back seat driver, with the erroneous belief that I had to control the process. Letting go of control is part of the healing process. I still have responsibility to choose what I desire, but then I must let go of how that manifestation will occur.

Aaron's words helped me to let go of the duality I was creating and to be more comfortable with the experiences of mind and body. I began to see my old pattern: the human who sought perfection and condemned itself for streaks on the window. I further understood that this pattern of self-judgment was a way of maintaining the illusory safety of a self that was in control. We all have a shadow side. If our intention is to be loving, we fear that shadow because at some level, we do know our power and our ability to do harm. We see the divine in ourselves and condemn ourselves because we cannot fully live that divinity. What if I truly was unlimited? Had I matured enough to handle that degree of power and to know I would not use it to do harm? I had to bring together the human and the unlimited divine in myself, before I could go further.

At this point I began to look again at any resistance to hearing. I said I wanted to hear, but did I really want that? Was I willing to hear all of the world's suffering, the cries of anguish and despair, knowing that I could not save the world from its pain? With deafness my hearing is selective; I need turn only to that which I choose to bring attention. It is easy to look away from anger or pain. While I had already explored this question, it was time to revisit it. Here I was able to use a past life to help me understand the fears.

In the final week of my 2004 visit, I asked the Entity incorporated in Medium Joao's body that morning if there was still karma around the deafness. He smiled and said again, "I am helping with the karma." In meditation in the Current Room that day, a memory spontaneously arose of my death in the lifetime just before this one, a death I had first seen in meditation many years before. This young man was a chaplain on a large ship in World War One. The ship was torpedoed at night in rough seas, and was sinking. He bravely gave his lifeboat seat to a terrified non-swimmer with a family, put his trust in his capable swimming abilities and his knowledge of the sea, and dove into the water. After surfacing from his dive, he was comfortable though cold for a few moments. The waves were big but he knew the ocean, and his life vest helped him to float. He trusted that rescuers would come. Then a fire spread over the sea, depriving him of oxygen as it burned fiercely around him, and burning alive those in boats that rested on the water. His last conscious awareness was of the nightmare of tortured screams and his helplessness to aid others or himself. I could see him attempting to shut out the sound, which is the last of our senses to go as we lose consciousness into death.

Remembering this ancestor, I asked myself, "What have I not wanted to hear in this lifetime? What might I wish not to hear now?" I knew that this knowledge would not cure the deafness, but it could bring deeper healing through compassion and forgiveness. That day I began to work with a forgiveness meditation for my ancestor, for those who battled on the seas, for those who suffered in the fire, for all who scream in pain and terror, and for all that acts as a cause of pain and terror. As I worked I could feel the release of long-held energetic knots, although it wasn't clear to me exactly what they were. I felt the kind of contraction one might feel when seeing something one once abhorred. The immediate fear might be gone, but a tension remains and is triggered. Now I felt the tension releasing.

Aaron reminded me to think of karma as a contraction, a ripple in the smooth flow of experience, which is held until it creases and creates a knot. Remember Aaron's image of a knotted sheet that will be untied and then ironed smooth. The sheet is uncomfortable to use as a sheet while it is knotted. It does not have to be ironed for use as a sheet, but smoothness is the highest level of its expression and it seeks that perfect expression. My work with this karmic ancestor was literally untying the knots and releasing the wrinkles to bring myself to the least contracted state possible for me in this moment, but without grasping at perfection. Remember that at one level all experience is already, and always, perfect.

Where a knot is perpetuated, the distortion that is an expression of that knot can be resolved, but it will recur unless care is taken to also attend to the conditions that created the distortion. I think of the seat belt in my car that sometimes twists in the anchoring hardware. I can twist the belt to fasten it, but if I don't smooth it through the hardware it will just twist again the next time I reach for it. In bringing attention to that karmic ancestor, I was attending to the conditions that created the knot, not just untying the knot.

I began to understand how this work was supported at the Casa. Continuing the above metaphor, when the Entities first see the human, they see the fabric that is open, the knots, and the conditions that create knots. Some knots are based only on habit energy, and some knots are still fed by misunderstandings, or by karma that is still active. For example, if I enter the Current Room feeling annoyance at the movement around me, and contract with this irritation, when I bring attention to my feelings the contraction will easily release.

The Entities also see the tighter knots. These are the knots that the human either has not yet acknowledged, or has not yet begun to resolve. They involve deeply-held beliefs and opinions. What the Entities seem to do is to seek the most effective way to release the knots that are tightly held, and to determine whether the best release for those knots is through surgery, sitting in the Current, or another means; and to then press smooth all the unknotted fabric.

Now I was acknowledging two very human knots—a knot of preference to avoid pain, and one of shame at feeling unable to save others. By working with forgiveness, I released the knot or habit energy itself, as well as any shame or discomfort about this tendency. I began to trust that I had the capacity to be present with pain and, therefore, did not separate so much into my pain and others' pain. Thus, I began to trust my readiness to hear.

As the karma was resolved, a new question arose. I wondered, when there is little remaining karma around the distortion, as with my present situation with deafness, why don't the Entities just release the physical distortion?

Aaron: *Although the karma around the deafness is mostly resolved, some karma remains. And there is still a knot on the form level of the physical body. This is the knot of distortion presented by the dead nerves. Here the Entity must work on a fabric where one simple pass with the iron does not remove the wrinkles, although they are no longer karmically bound.*

You are able to truly hold the Ever-Perfect in your mind, knowing the complete possibility of bringing it into expression. One might ask, "What prevents that instantaneous expression?" Resting in pure awareness, resting in pure spirit body, you are resting in a very high frequency vibration. The mental body is also expressing at a high frequency. In this case, the emotional body distortion is released, but the physical body has a slower vibration. The imprint can be made on the etheric level, as it was before the visit to the Casa. It can be made on the energetic level of the physical body, as was also done before the visit there, but left to your own devices, you do not have the skills to bring forth that shift on the physical level.

The work must be done gradually because the heavy density cannot tolerate a quick integration into the higher frequencies; therefore it must be done on a level that the form body can easily integrate.

Thus, even when the karma is resolved, the physical level healing may be slower. When it is more instant, much work is still needed to support the shift.

We go on to a question that is directly relevant. When there is a karmic knot, or several, the Entities may work around those knots in such a way as to release a cancer, or restore the functioning of a limb. This is deeply compassionate. Perhaps such ease from pain, fear, and limitation will enable that human to turn inward and work more deeply with the karma that brought forth those conditions. If not, it is not only possible but also probable that a related distortion will occur in time. But sometimes when there is such immense physical suffering, the human cannot get past that suffering, so we start the healing at one end. Consider the fact that you cannot teach too much to a starving man, as he is too hungry to listen.

Each being has his/her own personal guides. The Casa Entities form a support network with those personal guides so that when visitors go home they will have this helpful support to turn to and work with in order to bring forth that which is most deeply desired. So if the clarification of the karma is deeply desired, it will happen in time.

I personally do not have such healing skills as the Casa Entities, on the physical level. My own deepest work is from the opposite end of the corridor—teachings: which lead to the release of habitual karma; for the transmutation of karma; for the understanding of the difference between habitual and rooted karma; and for understanding the nature of the roots and how to release those roots. I also teach how to rest in the Ever-Perfect and thus, to temporarily transcend the karma. One must still return to resolve it, but one returns with much more spaciousness and ease.

It always returns to us: our free will, our ability to bring what we're learning into the physical plane, our courage, and our love.

INTERVAL III

Vipassana Instructions[1]

Beginning: Posture, Smiling, and Breathing

It is helpful to establish mindfulness (awareness) of the body at the beginning of practice. We tend to "live" less in our bodies, and more in our minds and the contents of thoughts, as we go about our daily lives. When we engage in a formal practice such as sitting, standing, or walking meditation, we first need to learn to be more fully in the body. Awareness of posture is helpful here, as is an awareness of breath and of the physical sensations in the body. Then we can expand our awareness beyond bodily sensations to an awareness of the emotions and other aspects of the mind's activities.

If you sit on the floor to meditate, you may be most comfortable with a *zabuton** or some other type of cushion or blanket underneath you. A *zafu*,** folded blanket, or other cushioning placed underneath your buttocks will raise your spine. Position the cushion so that you're not sitting on the flat surface and rolling backwards, but rather sitting on the forward edge of the cushion so that your pelvis tips under and the spine is naturally lengthened upwards. You may also sit on a chair. It should have a flat surface, or even tilt slightly forward. Place your feet flat on the floor and slightly apart. Sit with your back erect. Whether you sit on a cushion or a chair, let your hands rest comfortably on your thighs or let the hands be cupped on your lap, one inside the other.

---

*Zabuton: a large, flat, rectangular cushion that goes under the body and feet.
**Zafu: a small, thick, and fairly dense, round support cushion that rests on the zabuton.

Take a few deep, long breaths, inhaling and exhaling slowly. As you exhale, allow your body to soften and relax, releasing tension in those areas where you habitually hold it. Bring awareness to your posture, starting at the base of the spine. If you are seated on a zafu, notice that the position of your buttocks and knees resembles a tripod. Bring your attention to this foundation. Notice the position of the legs and the pelvis. Bring awareness to the erector muscles on either side of the spine; these lengthen the shoulders, chest, stomach, or the back. Lift the spine gently upward, towards the shoulder blades. You may feel as though gentle hands are supporting erectness by lifting you up under the edges of your rib cage and shoulder blades. Allow the lower back muscles to relax. As you experience this gentle lifting, notice that there is some space created between the bottom of your rib cage and your pelvis. Feel it lengthen. Roll the shoulders back; let the tops of the shoulders fall away from the ears. Let the tops of the shoulders be relaxed. Notice that this permits some roundness and curvature where the upper arm meets the shoulder socket.

Tuck in the chin slightly. Let the lower jaw hang open so that the lips separate a bit, which releases any tension in the joints of the jaws while the throat remains soft and relaxed. Invite the facial muscles to soften, relaxing them from the inside out. Feel a sense of gentle hands lifting the head, just below and behind the ears, with the skull softly lifted to erectness. Relax the skin of the forehead downward toward the eyes. Let the eyes be soft, with the eyelids gently closed, unless you are used to meditating with your eyes open. The area behind the eyes is relaxed, and the corners of the eyes are smiling. You may wish to focus the closed eyes on the inner wall of the forehead. See this inner wall as a blank screen upon which the inner gaze rests.

Invite a slight smile in the corners of the mouth: the inner smile, a Buddha smile, a feeling of lightness in the corners of the mouth. Smile into the moment and into your body. Be aware of any sensations as you smile into your body. Bring gentle awareness to the throat, smiling into the mid-area of the throat, the Adam's apple area. Move awareness down into the base of the throat, into the jugular notch.

Smile down into the chest; into the left side of the chest, left lung, right side of the chest, right lung. Smile into the whole body. Experience it. Establish mindfulness in the present moment, mindfulness of the body.

Smile into the heart center, in the area of the physical heart. Touch the heart with awareness.

Smile into the abdomen. Take a deep breath into the chest or the abdomen. Take a deep breath, hold it momentarily, and then slowly exhale. As you do, feel the chest and stomach relax. Do this two or three times with silent, deep breaths, and each exhale offered with awareness. Relax into the body and let the abdomen be soft, without tension. Soft belly, Buddha belly. Let go of fear.

Right now, you are breathing, a natural function of your body. With mindfulness of breathing, you simply turn your attention to this natural process that is already occurring. Take one breath at a time and simply be aware that you are breathing in, and aware that you are breathing out. Breathing in, be aware of the whole body. Breathing out, be aware of the whole body.

Focus on the breath as the primary object of your attention. Be aware of the breath at the nostrils, mouth, or wherever the feeling of the breath is clearest for you. Notice the physical sensation of the breath touching at the mouth or nostrils, the coolness of the in-breath, the warm softness of the out-breath. Allow the breath to find its own rhythm and flow. You are not controlling it, just observing it, trusting in the body and the breath to function naturally. Let your breath become the focus of your attention, the primary object.

Sometimes it can be helpful to extend and lengthen the breath at the beginning of a sitting, so that you begin to focus on the entirety of the inhalation and the exhalation, as well as on the pauses or apertures between the inhalation and the exhalation. This pause between the breath is the now, just this very moment. Noticing this aperture helps to bring you more deeply into the present moment and concentrates the mind; this awareness can also bring us more deeply into the heart center.

Experience your breath as a circle. There are beginning, middle, and end portions to the inhalation, a slight pause in the breath, and then the beginning, middle, and end of the exhalation. After a slight pause, the whole cycle begins once again. As you allow the breath to become more subtle and natural, you may not sense the entire length of the inhalation or the exhalation. That's okay. Become aware of as much of the breath as possible. Breathing in, allow the whole body to be calm and at peace. Breathing out, allow the whole body to be calm and at peace. As the mind begins to slow down, and becomes more calm and focused, awareness penetrates more deeply. The full length and duration of the breath and the pauses between the exhalation and the inhalation become more noticeable.

Natural Concentration

The breath is the primary object, but concentration is not held there with force. With natural concentration, you focus attention on what is dominant in your experience, in the moment. If a physical sensation, thought, image, or emotion pulls the attention away from the breath, be aware that the attention has moved from the breath. Know that the attention has moved to a physical sensation, to thinking, to an image, or to an emotion. This object has become predominant. People sometimes think that because a strong sensation, thought, image, or emotion draws their attention and they're not with the breath, that they're not meditating; that they're being distracted or that they're not concentrating. Actually, focusing upon that strong sensation develops deeper concentration, because the mind is holding to an object. That's a very powerful focus. It's a fine opportunity to develop concentration and mindfulness. Remember, it's not better to be with one object than another, not better to be with the breath than with a physical sensation, image, thought, or emotion. Be with whatever is the predominant experience in the moment.

If you find that an intense sensation keeps pulling your attention away from the breath towards that sensation, turn your attention to it. Lightly note it, creating some space for the experience, placing awareness on the sensation. If the sensation is unpleasant, watch the tendency to want to push the sensation away, to want not to experience it. If the sensation is pleasant, watch the tendency to want to hold on to it. Without judgment of that experience of aversion or attachment, just notice what arises. Move deeply into the sensation with merciful, nonjudgmental awareness and see how it may change, how it may not be one block of pain, one intense sensation, but little sensations that are arising, changing, and ceasing with varying levels of intensity. How does attachment or aversion toward the sensation change with awareness? Are some sensations neutral, calling up neither like nor dislike?

As you create room for a physical sensation, you may find that it moves to another part of the body, from the shoulders down to the back, to a different part of the back, or to the legs, for example. Stay with the experience as long as you are able to, without doing violence to your body or to yourself. When a particular physical sensation becomes predominant, turn your attention to the sensation and note it three times: *sensation, sensation, sensation.* If you prefer, note it more specifically as, *tingling, tingling, tingling,* or *itching, itching, itching.* Don't note it as *I have pain in my right knee,* which snares you into the story of the pain and a story of the self who owns that discomfort. Just observe the sensation and note it in any appropriate way. As you turn your awareness to the sensation, notice what happens to it. Does it disappear immediately? Does it fade gradually? Does it intensify? Lessen in intensity? Move about? Change into another sensation? When you find a sensation changing in any way, bring your attention back to the breath as the primary object.

As you are aware of your breathing, thoughts may arise, just like sensations. If the thoughts become predominant, if you find yourself more with the thoughts than with the breath, bring your attention to the direct experience of thinking, without entering into the content of the thought. Note a thought of the past as *remembering, remembering, remembering.* Is there a planning thought, a future-oriented thought? Note it as *planning, planning, planning,* or as *fantasizing, fantasizing, fantasizing.* Watch what happens as you note it. Does it disappear immediately? Does it fade gradually? Does it persist or turn into another thought? What's the nature of it? Watch and see how it changes as you watch it. When it changes, gently bring the attention back to the breath as the primary object.

You may have an image or an emotion that arises in your mind. Treat the image or emotion the same way as the sensation or thought. If, for example, an image arises of you seeing and talking to someone, and if that experience is strong enough to take your attention away from the breath, turn your attention to that image. Note it as *seeing, seeing, seeing.* If an emotion arises and predominates, know that you are experiencing that emotion. Note it as *anger, anger, anger,* or perhaps *fear, fear, fear,* or bliss, joy, jealousy, restlessness, boredom—whatever it may be. What happens to the image or emotion when you touch it with awareness? What is the nature of this object? Does it change when you focus your attention upon it? When the emotion or image no longer predominates, bring your attention back to the breath as the primary object. Know when you are breathing in. Know when you are breathing out.

Deepening

If the sensation, thought, or emotion returns and becomes predominant, then it needs to be investigated, not by probing and theorizing but by observing, by being fully present with that sensation, thought, or feeling, and allowing it to be present within the mind-body. Let it be a gentle, choiceless awareness that moves to whatever is predominant in the mind and body.

Allow yourself to enter a state of choiceless awareness. No preference for the breath, the thought, the sensation. Just being fully aware of, and present with, whatever is. No judgment. Observing. When sensation, thought, or emotion changes or is no longer predominant, invite awareness back to the breath.

Mindfulness of physical sensations can teach us a lot about our relationship with our body and about our patterns of attachment and aversion. If a pleasant sensation like tingling, the moving of energy, or a feeling of lightness in the body becomes predominant, turn your attention to it and note it as *tingling, tingling, tingling,* or *lightness, lightness, lightness.* What happens to it as you touch it with awareness? Does it fade gradually, intensify, disappear immediately, or change into another sensation? How do you relate to the situation? Is there a tendency to want to hold onto the sensation because it's pleasant? Can you experience the bodily sensation with equanimity, noting it while simply observing what happens to it? What if it is an unpleasant sensation, like pain, tightness, or burning? Can you just experience the unpleasant sensation with equanimity, noting it and watching to see what happens to it?

Notice how the predominant object changes. First the sensation may be predominant. If it is an unpleasant sensation, aversion may arise, followed by a great desire to be free of the sensation. There is a shift in experience. The sensation is no longer predominant. The desire energy now holds the attention. See this shift in the object and return to the breath. If the aversion or desire comes back, note it as *wanting, wanting, wanting,* and be with it until it changes or dissolves.

Notice the same process with the arising of thought, image, or emotion. Is there a desire to hold onto the pleasant, to get rid of the unpleasant? Can you watch that liking, followed by the next primary object, desire, or attachment—wanting to hold on to it? Can you watch aversion, followed by wanting to get rid of it? What happens to the attachment or aversion when you watch it? Remember that the sensation or emotion is no longer primary. Let it go gently, and be with the mood of mind that has arisen with the object.

Can there be no judgment of what you're experiencing? If judgment arises, note *judgment, judgment, judgment.* Judgment is just a mental formation, a specific kind of thought that also carries a body tension. As you note it, see what happens to it; see its impermanence, its emptiness. Can we watch with equanimity as judgment arises, without judgment of that experience? When judgment is no longer predominant, bring the attention back to the breath as the primary object.

If the predominant object is a very unpleasant physical sensation and is accompanied by such strong aversion that it no longer feels possible to stay with it, you can move the body. However, before you move, see the intention to move. The body doesn't move automatically. The mind must give the impulse for the body to move. If pain leads to intention to move the position of the legs, for instance, be aware of that intention, and then mindfully shift position to ease the discomfort. Be aware of the sensations, aware of the intention, aware of the movement. Meditation continues; there's no break in the continuity of the awareness. Note the ease also, then return to the breath, breathing in and breathing out, breathing in, pause, breathing out.

As thoughts arise, if they're strong enough to draw attention away from the breath, treat them the same way as bodily sensations. Sometimes an emotion feels intense. You cannot shift bodily positions to escape the pain of thoughts or emotions. Can you watch them and make space for them? What happens to the emotion or thought as you note it? Does it disappear, fade, intensify, lessen in intensity, or turn into another memory or thought pattern? See its impermanent, empty nature. It changes or dissolves in time. When you see a change in some way, and the specific thought or emotion is no longer predominant, bring your attention back to the breath as the primary object.

Remember, that which is aware of a painful emotion like fear or anger is not afraid or angry. Learn to rest in that awareness, not as a way to escape the painful experience, but as a way to create more space around such experience. When awareness watches fear, see the simultaneous possibility of fear and non-fear. It is not necessary to destroy fear to find the fearless. It is not necessary to destroy anger to find lovingkindness. Both exist together.

It may be helpful to feel the sensation that the emotion brings to the body, such as tightness in the belly with anger, and focus there. Soften around that tension with a kind presence. What happens to the anger when the belly softens?

Insight

In Insight Meditation, we want to see the nature of body and mind and of all the five aggregates—form, feeling, perception, mental formation, and consciousness. Watch them arise and pass away. Watch them change. Notice the interrelationships among them, not thinking about these interrelationships, just noticing, and observing the constant movement.

You may have a deeper insight into the impermanence of these aggregates and the emptiness of self therein. Observe body and mind, sensations, thoughts, feelings, perception, consciousness.

You may begin to notice that all phenomena, which are empty of a separate self, arise when conditions are present to lead to their arising. When those conditions cease, the phenomena fade.

Let there be no judgment of what is seen; have no preference for the place wherein awareness shines. Be fully present with what is, just observing.

If preference or judgment is seen, notice it as *preferring, preferring, preferring,* or *judging, judging, judging.* No judgment about the experience of preferring or judging. There is space for it all to float in choiceless awareness.

When a sensation, a thought, an image, or an emotion changes, or is no longer predominant, move awareness back to the breath.

Objects arising, dissolving, always in motion, impermanent, empty of self.

See the illusion of a permanent self dissolve as awareness penetrates and knows the illusion. Moving deeper, beyond the small self, beyond aversion and attachment, beyond ignorance.

Find space for all experiences to float in the heart that we all share. Rest in the vehicle of choiceless awareness.

Become aware of awareness itself. See objects arise out of spaciousness and dissolve back into spaciousness. Become aware of the nature of that which sees, that which knows. Gradually, you will rest in the

Unconditioned itself, seeing conditioned phenomena come and go like clouds through an empty sky.

Grasp at nothing. Cling to nothing. Push away nothing in your experience. Be present. Be mindful. Be aware.

It is a gentle, timeless process. Just watch it all unfold. In choiceless awareness, all experiences float in the open heart.

CHAPTER 13

Positive and Negative Polarity

IN MY FIRST trip to the Casa, I saw that much of the work there involved the release of negativity. It is important to remember that energy is not negative or positive; it is simply energy. Spiritual energy may have a negative or positive polarity, like the charge on a battery, but the words are not moral judgments. Like negative and positive poles on a battery, however, negative and positive spiritual energies help determine the character and flow of energy in individuals, between people, and in the general environment.

Energy with a negative polarity enters our lives on a daily basis. When you feel irritation, impatience, or fear, this is an expression of negatively polarized energy. Our innate expression is one of being loving; yet negative thoughts repeatedly arise, and we often act on them in the world. Then we experience their painful results. When I snap at someone, she's likely to snap back. When I give in to the stories of fear, they escalate. It could be said that a basic reason for our incarnate experience is to learn to relate lovingly to these negative impulses. They are not a threat to us, but are conditioned responses that give us a daily chance to make a choice for love, even when fear, anger, greed, or discomfort run deep. Negativity is not the master.

Aaron pointed out to me long before my first visit to the Casa that my work was not to wage war with negatively polarized energy, but to cease to get caught in its stories, in self-identification with it, or in judgment of it as it arises. Everything arises out of conditions and ceases when those conditions cease. Judgment doesn't help; it only adds more negativity. My first experiences with this lesson came early in my time with Aaron.

Journal, December 30, 1989

As I was sitting here typing this journal, Davy came down and asked, "Where's my breakfast?" I told him to toast the bagel that was on the kitchen counter; I was working. He looked disappointed. Of course he could fix his own bagel, but he was expressing an emotional need to be cared for, especially since he has been sick. I realized that I needed to do it, and with love, so I got up and went upstairs. He had put it in the toaster. I spread cream cheese on it, poured him some milk, and carried it out to him. His face lit up and he said thank you.

I asked Peter if he'd like me to make him one too. He said no, and ran downstairs to play, so I went to my desk. I had just sat down at the computer when Peter came in and said, "Where's my breakfast?"

"Darn it, Peter. You said no you didn't want any, and ignored me. Go get it yourself." I was angry! Of course I knew I had to go and make one for him—with love, Aaron reminded me. "Do it with love or not at all!" I made the bagel for Peter and came back down. Over the next fifteen minutes, Mike and Hal came one at a time and asked for breakfast. Each time, I became irritated at the interruption, then I caught my reaction and made breakfast for them with love.

Aaron keeps reminding me that I'm not trying to get rid of an impulse toward grasping but am learning to relate to it in a loving way. As long as we're human, negative thoughts will continue to arise, and Aaron constantly asks me to watch how I relate to them. But the tendency to want to get rid of the negativity is intense.

I fight with letting go of wanting, and not grasping at anything, every school "vacation" when my days are so full of the needs of others. I exhaust myself trying to meditate from 5:00 to 7:00 a.m., stay active through a long, long day of activity, and then meditate again at midnight or so, with only a few hours of sleep. Aaron asks me why I'm so attached to having to meditate in those early morning hours. Why not put it aside for a few days, sit just a half hour instead? I don't know why. My whole being cries out for that interlude of solitude, but I see that the issue is more about grasping than any real need. I asked Aaron how to let go.

Gently, and with love, child. This time is essential for your spiritual growth and I would never advise you to let go of meditation on a long-term basis. But you are attached to the idea of it, as much as the practice. It is less a letting go of the time for a few days than it is working with the feeling of compulsion. Simply be with what is there. Do what needs to be done, with love. Stay in the moment and do whatever is in front of you. You are using your frustration as a weapon of righteous anger.

Your resentment comes when you see what you incorrectly perceive as your needs balanced against their needs. But there is no self or other here. Deep inside you know this. Service to others is service to self. And both are service to God. I have said this to you before. Do not suppress your needs; rather, notice them and their intensity so that you can more lovingly put that urgency aside and do whatever needs to be done. This is the essence of what you're being asked to learn.

You cannot renounce your needs, cannot just say "I won't need. . . ." and go on from there. You know this is dishonest. Your sense of needing must become transparent through constant awareness of it, until it simply becomes a background tension: feeling a need that is noticed and observed. Otherwise there will always be resentment; and resentment and love cannot coexist. "I need" is a story based on fear. By "story" I mean a habitual line of thinking that avoids the direct experience. "I choose" is a straightforward response to the moment. You may choose to make the bagel or not; to serve another or not. It is okay to say no, with love. You may choose to meditate. Do it with presence that perceives the choices of the loving heart.

When you carry this through to its end, the oneness of self/other will predominate and the conflict will dissolve. But you will always notice the occasional need of self calling out, just more ego to be mindfully acknowledged, with love and compassion for the self-centeredness that generates it. You are human, and

certainly not a saint. Allow your feelings, be aware, and make the conscious deci-
sion to skillfully and lovingly do what needs to be done. Just follow your heart. It
becomes easier with practice.

I still wondered how it could become a service to others to acknowledge that I do need some solitude, and need to say no to their needs.
It seemed so harsh and selfish to say "no" and to use that time to
meditate.

On a day-to-day level, I seemed to either do for another or myself.
I began to understand it was not what I did so much as what motivated the choice. When there was fear and grasping, I moved into
"self" and separated. When my choice came out of kindness to myself
and to all, it held me open to serving the highest good. Sometimes
that was to meditate and sometimes it was to make lunch. Both felt
right at the time. What I did for another was also for me. There was
no longer conflict.

I had to watch the grasping mind without self-identification. What
is the direct experience of grasping? I noted the tension in it. It is
unpleasant; there is a desire to get away from that energy; I often
escape into the story line that has shaped itself, into "bad" and
"good," "should" and "should not," "worthy" and "unworthy."
These are also stories; there is no bad or good, nor worthy or unworthy in any ultimate sense. When I am present with the direct experience of anger, fear, or grasping, the stories they bring are so clear that
it sometimes becomes funny to watch the mind trying to control the
situation. Behind the stories, there is just the negatively charged
energy and the unpleasant sensations that accompany it. I am no
longer trying to stop an experience, just to relate to it in a more openhearted way.

The same lessons came with anger. One day I was late for a school
concert and when someone "stole" the parking space I was about to
enter, I felt rage. I know that every emotion arises out of conditions.
I considered the various conditions, of guilt for the lateness, and irri-

tation that I was attending a concert and could not hear it. The anger is not bad, but I had to be careful not to use it in ways that would do harm. Like grasping above, anger is a contracted energy and is unpleasant. I was looking for a distraction from the anger. Blame is a distraction. There is the convenient story, "It's her fault," or even the story, "It's my fault."

With awareness, I was able to note each passing component of this experience—tension, preference, the contracted body and mental energy of anger, that this contraction is unpleasant, the move into a story of blame—and to remain present with the entire experience. Each component is conditioned and not Self, though I am responsible for it. Each is impermanent. I can find openhearted awareness that holds space for the anger and neither enhances it nor tries to deny or push it away.

Aaron repeatedly advises, "That which is aware of anger is not angry. Rest in that spacious mind and watch anger, or any emotion, arise and pass away. What remains?" When I do that, I release the self-identify with the emotions and can rest in the spaciousness of the open heart, regardless of what is experienced in mind or body. As I learn this, each catalyst to anger or other negative emotion becomes simply a reminder to love. These are teachers, not enemies.

That day I was able to remind myself of these things, pause for a few minutes, center myself, enter calmly, and truly enjoy watching, but not hearing, the concert.

Through the years, Aaron has impressed upon me the importance of our free will choice of harm or nonharm; to make choices from love, not fear; and to act in ways that are predominantly in service to all, not just self-serving. There is both positivity and negativity in the world. We're constantly offered the choice of service to one or the other. These forces aren't opposites, or dual in any way. Aaron sees positivity as light and negativity as the relative absence of light, not as an ultimate darkness. Yet in that relative absence of light, great pain and hardship can emerge, so we do need to make a clear choice.

We cannot simply use service to self or others as the definition of positivity and negativity.

Positive polarity has been defined in the past as service to others and negative polarity as service to self; yet, on the ultimate level there is no self or other. How, then, may we define these terms? We can define polarity most clearly within a discussion of energy and the contraction or non-contraction of the energy field. I believe that the contraction or non-contraction of energy is the best basis for determining positive or negative polarity. No being is totally positively- or negatively-polarized, so we do not have a totally contracted or open energy field. The relative bias toward positivity or negativity may be measured by the degree of contraction.

The deepest expression of positivity is the willingness to be a vessel through which energy—as abundance, as lovingkindness, as light—may flow, to draw for the vessel-entity that which is needed for its own sustenance and to freely pass the rest through without any holding. Thus, one does not deny or make a martyr of the self, nor does one do harm to another or withhold, out of fear. Ultimate positive polarity knows the infinite nature of source, so it has no fear that it must withhold things for the self or else suffer lack. Neither does it serve another in preference to itself for it knows that the needs of both will be met. When this pattern is in process, what I see visually is the clear flow of energy through the vessel-entity, circulating within its physical, emotional, and mental levels; then passing freely from it, to all who would receive it.

Please remember as I speak that negative polarity is a distortion of positive polarity. Negative polarity may be defined as the contraction of fear whereby the serving entity contracts its energy because it does not fully understand the unlimited nature of the divine. Fear leads any being to the biased belief that all needs may not be met. That being may hold back more than it needs, thus momentarily depriving another and thereby causing them real pain. Or it may be induced by fear to much deeper and more ongoing harm to others. An example would be one who habitually abuses others, one who steals, or even murders in the name of service to self; all from fear.

This being then might move to the opposite bias, serving others at the expense of itself, and thereby, depleting and even destroying itself. On the sur-

face, such movement appears to be positive polarity, service to others, but self is also an other. To do harm to any, even the self, demonstrates the presence of the contraction of fear. There is the distorted belief that there is not enough, or that the self is insufficient as a channel for that abundance. If one denies self, not including self in that sharing of abundance, there is then the distortion that self is separate from other. This being may be basically of positive polarity but still contain these particular biases of duality and its own insufficiency. Therefore, its energy field is contracted around the issue of meeting its own needs. It expresses a negative distortion within the positively polarized vehicle: rust on the otherwise open pipe.

The pipe that is clogged with debris reminds one of a contracted state, yet no matter how clogged the pipe is, it has the potential to open. The water pushes against that congestion just as light touches darkness, asking it to open, receive, and share. Openness is the true nature of the pipe or of any vehicle. It is the true nature of the soul.

What of the saint who truly gives his life, in love, to serve another? Here there is no contraction. The saint's deepest need is being met. That need is to do precisely what he has done, to accept the harm in place of another with a deep awareness that he is suffering no harm, but is merely willingly suffering damage to this particular physical body as a necessary means of service in the moment.

Thus, Aaron taught me to watch for contraction in myself, and to attend to that contraction as a way to cease to encourage negative thought. Unpleasant and fearful experiences will come. Whatever happens, we always have options as to how we will relate to them. This is true of the flat tire and the stubbed toe, as well as of serious illness, loss, and pain. Will we offer it hatred or kind attention? If contraction arises, will we see it and attend to it, or act it out in the world? A famous Buddhist scripture, the *Dhammapada,* contains the words, "Hatred never dissolves hatred; only love dissolves hatred. This is the truth, ancient and unchangeable." The question then is how to offer lovingkindness to negativity in ourselves and in the world.

I began to see how often I chose negativity out of habit. A situation comes to mind when my dogs had escaped through a door left open.

I had been very worried, and had spent the day searching for them, getting nothing else done. Now the dogs were found but I was frustrated and unaware of the ways I was holding on to my anger.

Barbara: Aaron, who's going to do all the stuff I didn't get to today?

Aaron: *You are, if it truly needs to be done.*

B: Then how can you tell me to let go when I've got to do twice as much tomorrow?

A: *Does fretting get it done faster or more efficiently, child?*

B: No, but ...

A: *Do you enjoy the doing of it more when you fret?*

B: No, but ...

A: *If you let go of fretting about it and just do the next thing that needs to be done, as mindfully as possible, might you enjoy doing it?*

B: Okay, yes. I see that I might enjoy washing the dishes if I can do it without thinking of the whole list of stuff to be done after that.

A: *Does thinking of that list make the dish washing faster or more enjoyable?*

B: Aaron, I'm back to "No, but ..." I understand what you're saying, but how do I not think of it all?

A: *I'd suggest you make some greater attempt at mindfulness, child. First notice how sorry you're feeling for yourself, and all the anger. Just sit for ten minutes, notice all of that anger and make space for it. Then go and wash the dishes. As soon as you notice thoughts, label them and come back to the dishes. This is not said with sarcasm; surely you've developed some amount of skill at this in the past year!*

B: So was today about remembering to be able to laugh at myself?

A: *Only in part. Tell me briefly what else you see.*

B: Just letting go. Doing what I can and noticing the tension and suffering I'm creating for myself. If it's not under my control, let go.

A: *So do you think you'll be able to do this without so much agitation the next time?*

B: I hope so.

A: *Then you've missed the point. You may not be able to do it with less agitation. The issue is not if agitation comes or not, but how you will relate to it. Per-*

haps you'll be able to see the humor in your situation a little more clearly and take yourself and your story less seriously. The awareness that was laughing at the agitated self will laugh a bit more freely. I doubt if you'll end the agitation completely but you won't need to identify with it as you did today. Please think about the difference.

When we experience great fear or pain, we're deeply conditioned to contract and go deeper into fear. So many stories come up about what may happen, why it's not fair, of feeling like a victim. It is important to recognize that this is just our conditioning and that we do have a choice. We can note the conditioning of the mind and not believe in the stories. We are not slaves to the negative response. To know this is the first step to freedom.

Another example comes to mind from many years ago of a particle in my eye. As I looked up, something fell from the ceiling. It felt like I'd been hit in the eye with a red hot poker.

After trying for a half hour to get it out, I went to the emergency room. For two agonizing hours they tried to wash it out with a saline solution that burned. There wasn't constant pain, but every time I blinked or moved my eyeball that red-hot poker returned again. I was feeling very isolated and vulnerable, as with the eyes watering I couldn't see to lip-read. I was cut off from communication.

Finally they gave up and sent me on to the Eye Center. There was some wait there while they called in a doctor. After much searching they finally found a particle that had embedded like a thorn on my inner upper eyelid, and removed it.

In the beginning I wanted to disappear from the scene by moving into a deep meditation state. But I needed to cooperate by moving my eye this direction or that. I ended up breathing with the pain, staying open, and sending love to the pain and to myself. There was anger, but I was able to know it as anger. I didn't shift into 'it's not fair' or other stories.

What surprised me is that I was able to stay fully open to the physical pain, the fear, the isolation and to allow myself to experience it all with no suppression of anything. I was grateful for the lesson. This is the fruit of practice.

Channeling was also a wonderful teacher. I did encounter negativity, my own and that of others. At first this scared me. Slowly I learned that it makes no difference where the negative thought originates. There is just one response: send love to it. If there is fear of the negativity, send love to the fear. I also learned to always challenge before I channeled. This means to state my highest principles, and to make the statement that no being may use this body unless it comes avowed to those principles of love and for the highest good of all beings. This challenge is useful not only while channeling but in every day life, holding the intention to not allow this life force to be a tool of negativity.

Just as we can change a balance bar by either adding more weight at one end or removing weight at the other, so too can we affect the positively charged/negatively charged energy balances in our daily lives by nurturing positivity and by taking care to release negativity as it arises. In 1996, preparation for abdominal surgery to repair a hernia[1] had presented me with a vital question: "What is wholeness?" We can live but still remain only half-alive when we refuse to acknowledge our innate wholeness. I asked myself, "What needs to change besides the belly tissue, in order to really live fully and manifest wholeness? In what ways do I still cling to the illusion of 'broken, incomplete, and limited'? How do I nurture inherent wholeness and release fear?"

At an extended personal retreat just after this surgery, a very profound meditation experience supported a more conscious and spiritually mature response to negative habit energy. Within the meditation I chose to make a vow of service to all beings, and saw immediately that if I was to live that vow, I had to constantly watch and release attachment to these old negative habits of the mind in order to remember my commitment.

In the meditation I spontaneously began to offer the intention to allow that wholeness for the good of all beings. I began to pray for help. A recent dream had me literally sitting in the shit of my old beliefs of shame and limitation. I felt ready to strongly commit to a more mature knowledge of wholeness, yet I didn't know how to proceed.

As soon as I began to meditate, I felt myself surrounded by a loving circle of beings I saw as "Elders." Feeling very young, I stated my intention to begin to live my wholeness for the good of all beings. I asked if I might join the circle. I had a sense that I didn't need anyone else's permission, that the decision was mine but that I must understand what I had asked.

What followed was not my imagination, but the fruit of a deep meditation process. I was conscious, but not experiencing from the personality self. Instead, a deeper awareness participated. A voice asked, "Who speaks for this being?" All week I had been rescuing ladybugs trapped inside windows, catching and releasing them. The ladybugs through their deva* spoke first, saying that I had been showing them great kindness all week. Then a spider spoke and said that I had done great injury to their kind whenever they approached me. I was asked, not verbally but with some inward gesture, whether I found this to be true. There was no need to offer excuses. I just said "yes." The one who seemed to be the central speaker said, "These balance and will be put aside. Does someone else speak for this being?"

I understood clearly that I was not being judged. The evidence of my life was being offered to me for my own evaluation, to decide for myself if I was ready for what I had proposed. This self-honesty was vital to the process.

A student, unrecognizable as to whom, spoke of all I had given. But I had to say that I had sometimes also acted from ego, and felt

---

*Deva in this context is the "overlighting soul" of ladybugs, or highest template upon which the ladybug is based.

like I had occasionally used people for my own ego needs. Again the words, "These balance and will be put aside. Does anyone else speak for this being?"

One son spoke about what a loving mother I had been. Another son spoke of his anger at me and the voice said that these issues were more his than mine, although of course I was imperfect in my mothering. There was no further "other side" offered. It was just left to rest there.

My old dog, Beau, spoke of how my patient kindness had taught him love, he who had been so abused and was initially so afraid of people. I heard, "This is noted with joy."

Hal spoke of all that I had given him and the ways I had harmed him. It was clear that there was growth and that the harm wasn't offered as objection. I could see what it cost him, because to offer this assessment of me, he had to speak from a place of his own dawning responsibility.

Through this process came the clarity that I was not supposed to be perfect. The question being raised was whether I now had sufficient maturity to live a vow to relinquish the "brokenness" and armoring, whether I could actually live what I proposed or whether I needed more practice, and if so, of what sort.

Many others spoke. I was able to accept as truths the places where I had failed, done harm, or retreated into ego. There was no building up of these realities, just noting them. I was able to accept without pride the places where I was mature and responsible and acted with love.

Finally there was no more response to the question of whether any being present spoke for me. Some High Beings, Jeshua, Maharaj-ji, and Aaron were part of the circle; but I understood that these would not speak, that the statements were left to my peers. This process, thus far, had been about one hour, as I noted just before the end that the incense I had lit at the start had ceased to offer scent.

Then there was a time of silence when I was asked to deeply consider my request in the light of all that I had heard.

There was no sense of grasping. There was absolute clarity that the decision must come from the deepest aspirations of the heart and from a place of truth. That deepest inner voice said, "Yes, but I don't know how. Help me." The response was, "All the help you need will be given." There was a feeling of great joy, of embracing.

I know this was a taking of the Bodhisattva Vow, a statement of intention to offer service to all beings, and to not seek one's own liberation until all beings are thusly liberated. It is a statement of readiness to put others' well being at least beside one's own, rather than selfishly to grasp at one's own welfare. If it is taken with sincerity, it leads to deeper awareness of feelings of selfishness and greed and the need to attend to these experiences with kindness, but also to work toward their release. Thus, taking this vow serves as a reminder to do the inner work. I see that having made this commitment, I can't take it lightly. If feelings of unworthiness, fear, or greed get in the way of my keeping it, I have to resolve them. This *bodhicitta,* or pure heart, is in us all and I see that connection with it is the strongest motivating factor there can be to release our own fears.

The ceremony continued. We were drawn into a circle and I was given a seat, between Aaron and a high being I did not know by name but whose energy felt familiar. I was asked to stand, to state my intention to the gathering and to ask for whatever sorts of help I thought I needed. I was told to be as specific as possible.

I asked for help in releasing old concepts, old patterns of limitation, and fear. I asked for help with patience, grasping, and fear of harm to this body. I asked for help in releasing any old concepts of unworthy, unwhole, unsatisfactory. I asked that my body energy be helped to open in readiness for this work. There was no single response, just a clear sense that I had been heard, and that asking for help is one sign of maturity. Such maturity means recognizing one's weaknesses without exaggeration or slighting, without aversion to or clinging to those weaknesses or blame of them as a reason why one "can't" manifest one's intentions.

Finally, the one whom I knew as Jeshua stood up and took my

hands. There was a sense of an intense energy opening that was painful after some moments. I asked for help and felt additional intensity and His energy flowing into me; that energy opened all blockage and the pain released. There was a flooding of light, all sense of self dissolved. Words failed me. I just rested there.

Eventually I returned to more present consciousness and heard, "That is enough for today." I was told that this energy work would be repeated daily for a while in order to "tune this instrument the best as is possible for its work." By that I understood that there would be support to raise the vibrational frequency of all the bodies.

The session drew to a close rather abruptly. The energy of all these beings withdrew, leaving me with Aaron who simply suggested I go for a walk. I did so. There were two hundred ducks out on the lake and a golden glow of the setting sun. The shoreline was knee deep in crystal shards of ice.

Although this happened many years ago, this experience prepared the way for further releasing ideas of limitation. This was my unique, even idiosyncratic process; the reader's process will be similarly unique. I was led to the place to which we must all come, a state of readiness to let go of old limiting beliefs and fears. We are motivated to do this by a strong intention to serve others with an open and loving heart and the related intention to do no harm. This intention is a spiritually mature response to negativity. Within all of us is both positivity and wholeness and also the potential to enact the negative. No matter the source, negativity must be greeted with kindness; with the intention to serve for the good of all beings and with harm to none; and with confident faith in the reality and supremacy of love.

CHAPTER 14

Exploring Negativity with the Casa Entities

MOST OF THE events recorded in my journal in the previous chapter happened over a decade ago. A certain maturing of my spiritual practice under Aaron's guidance has occurred since then. This maturation aids me in working with the negativity that arises within and around me, and with negative spiritual beings. Still, the predominant form of negativity that I encountered on my first trip to the Casa was of my own making. I felt angry, unworthy, and abandoned by the Entities because I had not healed instantly. Why did others heal and not me? I was telling myself a well-rehearsed story. As usual, Aaron did not judge, but patiently offered advice that was practical and focused on what I could observe easily within myself: He suggested, "Note the direct experience of abandonment, of anger, and even of despair. These arise and pass away according to conditions. What is the direct experience of despair with no stories? Can you feel it in the belly, in the breath? Now notice the stories that arise with these sensations. Can there be the experience of a story pushing itself forth, and no self-identity with the content?"

Aaron was teaching and reminding me of things I regularly teach to my own meditation students. This was certainly familiar territory, where I could work with my emotions skillfully. But the Casa also opened up unfamiliar territory, which forced me to step beyond my own experience and to broaden my understanding of the role that negativity and negative spiritual beings can play in disease and healing. Aaron's teachings and perspectives in relation to the Casa's were expansive and informative, offering a more complete view than he offers when commenting only on my personal experiences.

A being whose actions, words, and thoughts are rooted in contraction is acting, speaking, or thinking with negativity. I do not mean the occasional ripples of contraction that come with momentary habit energy, nor do I mean those contractions that ebb and flow in a balanced way such as with the beating of the heart or the passing of the breath. I speak here of the continuous contraction that is a hallmark of negativity. Positive polarity experiences occasional contraction but it is soon released.

A human need move only slightly beyond the 50–50 balance of neutral polarity to graduate from this Earth plane as a positively polarized being. It is actually difficult to move further out on that scale, positive or negative, within the human experience. To do so with intention to positive polarity when negative thought arises, one must learn how to attend to that negative thought with kindness. Here is the catch. Most humans notice the negative thought and then move into further negativity by judging that thought and the human in whom it has arisen. With practice, one can learn to observe the arising of negative thought, impulse, action, or speech. This ability is a basic fruit of meditation practice.

Many people aspire to positive polarity but do not have the skills to overcome the habit energy of negativity. The more frustrated one becomes, judging and attacking the self, the more vulnerable one becomes to external negativity. Such external negativity may not be strongly negatively polarized. Most negativity that the ordinary human meets isn't beyond that 55 to 45 percent range where the human usually resides. So it does not come as fierce negativity, just a quiet voice encouraging fear, doubt, greed, anger, or other negative expressions. It

might come as blame, suggesting, "Oh, you are right; he is wrong. Tell him so."
It may come as judgment, "He is never very skillful; he should learn. . . ." It is easy
to be lured into these subtle negativities; they arise within the self, and when they
surface, external voices join in.

I find one universal answer to such negativity—a deep breath, smile, and the
words, "Is that so?" That's all it takes to catch and attend to the habit energy in
a kind and light-hearted way. Such a response releases contraction. It returns
you to your inherently loving nature of being.

Occasionally the negativity may be far more powerful, but strong negativity
usually only interacts with other intense negativity, or in opposition to strong
positivity. To a certain degree, the more strongly a person aligns him/herself with
the light, the more he/she attracts the darkness, which wonders if and how it can
make use of this force. Eventually it may concede that there does not seem to be
any immediate access and steps back its efforts. It is still watchful, however and
awaiting opportunity and opening. This is why those of positive polarity must
always be vigilant of any subtle habit energies of negativity to self and others.
The practice always goes on; there is no point where one is finished.

When an external negative entity approaches any being, negative or positive,
we call it a negative psychic greeting. The same is true of a positive entity, except
that it offers a positive psychic greeting. The main distinction between these two
offerings is in the respect shown for personal free will. The positive entity will
never force or manipulate. It will invite positive action, or loving action and
speech, it will support such; but the free will of the entity it greets is fully
respected. Negative polarity disrespects free will and will use any means possible
to create fear, havoc, and contraction.

I repeat again that the one skillful response to a negative greeting is lov-
ingkindness.

I asked Aaron to define the distinction between negative greeting and
attachment and possession. I have learned that both are a large part
of illness.

The negative greeting is as I have described above. If one thusly greeted moves
into even further negative contraction, this gesture leaves an expanding opening
through which the negative greeting may flow. At a certain point one has taken

so much of that negative greeting into oneself that one thinks that this is one's own energy, and thereby becomes confused. Then the negative entity has more power. Let me give you an example: imagine that you have a plot in a community garden. There are small stakes that mark your corners, but they have fallen and been lost. Your garden neighbor begins inching into your plot a little more each day. You keep drawing back because of the concern of being mistaken in your boundaries. You are planting flowers. He has a thistle crop. Slowly his crop invades your garden and you come to believe that it is your crop, and nurture it. You have literally forgotten what you planted. This is negative attachment.

Negative possession is the deeper result of negative attachment. It comes at a point when, using our example above, there are no flowers remaining, only thistles. Thus this is a matter of degree. Increasing negative attachment, that is, the attachment of the negative entity to you, finally results in possession.

How does this relate to physical and mental health?

Negative psychic greeting, negative attachment, and possession are frequent contributors to illness. Physical distortions arise because of the contracted state of the mind and body and because of the various environmental and genetic factors that influence disease. Thus a negative psychic greeting cannot cause a broken leg. It can cause the mindlessness, franticness and fear that lead to carelessness. A negative greeting cannot cause cancer. If some conditions that may eventually lead to a tumor are present, and further conditions arise for cancer to manifest, the negative greeting will enhance those conditions. The negative greeting can cause mental symptoms such as what presents as psychosis. The illness can be enhanced by despair and loss of self-worth because the human cannot free itself of this visiting energy.

The negative psychic greeting brings those further conditions to the fore through both stress and chemical changes in the body. It may take years for the distortion to express itself. The person may have dealt with and released the negative greeting, but if it was present for many years, it will still have an impact on the body. Psychic negative attachment becomes like a whirlpool with a downward pull. The energy devoted to staying afloat drains the health out of the body. It is like ingesting a slow poison. Even if you realize it is a poison and cease to take it, the body has already been changed by the poison and cannot immediately revert to its pre-poisoned state. Here is a special case: One who has a strong negative polarity will not necessarily suffer ill health, so long as he/she is content with the polarity.

I began to see that a predominant part of the work at the Casa is to help us learn to work skillfully with the types of negativity Aaron described. I've been told that the Casa Entities say that many of the people who come to the Casa are experiencing a visitation from some type of external entity. This kind of visitation or possession may sound odd to people in our culture, but is a very accepted phenomenon in many cultures throughout history. These visitations, rightly understood, are only extensions of already indwelling habits and dynamics.

Attachment or possession by negatively polarized entities as a cause of illness has been my experience too, as I work with students with physical and mental ailments. Another related cause of illness occurs when parts of the spirit, or soul, fragment off during a traumatic experience. Shamanic healing throughout many cultures addresses this with soul retrieval techniques. Soul retrieval finds that core aspect of the being and supports re-integration, often by returning to the moment of fragmentation and introducing a new possibility that maintains integrity. Finally, we see various kinds of black magic such as magnetic and other psychic implants as a cause of illness. For the most part, Western medicine has no direct way to treat the causes of such illness, but only the results. At the Casa, the Entities attend to the causes.

On my second trip to the Casa I had the opportunity to talk in depth with a man, let's call him T, who was struggling with negativity. His situation weaves many of the points Aaron discusses into a compelling personal narrative. The official Western diagnosis at the time was that he was experiencing atypical brain seizures. Although doctors could see through the EEG that his brain was seizing up, they could make no sense of the symptoms. They had no idea what type of condition it was, so they called it atypical. He saw many healers, and medical specialists in the U.S. and elsewhere, and became increasingly ill. This is his story much as he told it to me again in 2007:

Interview with T

"When I was twenty-four, I experienced a major spiritual breakthrough where I encountered God and then made a decision to turn my back to God. I wanted a temporary break, a time out to figure out what this God experience meant. Since then I have been trying to come back to God.

"In early 2000 when I had a nervous breakdown, I came into contact with a very negatively polarized psychotherapist. As she treated me she started to do some black magic work on me. I clearly remember that she did something to me under the guise of balancing my chakras in one of the sessions. From one day to the next, I had a constant pulsing in my head that was like a sound and that prevented me from coming into a restful state. I now understand that this was clearly a psychic implant and one that I believe provided an opening for other implants to follow.

"After the pulsing started, she invited me to come to a class on magic. I had my misgivings about that, but I went because I was curious. When I arrived there, I saw forty to fifty of her students. They looked gray in the face. I suspected that she was taking energy from them and using it for her own purposes. She was a radiant being, positively radiating energy.

"I left, but she told me, 'Oh, you can go, but you won't go very far.' Three years later in 2003, this constant pulsing in my head started to develop into some real physical problems. The doctors couldn't find out what it was. I was desperate to get rid of that pulsing. The official Western diagnosis at the time was that I was experiencing atypical brain seizures, but they really could make no sense of the symptoms. By the time a professional exorcist looked at me in 2004, four years after the initial insertion, she saw a multitude of implants throughout my energy body.

"When I was told this was black magic, I was willing to accept it at that time, but I was more interested in getting relief and getting a cure than in the diagnosis. The psychiatrist and the neurologist gave me an antipsychotic drug. The symptoms seemed to decrease, but they came back if I didn't increase the dosage time and time again.

"One time I tried to exorcise the therapist/black magician, because I could see her in my energy field; every time I grounded myself, I saw her sitting in the very middle of the Earth and what happened was that instead of saying: 'In the name of Jesus the Christ, I order you out of my energy field,' what came out of my mouth was the exact opposite. These implants were clearly dark, connected to powerful dark beings capable of manipulating my thought and voice, and definitely not operating in accordance with my own volition. All I was able to do was to accept them and not to react or fight with them, because they seemed to get stronger when I reacted. I was reduced to relying on implicit faith, by relying on the knowledge that no soul is more tested by God than it can bear.

"After unsuccessful experiences with several healers over many years, I heard about the Casa and instinctively knew that this was the place where I would find my healing. When I first came, the Entity incorporated in Medium João had a long look at me and talked to me for a good five to ten minutes. The translator said, 'Well, you are a unique case. I've never heard of this before but Medium João cannot operate on you at the moment because your system is too weak and would not support the operation. So he has to put you on observation for a period of between eight and forty days. You just take herbs and the Entities will observe you and see what needs to be done.'

"Here in the Casa's Current Rooms I got to see these implants directly. The Entities showed me where they were; they showed me how they were linked with each other; they showed me what type of external circuits they made, and how the energy ran. The Entities also showed me in Current how they intended to remove the implants, by bombarding the attachment points with a green light. But their initial attempt wasn't strong enough. So even here with the Entities, it took eight attempts to finally release those implants.

"I still don't know exactly what energy implants are, other than they are a kind of energetic object that manipulates your etheric body. Energy implants were apparently used in Atlantean times to speed up an individual's evolution. I'm well aware that at a higher level, these things were actually intended to speed up your growth in a good way. And I also know that implants on the surface may look like something negative, like a psychic attack. Darker entities abused implants in Atlantis to create fear and to control other beings. My feeling is that whenever implants are used against the volition of the people who are implanted, this is definitely a negative purpose. But that doesn't mean that the person who is subjected to an implant in the end does not benefit from it. In the higher order of things, nothing escapes God's will and attention. Even these very negative experiences can be the catalyst of personal and spiritual transformation.

"I see now that my problem was that I wanted mental control over spiritual experience. Remember that I told God that I wanted to figure this all out? I got an experience of other beings trying to control me. So I got to experience first-hand the consequences of rebellion and the aim to control things. I now know that I will no longer try to control things. I can surrender at a new level of wholeheartedness. I think that's the ultimate lesson of my experience. And I'm still learning it every day."

I found T to be very inspirational through the five years I saw him at the Casa. His intentions to himself and others were very loving. I wondered, how could a positively polarized human unconsciously receive a negative implant or experience negative possession?

Later at home, during a discussion on working with negatively polarized energy, I asked Aaron.

Nothing can attack you without your participation. The most common way to participate is to turn to the anger energy or contracted energy for power, and then to use that power to fight back. There are some negative entities that will collapse under your attack, but you will still be left with your own negativity. More often the negative entity will call for reinforcements. If you are working from a positive place you can also bring forth reinforcements, but if you are doing combat from a place of fear and contraction, your resources are limited. The first lesson of this situation is to investigate the habit energy. Does one habitually turn to that contracted fear-based place in the self for power; or does the negative catalyst remind one to ground more deeply in one's own divine nature?

T's experience with the black magician was not thrust upon him by an outside entity, but instead was invited by T's own habit energy from previous incarnations. T unconsciously agreed to energy implants as his habitual way of coping. By energy implant, I mean something similar to the person who takes a drink to calm his nerves, or one who drinks an energizing tonic before an athletic event. One can call forth that energy but not in a balanced way for a human being. The implant was then further fostered by those negative beings that were greeting T, until he was over-charged and unbalanced.

What is the difference between an implant and a possession?

A possession involves another entity that moves itself into your energy field. An implant involves some energy or object that is urged by another entity, for you to accept into yourself.

Could a positively polarized human unconsciously receive a negative implant or experience negative possession?

Yes. We see how this has happened to T. The most common situation would be for the being who aspires to positive polarity, but still attacks him/herself when negative thought arises. Such a being can be vulnerable precisely because of the aspiration to be loving, and the lack of skills needed to manifest that lovingkindness. Here it is naiveté that accepts the implant. This negative greeting, possession, or implant is more easily released because of the intention to love. The obtaining and release of it may be an important part of the learning process.

You say we all have free will, always. Why can't that free will overcome the implants?

You always do have free will and it did overcome the implants, with the help of the Entities. At some level T chose to invite the implants of his own free will. Once invited, one must work with the results of the choice. For T, those results had the effect of deepening faith. This was his learning here. The implants were in fact a positive influence because they pushed him to understand that he is always responsible for his choices. He demonstrated this responsibility by making the wholesome choice to go where he needed to go when he was ready to release the implants.

Remember that you always teach and learn. He was not a victim, but rather a teacher to the negatively polarized forces that held him. Through him, they learned the power of love. He recognizes that in this participation, he has balanced much karma.

What will help you in such circumstances? Just what T says in his message: "faith, and relying on the knowledge that no soul is more tested by God than it can bear." This entire passage has been a journey for T to remembering the power of faith.

One major cause of T's initial acceptance of negativity I see is, as T phrased it, "the attempt to have mental control over spiritual experience." Any grasping at control comes from fear, and leads us into a negative path. This specific kind of attempted control is one of the most common I see among my students, trying to control the duration and direction of the meditative experience. It takes courage to sit back and let things unfold. This is the fruit of practice and of growing faith.

I asked Aaron to explain further how the Casa Entities aid Casa visitors to work with the types of negativity described above:

The Entities work in two ways. The first is to support the human with a high energy vibration. The human is better able to resist being ensnared by negative psychic greeting when its energy vibration is more clear and high. A high vibration repels any negativity. Free will is always respected. If you provide a high enough vibration, negativity will be sufficiently discomforted to decide to depart of its own free will. The high vibration also supports the body's healing.

As the Entities help the human to find more self-love and caring, and release feelings of low self-worth and of antagonism to the self, the human is less vulnerable to negative greeting of any sort.

The Entities may also directly approach the negative entity that is with the human to inquire how they may be of service, and to help it understand that it harms itself by harming the human. Keep in mind that there are two beings suffering, the human experiencing the negative psychic greeting or possession and the spirit entity delivering it. The human experiencing it has come to the Casa. If the spirit delivering the negative greeting truly wanted no part of the Casa experience, it would have left upon the arising of the human's intention to come. Since it has not left, it is making its free will statement of willingness to experience high vibration, and willingness to experience love. So the Entities are treating both beings. There are even situations where the person experiencing negative greeting has unconsciously agreed to it as a way to assist the negative greeter's growth toward the light.

Often a possessing entity, or even one offering negative psychic greeting, has some karmic connection to the one with whom it has paired itself. There is often some unwholesome codependence. The human who comes to the Casa does not consciously seek the benefit for the one who greets or possesses. It is only later that he/she will understand that result. Through this service to the other, he/she balances old karma.

If a negative entity has attached itself to a person and the Casa Entities help release that negative entity, where does it go?

If they are able to successfully communicate with the entity and teach it, it will go toward the light. Whatever density it is, it will find loving helpers to support it further on that journey to light. If the Entities are not able to reach the negative one, only to provide a high vibration so that it lets go, it may seek another place to lodge itself. The Entities are watchful for this and take care that it will not simply move from one human to another.

How could one receive a negative greeting while sitting in Current with so much love and light all around?

Have you ever watched a beekeeper and several assistants move a hive? Their energy may be loving. Still, the bees may become frightened and agitated. If there are several observers who are also frightened and begin to swat at the bees, it further agitates them; they may sting even the beekeeper.

Can't the Entities protect us?

There is always free will. Sometimes there is the intention to work with the agitated bees in order to learn how love invites peace and ease. Sometimes there is the intention to learn more about appropriate response to negativity by inviting some low level participation with it and investigating the process. This can be a wholesome exploration, much as when one investigates the nature of one's own anger. Of course, there can also be self-sabotage, inviting in negativity in order to prove a distorted belief in one's own innate imperfection. There is still free will and if you insist on doing that, all the Entities can do is to say, "We will not support your negativity."

Please remember that every being has some balance of negative and positive. You are not asked to become wholly positive, only to learn how to respond to negativity with love rather than fear. A large part of the reason for your incarnation is to practice just this, to speak love to fear. The Casa Entities will not remove your opportunity for practice, only help support you to keep it workable, so that you can learn what you came to learn.

"Speak love to fear." As I reread this, I am aware of how many questions asked of Aaron are rooted in fear or in a desire for control through understanding. His gentle, simple answer speaks from a place of confident strength. How do we say no with love? When we're in touch with our fears, and see the stories mind obsesses over, we see too that we have a choice, to go with those stories or let them go. Our kind attention to our own pain allows the letting go.

I may continue to experience negativity in both others and myself throughout my life, as negative thoughts do still come. I no longer fear them. Negativity more properly understood is one note in the divine orchestra, one that might sound dissonant if heard alone, but part of the melody when heard in the proper context. Taking responsibility for the emotions we generate, coming to know our innate wholeness, and learning to compassionately refuse others the opportunity to harm are all lessons we can glean from our dealings with negativity. As they teach and heal, the Casa Entities model a positive ideal, and help even very negative beings toward greater wholeness and wellness.

INTERVAL IV
Consciousness

Through the years, Aaron has spoken of raising the human conscious-ness as a very important part of our work on Earth. I have become increasingly aware that this is also at the heart of the direction pro-vided by the Entities of the Casa, although in their great compassion, they also offer whatever healing is possible as we work toward higher consciousness.

In this context, what is meant by the term "higher conscious-ness?"[1] It is helpful to think and speak from a common vocabulary and shared understanding of humankind's evolution toward con-scious divinity. Aaron attempts to fulfill this need by using a threefold division to categorize the broad range of possible human forms of consciousnesses as gross, subtle, and causal. We use these states when we brush our teeth, drive, converse, read books, sleep, and otherwise navigate our world. These states are based on conditions, and there-fore, are fundamentally temporary and subject to change at any moment.

Gross Consciousness

Gross consciousness is of the everyday world. Awareness remains focused exclusively on the physical level. Gross consciousness is the usual waking state wherein we are only aware of mundane mind and body senses and experiences. Mind and body senses make contact with mundane objects; with this contact comes the arising of mun-dane consciousness. For example, as the eye makes contact with a visual object, seeing consciousness arises with that contact. The mind touches a memory and mind consciousness results.

Subtle Consciousness

Subtle consciousness goes beyond the physical senses. Here we move away from the mundane-only perspective toward a knowing of more refined states of being. Higher vibrations and energies are perceived and embodied. The world of spirit can be known and understood. Stated differently, subtle is everything in between gross and causal. Subtle consciousness serves as a bridge. This state of consciousness is firmly grounded in both Gross and Causal. Subtle consciousness is linked to the dream state, apart from the solid reality of the senses; yet with thoughts, images, etc., based on gross input.

Causal

Causal consciousness is the highest conditioned state. It is given this name because it goes back to the root "cause," that-which-is. Another way of saying this is that because the Unconditioned exists, the conditioned may exist as an expression of the Unconditioned. Causal consciousness, however, still touches the world of conditions. Causal is sometimes likened to the state of sound sleep, where all gross and subtle phenomena cease. High causal is one step beyond causal.

Other states of consciousness exist besides these conditioned states. For example, Aaron's consciousness is not temporary, not based on conditions, and not subject to change. He describes it as being "beyond the causal plane." The full awareness of unlimitedness and divinity is immediately present. This supramundane state is also accessible to humans, but usually only in a limited way. Aaron and others describe this state as "nondual," because it is characterized by an intensely felt sense of oneness and is not fundamentally separate from the mundane states of consciousness.

The explanation above subtly suggests a sequential relationship between these states, as one in which people progress from the lower vibration of the gross state, through the subtle and causal, to a realization of nondual consciousness. Aaron offers a less distorted and more nuanced image:

When you think of the states of consciousness, it's important not to think of linearity; but rather of a nested set of round balls. The gross state of consciousness is always surrounded by the subtle state, but if you're totally caught up in the

gross state, you won't be aware of the subtle state. The causal state of conscious-
ness surrounds the subtle, but if you're focused in the subtle, you don't see the
causal. The state beyond the causal surrounds all the mundane states. All states
exist simultaneously. Most humans are centered in the gross state of conscious-
ness, the physical body and the mundane level of mind; and only occasionally in
your meditation practice do you break through this limited consciousness. The
highest states are always there and accessible, if you would but open to them.

You don't often connect that outer space with the mundane experience, but
of course it is connected. There is no firm line between these states. So you must
move beyond any duality and begin to understand that gross, subtle, causal, and
supramundane are one whole piece like the nut and its shell—one nut alto-
gether.

We all experience all three of these mundane states of consciousness, daily. Even the infant experiences them. Normally we just fall into one level or another. In our daily lives, we see forms and objects as solid, from the level of gross consciousness. Most people can only enter the subtle and causal levels when asleep. In dreaming sleep, there is only subtle consciousness and the idea of physical form. With lucid dreaming, we experience the subtle realm with an awake consciousness, rather than only in the unconsciousness of regular dreaming. Beyond dreaming, in the state of sound sleep, all gross and subtle phenomena cease. The causal level remains, but we are unconscious of it. In meditation, we learn how to open to the subtle and causal levels of consciousness while awake. Within the enlightenment experience, we experience the causal level and the supramundane consciousness simultaneously. The fully awakened mind can direct itself to and rest at ease in any of the three mundane levels.

Aaron also introduced me to the different developmental stages of consciousness that humans move through as they mature emotionally, intellectually, and spiritually. Let us be careful with the words that we use here. The *stages* of consciousness that I describe below are distinct from, but linked to, the *states* of consciousness that I described above, but some of the words are the same. Aaron borrows from and gratefully acknowledges Ken Wilbur for first developing this framework.

Aaron explains consciousness states and stages in these words:[2]

In a very brief capsule, we first find the magical consciousness *of the infant and young child. The infant doesn't have too much of a sense of reasoning. If he cries and a bottle appears, he doesn't see the whole chain of events, only feels that by some magic his cry brought forth what he needed. He doesn't yet recognize any boundary between self and mother. The older child advances into* mythic consciousness *with a deep set of beliefs, often based on the magic of which he has dreamed. Within mythic consciousness there is a clear sense of good and evil. Everything is in terms of black and white, no grays. The fundamentalists of any religion are often deep in mythic consciousness, unwilling to release their belief systems even though experiential understanding brings new information.*

The next stage is the rational consciousness *level. Here we begin to use the physical senses and mind to understand the universe. This attempt at understanding is predominant. Before rational consciousness, there was only the attempt to force new and different experiences into a particular belief structure, as one might attempt to force jigsaw puzzle pieces into the wrong spot in a puzzle. Rational consciousness is totally empirical: only what the senses can see and tell.*

These three stages—magical, mythic, and rational—all belong to the gross state of consciousness. Awareness is focused exclusively on the material world, interpreting the inputs from the mind and physical senses.

Vision logic consciousness *is still based in the rational, the logical, but it climbs a step up the mountain to a bigger perspective, begins to see with a clearer vision, and touches more on intuition. This is the opening to the subtle state. It is not yet fully open to the subtle energies, but it allows the possibility of data beyond the empirical, both from the outer world and from the self as intuition. There is a gentle detachment from reliance only on empirical fact that is measured solely by scientific instruments and techniques. Vision logic consciousness has one foot in the gross state of consciousness and one foot in the subtle state of consciousness.*

With psychic consciousness, *the various nonphysical senses open: clairvoy-*

ance, clairaudience, all forms of telepathy, and so forth. These are all the ways we have of knowing beyond the physical senses; extraordinary knowing. We know in this way through extensions of all the body senses. As this stage is heightened, we open further into the subtle stage of consciousness in which energy is experienced and exchanged. People begin to feel assurance about auras and read information from them. Whereas in early subtle consciousness the aura was glimpsed, but not trusted or understood, now when you walk into a room, you not only feel the energy in the room, but you trust and can interpret and understand what you feel. When talking to another individual, the nonverbal and energetic cues are more important than the verbal.

The psychic and subtle stages of consciousness belong to the subtle state of consciousness. Both the subtle state and the subtle stage of consciousness, end in what the Christian mystics call the dark night of the senses. This "dark night" also arises during what the Buddhist tradition calls the experience of no-self or ego dissolution. In this passage, the perceiver begins to see how much all of this observation has come from the personal self as a center of the experience. As self disappears, or its observations feel unreliable, a period of despair arises wherein it feels like nothing that has previously been known can be counted on as truth. Within the passage of this dark night we shift almost completely out of what has been a mundane state of consciousness, involving the etheric and astral bodies, and gross and subtle states; and into the causal state of consciousness. This consciousness is also sometimes called Christ consciousness or Buddha nature, living from a place seemingly of no self, knowing one's deepest connection with All-That-Is.

Even this is not the end because in the causal state there is still a self, no matter how subtle. We are still bound, albeit in an elusive and delicate way, to an everyday, mundane consciousness that interprets and reacts to external events through the lens of personality.

With the disintegration even of that sense of self, there is the breakthrough into nondual consciousness or pure awareness. This is perceived at that time to be the highest level of consciousness. With the first breakthrough into the subtle state, we understood that which we have called self to be a collection of temporary phenomena such as body experience, thoughts, feelings, impulse, and consciousness; that which Buddhism terms "skandhas." They were seen to arise and dissolve out of conditions and did not denote a separate self. Although there was clearly something beyond these skandhas, we could not say what it was, only what it was not. Now we return to that experience at greater depth.

The awareness that notes these phenomena arising and dissolving is not mundane consciousness. Awareness then becomes aware of itself, and knows that it has no boundaries. However, the nondual state is not a static experience but ever-changing and deepening. If you were to drift in space it would seem vast; your first experience of this space would know it as unlimited and as undifferentiated in nature. As you get to know that space, details come forth and there is some recognition of the variety within the Oneness. This experience of the Unconditioned is similar. It is limitless so the experience of it will constantly deepen and not be stagnant.

This has been just a very brief map. As you raise the consciousness, you move out of the personal self and toward the nondual self, and then begin to be able to relate to the world around you with more lovingkindness, and much more wisdom and compassion. Fear falls away. There's really no longer a fear of anything, because with the opening of nondual consciousness you know that the deepest core of Being is indestructible. However, you will not stand in the middle of a highway inviting a truck to smash into you; in fact, there may be even greater respect for the body because the body is seen as the vehicle for growth in this incarnation. But the respect is based on love, not on fear.

The stages of consciousness are like intersecting planes. We move back and forth between them, although one is predominant at any given time. But through any particular day, we may touch on many stages of consciousness. The mythic consciousness of the child may appear in a somewhat whiny, "I want that; I don't like this," type of thought. A deep moment of compassionate seeing may lead into Christ or Buddha consciousness. Yet neither deep grasping with mythic consciousness, nor high compassion and nondual consciousness are the norm for that person at that time, so neither is held very long.

We interpret our experiences through the lens of our highest stable stage of development. There's a big difference between having a "peak" experience— perhaps a short-term experience of the subtle or causal realm—and being able to integrate that experience into the rest of one's life. Movement into a peak experience of the nondual will be differently interpreted by someone who is stable in the stage just below the nondual, than by someone who is in a very early stage of consciousness. With the peak experience, one has suddenly touched the mountain top; but one doesn't know how one got to that peak, or where to turn from there. With the integrated experience, all the levels that led to the peak experience are always available.

Before I present any more information, let me show you graphically how everything is related. It is difficult to present this information in a two dimensional format. Please remember that our actual experience is far more complex than any graphic. Within each state we might encounter all the bodies and aspects of all the stages. Below is an illustration.

Let me discuss the Bodies column. The energetic expression of the physical level is called the physical etheric (from "ether"—the state between energy and matter) body. Here we find the elements that support the physical body, in their material and energetic components. This is part of the gross state. This material and energetic expression body exists in our everyday space-time continuum. Within this etheric body are the gross tissues of the body as well as the energy meridians and chakras. The next energetic expression is the subtle or astral body, which is transitional between the Gross and Causal states.

The astral body exists at two levels, one that transcends space, and one that transcends both space and time. Within the first level of the astral body one still finds emotions and the nonphysical senses, which include clairaudience and clairvoyance. These senses allow an enhanced range of body and mental perceptions. This experience of the astral body transcends space. There is no need to be physically present in order to have this experience. The second level of the astral body, called the thought level, is sometimes seen as a separate body; but I experience it as an upper floor of the astral body. This level transcends both space and time. Here everything is understood as simultaneous. In dreaming, we are on the astral plane.

Last is the causal body. The causal body is at the edge of conditions of any sort and yet, through the human connection, still touches the world of conditions. Here, awareness knows both the mundane experience that arises out of conditions, and also, that nothing ever arose or ceased; but simply is. It is here that true healing occurs. In the mundane body, Barbara's ear nerves are dead and nonfunctional. Beyond the causal plane, there has never been any distortion to the ear nerves. Barbara simultaneously works to heal the ear nerves and to know the Ever-Perfect, beyond all distortion. It sounds like a paradox, but there are also no paradoxes.

Within each state, all three bodies appear. Thus, the gross state has etheric, astral, and causal bodies, though we are only usually aware of the etheric one. The causal state also holds all the bodies. Even beyond the causal plane, the three bodies are found. This is challenging to understand through the conceptual mind. The Buddhist Heart Sutra says it well as, "Form is emptiness; emptiness is form." Another statement is from the Buddhist poem of the Dzogchen tradition, "Flight of the Garuda."[3]

> Let your mind spontaneously relax and rest.
> When left to itself, ordinary mind is fresh and naked.
> If observed, it is a vivid clarity without anything to see,
> A direct awareness, sharp and awake.
> Possessing no existence, it is empty and pure,
> A clear openness of nondual luminosity and emptiness.
>
> It is not permanent, since it does not exist at all.
> It is not nothingness, since it is vividly clear and awake.
> It is not oneness, since many things are cognized and known.
> It is not plurality, since the many things known are inseparable in one taste.
> It is not somewhere else; it is your own awareness itself.
>
> The face of this Primordial Protector, dwelling in your heart,
> Can be directly perceived in this very instant.
> Never be separated from it, children of my heart!

When the predominant stage of consciousness is the nondual, this is usually the end of the physical, etheric, astral, and causal bodies. This is a transcendent, liberated state in which these human bodies are no longer karmically necessary.

One might ask, "Of what use is all this information?" Aaron said,

State	Body	Stage	Usual Chakra	Tone	Color
Gross	Etheric	Magical	Base	C	Red
		Mythical	Sacral	D	Orange
		Rational			
	Low astral	Vision-Logic	Solar plexus	E	Yellow
		Opening to the Subtle			
Subtle	Astral	End of Vision-Logic	Heart	F	Green
		Psychic	Throat	G	Blue
		Dark night of the senses			
	High astral	Subtle	Third Eye	A	Indigo
		Dark night of the soul			
Causal	Causal	Christ / Buddha Consciousness	Crown	B	Violet
Beyond the Causal	Causal	Nondual Awareness	Above the Crown	C	White

The basic work of the human is consciousness-raising. And then we must ask, "What helps you to raise your awareness of the already existent higher consciousness, and what gets in the way and keeps you stuck in lower consciousness?"

Having the map of consciousness doesn't promise us the transcendence of lower consciousness. Rather, such conceptual knowledge makes us more aware of our potential to truly dwell in nondual consciousness. This awareness is a key to living our wholeness in the personal sense, and a key to a peaceful world where all beings may find happiness. Without such awareness, we think only in terms of the limits that are revealed at the present level. Then we perpetuate the limitations instead of opening to the unlimited.

With such awareness, we recognize the old patterns that hold us to lower levels of fear-based consciousness. We always have a choice, not of what may arise in experience, but of how we will relate to it; and whether the response will be of a lower consciousness and vibration based on old patterns of fear, or a higher consciousness and vibration grounded in nonseparation and love for all beings.

When the pattern is fear-based, the physical, emotional, and mental bodies move into an unbalanced contraction. There will always be contraction, such as comes when we inhale or exhale, or reach out a hand to receive an object. But these contractions are quickly released and create no long lasting distortions. The imbalanced contractions are what hold us to patterns that lead to illness. More importantly, these contractions are what hold karma.

Karma is based on intention. As long as there is even the subtle intention to hold a pattern based in fear and contraction, it influences all the bodies and holds us in lower states and stages of consciousness. If the intention is to be kind, but there is also an intention to protect the self at any cost, then when something comes that feels threatening there will be a contraction drawn from these conflicting intentions; and the whole idea of a separate self will blossom large, blocking loving action and thought. Once we deeply realize that whatever hurts another hurts the self and vice versa, we stop trying to control everything. We relax and invite in whatever is for the highest good. Then we stop holding these contractions that create dis-ease at all levels. And the karma can be balanced and resolved.

It's valuable to remember that we are beings of matter and energy who exist on many different levels. When there is a physically or emotionally unbalanced contraction, it affects all levels. It's circular. Whatever arises in our experience is the result of conditions and in itself becomes the condition for future arisings. Any contraction or distortion is influenced by and further influences everything within and beyond the self. Everything is connected. This fact is part of the law of karma. You've heard the expression, "What goes around, comes around." Whatever we do is returned to us, as reflection, so we may again have the opportunity to attend to it, and finally to have that motion cease.

Consider the previously related myth of Sisyphus, who had the karma to push a boulder up a hill daily, and have it roll back down every night. The harder he tried to make it stay at the top, the more he suffered. Only by relaxing and understanding the laws of cause and effect in this mundane world can we stop the momentum and cease to push the boulder. We can relax and attend to things as they are, with kindness and compassion, but without the contracted state of fear. But if the boulder must be pushed, can it be pushed without a self and its stories? In either way, the karma can resolve.

There is no first cause. In healing we must attend to the whole. Our human path is to evolve into higher consciousness for our own sakes, and for the good of all beings and the Earth itself. As we do so, we heal the distortions and balance old karma. As the karma resolves, we may find unimagined healing.

CHAPTER 15

THE BIG WAVE

EXITING THE PLANE in Detroit after my first visit to the Casa, I felt enthused about both my trip and my prospects for healing. I had learned much, my mind had expanded, and the possibilities were endless. I felt like I had a clear plan of action and a healing practice that I could work with. Yet, there was also a sense of failure. I still could not hear and there was both anger and sadness. I would learn more in the weeks and years ahead, but not in a manner that I could have foreseen.

In April of 2004, I led a retreat in North Carolina, at a facility located on the beach. I'm a strong swimmer, and love to play in the waves. I find it helpful to hold on to a small surfboard because of my poor balance. I was playing happily in the ocean when an unexpected series of large waves scooped me up and threw me to the ocean floor. My face hit the ocean bottom hard, twisting my neck and breaking facial bones including the nose and orbital bones around one eye. My legs went numb and I lost control of them. My surfboard broke, knocking the breath out of my body and smashing several ribs in the front and back.

There were short lapses of consciousness, mixed with moments of lucidity; I was aware of terrible pain and that I was drowning, but felt helpless to change the situation. I didn't know which direction was up, as the surf tossed me about. I thought my back was broken. Yet interestingly, there was no panic. The noting mind of meditation came through, *great pain, dizzy, chest burning, no air. . . .* It wasn't a conscious thinking process, which at that moment I was incapable of, but a deeper level of awareness. Then came that often-described "tunnel of light," an alluring exit in the face of intense pain. In that radiance there was such spaciousness, ease, joy, and peace. As I wavered between life and death, knowing that to choose the light meant leaving the body, something within made a conscious decision for life, not out of fear of death, but from a conscious realization that my work here was unfinished.

I had no idea what kind of body I would have when I returned. But the decision arose spontaneously and was stable; the fruit of a long spiritual practice. At that point, I felt spirit support me to move my arms and rise to the surface. With my face streaming blood, I was able to give a feeble call for help, and I was seen. Hands grabbed me and that was the last of consciousness until my eyes opened, and I became aware of my body lying on the beach.

Blessed now with the perspective of distance, I can see how this seemingly horrible accident fits into my journey. Before that first Casa trip, Jeshua had said that what I would need most was courage. I really did not understand, then, how prophetic Jeshua's statement would prove to be, on many levels. When He had spoken, I thought He had meant the courage to heal my ears, resolve my past karma, and break through the feelings of separation from the world that my deafness fostered. I thought He had meant the courage to go to Brazil and invite healing at all levels. These meanings were both true, but much more would be asked of me over time. Healing would take longer than I had expected, and would require a greater transformation than I had thought possible. "Having faith" became words and a concept that held my attention.

On the plane to Brazil I had read a book called *The Desert Pilgrim.*[1] The section on a monk's healing of a deaf child resonated with my growing understanding of faith. The monk is speaking:

"When you're on the spiritual path, you're on the right road. Listen, there was a mother who brought her young daughter here the other day. The daughter was deaf. The mother had taken her to doctors, but they could do nothing. 'Oh Papa, won't you help my daughter,' the woman begged. 'I can help your daughter and I will,' I said. I sat her down on the bench right where you are. I spit on my two fingers and placed them in the daughter's ears. The girl closed her eyes and I began to chant a prayer of healing in Russian.

"'But what if it doesn't work?' the mother cried. 'What if it doesn't work?'

'And it's not going to work with you asking that question,' I said. 'You of little faith, go on out of the room right now, immediately.' I kicked her out and returned to the daughter, the girl who had perfect faith. I spit on my fingers again and placed them in her ears. I chanted. I asked that God's healing powers come down upon her. We joined together in our prayers and after a few minutes the girl said that she could hear my voice. She raced outside and found her mother and told her that her deafness was gone.

"So that's the kind of faith you have to have, the faith of a little child. You must come to the kingdom of God like an innocent."

Faith had deepened on the trip, as I saw the miraculous healings taking place around me. However, faith and equanimity are not the same. Equanimity allows us spaciousness, and rests in wisdom, but in part it's logical or at least has roots in logic. Equanimity grows as we see that everything truly does arise from conditions and then passes away; thus, there is a logic to allowing things to be the way they are. Faith is total surrender to things as they are. In faith there is equanimity; but also courage, deep love, and joy. Faith brings me home.

Yet when I returned from Brazil, I was angry, disappointed and felt abandoned. I felt like I had failed somehow because I could not bring forth hearing, despite my rosy concepts of faith, and despite my conceptual understanding of what was needed. I didn't yet really believe that hearing was possible, despite all I had seen at the Casa and despite the Entities' promise to help. It became clear that this faith that I thought I had, was actually based on conditions, and that I had not completely surrendered to things as they were. My faith in healing and in spirit, already troubled by my lack of healing, was further shaken by the accident. I found further wisdom in *The Desert Pilgrim*. The monk is discussing the Dark Night of the Soul with Mary:

> Monk: I told you that you want to sink down into the dark night and stay there. You are fighting so hard to get out. You must enter into that void because then you make the great discovery that God is in the void. God is the dark night.
>
> Mary: How could God be the dark night?
>
> Monk: ... You'll find the Divine in paradox, in contradictions, in moments of surprise. You are not going to find the Divine in some safe, cozy apartment where everything moves along at a predictable pace.

The Monk's words certainly spoke to my condition, and would prove to be as prophetic as Jeshua's statement that courage was what I needed most. As long as we cling to some place of safety, we never surrender to the fullness of that void, which holds the intensity of love and fear, of perfect love and perfect peace. In my journal after the accident I asked,

Am I holding back? Having come so far, I feel like I have settled into a safe space, a safe enlightenment, only to be thrown out by this pain and confusion. I know that the enormous suffering that sometimes catalyzes growth is not necessary. We can enter the void *and* know the safety of the divine, at the same time. Can I find the divine in this battered body filled with pain? I don't know how to start.

It was out of that "don't know" that a more complete surrender finally came, both with the continuing deafness, and now with these new injuries. The body was devastated. There was constant pain. I could not even lie down as ribs were broken in front and back. For weeks I slept sitting in a chair, head cushioned on arms resting on a table to avoid any pressure on the body. I had nothing left with which to fight, I could only let go and be with this body as it was.

I found myself ready and willing to work on gradual healing, with a deepened faith in the possibility to heal. There was an awareness of the need to look at any doubt and not to be caught in the story of doubt. If healing was not immediate, it was because that was the deepest, though unconscious, intention for the highest good. I needed courage to find and demonstrate healing gradually, the courage to persevere through bodily pain and loss of function. I needed patience to learn the skills that can be passed on to others, for that transmission is my higher intention, not just ease and comfort.

In order to survive that day in the surf, I needed to make an instant choice for the highest good. In that moment, I released old karma related to the small self, holding back from the world for its own safety and protection. I made the choice then to do what serves light and love most completely, regardless of the consequences. From then on, I would live the painful and transformative results of that choice willingly made. Skillfully attending to and experiencing these results is the process of karmic balancing. That moment seemed like an initiation of sorts into a long period of unexpected twists in my health and seeming detours in my progress toward healing.

Four months of rehabilitation followed. My picture was brought to the Entities, requesting their help and they responded in many ways. Broken bones healed more quickly than expected. When pain was severe, I felt them near me, helping to release the physical agony. I would feel their presence and a warmth and softness wrapped around me, allowing me to sleep.

My back and face began to feel better. I was able to walk and swim again, although walking was painful. My left knee, on which I had had traditional surgery years earlier to correct torn cartilage, was very painful and swollen. It had been reinjured in the accident. Hip and lower back pain also made walking a struggle. However, it no longer hurt to breathe, or to open my mouth to talk or chew. A spot on my lower lip bled profusely several times a week, when I talked or ate. The medical doctor said that an artery must have been punctured. Since surgery would leave a scar, we left it alone, hoping that it would soon heal on its own.

Now that I wasn't feeling overwhelmed by the physical experience, I could begin to gain insight into what had happened to me. Before the trip to Brazil, I had explored the simultaneity of relative and ultimate reality. On the ultimate level there was nothing left to heal, while on the relative level there was deafness. I began to understand how to hold the truth of wholeness, and to still be with the body as it was. There can be no denial of either reality. I also see now that I needed to learn how to invite the healing of the body, of broken bones and torn tissues, before I could do the work on the ears.

Through the late summer, Aaron spoke to me of healing the body and spirit with harmonics and vibration. He said the healing that I was seeking was part of the core of my work here on Earth, and truly, of all of our work. That work is to carry a high, love-based vibration, regardless of our mundane experiences. A lesson came when a horsefly followed me as I guided my kayak around the lake one day. I became agitated. Aaron spoke to me and seemed to suggest that holding disharmony in the physical body limits the ability to face negativity with love. It was an unpleasant outing and I returned to my cabin filled with tension. I began to meditate, but my agitation followed me. Finally I began to speak with Aaron.

First let us address the rage at the horsefly. You were enjoying the boat, enjoying the lake, but did not want to be bitten and he kept returning; attacking, as you felt it. You understood that he was merely being a horsefly. There was mindfulness about the anger he brought up. Yet you would have killed him if you could, so you could enjoy your lake in peace. How can there be peace at the cost of killing a bit of the divine?

You are about to say, "Do I just sit there and let myself be eaten?" No, nor do you need to kill. Here we get to vibration and sound. The angry cells literally give

off a vibration that says, "prey" and invites the fly to bite. The high, centered
vibration gives a very different message of saying no to negativity, but with no
fear or hate.

To say no in this way, it is not necessary that there be no fear, but that there
be no self identity with fear; that is, no building up of stories based on the fear,
just knowing that fear has arisen in this mind and body based on conditions, and
will pass. In the same way, it is not necessary that there be no cellular distortion,
but no self-identity with that distortion. Even if the cells still express some dis-
tortion, when you hold the mirror of the Ever-Perfect as truth and embrace both
the distorted and the Ever-Perfect, it is that openness that gives the highest vibra-
tion. The cells will heal as they are able. On the relative plane, the distortion still
may exist, but it is embraced and transmuted. What expresses out is the highest
level of being.

I asked him if he meant that distorted cellular tissue normally gives a
lower vibration; but that tissue will not give a lower vibration if I
don't relate to it as the self.

Not quite. It still emits the lower vibration if it is diseased or distorted, but
that vibration is not broadcast. Rather, the lower vibration is held within a con-
tainer of the highest, most loving vibration, and that is what is broadcast. There
will always be distortion in the body, just as there will always be some emotional
distortion. Emotional or physical distortion actually strengthens positive polarity
when we are able to offer love to the distortion. You embrace the human, and
know the Ever-Perfect in all the bodies as true self. You also work on the relative
plane to balance the distortion, without taking it as self. That which presents as
"distorted" on the physical level, such as an unhealthy cell with low vibration,
has an Ever-Perfect component. Even when the cell broadcasts at a lower fre-
quency there is no difficulty if there is recognition of the simultaneous Ever-Per-
fect, a loving embracing of both, and the intention to help invite that of low
frequency into a higher vibration in gentle and loving ways.

So what makes it difficult to greet the negative with love is the
untended low vibration in body or emotion.

Precisely. Please return to your meditation.

As I looked at the horsefly experience, I saw that there could be both the low vibration of discordance and the higher vibration of the loving container. The lower vibration still exists; therefore, I had thought it would be broadcast. Yet when I look at the emotional experience rather than the physical one, I see that the lower vibration of negative emotions exists on the relative plane, but that it is almost irrelevant, like waves on the surface of the lake. There is anger, for example, and the compassion that holds space for anger. The compassion absorbs the anger just as the large body of water absorbs the waves. I asked Aaron if this was what he meant about the physical body discordance? He replied, "Yes. The waves do not affect the quality of the water."

While the learning came from an incident with a horsefly, I was very clear that these lessons applied to healing more severe physical distortions, such as my deafness, and even to potentially lethal trauma, such as my accident in the spring. They differed only in degree. Healing energies become available to us when we can tend to negative, discordant experiences of the mind and body with awareness, kindness, and love.

The Entities offer several ways to raise the vibrational frequency of the body, including prayer, meditation, and drinking their blessed water. After the accident, my instructions became more precise. In meditation, the Entity Dr. Cruz asked me to purchase tuning forks* that he directed me to use in very specific ways, and to use specific Casa crystals blessed by the Entities.

This work brought together firstly, the intention to open for the highest good of all beings, secondly, a willingness to see what held

---

*Eight weighted tuning forks of good quality, from lower C at 64Hz to the next octave C at 128Hz, specifically: 64 Hz, 72 Hz, 80 Hz, 85.33 Hz, 96 Hz, 106.68 Hz, 120 Hz, 128 Hz.

the chakra closed and attend to it, and thirdly, the tuning forks and crystals, which I often placed on my chakras as I chanted. The exercises included hearing with the body, feeling the vibration, and chanting specific syllables that are harmonious to each chakra and supportive to the health of body tissue. The Entities didn't tell me what to chant, only the tones. I used a sacred syllable, "Om," beginning with the musical note C at the base chakra and working up to the crown chakra at B, then to the higher C several inches above the crown. Sometimes I would repeatedly chant C for the root, D for the sacral, and E for the solar plexus chakras, while working with the tendency of these lower chakras to close. At other times, I held the fork near first the right ear, then the left, as instructed, and chanted the musical note that I heard or sensed through the body and vibration. Then I placed the stem of that fork on the appropriate chakra point and chanted more. I worked intuitively with the body and chakras, singing to whatever felt closed. I found that my chakras responded favorably and that I was learning to hear in a new way.

As I sang to the body, I visualized it as perfect, while still holding the injuries with compassion. I stopped seeing distortion as something wrongful. Distortion became akin to the movement of my kayak in strong current, just a slight swerve that needed attention. This listening and vocal toning became a daily practice. Aaron told me:

The pure harmonic vibration serves as a template for the discordant vibration and invites transformation, just as holding the visual image of the Ever-Perfect offers a template for the material distortion. The Ever-Perfect is one bias: the distortion is another. Just as two currents push at each other to establish a third flow of movement, these two currents—of the distorted or lower vibrational frequency, and the perfectly harmonious energy—both dissolve into a third movement that both contains and is different from the first two. Think of your sailboat: the wind pushes the sail one way and the water pushes against the centerboard the opposite way. The boat doesn't move as pushed by wind or water but moves ahead, merging the two forces. This is the emergent expression. This is the process of healing. At the ultimate level the Ever-Perfect always exists. At the relative level it is always becoming, never here. Everything is in flux; everything is decaying. Yet ultimate equilibrium always exists. Everything falls apart and decays in the relative, yet it decays into the One, into harmony. Chaos slowly shifts into divine order.

In the same way, diseased and damaged tissue gives a vibration that has an harmonic element. The perfectly pitched tuning forks carry the Ever-Perfect pitch, reminding the distorted tissue with discordant vibration of its own Ever-Perfect level. As you chant, the cells come into greater balance. On the ultimate plane, there is the realization of the Ever-Perfect and the cessation of identification with the distortion. This whole then becomes the new relative and is played again into balance with the Ever-Perfect. The vibration continues to increase.

While meditating and chanting I saw the meaning of Aaron's words in my body. Cells constantly die away and new cells come, always with some distortion. As the body holds a higher frequency, the new cells are born into the higher frequency; the tissue becomes healthier, and the whole vibration becomes progressively more pure. When there's a focus on "fixing" the distorted, with contracted feelings and energy, that contraction lowers the vibration. While the idea is held to raise the vibration, it can't happen if one is practicing the contraction. When there is the openhearted intention to invite the higher vibration and to rest in the Ultimate Truth of that Ever-Perfect, the body on a cellular level, follows naturally.

The body wants to express its wholeness. The mind with fear shies away and holds the body back. Chanting and the work with harmonics is a kind of affirmation of the body's ultimate perfection and high vibration; and these actions invite the body's gradual move to that higher vibration.

Fear, expressed as contraction, is the limiting condition. Love, expressed as the uncontracted, is the release.

More recently, I had further practice in utilizing harmonics. In the summer of 2008, I had an opportunity to explore release from the belief that we are limited beings in everyday life; and to watch that release transfer from the mental to the physical body, as I experienced the healing power of harmonics. I was leading a horse who bolted and pulled me over. In the hard fall, I broke my big toe. A doctor estimated it would take six weeks for the bone to mend, and longer for it to recover fully. It was painful, swollen, and very discolored. One of the Casa Entities, Dr. Cruz, said to me in meditation, "It is all molecules; there is nothing solid there. Sing to it, and visualize the bone whole." He asked me to hold the foot tenderly, ask it what tones it needed to support healing, and to soak it with the Casa water. For three days I sang to it, just a repetition of the syllable "Om" in different tones. I held the image of the healed toe in my mind, not as a linear process, but envisioning the Ever-Perfect toe that was already there under the swelling. Over those three days, the colors changed, and finally faded. The pain diminished. By the fourth day, there was no longer any discoloration or pain at all. Dr. Cruz assured me, "The bone is mended. Be gentle to it for a time, as it is still a little fragile." Although it remained swollen for several weeks, there was no further pain at all. The X-rays several months after that healing showed no sign of a break.

Moving back to the late summer of 2004, some time after experiencing the horsefly in my kayak, a different fly gave me another opportunity to explore and practice. This time I had a very different response. I could feel myself tensing, being pulled out of awareness. Then came wisdom about the experience. I found equanimity with the fly, with being uncentered, with the tension—all of it. Without trying to fix anything, awareness watched an ancient desire to control and the feeling of helplessness. Meanwhile the fly kept buzzing me, and occasionally landing, and there was an aversion to being bitten.

I slipped into the water to avoid the fly and floated there. Aaron often says "that which is aware of anger is not angry." I have learned to rest in that state of awareness and watch. Awareness could compassionately see the small self grasping and preferring, acting according to very old karmic conditioning. But it was clear that I could not choose to escape into awareness to avoid this experience. Pure awareness is never an escape. If anything, awareness directed at the pain of the fly's sting would increase the experience of pain, because the relative mind is focused on the pain as the predominant object. Whether suffering occurs would be a function of my level of equanimity at the moment. If the intention was to withdraw from the experience, and it seemed inevitable to kill or be bitten, I would experience resignation, the near-enemy of equanimity, which would tighten another karmic knot.

As I continued to float, the tension released, and my experience merged with light and space. My awareness felt very open, and nothing was solid. I doubt if this would have happened so easily if I had stayed on the boat with the fly attacking. It was as if I could see the knot and ten thousand events that had created it, all floating in space, no self, just conditions pouring forth, and there was no need to hold it any more. It was a very powerful shift. I floated there about ten minutes, just resting in awareness, feeling all tension released.

Once I climbed back into the boat, the fly was back and persistent in its effort to bite. It was unpleasant, but the experience no longer pulled me hard into aversion or into a personal self. Instead, there was spaciousness with the unpleasant feeling, and a strong compassion for this hungry fly, though not strong enough to let him eat. Finally I got back into the water, tied the boat rope to my waist, and swam back to the dock.

Looking back on my experiences after the ocean accident and through the summer of 2004, I am amazed and humbled at the healing I underwent and the teachings that I was given. Even biting insects became a blessing. Inwardly, this ongoing dialogue and exploration led to a deepened faith. The faith I had during my first trip to Brazil, I now realized was similar to the simple faith of the child in *The Desert Pilgrim*. My belief had been wounded by my lack of healing in the same way that the child's faith would have been shattered by the mother's disbelief. Out of that wound, and with Aaron's words and my experiences, I found a faith based on the more solid foundation of knowledge and wisdom. But even as I relaxed into this new understanding, new trials would lead to new learning. My healing would continue to happen gradually, with almost constant setbacks and unexpected difficulties. I needed the strengthened ability to surrender to the reality of my experiences so that this new faith could more easily survive intact, and grow.

CHAPTER 16

The Beginning of Letting Go
and Knowing Wholeness

IN SEPTEMBER 2004, just as my body was feeling stronger and more free of pain, my eyes began to bleed. I awoke one morning to very cloudy vision, unable to read or see details, and barely able to lip-read. The eye specialists were uncertain of the cause of the bleeding in the left eye, but diagnosed a ruptured blood vessel in the right eye. It had probably been damaged in the accident, and then suddenly tore when I began to resume a more active lifestyle including exercising. They had no easy resolution, or certain prognosis. Here was terror of being blind and deaf.

I went through traditional medical treatments, steroids injected into the eyes, eye drops, laser surgery, and more, but there was no permanent change. With each treatment hope arose with a brief improvement of vision, then anger and fear returned as the treatment ultimately failed to work. I could see that I was letting go of personal responsibility, and asking someone else to fix me. I was handing the choices to the retinal specialist and not trusting my intuition and inner ability to heal.

I found myself in a place akin to where I had been three decades earlier. Back then I faced deafness; now I found myself facing the very real possibility of blindness. I had found a level of peace in all these years of deafness, but only after a decade of rage and suffering. This time around, I was able to relate to my difficulty with more wisdom and love. Three weeks after the vision problem began I went to my cabin in the woods.

Journal, October 2004

At dawn I was sitting on the deck, a favorite spot. But the trees were all blurred. Anger and despair came, and fear and grief. I sat and cried for a while. Then there was the lovely smell of wood smoke; sweet apple I had cut last month, burning in the stove. Hal brought me tea. I looked out again and it was not as it used to be, but it was lovely, the blurred edges softening the trees as the dawn sun filtered through. Just this moment, perfect in itself!

I found myself very humbled, aware that all that we work so hard to build in the world can crumble in a minute. I have been letting go. I am not depressed really, and not resigned to blindness—which may or may not come—but I am letting go of so many attachments; learning how to live with things as they are. I'm just beginning to understand how to continue to live passionately, even though nothing matters. To say that thought more completely, nothing matters, yet everything matters; and I saw how we must hold that balance.

Here was the greater healing, not yet of the vision but of the heart. It was clear immediately how it related to the earlier experience of deafness. I was learning to be with things as they are, with an open heart.

In January 2005, I returned to Brazil not only deaf, but also legally blind in one eye and with limited vision in the other. The Entity immediately said to me with compassion for my fear, "You will not be blind," then sent me to surgery. Afterward, the Entity, speaking through Medium João, said, "No reading for forty days." I explained to the Entity that I'm deaf and with no one to finger spell, I need to read to communicate with people, and asked permission for that much reading. He gave me a long, penetrating look, smiled at me, and then said, "Yes, it is more difficult in your situation, but no reading."

So I spent the following weeks alone, watching the desire to escape from any discomfort into the solace of a good book or conversation.

Journal, February 18, 2005

Why am I not content with this silence? I ask this with a laugh, noting that in March I'll have two weeks of personal silent retreat that I am looking forward to experiencing. It's fascinating to watch the impulse and habit energies; wanting to do something, wanting entertainment, wanting social contact, wanting escape from this moment, which is not an unpleasant moment at all.

I became aware that part of the difficulty was in watching the people around me talk. This has always been a part of the deafness, the difficulty of sitting with a table full of strangers and being unable to converse. I wasn't really lonely. I had met several people with whom the one-to-one conversations were rich and rewarding, thanks to their willingness to slow down so that I could read lips. I knew that much of the group conversation at the table was social chitchat. But the mind was caught up in old habits, and came forth with its fearful question, "What am I missing?" I realized that at home I rarely experience that grasping, not just because it has been outgrown, but also because my life there has been shaped in a fashion that spares me this situation of exclusion. There are almost always family or friends around to finger spell for me.

That week I was forced to look at the habits that arise when my support system fails. I read! I am an eager writer also, always journaling. Reading and writing are not harmful activities. They can bring real enrichment. The harm is not in the process itself but in the motivation that brings forth the process. To do anything from a place of fear, reactivity, and habit can cause harm.

Journal, February 22, 2005

There's a first line of a Sufi poem that says, "Pilgrim, first do the purification. ..." Just after "no reading" I awoke at midnight with chills and what seemed to be a high fever. It has gone on for four days, alternating profuse sweating with shaking beneath a pile of blankets on a tropical summer afternoon. The body aches like a truck has run it down. There is a constant cough, and draining from every cell of the body. It feels like the body is releasing a lifetime of toxins through skin, sinuses, and abdomen. I drink three liters of water a day, but have eaten little. I've talked to almost no one.

Needless to say there has been a lot of time to lie in bed, a cool cloth covering my eyes, while reflecting on the question, "Why am I not content?" I have been promised vision. Why am I not rejoicing?

The next day the translator asked the Entities about the prolonged fever and they only said, "Cleansing; we are watching it. Sit in my Current." Through the three Casa days, I struggled to carry my fever-weakened body into the Entities' Current Room, sit there during the sessions, and then return to bed.

Our conditioning to move toward comfort and away from pain goes deep. It's not just related to the physical body. I went to the dining room for meals; sat in silence either alone or with others at the table, and felt the yearning for connection. This was not a personality level issue. I saw the deep separation we have, each in our own skins, each trying to connect with one another; but often failing. I think we each carry a memory of experience on a plane where there was total communication, before we moved into these insulated minds and bodies. We yearn to return there. Where is love? Where is God?

I see the ways I've transcended the existential pain I experienced that week through loving relationships, deep meditation, service, and connection with spirit. There is much authentic joy and meaning in my life, and I honor it.

Those experiences are the fruits of skillful choices for the most part, but during that week I also remembered the ways I had coped in the first years after losing my hearing, by closing my heart to isolation and pain. My heart now was much more open than it was in those first years, and the pain is mostly impersonal, but I also saw the habit energy that remained. When an experience was painful, I would subtly close myself and move into an insulated space of joy. I may have stepped into a meditative space, or into creative work or physical activity; each of these was meant to restore the feeling of connection. Thus, I consciously chose connection, a wholesome choice, but I did it while turning my back on pain. Such movement freed me from the need to open the heart enough to investigate the pain.

Aaron talked a lot that year about the pole meditation. He emphasized that we must hold both spaces. "On the ultimate level, everything is fine; while on the relative level, everything is shaky, unbalanced, and falling apart. You cannot hide out in the ultimate, feeling that everything is fine and turning your back on the human experience; but you also cannot get lost in the human experience and insist that everything is fine. ... You cannot hide in either space and still do the work for which you came into the incarnation. You need to hold the whole pole; to be deeply connected with the human experience and deeply connected with that which is whole and radiant— that divine essence of your being." That week I saw how easy it was for me to shift to the top of the pole, where there is peace, ease, and joy, regardless of the relative experience. Then the mind and body are abandoned. As I watched to see when I made that shift, I realized it was an almost automatic reaction to discomfort.

Lying there on my bed at the Casa that week in February of 2005, my heart broke open in compassion for the human experience of isolation; each of us caught in our own skins and in our own minds. Wisdom knows this is illusion, for nothing is truly separate; but it's the illusion to which we are all prone. When I become the pole, as Aaron would phrase it, I find a much deeper level of peace because nothing needs to be excluded. I find a new ease. Resting in the ultimate need not be an escape. Such resting does not end pain, but stretches the heart so that there is space for the pain, and therefore no need to avoid it.

In early March, I returned from Brazil. Tests at the retinal clinic confirmed the vision improvement. The right eye vision had shifted from 20/400 to 20/50; the left eye had, with glasses, changed from 20/100 to 20/20. There was real joy at this gift of restored vision, but I still had to battle the impulse to read during eighteen more days of restriction. By now I understood the reading rule as a gift from the Entities. When the impulse arose I found more ability to pause and ask myself, "Is there any experience the heart wishes to avoid?" The answers varied; there may have been tension, aloneness, or body discomfort. Even deep silence sometimes came as an answer; wanting distraction from that place where ego dissolves. I found myself better able to make space for these discomforts. With deeper presence, there was less of an impulse to escape the human experience.

Journal, March 21, 2005

Today is "reading day." This morning I read the front page of the newspaper. I am typing this page myself. It isn't as big an event as I had anticipated it would be. It's a delight to read, but the energy around it is different. All of our actions are a result of a variety of conditions, some based in love and some in fear. The slowing down required in the last six weeks enabled me to better see the conditions unfold, to release identity with those more based in fear, and to act in many of the same ways from a more loving place.

As I look back on this second Casa trip and the weeks that followed, I feel enormous gratitude to spirit. Both Aaron's and the Casa Entities' support was invaluable. I never would have brought myself into that lonely situation with conscious resolve, but it was clearly exactly what was needed. There was greater ease with difficult experiences, and more trust of such experiences. I began to understand the Entities' processes better. My intention was to heal, but also to learn and to serve others. The Entities hear all my intentions and help to show them to the conscious mind. Together, the Entities and I then cocreate the highest healing possible, on all levels.

Three months after returning from Brazil, the retinal specialist at the eye hospital said there were erratic blood vessels growing in the right eye, and that unless he removed them with laser surgery, I would certainly lose all vision, despite the fact that it was so much improved. He is a specialist; I decided to allow the surgery.

Journal, May 2005

The surgery on the right eye at the hospital was Thursday. Friday when the bandage was removed, there was no vision in the right eye again, just light and dark. Despair comes. I'm not able to say "Thy will be done." I don't want to be blind. It scares me. Yes, I can do it if it is necessary, but I don't want it. And I find myself asking, "What am I doing wrong? If I'm working with this situation skillfully, why did the vision fail again?"

Testing revealed that my right eye vision had degraded to 20/400. Meanwhile, the left eye started bleeding again. Several months of treatment by steroid injections in the right eye caused a cataract, which was surgically removed. None of this brought any improvement in vision. I had come full circle; after losing my vision I had healed. Now I had lost my vision again. It led to new internal struggles, which were by now becoming a familiar pattern. My journal continues:

I know that this is all just fear. I don't know how to rest in the faith and deeper knowing that all is well and that all will be well. Love knows that anything else is just the ego. Life will be full, vision or not. But there's such sadness at the idea of loss of the function of this eye.

Jeshua and Aaron tell me that I will not be blind. They also tell me some or much hearing will come back. The ego needs to let go and allow what is to come, to come as it will. But love does choose wholeness. Why should it be necessary to be deaf, to be blind, when the wholeness is right here, as close as the next breath? How can it be loving to allow that distortion? How can it be divine will to hold that distortion?

Through the next few months I was able to let go of struggle at least partially. Thankfully, the rest of my body continued to heal from the wave accident, so I could walk well again, and was mostly free of back, facial, and neck pain. I continued the tuning fork work, and reached a point where these deaf ears could differentiate the notes within the octave and I could repeat them with my voice. I was able to see many relevant past lives, to release much fear and resolve old karma, but my eyes still did not heal. The question still came, "What was I doing wrong?" Maybe if I did everything "right," the healing would happen. I was grasping after physical healing. This grasping arose out of a subtle state of fear and confusion. When I addressed the grasping—seeking equanimity with the losses, as Aaron had trained me to do—I ended up with resignation, which is a low energy, negative state. I was stuck.

Is healing really possible? Doubt arose. My beloved spirit friend Jeshua said to me (through Judith Coates, through whom he speaks), *"That which you can manifest you can unmanifest, very well."* Was I to disbelieve Him, whom I so deeply trust?

How do we manifest? How do we unmanifest, or release distortion and return to the Ever-Perfect? So much of this is about beliefs, and at some level, I continued to hold a belief in limitation, and the idea that something had to be fixed. Jeshua said to me of the swollen right eye: *"Visualize the swelling decreasing, see the appearance minimizing, the unneeded excess flowing/draining away. Know that it is returning to its perfect size and condition. Know it. Use My knowing, if you desire."*

Journal, 2005

I realized immediately as I read Jeshua's words that the eyes are already perfect, but keep expressing the distortion. Then I'm led directly to the old attitudes that underlie the distortion. As long as I keep bringing forth old attitudes of fear and limitation, they provoke the re-expression of the physical plane distortion, which further reinforces fear. It becomes an endless circle.

What needs most to be released then is not the distortion, which is a result, but the attitude, which is more directly the cause. The attitude is also a result, old conditioning that believes in linearity, and in an unrelenting karma.

Looking at all of this, it feels like this trip to Brazil was to remind me once more of our innate perfection, to rest in this space of love and wholeness, to feel gratitude for all we're given, and just to deepen the capacity to hold love and faith. It seems there is nothing else that I need to do. The eyes are healed. The deafness is healed. The outer expression of healing will be fast or slow, or even nonexistent, in whatever way it happens. I surrender the desire to want control over the outer process. I rest in love. I rest in knowing the innate perfection of everything. When the doubting mind and fear come to visit, I just note them and smile. They're only habit.

But habits run deep. There was much confusion around making a free will choice; how to state what I choose and know it as already present, without the denial of relative reality.

Aaron said to me:

You are still holding a duality between the Ever-Perfect and the expression. The eyes present a distorted expression, swelling, bleeding. You cannot deny that reality, but must attend to it on the physical level, as you are doing through traditional and energetic medical intervention.

To hold that as a "real" condition is important, but do not mistake the distortion for the true condition of the eyes. As long as you "fix," you repeatedly return the eyes to the distortion out of disbelief in the innate perfection. The work is to hold the simultaneity of distorted and Ever-Perfect and, as Jeshua has instructed, "visualize the swelling as decreasing, see the appearance minimizing, the unneeded excess flowing/draining away. Know that it is returning to its perfect size and condition." "Know it," He says. "Use My knowing, if you desire," thereby releasing the distortion so that only the Ever-Perfect remains. This is not denial of the distortion but knowing the nature of it, merely as an expression of the Ever-Perfect.

"Use My knowing" is an important phrase. When I use His knowing, I rest in pure awareness, which knows the innate perfection. There is no longer any need for faith; there is perfect knowing. "Use My knowing" also highlights that spiritual growth is at its essence an impersonal process—other beings are always available for guidance and support, and all share when one finds healing.

I wrote to Jeshua again, asking Him to tell more about how He healed others and Himself. Perhaps he could teach me. He replied in part:

> "Beloved one,
>
> "You have come so far. Yet you still hold me to be above and better than you. There is no difference between us: 'That which I do, you will do, and even greater things will you do.' There is but one consciousness, nonduality, which does function even in this world of seeming duality. The perfection that you seek, even of body, is yours right now. You have discerned well that the karmic residue is of belief.
>
> "The Father and I are One, as you are. Does the Father know limitation? It is not divine will that you should suffer or be in any way hindered."

My meditation practice had taught me to rest in awareness, in a centered space that is largely egoless, and from that space, to know the Ever-Perfect. Years earlier, Aaron had led a three-year healing class for body workers in which he emphasized this process, going to the Ever-Healed and reflecting it back to the distortion, inviting the distortion to resolve. For although the distortion is "real" on the physical level, on the deepest level there has never been distortion.

He used the image of a perfect underground spring of pure water. The water pours out of an opening, and down a slope to form a stream. A mile down, the water has become muddied. He asked, "Where is the pure water? Can you see it there in the muddy shallows?" Yes, the water is muddied, but the pure water is also there. One must filter it in order to drink, but there's no need to go back to the spring. Just filter out the mud.

When we are fixated on healing the distortion, we often fail to see the Ever-Healed. Aaron has repeated the phrase so often, "Right here with the anger is that which is not angry, but loving. Right here with fear is fearlessness." The practice involves holding both, knowing the anger, fear or body distortion but not getting caught up in the idea that that's all there is. So we must learn to be present with both relative and ultimate reality. Neither is more real. Neither is more important. But only by holding both can we refrain from becoming "fixers" with grasping energy, which sabotages the true healing. Instead we can relax, invite, and open into the Ever-Healed. Fear and grasping will arise. When we become caught in them, and fail to see the nondual truth of the distortion and Ever-Healed, we simply perpetuate the karma and the distortion.

I learned more about this through the experience of the frequent pictures taken of my eyes. The radiologist would insert dye into my arm vein through an IV needle. It caused immediate nausea and vomiting. Through that discomfort, I'd sit with my chin in a frame while he took pictures of the eyes. It got so that as soon as the doctor asked for pictures, I'd begin to feel nauseous, long before I reached the photography room. Ironically, the picture session itself was not painful.

During one appointment I sat for a while in the outer room, terribly nauseous and dreading the dye injection. After a time, I was able to see the experience of nausea arising from the body's conditioning, and also to know the place of no nausea. I sent loving thoughts to this body and the discomfort it was experiencing because of its conditioning. I stopped fighting with the body and just let it be as it was. By the time I was called in for the tests, the nausea had settled somewhat.

The radiologist inserted the dye, but this time the resulting nausea was just nausea—I wasn't upset. I could see the part of myself that was not nauseous right there with the nausea. There was no vomiting. The next time I needed this test, no nausea arose until the dye was put in, and then only briefly. No vomiting. Presence with ultimate and relative depends on nonseparation. I had been separating from my body, so had not allowed this settled and open level to show itself. This was not a miraculous cure of a life-threatening disorder, but this small experience demonstrated to me once again that a measure of ease and peace, even healing, was genuinely possible and attainable through the techniques and meditation practices I was learning.

We can learn to maintain connection with both relative and ultimate experiences when we move past the need to separate from painful things. I began to understand this many years ago during a challenging situation while traveling to lead a retreat.

The night before the retreat, I stayed in a house where one person had a drinking problem. He got drunk that night and at 2:00 a.m. woke us all up cursing, raging, and breaking apart furniture and a large glass mirror. I have rarely experienced such raw rage, fear, and grief, from the drunken young man and others who witnessed the scene. Yet it was also a relief because it was so honest!

I saw the reactions in myself, wanting to disassociate myself from the pain because it mirrored my own. I saw how I've chosen and maintained normalcy, how that kept the reality of brokenness at bay. My parents, husband, and children don't drink or throw furniture at one another. But both wholeness and that brokenness and despair are in ALL of us. Part of it is an existential despair and part of it is personal, based in our own karma, personality, and psychological makeup. Much is healed in me now; by "healed" I mean there is no longer self-identification with the emergent thoughts. Thus, the texture is different: without self to it, such thoughts lead me to compassion. Sadness, which remains, deepens connection rather than enhances separation.

My understanding of healing changed that night, or rather, I consciously saw in a new way, something I have not verbalized before. We're never fully healed. Healing isn't the doing away of those old reverberations of fear but total peace with them when they surface.

The drunken son left about 6:00 a.m. and the parents and sister began to sweep up, saying, "It's only glass, china, whatever. ..." What numbness was there? What right have I to make any attempt to draw them out of that numbness? What fears did I have that led me to wish to join into their numbness?

It was clear that they all loved one another. However, there was also tremendous hostility, fear and betrayal from one to another. None of them could see it. The young man was too drunk for coherence so I was speaking with the family. I saw that the only way to hear them and help them to hear one another was to hear all of my own fear. This was my son, my husband or father. I was these parents and siblings. How do we find compassion and forgiveness for all the denials and defenses of our own lives? How do we keep our hearts open to all that pain? How do we learn that we can't always do that, and that that also is okay? We really are fine, just as we are. With that insight, I took a broom and began to sweep.

Aaron said to me later: *The work is to hold both: the real pain and that which is truly beyond pain. There is nothing to fix, only love to be offered; yet one must still sweep up the ruins, embrace those who weep, and be fully present as a human. At first as the young man was raging, you believed that you had to fix the situation, but there was no way to touch his anger or the family's fear and grief. When you tried to fix it, it seemed to backfire, creating a gap between those who suffered and you who did not. Only when you acknowledged that this was your family, your sons and parents, and stopped fixing—just opened the heart and were present knowing the fear and sadness—could you also touch that which is not sad or afraid in the self, that of unconditional love. Then your calmness and centeredness allowed them to find their own calmness, to talk to the young man in ways that could reach him and to one another in ways that took them beyond despair.*

I was reminded of experiences from the 1960s when I had lived in New York City. My Fourth Street storefront studio near the Bowery had a recessed doorway; in the morning there were often drunk bodies in that small shelter. I had gotten into a habit of serving a pot of coffee, my attempt to fix the pain. Then I'd go back inside and lock the door, lock myself safely away from their difficulties. The situation overwhelmed me; I didn't know what else to do.

Walking through the neighborhood on a recent visit had brought these memories back. I had not been there in many years. I remembered seeing clearly so many years ago how much I was keeping my own fear at bay, how hard I had to work to justify working behind that locked door, denying the reality of cold and hungry bodies outside, feeling angry and helpless. I couldn't allow the reality in, that I was not separate from these drunk and homeless men; it was me shivering out there on the pavement. Here was the reality of my own suffering.

While I'm sure my coffee was welcomed, I realized then that it also enhanced separation, that I was assuaging my guilt and hiding from myself by being "the good helper." I was holding on to my illusion of personal nonsuffering. I remembered how uncomfortable I'd been thirty years earlier with helpless feelings and with my own fears, and the seeming dishonesty of covering up by serving coffee, trying to make it all normal.

We must be willing to acknowledge our fears and the desire to escape. At a meditation retreat[1] at the beach, Aaron gave instructions:

Energy contracts and releases. That is the nature of energy. The contraction is motion. At the end of the release is stillness. There is space in both motion and stillness. You have learned how to rest in awareness and watch mundane consciousness observe the arising of conditioned objects and the unconditioned space between. Mundane consciousness cannot perceive the unconditioned aspect but awareness can. Thus there is seeing on two levels. Mundane consciousness perceives the conditioned expression of space. Awareness knows the unconditioned essence of space.

I want you to try an experiment with me. I'd like you to think of something painful, unpleasant. Think about it as if it were really approaching you, a person you don't like, whom you see walking down the beach, a big storm blowing in from the sea, or sharp pain in the body that might be building up. Feel the tension around it. Allow yourself to feel contraction. I want you to be able to label, "This is contraction."

(long pause.)

Now release it. Send it on its way with the wind.

Now bring in a very pleasant thought. Something joyful, perhaps a thought of gratitude: how wonderful it is to be sitting on this beautiful beach sharing the dharma together. What a gift! Feel the joy. Can you feel the spaciousness in your body? Can you feel that it is a very different experience than the contraction?

Resting in awareness, when your painful thought comes, see if contraction pulls you out of awareness. If so, the instruction is to ask, "Is there anything here that is other than the Unconditioned?"

Your ability to answer that question is dependent upon your meditation practice, at first. If I addressed the question to somebody who doesn't have any clue about what the Unconditioned is, they can't say, "Yes, this is an expression of the Unconditioned." How would they know that? What is the Unconditioned?

But when you've done some meditation practice and have rested in that space and had glimpses of the Unconditioned, you start to be able to answer with more certainty. This negative thought, this angry or grudging thought, it's just an expression of the Unconditioned. This itch, this heat or cold, it's only the Unconditioned expressing itself in myriad ways. You have learned not to create something separate. You know such thought is just the dualistic, mundane mind reciting its mantra.

So you have periods of time where there is the ability to touch deeply on awareness, to respond to the world from awareness, but then boom! Something happens. You snap back into the everyday mind. The self returns and with it, karma returns.

Here is an example. Let's say that you've been sitting, eyes opened, relaxed, nothing separate, very open and connected, experiencing a lot of joy. Objects are clear but there is no sense of a self and no fixation on what arises. Suddenly a very wet sandy dog leaps up onto your lap. You contract. You look at it; is there anything here that is not the Unconditioned? No. You relax and shift into awareness. And then the dog is licking your face, trying to climb on you. You move out of awareness again. There's irritation.

At this point we shift the practice, and bring attention to contraction itself. Can you see the light and space within the contracted experience? We literally release the contracted experience, and allow it to dissolve into light and space.

Now you can't think your way through this, so just like the baby learning to walk, we have to take some baby steps. You can't just say, "Now I'm going to release this." So we practice in a very specific way with light and space.

We begin by resting in awareness; deep presence. When something comes in and pulls you out of awareness, instead of asking, "Is there anything other than the Unconditioned that is present here?" and finding your way back to awareness, you bring attention to the nature and texture of the contraction.

Whatever out there drew you out of awareness, like a loud noise or the sloppy dog, the contraction itself becomes the primary object. The practice is to invite contraction to dissolve in light and space. Once the contraction is dissolved, if you find yourself back resting in awareness, that's fine. If not, begin again as if you were at the start of a sitting.

Even though this nonduality approach had been at the heart of my meditation practice for several years, I was unable to embody it completely. Each time feelings of despair arose from my deafness and impending blindness, I could see that which was openhearted and joyful, right there alongside the despair. However, the seeing alone didn't allow the despair and fear to dissolve. There was grasping that I could not fully attend to, as I was caught in the contracted space of a belief in limitations.

I could see that as soon as I slipped out of that space of nondual mind, I began to grasp and then pulled back with an almost scolding tone of, *No grasping.* To release this condition, the open heart must be fully accessible, and my heart wasn't yet that open. I still wanted to "get it right" so as to attain special results. Letting go was still only a concept.

Years ago Aaron had introduced the term "karmic residue." The karma is no longer directly related to the eyes and ears. It is karma related to a belief in limitations, to a fear of letting go, and to the process of separating myself in order to protect myself. It is presently manifesting itself through the eyes and ears. Old attitudes and emotions are being expressed and are offering an opportunity for release through the eyes and ears. The predominant attitude is an old belief in limitations, held in place by the fear and anger of karmic ancestors, and is literally being held in the cellular tissues of the body. The good news is that this situation offers the perfect opportunity for release and balancing of the old karma.

Journal, 2005

I sat a half hour in the chapel of the retreat center, which I entered for a period of prayer before sleep. I was in the near darkness behind one of my students who was weeping. All I could do was to offer silent, loving prayer to support her through her grief. It's a simple, modern chapel, with a large crucifix in the front, a figure of Jeshua in much agony. Tonight, I saw that the pull we feel for that image is because it represents our human agony. We feel less alone when we see it. And Jeshua transcended the experience, reminding us that we also can transcend the conditions of human ignorance and fear, and can ascend into nondual consciousness.

I sat behind this crying woman feeling my heart closed a bit, going through the proper motions of offering love (silently; we weren't talking or touching). But I have been noticing today the subtle separation I create: *Not my suffering.* . . . The heart is not yet fully opened to it. I wonder: what is this suffering that I don't want to see?

Aaron speaks of opening as compared to a "dimmer switch." The light is definitely on, but not completely. What does it mean to turn my heart-light fully on? Can any of us do that in human form? Yet, I know that Jeshua did. How much more can I love? What blocks that love?

What would it mean to allow complete intimacy with the world? These situations I have remembered show me where I can break through the belief in old limitations and open more fully. Like the deafness and possible greater vision impairment, that intimacy is also fully there on one level; only the belief in limitations prevents its expression. I must stay with both the ultimate truth of already existent full openness and the relative experience of closure.

It isn't necessary to resolve all limitations in order to demonstrate either deep love of the human condition and compassion for it, or the ability to transcend that human condition. I can accept this seeming limit and still move ahead in faith, doing what needs to be done.

INTERVAL V
Mediumship

Since much of this book derives from a discarnate spirit talking through me, and since the healing work at the Casa would not be possible without spirit having a willing human to work through, a brief discussion about mediumship seems appropriate. João is a trance medium, a person through whom spirit can work and speak by fully incorporating into the physical human body. João is unaware of the body while the entity is incorporated. Other forms of mediumship are done while the medium is conscious.[1] When you have an intuitive sense about something, you—the ego-based human—are probably serving as a medium for your own higher self, that wisest aspect of your being. In fact we're all mediums, but most of us have never learned to nurture this skill. We all have access to spirit plane guidance and can learn to hear that guidance for ourselves. Some gardeners seem to hear the needs of the plants they raise; some people are able to hear animals quite clearly. Some people have a close connection and intuitive sense about weather; others seem forewarned about dangers. Artists of every genre are often serving as mediums for their highest self or an external guide. These are all forms of mediumship.

The past twenty years of my life, and João Teixeira de Faria's extraordinary healing work, are both powerful testimonies to the reality of spirits and the spirit world. They can communicate with us, if we can learn to hear them. Aaron says that the door is always open from their side. It is we who have not learned to perceive spirit presence. In the many workshops I've led on how to channel, I have found that most people are capable of hearing their guides and/or higher self clearly. The issue is usually less one of skill, than of trust. We are so doubtful that although we hear, we find it difficult to believe that it is real.

What is the benefit of hearing our guides? In some ways, we are much like a person, newly experiencing blindness, who is still staggering around the Earth plane with a not yet developed sense of direction. We agree to come into the incarnation, but forget our true nature and our reasons for incarnating. Aaron sometimes refers to this near universal human situation as the "veil of forgetfulness." Our guides can help us to remember why we came, help us to stay on track, and help us accomplish what we came to do.

Imagine yourself walking into a vast sea, water closing over your head, able to breathe with a breathing apparatus; but unable to see. Ahead of you is a complex maze on the surface of the water, through which you're asked to find your way. But you can't see. Your guide is like a figure sitting on your shoulders, head out of the water, with clear vision and who can point out the way. Our higher selves have clarity, and a broader perspective.

Why would we incarnate with this "veil of forgetting?" We are here in large part to learn faith, not to walk a path of blind obedience through the forced suppression of choice. If everything were clear to us, the question would only be whether we were willing to follow the track that lay before us even if it looked steep and rocky. But even with spirit guidance, the way is never perfectly clear; therefore, all we can do is to open our hearts and step ahead with as much love as is possible. So we can learn to open to the guidance available to us, and to let it shine a light on an otherwise dark path.

I have spoken in previous chapters of positive and negative polarity. When we open ourselves to spirit, it is vital that we first state our intention, be it service to self or service to all beings. This step is a bit like sending out invitations to a party. To whom do we wish to send the invitation, that angry crowd who gathers on the street corner to dispense hate literature, or those folks with whom we perform volunteer service work?

Once we decide whom to invite, we open our energy to receive, but we also challenge. This would be like having a watchman at the door to check, "Are you really from the service group, or are you someone from the hate group in disguise?" I've found that the best way to challenge is to state my own highest truth, and ask, "Do you come in harmony with these values?" If the watchman at the door states that only soft drinks are being served, the one seeking whiskey will probably choose to go elsewhere.[2]

Each of us has to find our own statement. I use the challenge, "Do you come in service to all beings, with love for all beings, and with no intention for harm, but only for the highest good?" I often add that my own energy is consecrated to the Christ and the Buddha and that none may speak through me who is in opposition to the values that They cherished and taught. If I feel any hesitation on that entity's part, I stop. I make it clear that such a being may listen if it wishes, but may not speak. Then I invite again.

Negativity may show up. It is important not to listen to it, but it's also important not to fear it. It is simply a sign that points to something unresolved in the self. If I say that I want to channel in service to all beings, but there exists an unconscious fear that my needs will not be met, that suppressed feeling provides an access for negativity. When I am honest with myself and acknowledge any fears or other heavy emotions, it disempowers those emotions. They have arisen; but they will pass away. I don't build a self-image around them.

When I first met Aaron, he was speaking just to me. But soon friends began to ask if they could talk to him. My fear about channeling him wasn't about Aaron, whom I already deeply trusted. It was about my own ego and fear that it would distort Aaron's words. To channel Aaron well, I needed to clear my own energy field.

One day at a workshop a man began to talk about his past as a child abuser. At some level I judged him, even though I heard him say that he had stopped this pattern, was seeking forgiveness for the harm he had done, and was seeking to balance the karma through service. I have heard so much pain from people who have experienced childhood sexual abuse that my heart closed. So when I channeled Aaron's reply, I could feel my own anger and judgment, which created a kind of static around Aaron's thoughts. I had to tell the seeker that I needed time with his questions and to ask him to repeat his question the next day. That night I spent many hours in meditation, and doing lovingkindness meditation to all who had suffered abuse of any sort. I also offered forgiveness meditation for the abusers, who in turn were often previously abused themselves. Slowly my heart opened again. It was a wonderful lesson for me and I recognized the gift that he had brought to me. The next day I was able to channel Aaron clearly for this man.

Channeling has often pointed me directly to the places where I've been stuck and asked me to release those emotions; for the alternative is to channel without clarity, and thereby to risk doing harm inadvertently. Channeling for others asks total honesty of me, and that's not always easy.

When we serve as mediums for spirit for ourselves, it's easier because we're not about to harm another being if we're not clear. This is how we start, and most people use their mediumship skills only for themselves, to hear their own guidance. Still, if we follow guidance of a spirit that intends harm or even just mischief, it can bring us much pain.

Among other functions, the Casa is a training ground for mediums. People sitting in the Current Rooms often begin to hear the Entities and also to hear their own guides. The power of the Currents supports our energetic opening to spirit. I also find that the people who come to the Casa have at least considered the real possibility that the Casa Entities are real as they speak through Medium João, and do their healing work. If the Casa Entities are real, then their own guides must also be real. With this understanding, people become more willing to trust the guidance they hear.

Self-responsibility is important here. The Casa Entities are happy to help us, but also wish us to learn to help ourselves. As we learn to hear our guides and our higher selves, we can make wiser and more loving choices for our own healing and for the good of all beings. This is a healing beyond that of the body; it is an opening into the integration of body, mind, and spirit; a movement toward wholeness.

When I first met Aaron, and began to listen to him for myself and to make his guidance available to other people, the technique to which he led me was conscious channeling. I used and refined this method for many years. Simply put, I would hear Aaron's thoughts in my head. If Aaron was talking to someone else, then I would express those thoughts in words. My part was to find an appropriate phrasing to fit the thought. If Aaron wasn't happy with my choice, he would ask me to try again. When I channeled I was briefly aware of the material as it flowed through me, but I could only focus on getting each phrase correct. There was no time or energy to focus on content. So channeling took a lot of effort, constant concentration, and presence. This was a gift for many years, deepening my ability to stay present. But it was also a strain, especially over a long session.

During my second visit to the Casa, I spoke to the Entities in meditation about my exhaustion after channeling and asked for help to become a clearer instrument, and to be able to do the work without depleting myself. They told me that with the conscious channeling I was bringing two diverse energies into the body at once, and that this was harming the body. When we hear our own guides, they are not so much in the body; there is just the hearing of them. But Aaron was coming part way into my body so the body was carrying his higher vibrational frequency and my lower one simultaneously.

And there was the additional strain of the strenuous effort required to hear and translate his thought into precise words. The Entities suggested that I learn to leave the body and allow Aaron to fully occupy it, so that only one frequency was in the body at any one time. This also allows people to make eye contact with Aaron, since with conscious channeling, my eyes were closed.

How would I do this? There was a training period where I heard one of the Entities giving me instructions. I needed to have the teacher be someone other than Aaron so that I was not with his energy in the usual way, as that would have blocked the letting go that was needed in order to empty the body. Aaron told me later that the same Entity was instructing him on when to come in, for the first few times.

At the beginning there was some fear; where would I go? How would I get back? But Aaron seemed very comfortable with the idea and encouraged me, and I trust him fully. The first experience was confusing. Had I really been out of the body and Aaron in it? Others verified that this was their experience.

I soon realized that the most challenging part of this new mode of mediumship is that my body is empty for a brief moment, as I vacate it and before Aaron enters it. This means that it is vulnerable during that period, and is protected mostly by the power of my love and positive intention. It's like leaving a house door open. If there are gin bottles littering the doorway, someone different may be attracted to enter than if there are flowers. This fact has served as a further catalyst for me to be sure that I am clear of any negativity. Before I open the body to Aaron, I meditate and make sure that I'm not holding any anger, fear, or other deep negativity that would invite in someone who wished to use the body to do harm. That doesn't mean there is no negativity, only that I've acknowledged it and am certain that it's not the strongest force operative in that moment. If negativity is present, I send it loving wishes and watch to be sure that my mind is quiet. My final statement before I release the body to Aaron is "This body (meaning, these physical, emotional, mental, and spiritual bodies) is consecrated to the light." I rarely get through the whole statement before he comes in.

While this process applies to formal channeling for me, it's also something each of us needs to watch in our lives, for we're all channeling something, if only the ego or the higher self. Before we speak and act we should strive to be as clear as possible, and be certain that our words and actions are coming from a place of love and an intention to cause no harm.

The channeling itself is much easier now. I no longer have to think of the words to fit Aaron's thoughts. There is almost no perception of the body. I rarely feel discomfort or a need to move, eat, drink, or use a toilet. There is no perception of time; there is just a small bit of awareness able to respond when Aaron needs a precise English word and searches my mind for it. I'm simply resting in a light-filled space, in deep meditation until he comes to get me. Then awareness touches on Aaron's energy reaching for me, inviting me back to the body. I find that I can channel for many more hours this way and not be exhausted afterwards.

Now that he's fully in the body, the eyes are open and he has rich dialogues with people; individuals and groups. There is no longer a need for me to come out of the trance, lip-read the person's question, and return to trance. He also gets up and walks around. On several occasions he put my sweet, light tea aside and made himself a cup of black tea, which I don't enjoy. I've learned to make the tea he prefers if he is going to be in the body. For the most part, when he's in the body, physical needs disappear. There is no thirst or hunger or need to use the bathroom. He does sip tea or water if the throat becomes dry and scratchy at a long session.

Aaron and the Entities are just beginning to lead me into a new step in the mediumship process, to fully give the body over to Aaron yet to also stay present so that he can use my memories, vocabulary, and energy to support the process. At these times I'm aware of his presence in the body and that he's speaking, though with no personal connection to what he's saying. I am aware of the content in the moment, but it isn't retained afterwards. But during this form of channeling, he occasionally asks me to supply a word, or simply to send loving energy to the person to whom he is speaking. I do see the benefit of this method as, with my free will directing of my energy, I can enhance the process; for example, by sending energetic support or loving thoughts to a listener who is feeling pain or by allowing Aaron to inquire into my mind for a specific English word. Remember, English is not his native language.

CHAPTER 17

Supporting Karmic
Resolution and Balancing

THROUGHOUT 2005, in between my second and third trips to the Casa, my right eye was blind and I was still deaf. I spent much time dealing with the unresolved karma of this and past lives. As I have discussed before, there are two parts to the resolution and healing of karma: releasing and balancing. Once I expressed a clear intention to resolve the karma, Aaron and the Entities began to further support the healing of the physical, emotional, and mental bodies. This healing in turn supported karmic resolution, and allowed balancing to begin. All of these processes allowed me to attend to the karma more effectively. I was beginning to more clearly understand the processes behind the transformations I was undergoing. Much of the spiritual focus around this time centered on my immediate past life and the question, "What do I not want to hear?"

In a period of intense meditation I stated again the intention to hear, if that is for the highest good, and asked what blocks the healing of the ears. Again there was the memory shared in Chapter 12, of the death of a recent ancestor who died when his ship was violently sunk in World War One. *Dying; can't breathe,* as I've seen often before. I had an acute memory of the explosions, the screams of the maimed and dying, and of the great aversion to hearing all of that. It felt like I was watching this karmic ancestor as observer, rather than living his experience.

Aaron asked me to "breathe more deeply." I did so for a short while. Then he asked me to stop breathing, to feel the man's lack of breath as fire burned away the oxygen on the surface of the sea. I did, ceasing the breath; no air, no oxygen. I had a sense of darkness; there was no fear, just grief, and no breath. I was still hearing the explosions and screams. I felt cold; very cold. At some level there was the observation that although he was losing consciousness through oxygen deprivation as the flames burned, he was still hearing the terrible sounds. The noting was strong; seeing both the experience and the aversion. It was spacious in that way; awareness was not identified with my ancestor as a self, but there was deep compassion for him.

The scene shifted again, cold and dark, but no more screams or noise. I could feel my ancestor very closed off, his consciousness retreating into a small safe spot. I rested a short while and then Aaron asked me to focus again.

Here was my opportunity to release the karma involved in not wanting to hear the screams, and in wanting to close off consciousness from unpleasant experiences. But karma is specific; there was more.

I observed how he found himself out of the body; hovering above the body and seeing it floating on the water, and then sinking. There were so many corpses, not just his. I felt his rage and grief very briefly, then a sense of his disgust of the body. He was leaving it but where was he going?

My ancestor was aware of light but he was too closed off to reach for it. His identity with the body kept him trapped in the body, repugnant, heavy, and dark, sinking. Present awareness noted "Bardo state."* Here, I was identifying a part of the Bardo where conscious-

---

*Bardo states are the states between death and rebirth.

ness moves between lives; I noted "thinking," let it go, and then returned to the breath.

As I focused on the breath, I felt intense energy. I remembered the chakra exercise that I described in Interval II and had the impulse to combine it with the chanting described in Chapter 15. As the base chakra was full of red light and was spinning, an inner voice told me to chant the tone of that chakra, a C, as a full, rich "Om." I tried a few tones and felt one that seemed to support a deeper vibration of that chakra, and make it spin faster. I repeated it many times, louder, clearer, until I was certain of it.

Then I left the base chakra spinning and went on to bring orange light into the sacral chakra. When the light felt full and the chakra was spinning, I felt directed to chant the tone D this time. It was easier to find. The chakra responded, spinning faster with openness and vital energy. The solar plexus opened and started spinning easily with E; the heart chakra was more difficult. I was moved to switch from the F tone to the chant *Kyrie Elaison; Christe Elaison* ("Lord have mercy; Christ have mercy").

I felt myself flooded with body memories, walking in a line of monks of hundreds of years ago, chanting these words. I felt the heart open and found the correct tone. Often I felt moved to touch the outer area of a chakra on the body, just a gentle touch with fingertips. The touching process helped me to be certain of the correct tone.

The process continued up through the crown chakra and finally the upper chakra above the crown. I sat for about another ten minutes chanting to the chakras. I was able to "hear" these sounds in my head and body in a way I have not heard for at least thirty-three years.

Then I felt high energy. I recognized Aaron and several of the Casa Entities. They said they wanted to work on my ears and nerves. They asked me to lie down. Occasionally they asked me to chant the whole range of chakra tones. As I chanted, I was asked to move a light touch from one chakra to another and hold them until told to release. I felt the Entities' energy move through my hands. But mostly I just rested while they worked, hearing many tones in my head.

Here was the healing of my karmic ancestor's self-identification with the body and its experiences. Instead of closing down into a belief in limitation and death, there was an opening of energy and an awareness of choice. Now he is released to move through the Bardos, to begin a move toward the light. My conscious understanding of what my ancestor experienced, my work to open my energy field, and the Entities' work with the karma held in my body's cells, all contributed to a positive outcome. I was ready to look more deeply than I had before.

Finally I was told it was sufficient. The energy field was open and the heart was ready to see deeper, to allow that which I had held away. I lay still a few minutes, then Aaron asked me to pick up the meditation again, and to focus on the breath and be present with any image that arose. I began to see through the eyes of that karmic ancestor again, seeing his body dying in the water, seeing the other bodies, and aware of all the sounds of explosions and screams. I could feel his revulsion for the body again, and how he shut himself away; shut off sound. He moved through the Bardo states, moving toward light, but insulated in a way; not allowing full contact with anything or anyone, protecting, closed. I could see the source of radiant light at a distance and his decision not to approach that very high vibration. I understood that I came into this incarnation from that barricaded place; I had never released it.

I was shown something different, and he was allowed to see it through my (Barbara's) willingness to see, which was the cherishing of these dead bodies. On the sea were just the material remains but their energetic essence, their etheric bodies, were raised up and taken into the light. I watched with awe and love, as did the ancestor. The taking up was so tender, so loving. The essences were not just left discarded on the sea, but cherished. I could feel him open; feel the release of something that had been held in me too, throughout this lifetime.

I experienced enormous light, and was uncomfortable with the power of it. It is the light that will burn away everything of any heaviness or denseness. I have approached it, even entered far into it, but somewhere along the way I stop. This time I felt the presence of a great loving energy and I was able to accept the invitation.

All sense of self left then. There was nothing but light, very high energy, and heavenly music. Awareness spent some time there, before moving on to that place where destruction and creation meet, and through that to a place of stillness. Awareness rested there for some unknown period of time. There are no words for this "peace beyond understanding," but it is a familiar place. I've been there several times in meditation. I know the importance to stay in awareness here, not to get lost in the peacefulness.

I felt clarity far beyond words, of the nature of the Bardo states and passage through them. I saw more deeply into the nature of rebirth consciousness, and knew also that I had much more to learn. I also realized that the direct karmic ancestor was more healed, his trauma more released. Noting all of that, I allowed the eyes to open.

This meditation and the associated spiritual work set the foundation for deeper healing. Some karma was resolved. The next step, balancing, I am doing, in part, by writing this book.

When we don't heal, we can assume that something may be blocking the healing. When we ask to see that blockage, even if what we see is painful, we deepen the intention to understand and heal. We can use this intention toward resolution of the karma so that the karma doesn't serve as ground for a new area of distortion. The physical body may heal or may be beyond the ability to heal. Deeper healing is still possible.

As the karma releases, we are able to rest stably in increasingly higher levels of consciousness. Unwholesome karma equates with contraction, and with a lower vibration and consciousness. Freedom from unwholesome karma is a noncontracted state that allows higher vibration and consciousness. When the body doesn't heal, it is important to remember that we are not failures, and that we may have indeed found just the healing that we most needed.

We are spirit, here to grow and learn, here to support the higher consciousness to which we are all evolving. The distortions we carry, and even the karmic distortions, are our tools for learning. Speaking to a group, Aaron said:[1]

You are following a very beautiful path. You have moved through the entire illusion of duality in this and in past lives. You have struggled with believing the divine is out there and separate, believing you were not worthy to experience it; and then you have come to understand it's here, it's everywhere, and that the duality you believe in is a concept that you can transcend. But you cannot transcend it mentally; you must transcend it experientially.

We have come full circle. Once we knew nonduality, but as very young, innocent beings; much as a newborn doesn't experience a duality of self and parents. Then we tumbled off into the belief of duality, and have worked with the catalysts of fear, greed, hatred, and more. We have learned how not to succumb to such negativity. Now we are coming around to the other side of the circle, and we begin to see the possibility of nonduality again. But we cannot reenter that innocent nonduality of infancy. In the Biblical sense, we have tasted the apple in the garden.

Our present work is not to get rid of negativity and fear but to find the perfection in it, to find that which is whole, radiant, and beautiful. When we look at ourselves and see all the cracks and brokenness, we may now begin to know that we are perfect just the way we are. We still work to release distortion, but the innate core of radiant goodness cannot be lost and has never been lost.

It is not easy work. It takes enormous courage because our practice asks us now to look deeply at the brokenness and not to take it personally but rather to accept it as a gift, whether it be emotional wrinkles of negative thought, physical wrinkles of body distortion, or the mental wrinkles of outmoded belief.

Even when we open to deep insight in meditation, doubt can arise. We still tend to ask, "Is healing happening?" Here was a clue in dream form.

Journal, January 2005

Last night I had a beautiful dream. Earlier this week I had had several dreams about cars with flat tires, no brakes ... broken vehicles, unsafe to drive. Last night, near the sea, I had a sailboat to use. It was a little late, and the water was rough. Other people were coming in from sailing. I had just arrived and was overjoyed to see that I had a boat. I couldn't wait to try it out. People said not to sail out as it was late and might storm, but I just set up the boat, rigged it to be sure everything was in good shape, as it was, and looked forward to being able to sail the next day.

This dream said to me that the healing I had experienced was genuine and that I was ready to move ahead, to venture out to sea. The boat of healing consciousness and karma was sound and seaworthy. Tonight it might storm, but tomorrow it would be fair.

Several months later, I was preparing inwardly for my third trip to the Casa. Karma associated with past lives continued to be a focus:

Journal, December 2005

I asked Aaron, if we are soul mates, how did you get so far ahead of me? His reply led me to see a distant past life with our two souls coming in as twins. He was beside me in the womb. I saw fear in myself, as I pushed him aside to seek birth. He was not harmed, and waited patiently. We were born as healthy male twins. But at that point I created a self-view that limited my connection to the light because of a fear of misusing my power. We were loving brothers. Out of fear and shame, I constantly cut myself short and held myself back, while he constantly opened to the light, and thrived.

Since then I have made choices that cause me to hold on to limits and a lessened sense of self-worth. Thus I have held myself back from knowing my wholeness, and from enlightenment.

I knew this was one aspect of the karma that needed resolution now. To continue to hold myself from the light harms not only me, but also all other beings; as any one of us who holds back from expressing that radiance, diminishes it for all.

Several years ago in this present lifetime, a dying friend's final words to me were, "Finish it. Finish it for me." My friend was a meditation master in Sri Lanka; together we had reviewed the karma of numerous shared lifetimes. I've looked deeply at this phrase, "Finish it. ..." All karma must be cleansed and balanced; he would not have asked if this task were impossible. His words inspire me.

One night just after thinking of this friend, I had a clear feeling of the Entities' presence, energy work on the eye, and also Jeshua's presence. I experienced great love as a very high-energy vibration. Words came to me, "Forgive me, as I forgive you. ..." In order to heal completely, I need to let go of that whole karmic stream of feeling wrongness and holding to limits. That belief is what now limits the opening to healing. Let it go. But how do we let go? How do we find the strength to do the needed work? Through remembering that there is always support available to us.

Journal, Thursday, January 5, 2006

Last night I received a package from D, an exquisite prayer shawl in my favorite color of blue, hand knitted by his mother. In his note he said, "... it is a prayer shawl my mother gave me for Christmas, of royal baby alpaca. ... With each knit my mother said a prayer. Since my family was there when I opened the present, they said a prayer over it also. At that moment there wasn't much separation between giver, gift, or receiver ... Gratitude merged with generosity and there was joy. ... with me since at daily sittings. ... It is a very potent symbol of love to me, of precious gifts given unexpectedly. I don't have, nor will I ever likely have, another single object that I value more highly. I also know its value can only increase the more it is given away. I would love to give it to you for your trip to Brazil because it is the best I have to give. I want you to know that my prayers and joy go with you."

I was moved to tears when I opened it, aware of both the material beauty of the deep blue color and wonderful softness, and especially the love it conveyed, to D, and from him to me. I saw in it the mother love that regards all beings as "her child, her only child,"[2] wishes well-being, and holds all the world in her heart. But there was still a small voice inside that said, "I can't take this to Brazil. It could get lost or damaged there or in transit; too big to pack; too hot there to use it ..." I recognized that as the very old voice of fear, posing as practicality. There was still so much fear. But the learning continued:

Journal, January 6, 2006

So much has opened last night and this morning, sitting wrapped in this gift of deep love. The first image I had was that of my karmic ancestor, the young man Mark, who lived as an Essene in Galilee during Jeshua's Earthly ministry. He watched Jeshua's crucifixion with anger and despair, was later brutally blinded in one eye, and eventually crucified. I saw more deeply into his anger. He didn't have the advantage of the in-depth training that his father Aaron (named Nathaniel), and Jeshua had. Jeshua's crucifixion and the political turmoil that followed took Mark away from the Essene school at an age when he would have learned more. He couldn't heal the eye; he couldn't love the ones who had blinded him. He was angry with himself, with his father and with Jeshua. He felt betrayed because he believed that he had been asked to walk a path that he hadn't been enabled to follow.

I had previously written to Jeshua expressing the pain around not being able to follow Him, and the feeling that the young man Mark had failed Him. His response provided the comfort, inspiration, and wide perspective that naturally follow from great compassion:

Jeshua: "*The one known as Mark revered me and my teachings but he did not have the benefit of the trainings that I had. He knew only that he wished to serve me and to follow my example. His plan/contract was to release the body in the fashion that he did. You have carried the trauma of that experience with you throughout many lifetimes, feeling guilt and rage at self and me. But truly the demonstration that you were asked to do, and did do, was the demonstration of prolonged courage, much as it is in this lifetime. People witnessed your courage and your method of releasing the body. And they said, 'I could not do that,' yet you had the courage to do it, and still you judged self for what you called your weakness. It was in truth your strength.*

"This lifetime you again teach by example of great strength. You show ones how to go forward independently, although there would be seeming disability. It does not hold you back. And you give to others a great example of the strength and vitality of life itself."

But I wasn't feeling courageous. I was feeling quite helpless, resentful, and impatient in the weeks before the gift of the prayer shawl. It felt like there were numerous tasks ahead of me and that if only I could perform them adequately, I would be given the boon of hearing and seeing; as if this were another series of tests. It was at this time that my faith fell to its lowest point. I found within myself a deep rage, and also feelings of unworthiness that came with the inability to love unconditionally. My meditations took me to a profound knowing of Oneness, yet the human experienced separation. Sitting with that shawl of unconditional love wrapped around me broke through all the stories, and took me back to love.

Journal, January 6, 2006

Writing again later, wrapped in the prayer shawl; I see how I've used reason as armor throughout this lifetime. That state of connection, of noncontraction, is easy in meditation but risky in life. I approach it but never fully engage. It is that small separation that I've felt so often, the Oneness regarded as concept; as the ego comes forth yet again, with its schemes for self-protection.

Yet nothing less than this Oneness will allow the healing of the body or the heart. I see that I must bring the heart to Brazil and leave the brain at home. Logic, reason, the "what if my luggage gets lost," that all remains here. Just love and shawl come along. It is only that perfect love that can allow sight and hearing. The shawl is the doorway. I can walk through.

Journal, January 7, 2006

I sit wrapped in the shawl. Its magic continues; I had a very deep meditation today that has left me in a state of openhearted wonder and joy. Today was the first day of sunshine in the past ten days, and as dawn came the room was flooded with light. I began by chanting, and was asked to work with crystals too. In a few minutes I once again felt myself in the Circle of Blessed Ones. During my first visit to the circle, I took a vow to serve all beings, and to support their enlightenment and liberation. After such a vow I could no longer hide behind self-limiting beliefs and feelings of unworthiness even if I could not totally release them.

This morning I sat in that same circle for an unknown time, no-self, just that energy and light. I was returned to the circle today as a reminder of the Vow. No clinging to old limits and views for self-protection. The shawl was wrapped around me. I had the impulse to offer the ends to the circle; and it was big enough to go all the way around, "All beings, one body."[3] There was a sense of total merging within that blanket of love. The words to the Metta Sutta came again, "just as a mother protects with her life, her child, her only child. ..." There is only one child, and we are all that child, beloved of the Mother/Father/Divine. There is so much mother-love in this shawl.

The Christ Energy was part of the circle. Gradually the full circle faded so there was only Jeshua. *"Come with me,"* He said, and He held out His hands. I asked where we were going and was told it is a new baptism. I expected a sea again, actually saw the image of that sea and a wild surf; I drew back a bit from it, but then was told that that wasn't our destination. Backs to the sea, we entered a desert. The space was flooded with light and felt dry and hot. We walked what seemed like a long time, hard walking; Him in front, and me following with joy, but not without real effort.

Finally there was an adobe chapel, small from the outside but as we entered, it seemed huge and illuminated with a brilliant radiance. Some time was spent just sitting in that Light. I use the capital L because it was not an Earthly Light.

Then He spoke. *"This is a new baptism that is offered."* He explained that it is of a second level, beyond the first baptism of eighteen years ago, and beyond the Bodhisattva Vow of ten years ago; yet including both in some ways. In that vow there was still a self that took the vow. Now it must be love that takes it, and love that allows the fuller dissolution of the ego. The blanket symbolizes the merging, coming fully away from the self and into the circle, yet in the outer world the small self must also participate, as there is always free will at that level of self as well.

The first was baptism by water. This one is baptism by light, a fuller merging into that Light. It touches on the vows in that there must be the awareness of the depth of one's responsibility. It is not an honor; one does not seek this to receive personal honor, or any kind of personal gain. It is maturation; a willingness to rest within that circle despite any murmurs of fear or discomfort from the small self; to hold that self with love, yet even more, to hold the space of fearlessness and connection. It seemed to be a stepping up from the novice in the circle to full participation, like monastic vows that move one from novice to fuller ordination, and within that fullness, that ask an even deeper commitment.

My words here cannot begin to do justice to the profound depth of His explanation, nor to the power of the light and love in which I was held. He spoke for about half an hour.

He finished speaking and asked if I had any questions. I said no. He asked if I was ready to proceed. Yes.

Then the light intensified. It was as if the roof came off the building and light beyond light flooded through. It felt like that light was burning away all self. I pulled back, felt the comfort of His hands take mine, not to pull, but to support me until I was ready to walk further into the luminosity. He reminded me to take the ends of the prayer shawl in my hands and to hold them as if they were His hands. I must go on alone, yet we are never alone. I stepped forth. Again the light intensified.

There was a voice then, beyond even His, that sound of the Divine I've known only rarely before, a rich, deeply resonant voice that seems to come from everywhere.

"What do you ask?"
"To serve You."
"What more do you ask?"
"To know the full healing of this body, to hear Thy heavenly music and all the expressions of that music on Earth. To see fully, Thy glory and its expressions on Earth."

"Do you wish to hear ('able to bear' was included in this thought) the cries as well as the joy?"

"I am willing, yes."

"Do you choose to see the terrible distortions as well as the lovely ones?"

"I am willing."

"But do you choose it?"

"Yes."

My answer seemed sufficient. In that moment I did not discern the distinction between choice and willingness. Yet this willingness was enough for now. It was clear that this answer had to come from both the small self and the greater self, yet there was no sense of the small self in those moments. There was only Oneness; only light.

Then the baptism, of light, of fire! It felt like the body would shake apart, yet there was no fear, only a welcoming of that burning away. There were no more thoughts. There was an image of a mountain of snow and the sun melting it into a fiery sea. It just burned. There is the memory of strong energy releases, but there were no thoughts as this occurred.

It came in three waves, with each the statement of the baptism, in the name of the Father, the Son, and the Holy Spirit. Then I settled into a long and profound stillness, but there was no "I," only the awareness of light.

I am moved here, as I write this, to look back to the words in my journal from that first baptism, when I was asked if I understood the meaning of it. April 22, 1989: "He asks me if I understand what baptism means. I say no. He says that it is a confirmation of my love of God and my willingness to follow Father/Mother/Divine Love wherever God asks me to go, and to follow with gladness and no holding back."

The meaning now is the same, but it goes deeper. There is the commitment to never forget the Oneness. When thoughts that are self-centered or mean in any way appear, they must be known as "old mind" and noted, but with no involvement in the stories. I understood that I must stay wrapped in the shawl, and offer that completeness as outward expression. I must take responsibility for all of my thoughts and actions, and do so with joy. Only by fully opening the heart to this self, can there be the fullest opening to all beings, and a release of judgment for the horrors that humans create. What remains is just compassion, an inward focus on our innate capacity for love, and the intention to balance the energies that surge through us.

Journal, January 7, 2006

With each wave of light, the body shook. The ice cap of the heart that has been frozen by many lifetimes of anguish, softening now; releasing. All the chakras opened. Three times the wave of fire came. Then a profound stillness, for a long time. Just sitting in that radiance. No self.

After an unknown period of time, I felt Jeshua's energy again, and Aaron's. Also I felt two of the Casa Entities, Dr. Cruz and one of the Fathers. The light dimmed a bit. There was an awareness again of the gathered circle, singing a version of the Lord's Prayer in a foreign language. Somehow I understood the words, which were sung in a beautiful harmony and richness that these human ears have never heard.

The light faded further, receding into the morning, as I finished the sitting on my meditation cushion. As I opened my eyes, awareness arose of dog needing to be fed, and the remembrance that it was way past the time for my daily call to my mother. A moment's contraction, "But I want to write this down. . . ." followed by the immediate clarity that I first had to take care of the needs of Mom and Sulu. I thought of that old teaching, "Do it with love or not at all." Love fed Sulu, called Mom, and even talked to Peter for a while; he came in just as I was starting to write.

Now the shawl was packed, and I was ready to leave for Brazil once again.

♦

CHAPTER 18

Returning to the Casa

MY THIRD TRIP to the Casa in January of 2006 began with this deeper intention: to offer my own healing in service to all beings. Any choice we make can come from a place of self-centeredness, "for me," or it can be made from a place that recognizes our interconnections. One person's healing serves us all. There was an openness to see and hear not just the joys and beauty present in the world, but also the sorrows and pain. On the first day of my first Casa session, I was immediately sent to surgery. Sitting with eyes closed, I began to feel a profound energy around me. Many people were there having surgery that morning, maybe forty. I found myself in the Circle of Blessed Ones, holding the space with joy and gratitude.

Journal, January 12, 2006

I sat for some time, very focused, feeling the high energy all around, supporting the holding of space as one or more beings were brought into the center of the circle. When my turn seemed to come, I noticed that I had been creating a subtle duality of giving/receiving. This in turn stemmed from an old habit of wanting special attention and recognition. But it is not "better" to hold the space than to be in the center. The circle gives to the center; the center receives what is given. Each position gives a needed gift to the other, and each is enriched. Both are a part of the whole.

I felt myself embraced. Immediately there was a strong energy around the eyes and I was asked to be very still. Dr. Augusto worked on the right eye. I felt pressure there for about one minute, then that specific energy faded. I felt other energies/Entities working in my sinuses, ears, and eyes for about five minutes. Then I found myself just being held, wrapped in caring. Aaron was there, and I briefly felt the hand of love on my head. Then Aaron indicated that I should take my place back in the circle again.

The surgery ended. I took a taxi to the pousada and slept most of the afternoon and evening. I had a somewhat restless night, no surprise after sleeping all the previous afternoon; I woke up early to meditate outdoors. I was in a very connected place, at ease and filled with joy. Then a thought about the eyes and ears came and there was contraction. *Will I get what I need?* A soft breeze was blowing, and the sun felt gentle on my face. Aaron asked me to notice that the breeze and sunshine touched everything with the same presence; that they did not choose one object to caress over another. Grasping at healing, wanting to step ahead and be noticed so as to receive, to be born into the light before my twin, are such old habits for this human. Aaron asked me to just rest in that full presence of love, expressed now as breeze and sunshine, and to feel the non-contraction as I rested there.

After some time, Aaron asked me to feel the healing energy also present around me, touching everything, not choosing to go to one because it was more worthy or called more loudly. He suggested that I rest in that energy in the same way that I was resting in the breeze and sunshine. I was able to do that, and experienced a deep joy and peace with none of the previous contraction.

Eventually a vision came of a still sea, lit in brilliant silver, while above me I felt a very brilliant light. It was the sea that I have seen before, where small animals come to drink and are reflected in the stillness. All is complete in the sea, with nothing separate. Everything else stopped. The light and stillness remained for a long time.

Several days later, in meditation, I felt a deep quiet. I found myself resting in the gathered energy of the circle. I felt moved to state my intention to the gathered circle and my request for help, to heal the eyes and ears. My heart spoke the intention to fully hear and see, and to be intimate with everything. I was asked if I felt able to hold all that joy and sorrow. I replied that it wasn't a question of whether I could, but whether I would. If I will, then I can learn to. I will it. I choose it. That reply seemed to be accepted.

That afternoon Aaron spoke to me about healing:

On one level there is nothing to heal. On another level, there is a distortion of the Ever-Perfect that expresses on the mundane level. Here please use your previous work with emotions. You understand that trying to "fix" an emotion, and giving it the slightly contracted energy of "fixing," only holds it in place. To heal the emotions, you must hold them lovingly, acknowledging them but without the contraction caused by fear or aversion. Within the field of equanimity, contractions dissolve.

The same is true of physical distortion. It must be acknowledged and held lovingly with an intention to release it to the Ever-Perfect, but the distortion must be held without contraction. This you have been learning to do. So long as there is still the tension of, "Can I do it?" you have an I and a self; contraction, therefore, will be present.

Come now to the place where it is already done. Know that space. Rest there, knowing the innate perfection of the physical body as you know the perfection of pure awareness. Rest in awareness, rest in the circle, and look at the physical body. See the various expressions and consciously release the distorted ones, but with no aversion, just the clarity that these are not useful to the self. Do it, as you would rinse garden soil off the hands after gardening, with appreciation for the soil but awareness that it is not useful to carry it indoors.

The following week I went through the line for surgery review and gave Heather some questions to ask. The incorporated Entity, Dr. Valdivino, didn't look at me or answer my questions, just said to go to the surgery room for removal of the last stitches. I felt unseen and unheard. I wanted attention, but I knew this was just an expression of ego. Eventually, I was able to watch the emotions I was feeling with kindness, and did not judge them or take them personally.

My vision was still very poor, so the question continued to arise within, "Are my eyes healing?" I was still afraid of becoming blind. After this Casa surgery, I could see some shapes again, but with a large black hole in the center of the visual field. The left eye continued to bleed, for reasons the American eye specialist could not discern. Floaters from the blood marred the vision.

Journal, January 21, 2006

Last night I had a dream: I was stranded. Hal was to pick me up but the car had broken down. Then Hal appeared in a somewhat ramshackle Casa blue convertible! I said kiddingly, "What's this? Did you buy it?" and he said, "Yes." I got in, and he began to drive. I asked, "Does this thing have brakes?" as he made a somewhat too fast and wild first sharp turn. "Yes, you just have to learn how it works, and get used to this new vehicle." So we drove.

Things seemed to pass in a blur and someone told me to close the left (better) eye and see with the right, to bring the objects into focus, but I didn't know how. I was disoriented and wanted to use the good eye and kept hearing, "No, just the right one."

Then I seemed to be waking, but I heard a strong message not to open the eyes yet. There was an instruction to read some text appearing within the closed eye. Earlier in the dream, I had noted that I was reading the signs we passed with the left eye, but that when I tried to track with the right, they were blurry. Now I was told to hold a hand over the left eye as a reminder not to try to read with it. Focus the right eye and pick out the letters. First they were blurred, then slowly the images of the alphabet in capital letters began to appear in my right eye visual field, although the eye was still held closed. I was asked to stay with each letter until it became clear.

After reading the alphabet, which took maybe twenty minutes, words began to appear, although the physical eyes remained closed. I recognized the beginning of the Lord's Prayer. I was told, "Don't just recite it; hold each word or even each small group of letters until it becomes clear. If the straight lines bend and wiggle, hold the focus until they become straight. If the curves are blurred, hold until it clears."

At first I was reading the words one letter at a time, then getting whole words and holding them. Finally, I was able to get several words (all uppercase) and read more like one reads with normal vision.

When the prayer ended, I was asked to focus on a palette of color, and to hold each color. This was harder. I have not seen color in that eye in a long time. We went through the whole palette.

Finally I heard the instructions: "Vision will clear slowly. You may not read small print such as books with this eye ever, at least for many months or even years." I was told to practice this several times daily as we had done, using the Lord's Prayer or another text if I prefer. I will know when I've done enough and vision is clear, and may stop the daily practice then. If vision begins to distort at any time, return to the practice. Put Casa water on the eyes daily. Take enough home with me to last until it's clear or until my next visit.

That was all. Aaron sort of woke me up. The vision is still blurry at the periphery and has a black hole in the center, but overall, it has improved. If I cover the left eye and look at the doorframe as I was asked to look at the letters, the wavering line becomes straight and there is some vision through the dark center area.

Was I awake or asleep? It doesn't matter. In hindsight, the dream of the car was an interesting introduction to this particular exercise. Aaron says that everything inside a dream ultimately refers to aspects of the self. Hal is a male; a being of the opposite sex represents my subconscious mind. He was confidently driving a new vehicle, which represents my new eyes. The way my subconscious mind gets used to riding in the new car—that is to say, to see—is through these instructions. Later that day, spirit spoke to me further through a fragment of a news article in an e-mail:

BALTIMORE, Jan. 18 (UPI)—Johns Hopkins University

Scientists are studying how we "see" objects in hopes of eventually developing neural prostheses.

Paper co-author Charles Connor said, "Vision doesn't happen in the eye. . . . It happens at multiple processing stages in the brain."

"Vision doesn't happen in the eye. It happens at multiple processing stages in the brain." I became excited. The Entities were retraining my brain to take the visual data and interpret it in a new way, to literally see a ripple (which the broken central retinal vein will produce) and interpret it as straight. My eyes were also learning to distinguish a true curve from a curve caused by my eye's physiology, and finally to see through the blind spot in the center.

Journal, January 30, 2006

The eye sees the different forms such as the space around the "A" of FATHER. I'm told to hold the whole word (short) or syllable and focus on it until the letters are clear, and until the spaces around the letters are also clear. See the negative space along with the lines.

The font is very delicate and the letters are filled with energy and light. Sometimes they appear to be blazing, sometimes black, but they are always energizing to the eye!

Reciting the Lord's Prayer two or three times a day in such a focused way, deeply connects me to the energy of that prayer. Sometimes I feel Jeshua's loving presence beside me, and feel the strength of His energy as this prayer is offered.

Journal, February 2, 2006

I awoke at 5:30 a.m. and did the "Our Father" exercise in bed, with Casa water on the eyes. Energy streamed into the right eye. The letters seem to have narrow lines like cuts that allow the God-Light to come through. The words also have their own energy. Each has its own energy and vibration. Certain words, such as Father, power, glory, forgive, and Thy, carry a higher vibration, while others, such as us, in, and be, are more neutral.

One morning at the opening of the Current, the Entity Dr. Augusto de Almeida, who was incorporated in Medium João, had told the Casa mediums that he wanted to do intensive work on the deaf woman with the tuning forks, whom Heather had brought through the line yesterday. Heather knew he meant me, of course, and pointed me out, sitting in the Current. "Yes, yes, after the session."

Journal, January 26, 2006

I sat in the empty surgery room. As soon as I sat, I felt the gathered circle. I was immediately asked, very gently and lovingly, "Why do you wish to hear?"

I had been asked this question in a slightly different form during the baptism in the adobe chapel, and previously in the gathered circle. This time I was able to answer more clearly and completely, and from my heart. "I wish to hear Earth's beauty, the bird's song, waterfalls, children's laughter, music; to fully bring forth the expression of divinity that I am, and to fully participate in the incarnation. I am also willing to hear the anguished screams, the whine of dropping bombs, the roar of floods, and the helpless whimper and allow them to open this heart of compassion. I am ready to hear it all. I desire the beauty, and understand the need to hear the pain for the heart of compassion to fully manifest. That is the greatest service I can do. It is what I have not previously allowed."

Spirit asked me, "Do you feel able to hear it all?" I replied, "I can only try."

Spirit said, "It is noted. Why do you wish to see?"

I gave a similar answer, very much from my heart. Then there was a review of the life of the navy chaplain, and of other lives where there was some resistance to fully hearing and seeing the pain of the world. I was asked again if I was ready now to fully see and hear. "Yes."

Spirit again, "It is noted. Who speaks for this human?"

Aaron immediately said, "I speak for her." He said, "I feel she is ready for what she seeks. Beings are helping to lift the karma."

Then I asked the entire gathered circle if they would support me in this attempt to hear and see. The answer was completely affirmative. There was a feeling of profound love, compassion, and support.

Just at that point Heather entered with the mediums, three women. They asked me to lie on one of the surgery beds and to close my eyes.

I had not realized before that Medium João would not be present. I felt a moment of skepticism or let-down, thinking this was just going to be these three women doing some energy work, not direct help from the Entities. That showed my limited understanding! As they began to work, I could feel Dr. Augusto directing. Doctors Cruz and Valdivino were also there, perhaps one Spirit-Entity doctor working through each of the three mediums.

Journal, January 26, 2006

At first I had some resistance to letting in the Energy, which was concentrated around the head and heart. Aaron "held my hands" (hard to explain that sensation!) and asked me to relax and open to the Energy. Jeshua* then spoke to me and said, *"This is another baptism; you have been into the water and the light/fire; this is the baptism of spirit."* With that Love around me, I was able to let go. The mediums stood at my head, my feet, and at one side. Heather was watching and keeping track of time. Dr. Augusto had asked them to work for precisely twenty minutes.

They worked primarily on the eyes and orbital bones, but also the sinuses, nose, face above the front teeth, jaw bones just in front of the ears, and the ears—in other words, most of my face. My whole body was quivering with powerful Energy, almost to the point of pain. It seemed that the Entities would pour in Energy, let it settle in as deeply as possible, wait a moment until there was a little more space, then pour in more. It seemed especially deeply directed into the eyes.

Finally they stopped and helped me sit up. I felt tremendous gratitude to all of them and thanked them for their commitment and for sharing their gifts.

I couldn't imagine anything beyond this powerful energy work, but here at the Casa, the unexpected happens. The next morning in Current I was tired, restless and unfocused. Suddenly I heard Aaron say, "Wake up. The doctor is here and wants you." At first I thought he meant the incorporated Entity, as he does sometimes walk through the room and work directly on people, but I quickly realized that this was on a different, inner plane. As I sat up, I felt my whole body

---

*When I speak of experiencing Jeshua at the Casa, I ask the reader to remember that He is everywhere if we call upon Him. He does not incorporate as do the Casa Entities, and it is not necessary to be at the Casa to feel His presence.

enveloped in a radiant light and energy. I felt moved to sit up very straight, allowing the energy to move freely down the spine. The energy flowing in felt much like that of the previous day's energy session but this time there was no outward physical expression, only what I saw and felt in meditation.

It felt like spirit took my face in his hands, holding it with fingers spread just over and under my ears. I could almost feel physical hands, to the point that I opened my eyes for a moment, half expecting to see Medium João there, with the Entity incorporated. The energy stopped for a moment and there was the sense of being looked at deeply. Then energy began to build again, waves and waves of light, this time primarily focused around the ears, unlike yesterday where the focus was more on the eyes and facial bones. My body was shaking so hard I was certain the people sitting next to me would feel it. Discomfort intensified almost to pain, plateaued, then built up again as the capacity to hold it became available. I don't know how long this continued, maybe seven or eight minutes. Then the hands came away and Aaron said to relax the body, to rest. From my journal:

I rested a few minutes, coming back into awareness of the room, then Dr. Augusto approached again with Dr. Cruz and another Entity whose energy I didn't recognize. In my inner vision, Dr. Augusto was holding two glowing wires each about eight inches long. He held each one by one end. They had an intense radiance, and seemed almost alive. There was a moment of fear, and he gave a piercing look. Well, I did ask for this; I didn't say how I wanted it to happen but gave full permission to make it happen in any way that they chose.

An energetic hand on my forehead caused all sense of resistance to float away. Then Dr. Augusto brought these two fiery wires up toward either side of my face, still holding one in each hand. I could feel Aaron's reassuring presence. There was a touch just behind the jawbone, under the ear, the sensation of sharp stinging there for a moment. I was asked if there was still pain. No. He moved his hands slowly and seemed to be measuring, aligning, for a moment, the wire tips touching my face on either side. His eyes were firm to mine.

Aaron said, "There will be strong pressure," and Dr. Augusto thrust both hands forward, pushing these burning wires full length in to my face on either side. Then I felt his fingers as if they were pushing inside the openings. Once again, there was very powerful energy, a very high vibration that pulsed up through the area behind the jawbone and seemed to go up to the crown of the head. Again, energy poured in, plateaued, and poured in again. The energetic anesthetic kept me relaxed and peaceful. After a few minutes Dr. Augusto stepped back, looked deeply, then walked away again. Aaron again said to rest. I realized I was trembling and covered with sweat. I felt both exhausted and exhilarated. The work had not been uncomfortable except for the very brief sting of the wires, but the high energy left me shaken. At the same time, I had a very joyful sense that they were truly addressing the situation of the deafness and dead nerves.

Dr. Augusto returned in several minutes. He said matter-of-factly that they would not tune the left side now; I must do more work there with the tuning forks and toning. I realized that I had done much more practice on the right side.

Then Dr. Augusto seemed to be talking to the other two Entities, almost as if he were explaining a procedure. Again, a hand on the forehead, and a complete letting go from me; then he seemed to insert one hand into the jaw opening and one into the top of my head. It felt like someone was tightening something. I started to hear inner ear, tinnitus-like sounds, but very different than usual; rumbling, squealing. . . . He asked me a few times, "Is this higher or lower?" Or, "louder? softer?" I'd reply, he'd adjust, then ask again. I felt not pain but uncomfortable pressure. Finally he stopped, gave another piercing look, said "done," and walked away.

When Dr. Augusto walked away, Aaron told me that it was done, to slide my body down a bit in the chair, to stretch out the legs, relax, and rest. He asked me not to talk to him, just to meditate. I moved into a deep meditation. When the Current ended, I felt very peaceful. There was considerable tenderness at the insertion points on each side, and some throbbing, but not pain. It subsided in about an hour. The next morning, there was just mild tenderness at the insertion points and considerable swelling.

Here the trip ended and it was time to return home. The first morning at home, the Entities were present, asking me to do the vision exercises and chanting. I felt deep energy from them too, as if I still lay on the crystal bed. It was good to feel their presence and to know that the energy work I had been doing at the Casa would now continue at home. I hoped that the work with karmic resolution would continue also.

CHAPTER 19

Homecoming

AFTER A WEEK at home, I left to lead a senior students' retreat that was held at a Jesuit Center. At the Center is a small chapel named after St. Ignatius. Early one morning, I went there for prayer and meditation. I started by restating my continuously evolving intention for healing as I understood it then. The act of stating intentions can both reaffirm and clarify spiritual aspirations. It must be done often. In this way spirit is able to tailor answers that more fully meet current needs. By "spirit" here, I don't just mean an external entity, but that combination of my higher self, and the loving spirit plane guidance and support.

I spoke of the intention/desire to hear and see all the beauty of this Earth; to be a full and joyful witness of this Eden. I spoke of my intention to see and hear the fullness of suffering on the Earth in order to fully open this heart of compassion. I gratefully noted that Dr. Valdivino, speaking through Medium João, had said he was helping to release the karma. I also understood that this release ultimately is my responsibility. The gift from the Casa Entities and other loving spirits is twofold: what they lift from me, out of their compassion, and what they lead me to clearly see and resolve.

I asked about the subtle closure of my heart, which leads me to negative and judgmental thoughts. Powerful energy work has opened the other chakras more fully in the past few days, and the partially closed heart chakra stands out more clearly now in contrast. Wrapped in the blue shawl, I began to meditate. I started to see the image that hung on the wall beyond these closed eyes, Jesus on the cross. It led me back into a familiar and anguished past-life memory.

My karmic ancestor had been Mark, the son of Nathaniel, Aaron's karmic ancestor. Both lived when Jeshua walked the Earth. I had last worked with Mark's lifetime when I received the shawl. This time there was more detail. Mark as a young teenage boy disobeyed his father, and watched that crucifixion with terrible pain and a feeling of betrayal. He saw the bloody crown and whip, and the nails being driven into His hands; he felt that Jeshua, whom he loved as a mentor, could have chosen differently and did not have to die. Mark felt shattered, confused, and abandoned. He ran away, and argued with his father. He was blinded by the authorities with two knife cuts to the right eye, then was later crucified. He hated himself because he couldn't die with love. Finally I was able to allow both my heart and Mark's heart to open a little, with some compassion to ourselves. Clearly, however, I still had work to do with Mark.

The next morning I again arose early and went to the Chapel of St. Ignatius, as the Current was starting at the Casa, several time zones away. I sat quietly for quite a while, aware of the Current forming and people going in to surgery. My intention was simply to support the Current. After a while the surgery was finished and the second timeline had started. I felt an Entity come to me, look into the eyes and ears for just a moment, then leave. Aaron said to meditate and someone would return. A minute later I felt Dr. Valdivino take my hands, smile at me, and remind me that he had said that he would help me with karma. He asked me to open my eyes and look at the cross on the wall before me. Immediately the scene came back to me, of Mark's watching the crucifixion. I felt the agony of wanting to run up and demand that they stop; I was furious with Jeshua for not stopping it, and I felt Mark's fear that if he intruded in any way he would be killed. Somehow it didn't register with him that he could not have stopped it. He believed that he did not stop it out of fear for himself, and he felt intense shame at what he believed was his selfishness. So he blamed himself for Jeshua's death. Now I felt Aaron embrace me as I cried and forgave that boy, and forgave myself for all I have been unable to do.

It seemed to me then, sitting in that chapel, that I needed to understand exactly what had happened to this ancestor afterwards, and then, through the chain of lives that followed, to unravel the karma as one would unravel a knotted string. Dr. Valdivino said no, to just rest in the open heart. He helped me understand that to go back right now would just serve to give it all energy again. It is done. Let it be. I will see further into Mark's experience when I am ready.

I felt a deep peace and warmth in the heart, loving energy embracing me, and just rested in that space for a while. Then I felt Jeshua approach, take my hands, and ask me to look into His eyes. He asked me if there was anything remaining that I needed Him to explain. I saw the infiniteness of compassion in His eyes and knew that it truly was done, that there was nothing to explain. I just rested there for a while.

This was a very deep karmic resolution, and a clear answer to my prayers. Yet I remained filled with doubts and fears about the processes I was undergoing. A meditative experience in the chapel the next day addressed my concerns.

Journal, February 2006

I haven't experienced any energy work for several days, just quiet sittings. Doubt came. Will I remain deaf and unhealed because I am simply imagining my way into these powerful experiences? I tried imagining for about a half hour, just to see if I could. It was quiet and peaceful, but there was no sense of spirit presence. I let go of trying and sat there with eyes open, enjoying the peace and candlelight.

After another half hour of quiet, I began to see a procession of people moving in pairs toward a light in the distance. It became clear that each was a seeker with a guide. I watched for a short while, and asked for a guide. Jeshua appeared. It was a slow and peaceful procession moving toward a reflected light. As we rounded a bend, the light became brilliant. Then I stepped into the light, with Jeshua holding my arm. There was some hesitation, it was so bright. I felt it burn through me. Then I heard, "What do you ask?" "Can I hear?" was my question. I didn't mean it as "in this moment," but, "Is the work done? Is there still any block to healing?" "It is clear," was the reply. "Hearing will come. You will be helped." Then my turn was up and the light faded. The sense of Jeshua's presence also faded.

The response that came was very explicit: "Hearing will come." This was the reassurance that I needed. However, what *wasn't* said was also significant: "but not yet." The energy work resumed again and continued for months. Most days I began with silent meditation and then worked for an hour with chanting with the tuning forks, with eye exercises, and with the Entities.

One morning, almost immediately after my silent meditation, the Entities began to work on me. Then the energy suddenly stopped. No "goodbye." I asked Aaron if they were done for the day. Yes. I saw my desire to talk to them, saw my desire for a more personal relationship with them, as I have with Aaron. Aaron said that he and I have that relationship because of our past lives together, and that we are soul mates. He pointed out that I can feel the immense compassion in Dr. Valdivino's energy, and know that I am not just an object to be put aside, but I am cherished; but not cherished any more or less than any other being. He asked me to look at that which wants to be "special" in some way, to have a friendship beyond the one of co-creators.

But, I said to Aaron, if they work with me, there has to be trust. How do I establish that trust if there is no personal relationship? He replied, "On the basis of who they are and what you have observed of them. Any further desire is just ego."

At that point I felt Dr. Valdivino come in again. I felt his energy field wash over me in a loving way. Then he said, "We do not coddle.

The deepest respect I can offer you is the observation that you are whole and divine and need no affirmation of that truth from me. That I work and then leave you is a statement of my trust of your ability to hold that high vibration without fear, to take it as it is offered, and to not create your stories of someone special. For me to do otherwise is to do you a disservice and to enhance the ego's need to feel special."

Before he left he asked me to sit in silence and meditate with those thoughts. Again I felt his huge compassion wash over me and then he was gone. I wanted to talk to Aaron but he just said, "Silence, please," so I sat.

The next morning after the visualization exercise, the Entities were present and began to work energetically with the chakras. It was fairly gentle for about fifteen minutes, just moving up and down the body/chakras, which I could feel opening.

Dr. Augusto came in; I could feel the shift in energy. He asked my permission to proceed, noting that he knew I had a quiet day, but didn't say what he planned to do. I said yes, whatever he felt was useful. I was asked to relax and to open my mouth. Aaron said that there might be some pressure or discomfort. I felt Dr. Augusto's energy in my body, pressure around the nose and sinuses, then a burst of energy throughout that whole area. I saw brilliant flashing light in my closed eyes; then it felt like he turned what he had inserted so that it was pointed down into the body and directed the energy to different places in the body. It was uncomfortable but not painful.

The procedure ended and I lay still for a minute. Dr. Augusto seems to have left. Then there was some pressure on the abdomen. I had been constipated much of the time since returning from Brazil. I felt a lot of movement in the abdomen and Aaron said that Dr. Valdivino was massaging the bowels. When he ended, it was suggested that I go to sleep, and that I rest throughout the day. After sleeping about three hours, my bowels moved immediately and easily when I woke up.

I talked with Aaron and Dr. Valdivino when I awakened, and asked if he would explain a little about the work they're doing. I don't hear him in words; his reply was more in images and thought blocks, so it's hard to translate it into verbal thought. Aaron later did so:

The body energy patterns are conditioned by karma, genetics, environment, and more. Energy often slides back into old patterns as long as there is no change beyond the etheric body. So working on the etheric body is not enough. The work needs to happen at the astral and causal levels.

The causal template is the place where change can be held. This template is of the causal and astral bodies.* One never forces, but invites the causal template to more firmly hold the patterns of the cosmic template, and to reveal those patterns to the etheric level, which in turn reveals them to the physical level.

Think of a young animal that has suffered deep trauma and has brought forth distorted patterns such as backing away from loving attention out of fear. You repeat the positive feedback each time the animal approaches. At first the fear remains along with the movement to come forth. Slowly a new pattern is ingrained until the old memories literally die away. You saw this in your old collie, Beau, who shook with terror when he first entered your home as an abused foundling, and later became what you referred to as "the teddy bear," so loving and trusting was he.

As the Entities work with the cells themselves, and the energy patterns that hold the cells at a certain vibration, these changes will occur, literally changing the tissue at a cellular level, and changing the causal template so that if the cells are damaged, they replace themselves according to that new template. It is all at a substantially higher vibration.

Six days later I awakened at 6:00 a.m., and "read" the Lord's Prayer. When I finished, I offered thanks, and stated my highest intention. Then Dr. Valdivino was back with more gentle energy work. I felt so wrapped in it, so relaxed and filled with light. I slept on and off, waking only to some new energy sensation and his reassurances, and

---

*See Interval IV and Glossary to review these bodies.

awakened fully at 10:00 a.m. I still felt the cocoon of light energy wrapped around me. I felt him almost unroll the strands of energy. Then he wished me a good day and reminded me again to take it very easy. He said that this session felt far less intense, but to remember that it had lasted for four hours.

I felt very well, rested and energized. I also felt a personal relationship to both Dr. Valdivino and Dr. Augusto that day. It is interesting that they said "not needed" when my ego self wanted it, but then offered it when there was no grasping for it. The talking was brief with Dr. Augusto, but he was pleasant. His compassionate smile lit my heart. And Dr. Valdivino was very warm and friendly.

I had been looking at them with such gratitude through these weeks, afraid to state my needs other than the healing ones. But of course they're no different than Aaron. Like Aaron, they have no need to please in order to be liked. But loving spirit wishes to please when it is possible, just to give ease and joy to another. We have to ask, and to make sure our requests are reasonable and stem from the higher self, not the ego. I saw how the first request was from ego, and that Dr. Valdivino was correct to say, "We will not coddle you." Now I was able to ask from a clearer space.

One night a week later, I meditated and climbed into my bed. As I was falling asleep, faces began to appear, horrible, wounded, maimed. I saw blood pouring out of an eye, and another eye with a knife in it. Some were me, and in some I was the assailant maiming others. It was very frightening and I began to cry. I sat up in bed and began to meditate. I felt Aaron immediately, saying he was there with me, and also felt Dr. Valdivino. He didn't say anything, but Aaron reminded me that Dr. Valdivino had said that he would help with the karma. I felt very supported. I began to do metta, and ask forgiveness for any harm I had done, and forgave others who had harmed me. I did that until I fell asleep.

Soon after that night, the lower chakras were closed again, although the heart and upper chakras remained very open. Dr. Valdivino asked me why I do not want to be more in the body, to please reflect on that question. I could see the desire to stay in the incarnation, yet I also acknowledged a subtle weariness. Aaron said that I needed to focus more on the deeper intention, to be here fully, with full intimacy with everything.

The Entities were not too concerned about the blockage; they just told me to continue to do my work and to be patient. Dr. Valdivino said that there was no major blockage between the chakras. The energy is flowing. I'm just not taking in as much energy through the base, or allowing it to cycle over and back into the lower chakras. The energy stays in the upper chakras and creates a "pressure." I needed to be patient and let the process unfold. Day by day, it did so.

Journal, Monday, March 6, 2006

Dr. Valdivino did a very low-level energy session, just gently participating in my opening of the chakras, and supporting the body in a way that seemed to bring deep ease and relaxation. At the end, my body felt odd, like there were two bodies, one straight with energy flowing through it; and a second, overlaid, which seemed very distorted. I had a vivid image of a man being hung, not so that his neck was broken, but just so that his body was shaking in the wind, being pushed in all directions. Then there was the image of an animal, held by the neck, shaken and hit over a rock, and other similar images. I asked what to do with them and was told simply, "Forgive." I think some were me as victim and some were me as the doer. "I offer forgiveness to all who have harmed these bodies. I ask forgiveness from all whom I have harmed." There was no one central "story" or image, beyond these unknown, distorted bodies. Tears were flowing. I felt this body becoming more able to take and hold its true openness, its reflection of the Ever-Perfect.

Journal, Tuesday, March 7, 2006

Dr. Augusto and Dr. Valdivino did some high-energy work around the eyes and ears. Finally, Dr. Augusto noted that the sinus was inflamed again. He asked me to open my mouth. He reassured me that he was not about to put the forceps up my nose. He smiled as he spoke. He said there would be some pressure. He then moved my hands literally into my mouth and started directing energy through them into the soft palate, and up into the sinus cavity. It's an odd sensation to feel my hands move with certainty and the intense energy flow through them. I would not say that they are out of my control. I could stop the movement if I chose to, but when I relax, they move seemingly of their own accord. There is no plan or impulse in my mind before the movement.

There was very strong pressure, bordering on discomfort, but not pain, for about thirty seconds. Dr. Valdivino kept asking me to relax the body as much as possible and to breathe with the pressure and energy. When Dr. Augusto finished, he said that he wanted to do the surgery on the sinus and orbital bones on Friday if it felt suitable, with Kathleen's support. Kathleen is my chiropractor and is very open to working with Aaron. While in Brazil, Dr. Augusto had suggested he wished to do further work with her supportive presence if she was willing. He says that these facial bones were not realigned after the accident and, therefore, have healed crookedly, which the X-rays have confirmed. He also says that these various misalignments in face and skull are part of the reason for some recent blood pressure deviations and frequent nose bleeds.

My body felt like that dangling figure again, with a misalignment and the physical body out of balance. The experience was similar to seeing multiple lines and as the "shaking" stopped, they came into a straight line. Dr. Valdivino worked again for about five minutes and the body and energy field came easily into alignment. He asked me to be aware of this misalignment throughout the day, and to pause and bring it back; and to do the forgiveness meditation if useful, to aid in the release.

My heart feels so open and filled with joy. I feel so much love from and to these Entities and Aaron. I feel great gratitude.

Wednesday, March 8, 2006

After my vipassana sitting, I did the vision exercise and worked by myself in the lower chakras that were blocked. Then Dr. Valdivino came in and helped. It is very powerful to feel any one of these Entities' energies come into my hands and move them. He asked me to just invite energy into the lower chakras and to offer it in divine service. Then Dr. Cruz came in briefly and, using my hands, held the upper chakras while Dr. Valdivino's energy held the lower until all the chakras opened. Finally I was asked to try to hold the whole system open and to just rest in the Current, offering this energy to the Current. I did that for an hour, feeling very relaxed, joyful, alert.

I see that the chakras can open, but the habit energy to close them is strong. It will just take dedicated effort to pay attention, and to use the tools they have given me to reopen them when they close. Dedicate the energy to divine service! That way it isn't frightening to hold so much power.

Thursday, March 9, 2006

This morning both Dr. Augusto and Brother Sebastian, the back specialist, came as I meditated, to speak about what they would do tomorrow with Kathleen's help. Brother Sebastian also explained that the Casa Entities and Aaron were able to offer some support as the accident happened. Thus, I was saved from a broken neck. But there was serious damage, because my lower neck and back took the force of the impact. C7 and T1, vertebrae located approximately where the neck meets the torso, were pressing on the disc, which had been compressed since the accident. C6 and T2 and their discs were damaged. The middle thoracic vertebrae had impact damage. There was misalignment in the cervical vertebrae that was related to the high blood pressure. The lumbar vertebrae had some misalignment. The sacrum had misalignment at the iliac joints and also was compressed on one side.

Dr. Augusto will work after the spinal work is done. The bones are merely a collection of molecules, not solid. He is going to dissolve a number of the facial bones while Kathleen holds the energy on the human side, with craniosacral work. He will stretch the skull, then refit the orbital bones where they broke and healed into misalignment. He'll also work on a lower sinus cavity and the misaligned bones in the cheek. Then he'll bring them back to solidity. The whole process will take only about five to ten minutes. He'll give an anesthetic before he begins. I'll feel considerable pressure and high energy, but no pain. This opening of the space has to be done first. Finally he will work on the damaged retinal vein.

The next day I came into Kathleen's office and we began to work. In meditation, I invited the Entities into my body, not incorporated, but just as they are when they do the energy work. Dr Augusto told me that he would create an anesthetic so there would be no pain. I was awake but remember almost none of this phase. I felt very peaceful, blissful really. First Brother Sebastian worked on the back. Then I was asked to turn face up and Dr. Augusto began to work. I felt intense pressure and very high energy, but no pain. It felt like my face was dissolving, which I guess was literally true. Kathleen said she saw it like that. She was just holding the energy and watching. I have no sense of the time, maybe a few minutes.

After his work on the orbital bones, Dr. Augusto repaired the eye's torn central retinal vein. He said the eye was stitched so there was little movement; I could not roll my eye up, down or from side to side. It will move fine when he takes out the stitches. He also worked on the new hearing he is devising. When he finished, Kathleen did more craniosacral work. Then all agreed we were finished.

When I stood up I felt fine, a little shaky but I also felt like I fit correctly into my body, for the first time since the accident. I had been feeling like I rattled around in the body. Now it felt aligned.

Kathleen drove me home. It was about 2:40 p.m. I had a bowl of soup and went to sleep until dinner, then dozed through the evening. My back and face felt sore. At bedtime, Dr. Valdivino came and gave an anesthetic so that I would sleep without pain. First he checked over the body, to be sure that it all looked as it should. Then I felt a great warmth of energy wash over me. I fell asleep and slept very soundly.

CHAPTER 20

A Knife, a Bear, and Thunder

DESPITE DAILY ENERGY work, I could not consistently hold the base, sacral, and solar plexus chakras open. With Aaron's encouragement, I began to look again at two deaths in the very distant past that I had seen many times before. There is little detail; often I only get what is directly relevant to the present karma. The first karmic ancestor was taken captive in a battle and had been tied down on the ground, with his hands and feet staked out so that he was held motionless. His belly was slit and he was left there, in the hot sun, for birds to devour his internal organs. He died in agony and with great hatred for his captors and their cruelty. The second karmic ancestor was captured by an enemy who believed that eating the living heart of your courageous opponent would bestow strength and courage upon the self. This ancestor was likewise tied and held motionless, his chest split and the still-beating heart lifted out by the triumphant enemy. Again he died in agony and with hatred. That's all the detail I have ever seen of either lifetime. I have worked often in this lifetime with forgiveness meditation, for both of those past lives. I saw now, however, that karmic release was still in the conceptual realm. How do we allow the heart to open to such agony and fear?

Aaron asked me to reflect on these two lives, and to look for the gifts of healing they offered. In both of these lives, it was clear that the man would die. There was no hope for either man's rescue. But each did have a choice of how he would die, with hatred or with love. Each morning as I worked with the Entities and the energy, the belly was hard and closed. Dr. Valdivino worked patiently, helping to support the opening of these chakras, but I realized that it was not their opening that was my necessary focus, but their closure. The closed chakras were making a statement of something deeper that I had previously pushed away; something that I now needed to investigate. Nothing happens by chance in the body; when the chakras that have been previously open are closed, that closure relates to life issues that are now ready to be explored and healed.

How do we offer love to the thing that seems destined to destroy us? Is it possible to offer love even as one dies in agony? Can I offer love to the ears, to deafness and blindness, to the accident itself and to the ocean waves and sea floor that battered me? And what anger was I still carrying in other areas of my life? What was devouring me now?

One morning when the energy seemed very blocked in the third chakra, the Entities lovingly encouraged me to be patient, to use no force. Aaron reminded me to enter the level where the energy is always open, without denial of the blockage and resistance on the physical plane, to just rest in the Ever-Perfect, and in that openness, to relax. Let the body alone; let it be as it is. Hold it with love.

Journal, March 13, 2006

The Entities worked with, and helped to open, the half-chakra meridians.* Dr. Valdivino said, "The chakras are open, just not as fully as they have been. Relax.

---

*Half and core chakras: the half chakras lie along the back, each spaced halfway between the core chakras with which we are more familiar. The core chakras are named: base, sacral, solar plexus, heart, throat, third eye, and crown. They are located slightly more in front of the spine. See Interval II for a more detailed discussion.

Invite. Rest in perfection." I worked with metta and forgiveness meditations, the tuning forks, and chanting for about forty minutes. Then Dr. Cruz reminded me of how powerful harmonics are in working with the chakras, and asked me not to forget this. "Chant with joy, as an offering to God, and offer all the power of this belly energy to God as well." I can really feel the openness as I type. There is no resistance, no tension in the body. . . .

Hal just walked in as I was typing, irritated about my lengthy time at my desk. "Getting late. . . . haven't had breakfast. . . ." I can feel the anger coming up as I type. I was able to keep the belly somewhat open as he spoke, even with the anger; I tried just to hear him, reply, and not shut down. So now it's not as open as it was five minutes ago. Can I invite reopening easily, just with a minute of holding him and myself in my heart? . . . Yes. It opened right back up.

The next day I went into my meditation room very early and did more energy work. I worked first with the tuning forks until I could feel all the chakras vibrating. Then I tried to allow the energy to flow, but the sacral and the solar plexus chakras kept closing.

Journal, March 14, 2006

The Entities began to work very gently with the energy, helping me to invite the closed belly to open. Dr. Valdivino asked me to touch the belly. The center flesh was icy cold, even though the rest of my body was warm, tucked under a down comforter. Aaron asked me to reflect on a distant past life in which the person that Hal was, wounded me in the belly with a knife.

Recently more issues with Hal had been surfacing; there were times when we were combative with one another rather than supportive. I occasionally felt, sometimes unfairly, that I had to hold my ground or he would overwhelm me. We both participated in this pattern. He became combative when I held his knife in my belly. Control reverted to me when I held it and would not let go. Our life situation always offers to us the karmic situation that needs to be addressed the most.

The work of releasing this pattern between Hal and me has to happen on two levels. One area of work is talking and bringing this healing to fruition in our lives, thereby touching a deeper place of love and peace with each other. The other work must happen in the area of the body associated with the karma. I had previously done much healing of the wounded belly around the time of my hernia surgery, but something unresolved was still there. Healing is a process; each stage of that process leads us to the next one.

As I lay in bed one morning, I did a forgiveness meditation for any wounds to and from me, feeling a real opening of the heart. Then I "offered" the belly by bringing it forth for healing. I asked for help to release any karma around the wound in the physical or emotional bodies. I felt a long, icy knife and began to draw it out. As I did so, I could see how I had kept the knife there, as a way of protecting myself, holding on to old pain and anger so as to prevent the trusting that might lead to new pain.

It was very difficult to allow it to come out. After a few minutes of struggle, I was sweating and tears were near the surface. Aaron said that I was forcing rather than inviting. I asked for help. Jeshua appeared. He asked me if I would trust him to help remove it. I said yes. He very gently began to withdraw it. I felt the iciness of it, pulling through the belly, so deep in the belly, and gentle warmth entering; at least the possibility of warmth.

Jeshua proceeded very slowly, accepting this icy weapon as my body released it, rather than pulling it with any force, then filling the opening with light. There was a gaping wound and he offered it more and more light. He worked with me for about a half hour. Meanwhile, Hal slept beside me. I watched the tendency to protect myself from his energy field each time he moved or rolled over in his sleep.

In the end it seemed to be about one-third of the way out. The flesh was warmer. Jeshua pointed out to me that this was a process; it needed work on the karmic physical and etheric levels, but also on the mundane level in terms of working with this knife and its withdrawal in daily life. Aaron said we would do more each day.

I asked why the belly was so open several weeks ago when the Entities were doing so much crystal bed work. Aaron said that I was not ready then to address this issue; but now that I am, it can present itself for healing.

Later, I talked to Hal about all of the above, and about what I was learning. I asked if he would join me in trying to watch for and release these habit energies in ourselves. He said yes, gladly. These responses made me realize how much I do love and appreciate Hal. His habit is to throw the knife. My habit is to react by holding the knife, and by taking energy from the knife wound rather than by opening the heart. Then, I either withdraw or push back at Hal. We are always working together with those closest to us, teaching and learning through and with each other.

Later that day I meditated and did more energy work. I tried to allow the energy to flow, but the sacral and solar plexus chakras kept closing. I felt Jeshua come in again. Dr. Valdivino, Dr. Cruz and Aaron were also present. I was asked to open my arms, straight out to the side, what I call the "crucifixion position." Powerful, pleasant energy was brought into the palms and also through the soles of the feet. As the energy became more intense, I felt a sense of rising discomfort.

As I allowed this energy to go deeply within, Jeshua gently asked me to reflect on the past life memory as Mark, who saw Jeshua's crucifixion. He said that while Mark saw only the pain, for Him it was both painful and a gift, with joy for what He was able to give. Jeshua said that He was able to remove consciousness from the body enough to allow the pain to pass by, but to also stay in the body enough to transmute the energy of any sensations and emotions that arose.

Jeshua and Aaron have spoken in the past of a crucifixion initiation. We each participate in this initiation in our lives, each in our own way. This is not a literal crucifixion, of course, but is the place where we each face our deepest demons. An essential part of the crucifixion initiation is taking pain and transforming it with Love. All the bodies must be able to hold an extremely high vibration during the crucifixion initiation, in order to move on to the resurrection initiation. Jeshua has explained that if He had just felt pain, and the hatred of that pain, it would have lowered the vibrational frequency so much that the resurrection would have been impossible. The body simply would have died. The resurrection initiation is the rebirth, from fear to love, from hatred to compassion. We are reborn into the loving heart in each moment, but we often miss that opportunity for rebirth, so deep are we in our fears and old habits. These opportunities are called "initiations" because they initiate or commence a new way of being. Life leads us naturally to these moments, again and again; moments wherein we are faced with choosing fear or love.

Recently I was asked to reflect on the words from Luke 11:40, "I am the resurrection and the life" and to repeat them. My first reaction was no; that this was Jeshua's mantra, not mine. But as I complied with the request and meditated with these words, I saw that we each carry this responsibility; that we are each the resurrection, each responsible for bringing love and light into the world.

That day, Jeshua continued pouring energy into my hands and feet until they felt like they would explode. I was trembling and sweating; the experience was not painful, but not without pain either. He asked me to envision the nails that Mark saw driven into Jeshua's palms, to bless them as an instrument of the process of crucifixion and resurrection, and to release the sense of cruelty that they intrinsically elicit. Without the crucifixion there could have been no resurrection. This was the teaching Jeshua had sought to offer. Everything arises from conditions. What seems cruel on one level is teaching on another, and we must open to see all the levels. If Jeshua had not been willing, this would not have happened. He had co-created it.

I now understand that if I had not been willing on some level to experience deafness, then this "resurrection" of the learning of compassion and teaching that compassion to others, could not have happened. The acts of violence experienced by this body through many lifetimes offer the same opportunity. We each may learn, transform the painful lessons, and then offer that energy back out, as love, to the world.

Finally I was asked to relax for a few minutes. Then Jeshua asked me to turn to the knife in the belly. I co-created it. See it as part of my learning. See it with love, a tool of change and growth. But know that now is the time for its release.

He asked my permission to begin to withdraw the knife yet again, and my assistance in letting it go. He asked me to allow the light in, to soften the belly and release. He asked me to offer gratitude for this tool of change. We spent almost an hour. It was very difficult. The belly kept closing up; four steps forward and three back. He asked me to release any idea of how it should happen, to just allow vulnerability while staying present with love and forgiveness. I could feel heat and energy enter the belly as it softened.

What was most powerful was the new idea of the crucifixion initiation as a gift. I'm not sure why it seemed new. I deeply understand the gift of my deafness. I just never related my experience of deafness to Jeshua's crucifixion. Later Jeshua again emphasized the transformation of pain and base emotions. Unless we bring that high love energy to the experience, the vibrational frequency is reduced and there is no possibility of resurrection. This must be taken both figuratively and literally. In other words, to fully do this work, we must commit to it completely. There is no going only halfway.

Several weeks later I had the opportunity to speak to Jeshua, through Judi. He said:

"Beloved one, it is my pleasure to assist you in any way that I can. I love you greatly. When you were Mark and you witnessed the crucifixion, the rage blinded you to the divine blessing, which was happening in front of you.

"Part of what you experience now with the eyes is karmic in that the rage has subtly remained and has manifested as a partial blindness at times. However, the good news is you have worked your way past the rage. You have forgiven the others. You have forgiven me and most of all you have forgiven yourself for feeling helpless.

"You are coming into a great awareness of your divine strength.

"As you have understood the working of the molecules in restructuring the face, you recognize that all is energy. When the nails were embedded in the palms

of my hands I knew them to be molecules of energy, the same as I am. And there was a raising of vibrational energy with my acknowledgment that everything is energy, no judgment. It was a blessing to me to experience this Oneness."

I thanked him and said that while I understood this, there had been doubt about the whole opening process. It was helpful to hear His reply, especially His verification of the direct experiences with Him.

"Yes, it is the ego that doubts. You do hear me and you can trust that hearing, the inner hearing that at some point in this lifetime will become an outward vibrational hearing as well."

I see the process of healing and opening as a rebirth into the Ever-Healed. Each trauma was also a gift; and from this perspective, the karma is transformed. Then healing begins. That insight led me to look even more deeply at what healing means. Through these years there have been so many layers of healing. First, there was the release of the trauma, fear and suffering around deafness. Then the question arose as to whether physical healing was also possible; a direction I began to explore when I first went to the Casa. Now I began to understand healing more as a process, which is continually unfolding.

Journal, Thursday, March 16, 2006

I was working with anger today, and saw how I hold the anger in my back, causing lower back pain. I can choose to view anger in the way that I was shown by Jeshua. Anger is a nail driven into the palm; transmute it. Take in that energy and offer it love, by bringing it into the heart, which transforms it.

I was able to take these lessons back to the other two lifetimes, to the karmic ancestors with such traumatic deaths. One night in meditation, with tears streaming down my face, I offered this body to the birds that devoured my karmic ancestor's bowels, not grudgingly, but with joy, to feed them, nurture them. The birds symbolize everything in my life that tries to "eat" me, to devour or diminish me. But if the body and heart are offered freely, there can be no diminishment, only increase. I am everything, and everything is me. There is no enemy to steal the heart, only love offering itself to itself.

In meditation, I rested in a place of enormous light, with a sense of deep connection; there were no separate beings, just divinity. When my experience of love and stillness was powerfully present, I was asked to state my intentions. My prayer became to be the eyes and ears of God. This seems like the ultimate level of seeing and hearing, for the divine must see and hear it all, and with total unconditional love.

As the belly opened, I reflected on various traumas to the abdomen in this and past lifetimes: an appendectomy as a child in this life; a series of terrified kicks by a horse who had rolled over on me and crushed my leg, then reared over me and struck with his front hooves; and in past lives, the experiences I described at the beginning of this chapter of the two men who were cut open. I remembered my karmic ancestor who was stabbed by Hal's karmic ancestor in the 1500s. I also had an ancient memory of an insect eaten by a spider, held helpless, stung through the belly, then having had its life juices sucked out. We have all experienced such trauma in some past lives. Finally, the bear of the nineteenth-century lifetime came to mind one day in meditation as I lay with the belly very open. I felt myself surrounded by loving spirit all around, hands held, feet, head, shoulders, heart; as though I lay in a cradle of light, with the belly fully exposed.

I had not thought of him through all of this process. The bear lifetime is relatively recent. This karmic ancestor was a Native American shaman who had sworn never to do harm or take life. He was chased by a large bear, and cornered into a rock crevice where he could withdraw no further. With one swipe of his huge paw the bear sliced open his belly, then turned and walked away. Though the one I was had a knife, he did not use it to strike at the bear but was true to his intention not to harm. I have been amazed that the bear turned away, almost as if this slicing of the belly was an initiation. The wound festered. My ancestor, who lived alone at that time, washed the wound and sewed the belly closed. He shivered with fever for many days before returning to health.

In meditation, Dr. Valdivino asked me to try to stay as open as possible and to trust the Entities. They will support me. No harm will come. Allow this bear to tear open my belly, as he did long ago. Offer my belly to the bear as I offered it to the birds. Bless the bear as he opens the belly to the light, opens the last of the armoring. Thank him, praise him, and give myself fully to him. Thank God for this release of karma.

It was very hard, despite all the support. I cried, trembled, took three steps toward opening, two back. ... But eventually brother bear had done his work and the belly was fully open, with light flooding in. At that moment I recognized the bear as Maharaj-ji, my guru of this lifetime. It had always been Baba; I only thought it was a bear! Even then in the 1800s he was offering me this experience, to invite the small self to release. That Native American ancestor was determined not to kill the bear, but resolved to stop the bear from killing him. There was no hatred; there was deep compassion that said no to being killed. But when the bear did claw him, there was fear. He couldn't receive it as blessing, which was what Baba was offering him to learn, and what Jeshua had just taught me in this incarnation about the nails that entered his body. I know now that if my ancestor had not fled from the bear, the bear would not have killed him, just cut a little deeper and breathed his great breath into the wound.

With the light that the bear brought, and with these insights, came the experience of total bliss. All self was released. The chakras were all fully open, energy coursing through. I don't know how long a period of time passed. Time was nonexistent.

I came back to myself with the Entity using my hands, supporting my head, supporting the flow of energy. Aaron said it was holding the craniosacral flow open, supporting balance. They asked me to just rest, which I did for about twenty minutes. Slowly the other Entities left until only Aaron, Dr. Valdivino, and Baba remained.

I reflected that the Native American Shaman stitched the wound closed himself. He would not allow a loving healer to attend to it later when the scar was hard and painful, an armoring. That armoring was long-held. Now so much is released. The belly is warm, radiating light and energy; radiating life. Aaron has said that this release will allow the sacrum and lumbar spine to hold Kathleen's chiropractic adjustments much better.

I know that the next and perhaps most vital part of the work is to live this, not to close the belly in response to painful catalysts.

Journal, April 8, 2006

This morning, I went through the usual routine of eye exercise, tuning forks, and chakra openings. Dr. Valdivino worked on the chakras, until they all felt very open. Then he worked with the belly using very strong energy. My lower chakras still felt wide open, and he asked me to hold it that way, to allow light to enter. The energy was very intense, but also soothing and freeing. He asked me to offer forgiveness for all the times of trauma to the belly, seen and unseen. I saw the bear, with Baba's face, and then the terrified horse in this present lifetime, hooves crashing down on my belly and chest as I lay helpless and terrified, with my leg crushed. Dr. Valdivino asked me to feel those hooves as a blessing, to release the body's karma with those terrible blows. Then we turned to Mark. I had previously seen that several years after Jeshua's crucifixion, Mark had been captured and blinded by an enemy, and later he had been crucified, hung upside down by bored soldiers. Mark was filled with a self-righteousness that misunderstood Jeshua's teachings; he had condemned the world around him, as he condemned himself.

In meditation now, I didn't feel the pain, but was otherwise in Mark's body, seeing how he was held and blinded in the right eye. I saw how he had held that karma in the eye; in his eye, my eye, Everyman's Eye. Can I offer it? Can I transmute that trauma and release it? Can I do the same with Mark's crucifixion, feeling how he participated in creating the trauma with his righteousness, and releasing all traumas through forgiveness? My body shook with the releasing of so much old energy and karma.

They asked me to rest in a white light of a very high vibration. Again, I felt myself surrounded, as if held in a cradle of love and light. Then the white light began to shine into every cell, filling me completely until "me" just washed away; no thought, just light and peace.

I continued to do the tuning fork work, toning, visualization exercises and energy work with the Entities daily through the summer and fall of 2006. I meditated and did practices to release and balance old karma. I diligently did everything that was asked of me, but noticed few if any physical changes in my hearing ability, which was the original reason I went to Brazil. After the April 2004 accident in North Carolina, however, my body was a constantly changing grab bag of physical problems. Some were better, some were worse; some were the same as they had been upon my return from Brazil, ten months earlier. My eyes, which had briefly and dramatically improved in Brazil, were much the same, showing no further improvement. My right eye had some peripheral vision but a black hole remained in the center of my visual field. The left eye was still bleeding, but much less so than before.

After the healing session with the Entities and Kathleen, my body felt mostly pain-free, especially the back and neck. Even the knee was somewhat improved. I had had no further sinus headaches or nose bleeds. My lip had a large sore with a scab that would hold a few days, then fall off if I knocked it with a spoon or toothbrush. The sore would then spurt blood profusely for several days until a new scab formed. After two years of this intermittent bleeding, my primary care physician and I agreed that we needed to treat it. I had a surgical appointment scheduled after my return from the Casa. My body had become a ground for experimentation: what supports healing?

In December 2006, the Entities' work changed subtly. One morning when I began to meditate, a new energetic presence introduced himself to me. I had heard his name, Father Francis Xavier, at the Casa, but had not had a direct conscious experience of him. I asked him why he was here, instead of the now familiar energy of Dr. Valdivino. He told me that the new circuit between ear and brain that they had built over the past three years was nearing completion, but dormant. Father Francis likened the situation to an automobile that was fully built, but had no gasoline in the tank, and the ignition key was not turned on. The car is complete but will not run. His work is to teach me to open the new auditory circuit and to use it to hear. He cautioned me that the new circuit would not work like the old. The old neural circuit is dead. This is a new route that sound will take, to travel to the brain. He would be the one working with me regularly now. He said that Dr. Augusto would come often, to check on the circuits.

Father Francis' energy was very gentle and loving. When I asked him how we were to work together, he asked me to just rest in the Current of Divine Love, meditate, and allow him to support the opening of my energy field. I felt his participation when the chakras were less fully open, or when there were karmic issues.

In addition to Father Francis Xavier, another Entity new to me began to visit daily. St. Rita's energy was very gentle, yet I felt her strength beneath the soft exterior. Whenever she came, the room was filled with the scent of roses. She seemed mostly to hold me when I was sad, troubled, or in pain, just wrapping the warmth of her love around me, and wordlessly reminding me to allow myself to experience God's love. Although she introduced herself as Sister Margherita, her mother-like warmth led me to call her "Mother."

I felt like the next step was to go to Brazil and to stand before the Entities with this new openness, ready to fully receive what Love gives; and to express wholeness, for the highest good of all beings. Yet, I also saw the human part that was afraid of the power implied in this ability to express unlimitedness. We all have this power, if we allow ourselves to know it. I held in my heart a mantra that Spirit gave me several years ago: "Whatever I have and am comes from God, and I offer it all back to God."

With the new year, 2007, I found myself on the plane to Abadiânia for the fourth time, with great joy in my heart. Additionally, my dear friend and teaching colleague, John Orr, was accompanying me on this trip. John and I had been teaching meditation and dharma together since 1989, and he had encouraged me so much in my work. I was delighted to be able to introduce John to the Casa. The days, and the gifts of insight and healing that they brought, unfolded perfectly.

On the first morning for this visit, the Entity incorporated in Medium João came out on stage and performed an almost bloodless surgery, probably on a man's prostate, as the incision was low in the groin. The man stood so peacefully, with his back to the big triangle on the platform. I was in the front row and felt the strong energy. He did something I couldn't see in the area of the incision, then held his hand over the man's head, and thumped him firmly on the chest, and then the stomach. The man was then lowered into a wheelchair and taken off to the infirmary.

When I sat back down from watching, I immediately felt energy and was asked (in meditation) to put my hands over my heart and to be still. Unexplainable tears came, tears of intense emotion, not sadness, but joy and release. After about fifteen minutes, my everyday world and thoughts returned. Did they do surgery, as they sometimes do throughout the audience when the incorporated Entity is on the stage? I had no idea and Aaron would not discuss it. I went through the line. Dr. Valdivino was incorporated. He looked into my eyes for a long time. I could drown in his eyes; they are so filled with love and compassion. He pointed to a nearby chair and said to sit. I sat there in the front row through the rest of the morning and the afternoon session. I kept hearing the question, almost as if said aloud, *Why do you want to see and hear?*

I sat in the Current and again the question came: *Why do you want to see and hear?* This question had been pressing on me for months. I could see the changes in my answer, from willingness to see and hear even the painful things from a sense of duty to do so, to a more openhearted joy and desire for the full experience of being human and to invite deeper compassion. This is the birthright of us all as humans, to feel all the joys and sorrows, and to hold them in our hearts. I choose to see and hear, from a space of joy and love.

Dr. Augusto was incorporated, as I went through the line the next afternoon. He sent me to surgery. I sat in the surgery room and felt Aaron with me. Spirit's presence took me into a still, deep place. Then for a short time, I was just with the breath, and ever deeper into the space around the breath. I was asked to state my intention for the surgery. I began repeating the prayer: "May I be as clear a servant of light and of God as is possible. Please purify this body and energy to Thy service. Please heal this body, especially the ears and eyes if it is for the highest good, and whatever other healing you feel is appropriate. Help me to truly hear and see on the inmost planes, as well as the outer, physical one. Help me to hear and see all the ten million joys and sorrows." I repeated this for about five minutes.

I began to feel a lot of light. Then there was strong energy around the right eye, almost to the point of aching. Dr. Augusto acknowledged that it was he, but said no more. Then my ears began to feel pressure and heat. Tears were flowing and my body was trembling. It was the most intense surgery I have ever experienced.

Finally, I was told to lean back and relax a bit. I felt a lot of pressure to the lower and thoracic spine. Again the body trembled and tears began again. I was sitting that way, very erect, and trembling, when an attendant touched my hand to tell me to arise and leave the room, which was already empty except for the three people lying on the tables. I felt very weak, somewhat dizzy, and very disoriented. My ears felt hot and were ringing inwardly. They put me in a wheelchair and took me to the infirmary.

I had not been there before. A very loving volunteer sat me down on a bed, brought me water, helped me to lie down, and put a light covering over me, even though I was dripping with sweat. I fell asleep very quickly, and awoke in about ten minutes with severe back pain. Brother Sebastian was present immediately. I am not sure what he did, but the pain stopped almost instantly and I fell asleep again. I was half aware of the Entities continuing to work on me for some of that time. I awoke after an hour. A volunteer helped me to sit up, and brought me water, then the blessed Casa soup. I felt shaky, but much better. I went back to the pousada and directly to bed. There were some wild dreams that I cannot fully remember; one with swimming, one with a car that sideswiped another car, and the message that one must always be responsible for one's choices.

Learning flows; each new step builds upon the prior ones. While sitting in the Current, Father Francis Xavier began to give me instructions that could best be phrased as, "Don't do; be!" Later, Aaron asked me to look at the memory of infant Mike's crying and the tension that it had caused. This tension triggered karmic memories of situations in previous lives in which I could not save others or myself. Most vivid of all was the end of my last life, of the man drowning in the burning sea while dying people screamed all around him. I saw the fire around me, and the torpedoed, sinking ship. I saw myself panic, deepening the habit of reacting, of needing to do something because of my fear. Aaron said, "See the impulse on the relative plane; balance it. On the ultimate level, go to the place before it ever happened; all in balance, resting in spaciousness. Don't do, be!" Of course, it takes some doing first, before I can arrive at the place where I can just be.

Later that week I went through the line for the surgery review. The Entity sent me to the surgery room for the removal of any missed stitches, and then I was told to sit in his Current. After this interaction, I felt very deflated. I felt confident this morning that something big was going to happen. I really set myself up for disappointment with these expectations, but without expectations, how do we visualize what we wish to invite into our experience?

Aaron said that expectations are not the problem; one must see it not even as happening, but as already happened. With that insght, I must let go, with no grasping. If it has already happened, and one trusts that, then what is there to grasp at? Things are as they are. We just do what is in front of us.

The confusion comes when we don't clearly see what to do. Doing helped me to evade sadness, but I did not need to evade. I knew how to be with emotions. The doing is just more habit energy. The repetition of this pattern reflects a lack of trust that things are just where they should be in this moment. If it's hard, it's because there's something that needs to be understood; some grit is interfering with the smooth running of the wheel. We can then explore that direction in meditation.

That day I reflected on a recent, vivid dream. Someone came to me to tell me that the top floor of her new house had collapsed onto the lower floor. She was distraught, and I was aghast at first, seeing the destruction; but then it struck me. The weak beams were going to fail and the house was going to collapse no matter what. If someone had been hurt or killed, this could have been a much bigger tragedy. Now it can be rebuilt in a sound and correct manner. I said this to the woman and she brightened immediately, and then began to talk about how to rebuild better.

Looking at the dream, the woman is an aspect of my conscious self, and the "me" in the dream is a deeper level of awareness. The house (body) has collapsed, no hearing, no vision in one eye, as a way of announcing a weakness that needs attention. Instead of weeping, rejoice and rebuild with wisdom and love.

I can see now that through those first weeks at the Casa in 2007, I was remembering how to let go and trust; to allow the upper stories to collapse if they must, but to trust the integrity of the foundation, to invite the creation of a strong and beautiful superstructure, and to know that the complete house is already present.

Some years ago, there had been a period in which my daily meditations took me effortlessly into a vast field of light. There was very high energy then, and my self dissolved to the degree that there was no conscious thought. Aaron said the experience was related to the opening of the third eye.

That week Father Francis Xavier said that I needed to go more deeply into that light to awaken the new auditory system, and to also be able to allow Aaron more fully to incorporate into my body.

Aaron said that this is a deeper and more deliberate surrender to the light. I reverted back to "I don't know how to do it," then realized that there was nothing to do, to just let go and be. I know they're helping me.

Aaron: *If you seek to enter the light, child, it is because you think yourself to be outside that light. But how could you ever be apart from that which is your true nature? The more you try to enter the light, the more you deepen the illusion that you are separate from it. Just relax and be the light, and the depth of experience of that which you seek will open. Your work this week is nonwork, to relax and be. Effortless effort.*

I continued to ask for help to move more deeply into the light, to move past the resistance or at least to gain insight into the nature of it. I experienced a cave, a darkened area where people sat, and a brilliant light in the center of the room. The more I was focused on the darkness and trying to get to the light, the more I felt stuck in the darkness. As soon as I focused on the light, I was there and just sat immersed in that light and love.

I went through the line the following Wednesday afternoon to ask about the status of the hearing and eyes. Dr. Augusto was incorporated. He looked at me with his deep, penetrating gaze and then said, "You will hear. Be patient." Next, Heather asked him about the sore on the lip, which had been bleeding all week. I was holding a blood soaked handkerchief. He looked at the lip and said, "That we can help with now." He told me to sit back in his Current. But he said all this to Heather, and I didn't know that all that was said until later. I only knew that I was to sit in the Entity's Current.

Meditation went deep. One of the non-incorporated Entities, I am not sure which one, began to work through my hands on my body, especially on the head, face, ears, and eyes. There was much energy to the ears for an extended time. My body was shaking to the degree that I was concerned that I would disturb those sitting beside me.

There was deep, achy pain in the ears, and feelings of both congestion and opening, so I kept wanting to stretch, yawn, and swallow. I could feel the Entities conferring but couldn't hear them.

BOOM! BOOM!

What was that? I heard that! I sometimes feel the vibration in my body of a door slamming, especially in my feet through the floor, but this was undeniably different and in my ears. I opened my eyes for a moment and saw the bright flash. Then again, BOOM! People later confirmed that there were three loud bolts of thunder. This was the first thunder I had heard in thirty-four years. I sat there with tears running down my face.

About half an hour later, all my sinuses opened. It felt like a river running down my throat. I coughed so much I asked the Entities for help. They said drainage was necessary but they could release the cough mechanism. They moved my hands over the sinuses and throat, then the ears, back and forth for about five minutes. The coughing stopped though the drainage continued.

As I sat through that Current, I realized that my lip sore had stopped bleeding. After the Current ended I found Heather, who told me in full what Dr. Augusto had said.

Journal, Friday, January 26, 2007

This evening as I sat writing on the covered patio at the pousada, I heard thunder again, boom after boom resounding through the dusk. I ran from the dining area to the open lawn where I could see the lightning flash and began to dance in the rain. Many people joined me in this celebratory dance. I am hearing. It has begun. The lip has stopped bleeding completely. Dr. Augusto said he could heal it and it is healed. There is only a small scab now, just two days later. My knee, on which they operated last week, feels pain-free for the first time since the accident, and I have permission to walk gently, and may climb down to the waterfall. These healings are real. If he says I will hear, I will hear.

INTERVAL VI

Trainings

Aaron: *I want to speak with the reader directly, to give you a clear delineation of the basic trainings and initiations taught through many traditions. By "trainings" I merely mean those lessons on which you work, as a pathway to the growth to which you aspire. The initiations are the tests that life hands you, to see how well you have mastered the lesson. When it is mastered, the next period of training begins.*

These trainings are present in many traditions, but they are given different names. For example, the Buddhist tradition would call it training but does not speak of initiations. I will now delineate these trainings, giving some basic information about each. Trainings one and two may come in either order and usually are learned together. They are the trainings to observe the arisings within the physical and emotional bodies. One notes that sensations and emotions arise out of conditions, and that when the conditions cease, these sensations and emotions will cease. The intended result of the training at this level is development of a lessened self-identification with what has arisen, and the ability to allow more spaciousness with difficult body and emotional experiences. Training three does the same work with thought. The phrase, "Don't believe everything you think," distills the essence of training three.

These first three trainings are the essence of basic dharma practice, but Jesus taught the same thing in a different way. He did not give us the precise steps with which to transform difficult body sensations, emotions, and thoughts. He only reminded us that when one slaps us in the face, we can return love, not hatred. In large part, he did not spell it out because it had already been expressed by the Buddha, and by all the practices within the various mystery schools such as those of the Druids and Essenes and in related traditions. Jesus was speaking to all the people, but I think he felt it was sufficient to remind them to "turn the other cheek," and that those who already knew how to release the anger elicited by the slap would do so with this reminder. Those who did not yet know how would seek training. Now much of this wisdom has been forgotten so we must teach it again.

These first three were the trainings given to the youngest of children in the Essene tradition. They were taught never to despise even the most negative arisings in the self, but to recognize them as the result of conditions, to make space for them and to allow their release. Actually, even little children moved quickly into the sixth, seventh, and eighth trainings, which I will describe shortly.

The initiations for these first three trainings were freely given in life, through the stubbed toe, the rude remark that brought anger, and the restless mind with its judgments, fears, and complaints.

The fourth training was the first opening into the experience of selflessness and egolessness. It was the first seeing of the small self as a created mind object, and the first knowing of the greater self. There was as yet no stability in the ability to rest in that greater self, only the first glimpse of such resting seen as possible. This glimpse changes everything. If one has a deep commitment to nonharm because of the knowing of nonseparation, one can no longer act out of one's ego and fear and still be honest with one's self and true to one's values. Included in this training is the deepening of . . . I am hesitant to use the term Sila here because you may not know this term, but there is no other precise English equivalent. For those unfamiliar with the word Sila, it is a Pali language word. It connotes moral awareness, not a "Thou shalt not . . ." morality, but a morality deeply based on knowing the nonseparation of self and other. One does not cut off one's own hand. "Love thy neighbor as thy self." (More information can be found in the glossary.)

The fifth training is the opening into nondual Awareness. When it is understood that nothing is separate, and that to strike another is to harm the self, such abuse of others is much harder to enact. The fifth training is the fruit of the first four trainings. In this training, one more deeply recognizes relative reality and ultimate reality. Here is the first view that these realities are not dualistic, each to each, but that relative reality is an expression of ultimate reality. This means that when you are present with relative reality, the ground of the ultimate is also present. When you are resting on top of the ocean's surface, rising and falling with the waves, the stillness of the depths is still there. When you sink to the depths, the waves continue to rise and fall far above you. Mastery at the fifth level of training involves a more conceptual understanding. One who has mastered this level remembers it, but is rarely able to hold both places simultaneously. In Buddhist terms, this person is often at the stream-entry* level.

The sixth, seventh, and eighth trainings mirror the first, second, and third respectively, but at a deeper level. Here one is asked to bring awareness to what one understands about the conditioned arisings of physicality, emotion, and mind. These insights merge with the experience of the dissolution of the ego, and with the—at this point—conceptual, nondual understandings. One understands that difficult emotions will arise, for example, and one has learned nonreactivity to those emotions, that is, to not act them out or suppress them, but just to make space for them. But they will still arise. We understand that they are conditioned, and that this is the playing out of karma, or habit, but they still arise. When the training is internalized deeply enough not to react with negativity to their arising, but instead to bring kindness into play, then it is time to deepen the fifth training and to begin to use it as a tool for the transmutation of the heavier body and mind experiences.

Several practices are useful here. To summarize these practices, you turn to the Master of your heart's choosing for support, with gratitude that these models of clarity and love exist for your use. You see the negative emotion that has arisen, for example. Without a contraction, without a negative feeling about the arising, you experience compassionate regret that it continues to arise. You know it as a result of conditions. You understand that for the result to cease to arise, the conditions must change. You understand that you are stuck in this place. Then, the two levels of resolution arise. You resolve to clarify this habit energy on the relative level, and on the ultimate level you understand the already existent resolution of the habit. You can see here why training five must precede six, seven, and eight.

Within this ultimate level of resolution, you can clearly see the balance or antidote to the heavy energy that has arisen. For example, if there is jealousy, you do not try to feel joyful for the one who has received, so much as to find that already existent joy within you and the willingness to nurture it. When there is restlessness in mind and body, you both resolve to allow the release of restlessness and you see clearly the entire resolution of restlessness, which is peace, tranquility, and stillness. And you find those qualities already existent in the self.

---

*Stream-entry is the first stage of realization. See Glossary.

There is the willingness not to perpetuate the contracted energy of the restlessness, but to turn one's focus to that which is more spacious.

If you see a being act in a brutal way toward another, and a heavy judgment arises in the mind, right there with the judgment you note the possibility of compassion. You do not hold to the stories of judgment; you note that holding as an old habit. You resolve to allow the arising of compassion; you see the already existent compassion and realize that you have the choice either to hold on to the judgment, or to shift into compassion. You see the nondual nature of judgment and compassion, and that judgment is simply a distortion of compassion: a fear-based expression of the inherently compassionate mind. You do not have to get rid of judgment for compassion to be known; judgment will go when it is ready. The question is whether you will focus your attention on the judgment and become caught in its stories, caught in the negativity of judging judgment, or whether you will know judgment as a distorted expression, and joyfully release it. In either case, you may move to stop the abuser. The judgment mind will attack with negativity. The compassionate mind will stop the abuse with loving energy. It will know how to say no with kindness, and without fear or contraction.

The ninth training is a deepening level of the understanding of egolessness. Here one becomes more stable in opening to that deep interconnection of All-That-Is. When something pulls you out of that spaciousness and integration, you know that you are out. You understand that it is a temporary result of conditions. You do not take it as truth. You work with that experience of separation in the same way that you have worked with difficult body, emotion, and mind experiences in the sixth, seventh, and eighth trainings. Thus separation and the arising of the small ego self are seen through awareness. The greater self is readily accessible. You understand that you can go in one direction or the other by habit and choice.

The tenth training establishes the deeper resolution of duality. One experiences oneself as a pole, feet grounded in the relative, and we could say here the base and lower chakras grounded in the relative; the upper chakras grounded in the ultimate. The heart is that which holds it all together. At this level, you truly become an instrument of light. I do not want to suggest that those in the lower trainings and with heartfelt intention to transcend negativity are not instruments of light, but they are instruments of light in training. The tenth level is the first of more mature service to the light. It is the first level where the automatic response to negativity is to offer it love, to draw it into the light, to draw the negativity up inward into the light and bring the light downward into the negativity. This is possible because you are touching both. You cannot touch both as long as there is residual aversion to negativity, and as long as there is duality.

At this point, the vibrational frequency in all of the bodies is in the process of major transformation. The person at this level is increasingly able to experience negativity as a low-frequency vibration, and to understand experientially the power of light as tool. At this level, there still may be karma to resolve so there may not be full liberation, but there is the understanding that the liberation is in sight. At the full maturity of the tenth training and initiation, often—in Buddhist terms—is the once-returner.

The eleventh to fifteenth of the trainings and initiations repeat the cycle. In trainings eleven through thirteen, the adept is using his/her mastery of light in a continual way to transform negatively polarized energy as it arises in body, emotions, and mind. The fourteenth training often leads one to a more profound enlightenment experience and the ability to hold both the personality self and the Ground of Being easily. This may be the first experience of no-self, as contrasted with the dissolution of the ego. The fifteenth training and initiation is of the deepening learning to stably hold this light, not only into the inner experiences but into the outer world. Here of course we are at the level of non-returner, although many such beings choose to return in service. Karma is resolved to the degree that karma does not force return. There is still some karma. It comes to fruition quickly and is resolved with light.

Now we move to the higher training. I think you can see where this is going. Once this mastery is in place, anything may be done with light. The being that has done this work while deeply grounded in positive polarity, with deepest intention for the good of all beings, will use these deeper practices for healing. By healing I mean the healing of distortion on the physical, emotional, and mental levels, in itself and everywhere in the world, wherever that healing is requested. The Entities of the Casa are great masters of this process. The tools they use are those of light. Advanced practices such as cellular regeneration* are real on your

---

*This means the use of energy and vibration to regenerate cellular tissue.

present-day Earth, and are being remembered. As third-density beings, moving into fourth density, you are relearning these skills.

The work now is to teach the third density human to bring forth these practices that were once known, but were lost through the ages of heavy density human experiences. It is not necessarily the case that, just because you have a heavier density body, you cannot still work with light. In this process, the Earth and all upon it are raised up in vibrational frequency. All who are ready to sustain that higher vibration will shift into fourth density, including the Earth itself. And I think soon after, in cosmic time, into fifth density. Yet this new fourth and eventually fifth density will also be comprised of the basic elements: earth, air, fire, water, and ether, and will not have just a crystalline base as was the case in the time of Lemuria.*

Some of you are higher-density adepts, bodhisattvas really, returned to help carry forth this transformation. Some of you are third density beings ready for transformation, who have brought this forth through your courage and repeated growth through endless incarnations in this third density plane. You are all seeking one thing together; the movement of matter into light, without the loss of any of the beautiful qualities of matter. This shift has the power literally to transform the universe. That is why darkness so fears it.

Darkness wishes to keep matter at a low vibration, for darkness itself is a low vibration. It is based on fear, hatred, greed, and self-centeredness. Light understands self-centeredness as Self-centeredness, which means holding All-That-Is at the center. It understands that it is this All-That-Is. Negative polarity puts the personality self at the center. One is constantly at odds with the other; thus there is constant contraction.

The Entities of the Casa are not only assisting with physical healing. That is one gift of their work. But a core of their work is the bringing forth of the light into this Earth plane. We who do this work simply call ourselves brothers and sisters of light. You are also brothers and sisters of light, still in training, as we are still in training, all beings going into greater and greater light.

---

*Lemuria was an ancient and highly evolved civilization that existed prior to and during the beginning of the time of Atlantis.

CHAPTER 21

Other Healing Stories

WHEN WE COME to the Casa and ask for help, almost by definition we have the desire for healing, and at least the beginnings of a belief that such healing is possible. However, with many people and certainly with me, significant obstacles to healing remain. Often these obstacles take the form of belief systems that do not allow for spiritual healing. Such beliefs include, "I am not worthy," or "Miracles do not happen in real life; such things are not possible," or "God wants me to be this way." How can these beliefs be changed? One way is through the stories of others. There are many inspiring accounts of healing at the Casa, and many openhearted people who are willing to share them. I have come to understand that these tales support our paths in a vital way. Stories of healing often become a deliberate, even essential part of the healing process, for both teller and audience. As we hear these words, we are affected. We start to understand that healing is possible, and that miracles are possible. Beliefs in brokenness, lack, and limitation gradually shift into a knowledge of wholeness, abundance, and the unlimited nature of our divine essence. Trust in the process of healing grows. As our belief systems stretch and change to accept the formerly impossible, but now undeniably true information, we become more open to similar processes happening within ourselves. This opening in turn opens us more fully to the multilayered healing that we are then able to co-create with the Entities.

As I try to describe this process, the resurrection narrative in Matthew comes to mind. After the earthquake, after the angel rolls back the stone barring Jesus' tomb, after the guards pass out from fright, the angel speaks[1] to Mary Magdalene and the "other Mary": "Do not be afraid, for I know that you are looking for Jesus, who was crucified. He is not here; he has risen, just as he said. *Come* and *see* the place where he lay. Then *go* quickly and *tell* his disciples.... " [emphasis mine]. Here the angel is convincing the Marys of a miracle, a radical change from the expected. What is required to allow this new information to sink in is to *come* and *see*. The acts of *going* and *telling* are also necessary. Not only does going and telling help the teller to process and assimilate the experience, it starts a similar process inside the mind of the listener. Can it be true? What if this really happened? In this way minds are expanded and the news is spread.

On Sunday mornings at the Casa, an hour is devoted to expressing a communal love for the divine in whatever way the assembled individuals wish. On Sunday, January 28, 2007, several people shared inspiring healing stories. Later that day I was able to meet with two of them and hear the accounts in detail, while someone signed, and I recorded them for transcription. "Hearing" these healing stories deepened my trust in my own recent healing experiences; but at the time, I was unaware of the full implications of this process of telling and listening. These stories helped to create the necessary inner conditions for me to hear, by expanding my sense of the possible and by further opening my heart to my own healing.

The first meeting was with Beatrice who was healed of muscular dystrophy. Here is her experience. Minor changes in the transcript have been made for clarity:

"When I was a teenager, my father and aunt were told by doctors from the university that I had myotonic muscular dystrophy. My father and his sister both had it. They got weaker and weaker with walking. The disease is on the nineteenth chromosome. I experienced no symptoms, but the doctors predicted that I would develop a more aggressive form.

"My father and his sister were in wheelchairs, so I could watch the progression and know that I would have this disease. My father died at sixty-five; his sister, at sixty-four. Disease symptoms had started around age thirty-five; you could see the progression because they walked differently than other people do. I was shocked about this diagnosis because I saw how it would be for me. I did not talk much to other people because they started to feel so sorry for me that I had to take care of them!

"But I watched myself—for example, when I walked and there was a store window—I looked to see if I walked normally or not. Sometimes it seemed not. Also when I could not open a bottle, I thought, 'Now maybe it starts.' Or when my speech was not clear, I thought the same.

"I got many educational degrees because I wanted to be independent. I studied psychology because I would be able to sit and work in a wheelchair. I worked for three years as a psychologist, after the degree. When I was thirty-five, I realized that life was going by so fast. I thought, I need to fulfill my dreams before I am in a wheelchair. I will do everything I want now.

"So I quit my job, I left my apartment, and began to travel the world. I was very interested in spirituality and I was looking for help. So I went to India and lived in ashrams; I saw Sai Baba, Amma, and different gurus; and I took teachings with the Dalai Lama. I loved this life a lot.

"In Peru, I got to know a group from Holland. A man gave me a book on John of God and I read it overnight. I left almost the next morning to find this place. This was in the winter of 2002 and 2003. I went by boat over the Amazon; it was very adventurous. I flew from Manaus in the Amazon to Brasilia.

"At the airport I asked for Abadiânia and no one knew where this was. So I took the airport bus to the main bus station in Brasilia, and then people helped me to get here. I went into the Casa, and it was a really beautiful feeling, like coming home. But while I felt very good, my brain was saying, 'Watch out, this could be a dark thing.' Then I saw the picture of the Dalai Lama thanking João de Deus for his work, and everything was all right.

"When I first went through the line, I did everything wrong that you could do wrong. I went with closed eyes in front of the Entity. He was trying to get my attention, touching me, but I had heard that it would hurt João if I opened my eyes! So I kept them closed. But then the next time, he smiled at me, and said, 'Filia,' so I had the feeling I was at the right place.

"I did not ask if he could heal me of my disease because I was scared of the answer; I just sat in the Current. I had many very special experiences. First there was just Jesus and Sai Baba; they just came to visit. I cried a lot. One time, in one meditation, my whole body started to tremble, and I could not stop; I could not help it. There were only wooden benches then; so many people sat on one bench, but I could not stop trembling. The whole bench was vibrating. It was a long time, maybe twenty minutes. I thought my whole self would have been turned around: My whole body, every single cell. And then when it stopped there was a very beautiful light, so big a light, and I felt that I was one with everything, one with God. It was just unbelievable; I have never known this feeling before. I had everything, more than everything. It was soft and peaceful. Nothing was missing. I had everything.

"After five weeks. I went in the line and asked if he could heal me. Then Dr. Augusto took my hand and smiled at me, and he said, 'You are already healed.' And I knew it was true. There were not yet serious symptoms, but I knew I was getting the disease from the smaller symptoms. Before, I was unable to open a jar. Now, I can. So much weight has been lifted from me; I didn't even know I was carrying so much.

"From then on, my life changed completely. I wanted to go back and check the genetics with the university. And they said, 'We have done it once; your disease will never disappear because it is genetic. Just know that you are ill and must develop increasing symptoms. ...' So I didn't bother doing any more tests. The proof will be that I do not develop the symptoms.

"My illness was a wake-up call to go live another life, to go into spirituality, my path. I struggled a lot with doctors. I was mad at them for twenty-four years. They told me that there is no cure possible, that the disease is worse than my father's. Now I understand that they helped me to find my way. They came from God as well."

While listening to her story, and her gratitude to God, I was reminded of a man[2] I have met often at the Casa. He was blind with a progressive eye disease and was healed at the Casa. The eye doctors in California insist he's still blind when they examine his eyes. His optic nerves are destroyed, but he has excellent vision. He reads and drives a car. His story has inspired me for years, and is worth mentioning, if only in passing. On his website, he says, "I received a miracle in the form of restoration of my vision after being nearly blind. I am so grateful for God's healing grace working through the compassionate spirit guides of John of God." Our gratitude truly is important, not to God or Casa Entities who don't need our thanks, but to ourselves because of the way it opens our hearts.

That evening I met with Sarah. Here is her story of healing from epilepsy, translated from German:

"I have had epilepsy since I was twelve years old. I came upon João through my mother who is also very spiritual. The first time I came here was in August 2006. The Entity said that he could heal me, and that I should come back four times. This time is my third time and I have to come back only one more time to be healed.

"Medium João told me that I had spiritual epilepsy. When I have a seizure, I am attacked by negatively polarized energy that I can perceive. Now my third eye has opened, which enables me to see even more. I see a lot of colors and I see angels. Last week I experienced for the first time a negative entity that appeared in the form of a large black cloud, hunched over a woman. This entity told me that this woman did not have long to live. I was very upset. I ran home and cried. The next day I went to João to ask about my meditation. What happened last week was a test for me because for the first time I saw something negative with my normal awareness and did not lose consciousness. My last attack was on the twenty-fourth of December, four months after my first visit. Before coming here, I could not go a month without an attack.

"This week, the Entity told me that I would have my last operation. I am so happy that my healing is working out so well. After I am healed, I can continue on my professional path, and work on my own without having somebody next to me all the time looking after me, waiting for an attack. I can be alone with my two-year-old daughter. I thank the Entities from the bottom of my heart for everything that they have done for me, and that the healing has worked so well. This is a very, very special place for me. I know I will come back."

The Entities sometimes make requests as they did to Sarah, to come a certain number of times. For others they simply recommend that the person return, as they have for me; for there is no certainty how long the healing will take. A third story comes from friends who have never been to the Casa, who only had help through photographs. D and J had a beautiful son when J was forty-three. They wanted a second child and J was able to conceive, but after four miscarriages they had little hope that she could carry a baby to term. Their doctors in the United States were not encouraging. But Aaron had said to them that he thought they could have a healthy child. I was deeply involved with the beginning of their story at the same time I was collecting these other stories. Here is the story in their words, written over a year after the other events of this chapter. I include it because it is an inspiring story that shows how healing can work at a distance, and because their story further opened my heart to my own healing.

"After four miscarriages within a year and a half, my wife, J, and I had given up on the chance of having another baby. A top fertility clinic at the University of Washington confirmed that at age forty-six, J's eggs were just too old and that's why they never made it past the first six to eight weeks of gestation.

"In November of 2006 Barbara was visiting us in Seattle to lead a semiannual retreat that we organize. We talked with Aaron about our decision to try for another pregnancy. He heard from the Entity St. Francis Xavier that if we could come to the Casa, that they would be able to perform an operation on J that would increase her chances of having a baby. J and I discussed the possibility and decided that we (particularly J) could not withstand the enormous physical, emotional, and mental toll of yet another miscarriage. We knew that there was a little spirit that was trying hard to make its way to us, so we decided that if we cannot have it come to us naturally, then we'll simply let it come to us through adoption.

"Two weeks later we found out to our great surprise that J was pregnant again. We immediately sent notice to the Entities through Barbara and through Heather Cumming. The message back was that the Entities would do all that they could to support us and the baby.

"The pregnancy was progressing well and while we held out hope, we also knew that the odds were not in our favor. We contemplated having an amniocentesis, but decided to hold off knowing the risks involved with this test. J's midwife suggested instead to run a blood test in week fifteen that poses no risk to the baby, and that is supposed to be very accurate in screening potential birth defects. Unlike an amniocentesis, however, which looks at the actual chromosomes and, therefore, can give a definitive answers, this test looks at blood indicators and, therefore, gives a probabilistic answer.

"When we got the blood test results back we both went into shock. The test indicated a very high probability for Down syndrome (chromosome 21) and, even worse, a better than 50 percent chance of chromosome 18 being defective. Problems with this chromosome result in extreme birth defects (extreme disfigurement, intestinal defects, extreme heart defects, etc.) and the baby's chances of making it to birth are usually very small. If it did make it to birth, it would likely not live for very long.

"We were devastated and couldn't believe that we had made it through the first trimester, only to find out this horrible news.

"We sent an urgent message to the Entities through Barbara and through Heather. The answer back from the Entities was that they could not guarantee anything, but they are working with the genetic material, literally daily, as best as they could. Barbara told us that St. Francis Xavier said he was present with the baby every day. Our spirits lifted and J felt that the baby was going to be okay, but we were still feeling uneasy. It was suggested that we visualize the perfect baby in perfect health.

"We scheduled an amniocentesis for two days later and then waited nervously for the results.

"They came a week later—our little baby girl looked perfect and everything was normal. We were elated and very grateful to the Entities and everyone else's support.

"Our beautiful baby Sophia was born in autumn of 2007, at home with no complications. At the time of this writing she is four and a half months old and is happy, thriving, and adored by all, including her older brother Ori.

"As a footnote, we later found out from our naturopathic-midwife, who has over twenty years of midwifery experience and has delivered thousands of babies, that J (who was forty-seven by the time Sophia was born), was the oldest obstetric client that she had ever had by a margin of three years. We also found out that the doctors at the hospital where the amniocentesis was performed refused to believe that J's pregnancy was spontaneous (meaning, it did not require any medical intervention).

"Once again, we cannot express enough our deep gratitude and love to all the Entities, particularly to St. Francis Xavier, for their love, dedication, and support."

This fourth story is from a meeting on February 5, 2008, with Denise, who was healed from multiple sclerosis. Minor changes have been made for clarity.

"I found out that I had MS in 1987 when I had lost vision in my right eye. I was told there was no cure. My daughter, who is twenty-one now, was six months old, so I was full of dread and anxiety. I became very weak; had numbness, some pain, and difficulty walking. I was a nurse, but I didn't know what to do because traditional medical science said that there was no cure, no hope.

"I took the steroids that they gave me, and tried very hard to go on with my life while waiting for the next flare-up. I was full of anxiety because I never knew when I woke up if I would be the same as when I had gone to sleep. It was a life of always waiting for something to happen that I knew wouldn't be the best thing to happen to me.

"I realize now that I had had the symptoms since I was maybe nineteen, but I didn't know it. I would have three, four, five flare-ups every year. Sometimes the symptoms would stay. Sometimes the symptoms would go. I never knew. So there was a lot of anxiety.

"In 1995, I was remarried and had a lot of pressure at home. I was working very hard and trying to hide that I had MS. Then, in 1997, I had a very bad flare-up that I couldn't hide anymore. I went from my work to the hospital where they put me on steroids intravenously. A very bad flare-up; very scary, I felt like I was turning into concrete. I went on disability from nursing and felt very sad, disillusioned, and empty. I tried very hard to go on with my life but I never knew when I would have another flare-up.

"I walked with a cane, always a cane. Sometimes I couldn't get out of the shower. I would get in the shower and be so fatigued that I couldn't imagine rinsing my hair and getting out. I would be exhausted. I had handlebars in my bathroom. My friends bought me a scooter to get out to the store or to the mall, because it was hard for me to get anywhere.

"I had always believed in God. I knew there were spirits but I didn't know that they could help me. I had heard about healers, but I didn't accept it for myself. I thought that if God wanted to heal me, he would just heal me. So I made the best out of my life until February of 2005. I saw on TV the last five minutes of 'Prime-Time Live.' John Quinonas was interviewing Medium João, and immediately I knew I was going, especially when I saw the rich earth that you walk on, the color of the earth that I wanted to put on my face.

"I went to my computer. I looked up John of God and found a guide, and three weeks later I was in Abadiânia. I didn't know what to expect, I only knew to trust. I had faith that I would be healed in some way. I knew I should go. In the hotel room in Brasilia, a brilliant light came to me one night. The brilliant Golden Light was so huge I knew it was them, the Entities, and I wasn't scared because I knew that they were taking care of me. I knew that they were guiding me, that they were with me already, and I did not have to look for them, I was going to them. They were with me.

"So I came here and I followed directions exactly. I did what my guide told me to the tee. Everything. The Entity said, 'Go sit in my Current.' That was fine with me. Everyone in my group was getting operations. I didn't care. I knew I was where I should be. I cried a lot. I let go of a lot. I felt a lot. I felt vibrations. I felt wind. I felt movement around me. My heart was opening, in here. There was pain. It was finally coming out. I would look outside my window and see children playing, and I wanted to be one of them. I wanted to be as happy as a child.

"So one day I joined a parade without realizing it. Walking with my cane, I tried to keep up with many of the people who were in the parade. It was for Palm Sunday. It was very hot, but I didn't care, I just followed them and walked farther than I had in years. A couple of days after that, I put down my cane. I said, 'I don't need it anymore. I can walk.' So then I began to walk all over, up and down the street, with no pain anymore. I used to have terrible pain, pain that would make me want to lie in bed and die. I didn't feel that way here.

I opened the curtains, I wanted light, and I wanted to walk on the beautiful road I had seen on television. I walked and I laughed and I smiled, and my heart opened.

"Going back home, my husband brought the scooter to the airport; and he said, 'Where is your cane?' And I said, 'In Brazil! My cane is in Brazil!' He said, 'Do you want to sit in your scooter?' I said, 'No, you can use it!' No scooter needed.

"I was filled with energy. After that, I came back four more times to the Casa and saw Medium João in Atlanta. Now I have permission to bring people as a guide. I hope that they get relief from the pain in their lives, whether it is spiritual, emotional, or physical, or all—all are important. And I've gone back to work after eleven years of being unable to work. I'm a nurse. I work with an agency. I do hospice, and anyone who needs home care.

"I realize now that my body got me to Abadiânia and the Casa; but my spirit is the most important part of me. My spirit grows each day and will go on. I have been blessed that I have no symptoms of MS. Whereas before I had many, today I have none. Today I can walk. Today I can use the bathroom without help. Today I can see with contacts. Today I have no pain in my legs, no pain. No dizziness. I have freedom. To help other people is the most important part of my life, to come here to the Casa. I just brought my first group and I want to bring many more, to share with them the Entities and the blessings of one God for us all, who has given me love and my life back. I would like to thank Medium João, the Entities, and Beings of Light, the Angels, the Saints, and God, for healing me today; and for making it possible for my life to be better, and of use to others."

As I listened to the first two stories and the fourth one above, I was focused on getting the words, with the aid of the person who interpreted for me with sign language. On Tuesday, January 30, I had the opportunity to meet with Matt. There was no one to sign, but I knew the words would be transcribed so I was relaxed. I could lip-read only part of it, but I hesitated to interrupt him because the story was clearly an emotional one for him, and at times his eyes were filled with tears, his voice choked with emotion. So I just sat and listened to Matt with my heart. Perhaps that open hearted waiting and deep listening partially explains what happened near the end of Matt's story:

"This is my fourth year in Abadiânia, and I've had a life-changing experience here on every level. My story really begins in February 2003. I was working in a job that I really loved in the Rocky Mountains, with good friends. I felt like I was in a really magical, spiritual place; the views, the surroundings, everything was a little bit of a dream. But on the other hand, now I see that we were polluting it by smoking a lot of pot. That was something that was wrong in my life, I think.

"One day, I drove into work and I stopped in at the office in town before I went up into the mountains. I was doing some paperwork, and all of a sudden my head started to hurt, a migraine-type headache. It scared me. I lay down for half an hour or so, the headache went away, and I went on with my day.

"The next morning, I went through my routine again, and made it to the office in town. I got a headache again. It felt like the same headache, but today it was a little more painful and a little stronger. I walked it off, and it cleared in the afternoon.

"As the next week developed, these headaches became a daily routine. Each day at the same time the same headache would come, only each day's headache was progressively worse. After about a week, I went to the local doctor. He said, 'Migraines,' gave me some painkillers, and sent me on my way. After another week of the migraines getting worse and worse, I did some alternative therapies, some massage, and some chiropractic work. These would work great for about half an hour, but then the headache would be right back, just as strong as ever, and just as painful.

"After those two weeks, I was in so much pain, that my head would hurt for eighteen out of twenty-four hours a day. Everybody said, 'Go get an MRI. Go make sure you don't have something like a brain tumor.' At the hospital they found something they couldn't diagnose. All they could say was, 'There is a tumor in the center of your brain.' It cut off the normal free flow of cerebrospinal fluid, causing the pressure in my brain to rise dangerously. This was giving me extreme pressure headaches. The nearest hospital that could treat this was eight hours away in Denver. They said, 'Get there immediately. You have to have brain surgery NOW.'

"Some really good friends dropped everything they were doing, and they helped. We drove through a blizzard. We got to the hospital ten hours later, at 4:00 a.m. They were waiting for me, and I was immediately checked into the intensive care unit. I rested the best I could that morning. Then they had me scheduled for brain surgery. Their plan was to take a biopsy of the tumor to begin a diagnosis, and see what they could do about relieving the pressure.

"They implanted the shunt by drilling a hole through my brain, past the tumor, into the cavity where all the fluid was accumulating. That relieved the pain. That shunt was a godsend. That is where I thank Western medicine for their brilliance, for saving my life. I would not have made it to Abadiânia without the hospital, without the doctors. So God bless them.

"I was in the intensive care unit and everybody there has a very severe problem. I remember my one friend who strummed away on his guitar all day long. The whole ward was filled with music. It was so beautiful. I can only imagine the happiness that he brought to some of those people that were there alone and dying.

"About a week after surgery, somebody brought me the book that Lance Armstrong wrote about his victory over cancer. I read right through it and something stuck in my head that I thought was very odd, and that was the phrase, 'This cancer is the best thing that ever happened to me.' He wrote that down, and at that point I just couldn't figure it out. I just didn't get what was so good about something that nearly killed him. Something, though, told me to start putting this phrase into my head. And I think every single day since reading that quote, I see the truth of that statement more and more clearly. All this had to happen. I had to change my life. Something was going wrong. And this was my wake-up call.

"My diagnosis primarily was a stage I or stage II tumor, not super-dangerous, just something to keep an eye on, nothing that's really aggressive or dangerous. After a second biopsy and more biopsies of the blood and cranial fluid and spinal fluids, they eventually upgraded it to a stage III cancer, which is more dangerous and more aggressive. They still thought they could keep it under control with chemotherapy and radiation. Grade III was a little worse than grade II but not the end of the world.

"The day before I left, I went to see the doctor. He said, 'Well, I actually have some bad news. We've had a lot of doctors look at your report, all the biopsies, all the work, and we've come to the conclusion that this is something we have to deal with right now. Your tumor is a glioblastoma multiform stage IV: inoperable.' The tumor was too near the cortex, the center of my brain and they wouldn't operate on it. The doctor said to me in a friendly way, as nice as you can say this, 'It's a good idea to be near family, to start seeing people and saying goodbye to people. You have a 2 percent chance to be as good as you are or better in twelve weeks.' I accepted that as his way to say, 'Prepare to die, you don't have very long at all.' Inside myself, I said, *No, that's not right. I AM one of those 2 percent; I AM going to live.*

"I chose that day to live. The time leading up to it helped me make that choice. Seeing many people die around me in the ICU, watching these people die, listening to them die, I said, 'No way.' I chose to live and I think that a big part of healing is your choice and your positive thoughts, your positive feelings, your hope, your faith to live. It was so clear to me. Thank God it was the right message I got. And thank God for this warning, this opportunity to change my life.

"I flew back to Vermont with my mom and started chemotherapy and radiation treatments.

"I did all of my radiation treatment. I never felt good about chemotherapy. I never had before this all happened and I don't today. One of the brain's normal and natural defenses against poisons of all kinds is called the blood-brain barrier. So just to enter into the brain, a poison like chemotherapy has to pass through the blood-brain barrier, and maybe only 30 percent gets through to act on the tumor. Where is the other 70 percent of that poison going? All over your body, killing the rest of your body. And of this 30 percent that might get through, they said there is a 30 percent chance that it will do anything. So after saying no to chemotherapy for a couple of weeks, I said, 'Okay, I'll try that.' After about three weeks, I said, 'No more.'

"I slowly got stronger and stronger. I went to radiation treatments five days a week, and walked along the Appalachian trail every day. Healing then was a heavy, full-time process.

"In my time at Dartmouth doing the radiation, they told me, 'After this there's nothing we can offer you. We can check up on you every two months, but eventually this cancer will kill you.' Now, they didn't use those words, of course, they were very, very sweet. But they really gave me no hope. Then we talked a little about alternative therapies. My doctors couldn't really support them but they couldn't offer anything else. I had some friends who were getting into healing modalities, and we decided that as soon as I was strong and recovered from the radiation, we would set up a trip to work with a Peruvian shaman towards a cure. Everyone in the tour group I was going to travel with came to know my story, even folks I had never met. One of the women said, 'Matthew doesn't need to come to Peru, he needs to go see John of God in Brazil.' That was the first time I heard about the Entities.

"I looked on the computer and found the Friends of the Casa website.[3] I read about it and saw the picture on it and said, 'Wow, that's pretty weird.' I'm not from a past of religious faith. I haven't ever disbelieved in God, but I also didn't ever believe in any religion in particular. In other words, I believed in God, I just never believed in church. I found God in nature, in the woods, in the magical forests that really give you energy. The beautiful lakes and vistas, this to me was God. It still is. I think God is everywhere especially in the beauty He gives to us.

"I tried to cancel Peru. I couldn't. My trip was funded by donations from friends, so I didn't have any money to go from Peru to Brazil. And so I shut John of God out of my head.

"About two weeks before the departure date for Peru, I was in northern Vermont. The phone rang. It was a neighbor in a small community of about thirteen homes. The neighbor said, 'Hi, is this Matthew?' I said, 'Yeah.' She said, 'Hi, I live next door to you. I've been to John of God. And I would love you to come over, if you like, and I'll tell you my story, and we'll talk about it.' And I said, 'Oh, great! I'd love to meet someone who's been there.'

"So I went over and talked with her. I was there for about forty-five minutes, maybe an hour. When I walked back over to our house across the field, I had a ticket booked, I had a taxi driver ready to pick me up at the airport in Brasilia and drive me to Abadiânia, and I had the name of a woman in Abadiânia, with a pousada to stay in. My next door neighbor, God bless her heart, bought me a ticket. She said, 'You go. You need to go. Don't let money stop you. You can pay me back whenever you can pay me back. Don't worry, you just go.'

"So in two weeks, I was headed to Brazil and not Peru. Knowing nobody, knowing no Portuguese, knowing nothing, and on my own completely. Those two weeks before I left, I must have met half a dozen people, totally random, who had either just been to John of God, or their best friend had just been and had the experience of their life. They all said 'Good, good, good. Very good choice.' And that's how the Entities brought me here. I meet people all the time and I think, so many people, perhaps all of us, were brought here by the Entities, by God, by Dom Inácio. And it's wonderful.

"From day one, I didn't know anybody, I was a little bit lost, but I got by. I never had a guide or anything. I started living in a house by myself. I came the first time for two months, which I eventually extended to three months. It was wonderful.

OTHER HEALING STORIES 385

"I'm not very sensitive in terms of psychic seeing or hearing, even though I know we are all mediums at some level. But that very first night, before I ever went into the Casa, before I ever saw the Entities in person, I had a visit from the spirits, the first of several. It was so powerful I will never forget it.

"That night I was both awake and asleep, but definitely aware the entire time. I was asleep at the beginning and awake at the end but it was all the same experience from start to finish. I think that feeling is faith. It was love, it was perfection, it was health, it was kindness, it was bliss, it was everything wonderful. It was pure light, and it filled my body that night. I didn't even know this consciously yet, but there was something in that light that made me know that I was going to find healing here. This is where I would find love; I would forgive; I would give; I would find my health. I also knew my faith would grow stronger as well. My faith grew greatly that night.

"I spent part of one year going back and forth between Vermont and the Casa, staying each time at the Casa for as long as my visa would let me. Before I went home to Vermont, after my second visit, I passed the Entity and I asked him, 'Should I get an MRI?' The Entity said, while smiling, 'If you want to.' Very typical of the Entities not to give you a direct answer for a question of how you should run your life, or what you should do. So I decided not to get an MRI.

"The first and foremost purpose here, as I understand it, is to heal the spirit. And that's why we all come here. At least the Entities offer that to us. If we accept it, it's right there. And then behind that, slowly, as we grow into the spiritual healing, slowly the other steps manifest. In fact, it's just not very common to come here and receive your instant healing of the physical, even though an astounding number of people eventually experience physical healing.

"My faith is strong right now. I had a thought that if I go back and have an MRI, what if the tumor is not gone? What if it's a little bigger? I knew of stories of tumors growing before they shrink, of people getting worse before they get better, but also understand that this getting worse is part of this illness leaving your body, your spirit, your emotional levels.

"However, one day there was an opening. I said, 'Ma, I'm going to go get it. Will you go with me?' And she brought me up to the hospital to get the MRI. And I was really nervous. I told myself it didn't matter what that MRI says, I'm still going back and I still know this is working. I really do.

"I got the MRI and the tumor had shrunk. And it's the most wonderful thing I had ever seen in my life (crying). It helped a lot. I told myself it didn't matter, but it really helped my faith, knowing that I am healing, and this thing is going to be gone. I knew it. Now I could share it with my friends. One girl called me in tears. She had grown up in a medical family, her dad was a doctor, her mom was a nurse, so anytime they got a flu, anytime they got an earache, they'd go right to the hospital and the doctor would take care of it. And that's what they knew of healing. She said, 'Matthew, that's so wonderful. I know I supported you before this. I didn't know what you were doing. I didn't understand it, but I support you because I love you. You're such a good friend. But now, I understand what you are doing, and I support everything. Get back down there! Get rid of that tumor! This is wonderful!' That phone call was wonderful and powerful to me. This kind of feeling, this understanding, that comes from just hearing the story can help people change the medical world. I pray we can do this. My doctors were brilliant at what they did, but they had tunnel-vision. There's so much more to healing. There's a bigger picture. There's just so, so much more.

"This blessing of my tumor shrinking was for everybody that read that e-mail, everyone who hears this story. My healing is for so much more than me. I feel so little a part of this, really. My health is a huge blessing to me, but it's much bigger than me. So I came back here with even more enthusiasm the next time. And by this time I had fallen in love. This is another whole story, but I had found the partner for the rest of my life here. We're married now and living here full time, and she's just a blessing. I don't feel like I did much, I just opened up and let it happen.

"I spent so much time just sitting in Current sessions. I really had very few actual surgeries, and never anything physical, always just spiritual surgeries. I actually asked for a physical surgery once. The Entity came to me and said, 'No, you may not have a physical surgery now. What you need is spiritual work.'

"I later learned more about the tumor, understanding the spiritual part of it. I look at it so simply—so many people analyzing this and this and this—but it's so simple. It's a story of love and faith. And it's that simple. In that, there is healing. Just love: pure, unconditional love and faith. That's God, to me.

"One year later on my birthday, it was a Tuesday; we do a spiritual meeting at my house every Tuesday night. During the next part of that meeting, you receive a message. Somebody opens a spiritual book with short messages and reads the message on the page. That Tuesday night, I received the message, 'Blessing.' That Wednesday I sat in Current. Near the end of the Current session, the Entity came up to me, I had my eyes still closed. The Entity took my hand and he led me up to the front of the room, turned me around, and said, 'I want you to tell everybody in this room exactly what you came here with, and exactly what you have no more.' And that was when I was given my blessing that the cancer is gone. It's over; the tumor is no longer there. Later on, I did have a test and it's gone. There's still some scar tissue from the radiation, there's a lump of tissue there, but there is no brain tumor anymore. That is all a blessing from God and from the Entities and from love and from my friends and from everybody supporting and praying for me. That is just ... a little story of love. It's a very simple little story. (Crying again).

"So now I'm still here and I'm trying to give back. I'm helping out at the Casa. I guide groups, I bring people here, just as you are about to do.⁴ That's it. My life has changed. We're here for now. In a couple of years, who knows? We'll see. But I have a new approach to life.

It's so beautiful. Every day I wake up and I love it. I'm happy and I don't care if it's rain or sun or snow: it's beautiful. We have a short opportunity here on Earth."

Matthew was more aware of the dynamic between teller and listener than I was at the time. He clearly understood that part of his healing process was about listening to the healing stories of others. After his tumor disappeared, he felt he had a mission; his story was as valuable to his audience as it was to him: "My healing is for so much more than me. I feel so little a part of this, really. My health is a huge blessing to me, but it's much bigger than me." Telling his story has also become a part of his ongoing learning as a Casa guide, about how to lead a new kind of life: "It's a story of love and faith. And it's that simple. In that, there is healing." His story beautifully illustrates how one person came and saw; then went and told, just as in the biblical narrative.

In the transcript there is a brief pause while I considered how to share my experience of listening with Matt:

Barbara: Something amazing has been happening here as you've been talking. Usually I have somebody finger spelling for me. You were talking very slowly. I got maybe half of it, but I wasn't trying to lip-read, since I know that I'll read a transcript. I was just hearing you with my heart. As you were talking, I began to have pulsations and feelings in my ears and body too. It was a pulsation that came as I could see you forming the words. It started to feel like static, that you might hear sound that's not intelligible sound, but is as sound coming through a doorway in the distance.

M: Wow!

Barbara: But I, really, not the left ear but the right ear was hearing. (M: Wow!) And it's not intelligible hearing at all, but it's, there's something ... say a couple of words, loud, sharp.

M: Love! Love! Love! ...

Barbara: I can feel the vibration, but there is something more ...

M: Wow, really?

Barbara: It's like a pulsation, it's like if you have a radio that's tuned and you hear little bits of "t ..., t ..., t ..." Not a clear voice, but definitely sound.

M: It's coming back, it's coming ...

Barbara: There's something coming through, Matt!

M: Wow! That's so amazing! Oh, God bless you!

(Everyone celebrating and speaking at once, with tears of joy)

Barbara: Thank you.

M: Thank YOU!

Barbara: His story opened my ears. ...

My listening to the healing stories of others deepened my faith that hearing, an event that had not completely happened for me yet, was very possible. Then Matt's heartfelt telling of his story invited my deep listening. That dynamic created a mysterious alchemy that, although not complete, was deeply transformational. Afterward, my hope and faith did not have to be blindly pinned to a future event. My trust in restoring my hearing had finally become verified by experience, just as the trust in restoring my sight had been verified. The gratitude and trust I found that day in turn opened the door for further learning and healing in the months and years ahead.

Matt's experience and the other stories of this chapter have now inevitably become a part of my story. But I feel, as does Matt, that these accounts are bigger than just the individual. Ultimately, we cannot remain the sole owners of these experiences. We come and see the miracle, then go and tell, sharing the vision and its transformative power. As we both tell and listen, connections emerge between people, and differences fall away. The entire world begins to change.

I returned from the Casa without any other direct experiences of hearing, but with a firm trust of the hearing and healing as reality, now. Through the spring I continued to hear thunder, and other loud noises. I also noticed the vision clearing, so that the whole right eye receives images now, with no more black hole. There's still distortion, but I can see well enough to read my watch with the right eye, and to have binocular vision again, which supports balance.

More importantly, I have let go of grasping after a desired outcome. I rest in the perfection that is already present, with love and joy. The lip is healed. The knee is pain-free and stable. My back is better than it's been for years, even before the accident. I no longer have sinus headaches. The chakras are open and my energy is clear and loving. So much old anger and fear is released. Spirit told me that these things would come and they have. So I am confident that deafness will fall away. Yes, I will hear!

Healing is a journey. I look back and see all that I would have missed if the Entities had restored my hearing the first time I stood before them. I understand now that I needed to participate more fully in the healing, and that the hearing is almost trivial related to the deeper healing I have found. So much that was conceptual and not yet deeply rooted has taken hold and blossomed in these years. So "Yes, I will hear!" And it will take as long as it takes.

Several months after my latest experiences at the Casa, another experience of partial hearing, combined with explanations from the entities, illuminated the underlying processes happening with my healing. About once a month I had been doing a breath-work practice called Transformational Breathing with a facilitator named Julie.[5] In one session, I began to breathe deeply and almost immediately found myself moving into a very open space. It wasn't as deep as the usual breath workspace, but very relaxed and open. There was a lot of sound in my head, almost musical in quality. I felt Father Francis very present, urging me to trust and tone as I do with the tuning forks, repeating the sound. I began to tone with it and continued for a while. Julie, meanwhile, was seated by my head and holding her hands at the ears. After a few minutes Father suggested I ask Julie to tone the syllable "Om" with various tones as she felt moved to do. I opened my eyes and could see her face upside down above me, so I could see her mouth opening as she chanted. Father asked me to close my eyes and try to hear her. I felt like I was hearing the toning at some level, so he suggested that I open the eyes again, and use all the cues I had to repeat the tone I was hearing. Somehow I could tell when I was in tune with her, or off key. Julie said later that I got much of it right. It was very intense. I felt like the ears really were hearing her, and also the whole body. It took great effort to stay with it, but was also extremely beautiful, feeling a deep connection as we chanted.

I was starting to tremble and Father Francis suggested that this was enough; to pause. When we stopped, I was overcome by strong emotion and started to cry. There was a mix of joy, awe, and gratitude. There was also a fear: was I making it up? But Julie confirmed that many of the tones were a correct match to hers (not all, but enough). We took a break, during which time Father Francis began to talk to me.

When he first came to me last year, he had said that his job was to teach me how to use the new circuits that were being made. Dr. Augusto was the one taking care of the medical side of the hearing.

When my nerves died and I became deaf, the entire circuit of ears, nerves, and brain failed. The Entities did not replace the nerves that used to be there but created a new circuit. Now Father Francis said that in my normal state of consciousness, I'm so habituated to move into the old process of hearing with the ear nerves that no longer exist, that it has been hard to teach me to let go of that process. They've tried to do this in part through the tuning forks and teaching me to trust the hearing capacity of the body and its alternate paths of hearing. I can chant very much on tune now with the tuning forks, just holding them near my ears. There's some degree of body conduction since the hand is holding the fork and I feel the vibration. To some degree the ear bones are feeling the vibration. But in addition, I am also hearing in a new way because I'm relaxed and trust the process. As soon as I watch someone talking, however, I revert to the old pattern, trying to force understanding through the dead nerves.

The breath work relaxed away that old conditioning enough that I allowed the new channels to function. It's that simple. Father Francis reminded me of the interview with Matt at the Casa and how I began to feel that I was hearing him speak after I relaxed and just watched him speak, getting what I could and with trust that I'd be able to read it later. Matt was very emotional as he spoke and I was picking up his energy and feelings as well as many words. Slowly something shifted, so that as I saw a sharp consonant sound like p or t, I felt like I was also hearing it. It was a static-like sensation, where full words weren't coming through, but it felt like I was not just lip-reading but actually hearing parts of the words.

Father Francis said that I was in such a deep space with Matt that it was a similar consciousness to this breath work consciousness. Thus, I was permitting the body to hear in its new way rather than trying to force it back to the old patterns. When I heard the thunder it was similar. There was no attempt to lip-read, as there was nothing to see, so I wasn't trying to use the old hearing patterns. Thus, I was open to the new.

Aaron then reminded me of the friend I mentioned above, who now sees perfectly although the optic nerves are still dead. The Entities rerouted the vision pathway. This is no different; they have rerouted the hearing. But I need to release the old habits of trying to hear in order to use the new hearing. Aaron said right now, in some ways, lip-reading works against me because it's part of the old hearing pattern.

After this break and explanation, I was asked to lie down and begin the breathing again. No expectations, but if I did hear the sounds in my ears, to chant with them. If it felt appropriate, Julie would start toning again. We did this. At first I relaxed and breathed, and then heard the inner sounds and toned with them. As soon as Julie started, I could feel myself shift into more normal consciousness. I was trying too hard, not allowing but doing, which didn't work. I was able to get a few of the tones correct, and maybe more importantly, I could tell when I was off because my energy and consciousness were different. I could see when I was shifting into the old hearing pattern. That seeing in turn allowed me to release the old pattern in favor of the new.

Soon after this breathwork session, I had a vivid dream. I opened my eyes (in the dream, but it was so real I didn't know that I was dreaming) and the right-eye vision was absolutely clear and perfect: colors vivid, details sharp. I felt such enormous gratitude. I just fell on my knees and offered prayers of thanks. It was all so clear, awesomely beautiful. When I awakened and remembered the dream, Aaron said the vision is no different than the hearing, opening to a new vision pathway for the eye. This is why they've given me the eye exercise, to look through that right eye and see with no straining or grasping, just allowing and inviting clarity. He pointed out how much better the eye is now, six months since the last Casa visit. A year ago at this time there was no image, just dark or light. I really do know that I will see and hear, because I already do see and hear.

So with these experiences the Entities have confirmed that my healing is a direct result of my ability to listen deeply, without grasping or holding preconceptions. I learned long ago that hearing is a way of connecting with the world, and with people. Deep listening is reaching out with love and the open heart. This teaching was no longer a metaphor or conceptual understanding, but a vivid reality. On a very practical level, if I continued to react to my new experiences through the prism of old habits and perceptions, I could not hear—that neural pathway was long dead. When I found myself in a state where I could put aside those old patterns and be fully present with my experiences, my new circuit worked. If I allow this miracle of healing to occur, I will hear. Once again, the responsibility is upon me to accept or reject the gifts of spirit. I must choose to accept every day, in every moment, consciously, and in complete freedom. Now more than ever the commitment is deeper, the requirements higher, and the rewards greater, just as they always have been.

I often use the term "story" when teaching. This may be a product of a mind that is unable or unwilling to focus on the present reality. If we consciously or unconsciously respond to a story by either accepting or rejecting it, unwholesome results can arise. For example, reactions to stories, repeated often enough, tend to form beliefs that can hinder spiritual growth. Blame is a kind of story; a belief in unworthiness or limitation is another story. A story fundamentally is neither good nor bad, just the result of the conditions that caused it to arise, and nothing more. Like any other thought or emotion, a story's arising and passing in the mind are not subject to conscious control, and is not me or mine. I teach that the key to dealing effectively with stories and their consequences lies in our reaction to stories as they arise. The imaginative experience of a story is something to be noted and watched dispassionately, without reaction. My own stories about the Casa, and my unconscious reactions to them, at their worst served to reinforce the "reality" of my brokenness. Stories like this were more often than not destructive and unwholesome, best kept at the level of an object of meditation.

The healing path of the Casa ultimately showed me another more wholesome form of story, one with a content that can inspire healing. As I repeatedly reacted, joyfully and with an open heart, to the stories of healing around me, a belief in the potential for my own healing slowly solidified. At first this belief seemed like just another story, with all its unwholesome destructive potential. But instead I found that this emerging belief in healing supported my awareness of the Ever-Healed, that which has never suffered distortion. Eventually, with its use to me exhausted, my belief in healing faded. What replaced it was a deeper knowing of the Already-Healed, a more complete presence with the essence of things as they are.

We can distinguish between wholesome and unwholesome stories in part by their results. The wholesome story opens the doorway to light and love. I found stories at the Casa that deepened my faith and trust, moving me further toward my own complete healing and leaving me more deeply connected to the people and the universe around me. Now that I have a measure of what I have dreamed of for so long, I find a deep value in telling my own story to you. I am sharing my story and the stories of others with you in the hopes that you are inspired, that your faith is deepened, and that you can move toward your highest and most deeply held wishes.

CHAPTER 22

Balance, Amazing
Grace, and Wholeness

THE YEAR 2007 passed in a blur of life and activity; teaching and learning. My spiritual practice speaks to me of opening my heart to things just as they are. This understanding begins with awareness of both the conditioned realm in which we live our outer lives, and the Unconditioned, or divine, realm that is the core of everything. By "conditioned," I mean the everyday world where plants rise from the ground when seeds, soil, rain, and sun are present in their proper measure. Emotions similarly arise from the ground of our experience when conditions are favorable. By "Unconditioned," I mean that which exists beyond everyday conditions; the eternal aspect of being.

These two realms are not dual but exist simultaneously. Open your hand and look at your fingers as you wave them in front of your eyes. Each finger is there; no doubt about it. Your fingers represent conditioned reality. Now look through the fingers at the vast spaciousness beyond, which in this instance, represents unconditioned reality. When you focus in this way, the fingers don't disappear, but they are no longer the center of your awareness. In the same way, when we open to a greater awareness of what we are beyond this mind, body, and emotions, these aspects of being don't dissolve. We just see more deeply into the truth of who we are.

Deaf and hearing; blind and seeing; balanced and unbalanced; kind and unkind; patient and impatient. ... these expressions all come and go, each an expression of duality, a distortion of the One. Throughout 2007 I continued to investigate how easy it is to lean too far out on one side of an emotional or perceptual seesaw while ignoring the other side. Which old ideas of limitation, and of who I am, lead me to see the world through such an obviously distorted lens? Each time I raised that question, I saw the ways in which I had created a duality but still had not learned to move past it.

In January of 2008 I returned to the Casa for five weeks. Ever since I lost my hearing, I've used my eyes for balance; as the delicate middle-ear nerves that support the body's natural balance were oxygen-starved and had died along with the auditory nerves. In the 2004 ocean accident, the loss of the right eye function meant that I had lost binocular vision. Since that time my sense of balance had been quite precarious. Even with the Entities' help with the eye, there had not been good enough vision to easily support balance. Therefore, I could no longer walk at night without the support of two walking sticks. Even in the daytime I frequently used the walking sticks, and found them especially necessary when walking on an uneven surface.

When I came to the Casa in 2008 I walked from my pousada to the Casa with the walking sticks for support. The Entity said to me, "Put them aside and walk without them." I feared I would fall. I was asked again to walk and allow the Entities to energetically support me. They promised that I would not fall. I walked and did feel their momentary support, holding me when balance went, until I felt centered again. It felt like an energetic force field under the arms, just strong enough that I had a moment of support to re-center myself and feel the true balance of the body. As I began to trust that I could balance without the walking sticks, I began to rediscover my body's intuitive balance, on which I had not relied for thirty-five years. Within a week I was doing something I had not done for over three decades: taking long, easy strides and walking in a sure-footed way.

At the end of one week of walking, I had a new invitation. "Get a bicycle and ride it," the Entity suggested. With some trepidation I rented a bike, and promptly fell over trying to mount it. "That which is aware of imbalance is not unbalanced," Aaron reminded me. Anger came up, but I knew he was right. Find the balance right there with the lack of it. "Don't think 'I will become balanced,' but rather know, 'I am balanced.' Know the innate balance and trust it." I got up from the ground, swung my leg over the bike seat while allowing myself to feel the real balance, and rode off. For the remaining three weeks that bike went with me everywhere. I felt like an eight-year-old discovering the freedom of wheels again! In this newfound physical balancing, I found an apt metaphor for the inward balance needed to stop creating duality.

I was also rediscovering vision. The first day at the Casa I was sent to surgery. A week of recuperation followed. My right eye vision deteriorated after surgery, which had been the case in the past two years also. There was only dark and light to be seen. Then the vision began to return and I was urged to work hard with the eye exercises I had been doing for two years. Again I was reminded, "Know that which can see and cherish it. Do not think yourself blind, but know the vision that is there."

By the end of three weeks there was fair vision, blurred but without any blind spot, what I had thought of as a black hole. I was urged to close the good eye and walk, to depend on the right eye for seeing and to express gratitude to the eye for the real vision it was offering. At first I was reluctant, feeling that I would miss things; fearing I that would stumble and walk into objects and people. At the Entities' request I persisted; and discovered that which was able to see, right there in the eye with less than ideal vision.

Looking back, I see that these two areas of healing were offered, not just to heal balance and vision—though that was real and compassionate—but also because I needed these demonstrations in order to trust the reality of hearing. I've previously described how in 2007 at the Casa I heard thunder for the first time in thirty-five years; yet on some level, I still believed that that was all I could hear. I was still creating duality.

I learn about nonduality through meditation. For me, the center of meditation is presence in each moment with kind, spacious awareness. My meditation practice asks me to open the heart to whatever is predominant in the moment's experience, and to watch the movements of mind and body as they relate to that object. Are the heart and body open, or clenched tight? Is there ease and joy or fear and a need to control? We cannot choose what will arise in the next moment; sometimes it's pleasant, sometimes not. Sometimes there is great pain of body or emotion. I learn by long practice and repetition that only through full presence and kindness can we find the freedom to not invoke old patterns but to allow the heart and deepest wisdom to join together in each moment with love.

Many strengths come together to support that moment of openhearted clarity. We can train toward full presence, but may not be able to open the heart and trust enough to touch the most difficult moments. We can never force it. There must be kindness as we attend to these impermanent, yet sometimes very painful, objects. The natural tendency of so many years, of lifetimes even, is to flee. When great fear and negative thought come, what sustains us?

Returning to the fingers and the spaces between, the experience of that spaciousness supports heart opening. With each object that arises, I see the immense space that surrounds and accompanies the object. Aaron uses a metaphor here: he asks us to imagine sitting in a tiny box while he approaches with a tarantula, and points out how quickly we would leap out of the box. But imagine a much bigger box and we see the capacity to stay and observe the tarantula, even to befriend it. Eventually we come to know the infiniteness of that box, which is the Unconditioned or divine itself, and learn to rest in the spaciousness of the Unconditioned with full intimacy with the conditioned objects that challenge us. The balance of heart and mind allow both full presence and non-self-identification. We attend not to fix but just to witness and hold the space until the objects dissolve. With fear, for example, that which is aware of fear is not afraid. I rest in fearlessness yet am able to be lovingly intimate with the everyday mind-and-body experience of fear.

The Casa gave me the opportunity to further practice what my meditation and Aaron had taught me through the years. On the first trip to the Casa, the Casa Entity Dr. Augusto, speaking through João, said, "Possibly we can help with the deafness." The second trip he told me, "Probably." Was there grasping? Yes, and letting go, again and again. The third trip, Dr. Valdivino said (speaking through João), "You will hear;" but this brought up new grasping and a quandary. If I will hear, what delays that hearing? Why is it not now?

It was at that point that I finally investigated my beliefs in limitations, and how I was living my life in subservience to such beliefs. To believe that I am limited, less than whole, unworthy, or otherwise incomplete, leads me to enact such beliefs, to keep the scenario repeating; the proverbial, self-fulfilling prophecy. We stay in the rut, giving ever-increasing energy to holding on to things the way they are rather than glimpsing the reality of freedom from the situation. That which is aware of the rut is not caught in the rut. However, when there is no awareness, all we see is the rut, from which we desperately try to escape. Yet we keep recreating the rut out of the belief that it has some ultimate reality. We cannot escape, precisely because we cannot see that there never was a rut; except in our closed-minded belief. We become attached to the rut. It is uncomfortable, but familiar; true spaciousness may look even more uncomfortable.

When I hold a belief of myself as unworthy, for example, I begin to use my energy to prove myself worthy. I keep inviting situations in which I actually feel unworthy, and then repeat the impulse to prove that I am worthy. I can't prove I'm worthy without a situation that says I'm unworthy, so I keep the cycle going. I am believing, then, that I need the feeling of unworthiness in order to somehow, finally, prove that I am worthy. In some ways I'm attached to that feeling of unworthiness, painful though it is, and to the fight to overcome it. Similarly, if I have a belief that anger is bad and that I must conquer it, I continually invite situations that provoke anger so that I can try to destroy it. But in that situation I am merely giving my energy to the anger. I never see and nurture the non-anger, but stay focused on trying to defeat the familiar enemy of anger.

How do I handle the apparent reality that I am deaf? I could not yet apply these insights to my hearing. These ears have not heard for thirty-five years. The nerves in the middle ear and those that conduct sound to the brain have been declared dead medically. There is no response to any kind of impulse. Yet the Casa Entities have said, "You will hear." My experience with them has led me to have profound trust. If they say it, it will be so. I found myself believing the "You will hear," but also believing that "will" means in the future. Thus I cannot hear now. Here was a belief that it needs to happen in linear time, slowly. But if I *will* hear, I already do; as nothing can happen that is not already present. Just as non-anger is right there with anger, hearing must be right there with non-hearing. So my conceptual mind told me.

In confusion, I began to grasp at the healing I sought. I asked inwardly if I was unworthy of that healing, doing something wrong, or simply being rejected. I even went to Medium João when Dr. Valdivino was incorporated, and asked if I was doing something to block healing. He said no, I was doing exactly what they asked, and doing it perfectly. Then why does it not happen?

I went through a very painful few days, my mind doing gymnastics, seeking a way out. But in 2008 I was still profoundly deaf, and mostly blind in one eye, and in that moment, that's how it was, no matter how much I wanted it to be different. Meditation gives me the tool to see the grasping without self-identification with the endless stories of *Poor me* or *How can I fix it?* It is through infinite hours and days of this practice that one finally realizes the capacity just to stay present with the painful experience, instead of trying to get away. That day I realized that I wasn't being fully present but was still insulating myself from pain and diverting attention from that pain with the idea of "working to heal."

With that insight I let myself fully experience deafness and the sorrow I felt at how much the lack of ear-hearing cuts out so much of the experience of the world for me. I cried for several days, as I watched branches sway in the silent wind, saw bird mouths open and close in unheard voice, watched the soundless rain on my roof, and saw humans speaking, laughing, and crying. Once again I felt cut off, alone, and unconnected, as I had thirty-five years earlier. As that experience deepened, some profound wisdom said, as it had said many times before, "That which is aware of deafness is not deaf. Instead of being deaf in that moment, can I simultaneously allow and invite that which hears?" Yes. Yes! Something clicked, and the fruit of previous work blossomed into consciousness. I saw it clearly. The Casa environment and high vibration, combined with my intention and the actions of the Entities on many levels acted as a midwife, helping me to birth this precious knowing.

There is no duality. I rest in completion, in perfection, and yet with compassion for the human who does experience the limitations and distortions. When they arise, I know that they are not the full reality. We can learn to rest in innate perfection, with the heart open to the experiences of this moment, and let them pass away. We release limits, and the belief in limits, and live the ultimate reality. We are here to express our divinity and perfection. There is no need to continue to express the illusions of limits, brokenness, and fear. Rest in love and allow it ever more fully to express. What happened at the Casa this year would not have been possible without this realization growing within, not the balance or the seeing or the hearing.

When distortion remains, we don't need to believe we're doing something wrong. That distortion may be the perfect place for us in this moment. So my story isn't about some concept that says hearing is better, or more right than not hearing. The body may not heal. Moving beyond limitations doesn't just mean moving past deafness; it may mean moving past the idea that hearing is needed. The duality of hearing and deafness are part of this nondual reality. However, I am no longer holding the distortion through fear. It will remain as long as it serves some good. My highest prayer is not to hear but to serve for the highest good. But the Ever-Healed that is already present will show itself. Fear no longer holds onto limits.

I sat in the Current Room with this realization and with my heart opened to the pain of my deafness. One of the Entities asked me to relax and listen. "Your body has become an ear," he said. "You must learn how to hear with it."

They play many different kinds of music during Casa sessions, some very sacred and some popular songs, through the speakers in the Current Rooms. Some tracks are louder than others. As I sat there that day, I began to hear tones and rhythms. It felt like music. I listened with this body-ear for about half an hour. When the meditation session ended, I asked someone sitting near me, was there music with this kind of rhythm and melody, humming what I had heard? "Yes; yes."

Through the weeks, I found myself turning repeatedly to face what seemed like loud sounds. Frequently they were confirmed as a truck rolled by, or I saw a person who had just set an object on a table. One day I was talking to a woman when the friend seated behind me laughed aloud. She says I turned instantly and smiled at her. Did I hear it? It seems so. I am beginning to intimately know the "deaf" of so many years, but also the "I hear," which is a greater reality. Not, "I will hear" but "I do hear, right now." No, this is not yet hearing voices; yet it is real, and helps me move into this new reality. In every way I embrace my unlimitedness, and the unlimitedness of us all. We are all healed; and are moving into the fullest expression of our healing of which we are capable in this moment.

In January of 2009 I again returned to the Casa. "What would you like to hear first?" people have often asked me when they learn about my travels there. "My children's voices," I reply; "or the song, 'Amazing Grace.'" I only came to know that song after I was deaf. I learned all the words, and love them, but I had no idea of the melody or even of the rhythm of the music. Somehow I've always trusted, "I will hear this song some day."

On the first Casa day, I was sent to surgery. After several quiet days recovering in my room, followed by the post-surgery review, the Entity incorporated in João's body told me to sit in his Current. The third week, I sat in the Entity's Current on a Friday morning feeling a little low in energy and also a bit sad. I was three weeks into yet another five-week trip and little had seemed to happen. So I sat in the Current with these feelings, just noting *low energy, lethargic, sad, contracted.* Emotions and physical sensations will arise and fall away. My practice is just to note them and not become self-identified with them, or create stories about these mind and body states.

I was drowsing a bit when the touch came, a firm two hands on either side of my head. Sometimes, not often, the Entity incorporated in Medium João's body gets up from his chair and walks across the room, touches someone sitting in the Current or even leads them to another place. I sat, eyes still closed, feeling like a bolt of lightning had touched me. The hands held on both sides of my head firmly for about ten seconds and then gave it a small shake. Needless to say, I was no longer sleepy. My mind became very still and focused. I sat up straight and had a deep and energized three hours of meditation.

Besides the energy experience, I also felt deeply loved and seen, and that my needs were truly known and recognized. I was told later that it was Dr. Valdivino incorporated at that session, one of the two Entities who has been working with me most consistently through these years. He knew how I was feeling and gave that support. It's a good reminder that the Entities do know my needs and are helping me, as they keep reminding me verbally. As the hands released, a flow of my tears also released, along with tension that I did not know that I was feeling. My head continued to tingle there for the rest of the afternoon and evening and into the weekend. Doubt dissolved. I know that right there with deafness is hearing. My practice last year and this has been to focus less on "getting" hearing and more on knowing that which can already hear and supporting it. There is no denial of the deafness, just simultaneous acknowledgment that the basis for hearing is also there.

Every Sunday morning there is an English language Interfaith Service held at the Casa. I often go when there is someone willing to sign for me, but have never gone alone, as I would just sit with no way to know what was said. That Sunday I felt moved to attend, though I struggled with it a bit, thinking that I would regret it since I could not hear anything. The pull was strong though illogical; my heart said, "Go." When the service started, the man leading it began to talk and I just closed my eyes and sat meditating for half an hour. Then I felt a higher energy in the room, and some perception of music. I was literally hearing musical sounds, melody. I can't say how I was hearing it, whether in the body or the ears, but it was not just tinnitus, but true music. I opened my eyes to find the gathered group singing. One man was standing, and it was his voice I was hearing.

As my eyes focused on his face, I began to lip-read the words, "How precious did that Grace appear, the hour that first I believed." He was leading the group as they sang "Amazing Grace." I was hearing the music! I turned to face him and let the music come deeply into my heart. Each note reverberated there. We went through all seven verses. Each note had clarity and a purity of sound. My body was shaking so hard I could hardly control it, and tears were streaming down my face. As the closing notes sounded, I had to run from the room, sobbing. A friend came out to help me and learn the cause of my tears, then hugged me and cried with me when she heard the story.

When spirit opens doors, it does it in a wholehearted way. The singer was a well-known baritone opera singer named Stephen Salter who was at the Casa for a week for his own reasons. One person who read about this in my journal said, "What a classy reintroduction to the musical world the Entities have provided, by putting you within earshot of Stephen!" Yes, spirit doesn't orchestrate things halfway. If "Amazing Grace" is to be the first music I hear, as I had prayed, it would have to be with a world-class singer! When I spoke with Stephen after the service, he was as moved as I was. There are no accidents. We both highly valued this occasion.

Two days later he came to my pousada for a personal concert of "Amazing Grace" and other songs. At one point I had the opportunity to sing it with him; we had no word sheets; I was the only one who knew the words to all seven verses so I had to sing loud. Stephen said of my singing, "She is hearing it!"

The hearing is not consistent and is still connected only to music, not yet words. But in the remaining two weeks I heard enough music to know it was real and that it would grow and continue.

Growth seems to come in cycles: the proverbial three steps forward and two back. Even with all this healing and hearing, the Casa visit in 2010 left me feeling doubt again. "Am I doing something wrong?" "Are they displeased with me?" When I came through the line where Jose Penteado was incorporated, I had the sense not to ask, "What am I doing wrong?" Instead I asked him how I can best support healing my deafness. He saw through my maneuver; he looked at me for several moments, then said, "Love will support healing." He was holding a flower. He took my hand, opened my fingers, and placed the flower in my palm. "Here is my love," he said.

I spent the next ten days reflecting on his message as I sat many hours in Current and meditated in the garden. I do believe I'm a loving person, able to give and receive love from others. Yet as I watched the arising thoughts and my response to them, I saw myriad ways in which I was less than loving to myself. I saw that when a thought arose of *What am I doing wrong?* that I immediately condemned myself with a follow-up thought, *I should be beyond that kind of thinking by now.* I was amazed at how many judgments and "shoulds" I saw.

Yet the myth persisted. If I just did *something* right, I would hear. If he would just put his hands on my ears, surely he could bring hearing. I could imagine it happening! One day I was standing in the Main Hall during the session when the incorporated Entity came out on the stage, looked at me deeply, walked right toward me, stopped and looked into and through me for a long time. He then turned and put his hand on the head of the woman standing next to me. As he held his hand on her head, he continued to look me in the eyes. It was clear he was aware of my thoughts and was challenging me to transcend them. Twice in one day, the Entity walked up to where I was sitting in the front row of his Current. My eyes were closed but I could feel his energy approach. The first time he put his hand on the head of the woman sitting next to me, then moved her to a big chair right next to his seat. Another time, he called a different woman sitting next to me in the Current, to come up to talk with him, and asked her to stay another week so he could do more work with her. Each time, the same old habits arose. "I am invisible; unloved; imperfect." Each time these thoughts were noted with mindfulness, and I was able to skillfully note the tension and not build further stories. However, the thoughts still came, and judgment of them also came. It was a painful two weeks.

Finally, it was my last day, and I would pass through the line again. The logical mind did feel gratitude. The five weeks had been filled with many gifts. Body pain had diminished. Balance and vision were improved. I had been riding a bike with increasing ease and balance for five weeks. I was walking with greater ease. My first day here in January 2010, I had asked the Entities to help me find a way to bring this book out into the world, and they provided it. Almost immediately I had a contract for this book with a publisher I very much liked and respected.

Yet nagging and painful doubt still arose. Do these words, the words you are reading now, come from a place of enough emptiness and love that there is no distortion? So I asked the Entity what seemed at first to be another clear and innocent question; "Please help me to do my teaching and work with the book with humility, wisdom, and love."

Again the Entity, this time Dr. Valdivino, saw right through my question and into my fears and doubts. He gave me an exquisitely tender smile, and the kind of look a parent might give a beloved child, of "You still don't get it.... Please try now...." He took my hand, said very clearly, enunciating each word, "I love you very much," and placed two radiant roses in my hand. "Sit in my Current."

I sat and the tears came. There was such a deep level of healing, and with each tear shed, a profound release of old beliefs.

Are these beliefs completely eradicated? Probably not. However, hopefully the next time they emerge I will remember to smell the roses and feel spirit's love; to release the thought faster, and to rest in truth. We are loved. We are home. There is nothing to fear.

What is healing? How does this process work? Each time I take another step, I realize how little I understand. We move with faith and the intention for the highest good, and have no idea what will happen next, but need to trust the power of our loving intentions. My highest intention is not to hear, but to be in service toward whatever is for the highest good of all beings. The intention for hearing is there, but without grasping. Thus, I can't know what may come next. I can only trust the process and keep my heart open. Perhaps this letting go is the true healing, for only here do we release our self-identification with fear and the contractions of fear. When mind and body are uncontracted, we are truly open to the power of love in our selves and in the universe.

One afternoon during my first week back from Brazil, I went to the market, needing to fill my empty refrigerator and pantry. I could feel some small tension toward every day life and all the tasks it brings. My body was contracted and my back hurt. I was pushing, not flowing. As I was shopping, a student, not someone I know well, walked up to me with a loving smile and a large bouquet of pink tulips. "These are for you," she said, indicating with the receipt that she had already paid for them. Just that and a hug and she was gone. What a wonderful reminder; be present and love is here. Let go and live in love.

In the *Dhammapada*, the Buddha says, "We are what we think. With our thoughts we make the world." When I first began to write it, I believed that this book had to end with my full physical hearing.

I see now that it is not the hearing itself that is important, as much as the attitude and capacity for "knowing." My work here is to know my wholeness, embrace it, and live it; to know the world's wholeness and to support the highest expression of wholeness on this Earth; these are the reasons we have come into the incarnation. This is our path to love.

Bibliography

Bragdon, Emma. *Spiritual Alliances: Discovering the Roots of Health at the Casa de Dom Inácio.* Woodstock, VT: Lightening Up Press, 2002.

Cohen, Leonard. "Sisters of Mercy." *Songs of Leonard Cohen.* Toronto: Sony Music Canada, 1967.

Cumming, Heather and Karen Leffler. *John of God: The Brazilian Healer Who's Touched the Lives of Millions.* New York, NY: Atria/Beyond Words Publishing, 2007.

Dass, Ram. *Miracle of Love: Stories About Neem Karoli Baba.* New York, NY: E. P. Dutton, 1979.

Eliot, T. S. "The Waste Land." *The Waste Land.* New York, NY: Boni and Liveright, 1922.

Emoto, Masaru. *The Hidden Messages in Water.* Hillsboro, OR: Beyond Words Publishing, 2004.

The Findhorn Community. *The Findhorn Garden: Pioneering a New Vision of Man and Nature in Cooperation.* New York, NY: HarperCollins Perennial, 1976.

Heartsong, Claire. *Anna, Grandmother of Jesus: A Message of Wisdom and Love.* Santa Clara, CA: Spiritual Education Endeavors Publishing, 2002.

Kabir. "The Guest is Inside Me, and Also Inside You. ..." *The Kabir Book.* Translated by Robert Bly. Boston, MA: Beacon Press, 1971.

Kardec, Allan. *The Mediums' Book,* Paris, France: 1876. Translated by Emma A. Wood. Reissued as *The Book on Mediums: Guide for Mediums and Invocators.* Newburyport, MA: RedWheel/Weiser, 2008.

Kardec, Allan. *The Spirits' Book.* Paris, France: 1857. Translated by Darrel W. Kimble with Marcia M. Saiz. Brasilia, Brazil: International Spiritist Council, 2nd Edition, 2008.

Kornfield, Jack with Paul Breiter and Achaan Chah. *A Still Forest Pool: the Insight Meditation of Achaan Chah.* Wheaton, IL: Quest Books, 1985.

Levine, Stephen. *A Gradual Awakening.* New York, NY: Anchor Doubleday, 1989.

Levine, Stephen. *Healing into Life and Death.* New York, NY: Anchor Doubleday, 1987.

Marion, Jim. *Putting on the Mind of Christ.* Charlottesville, VA: Hampton Roads Publishing Company, 2000.

Mayer, Elizabeth Lloyd, PhD. *Extraordinary Knowing: Science, Skepticism, and the Inexplicable Powers of the Human Mind.* New York, NY: Bantam Books, 2007.

McBrien, Richard P. *Lives of the Saints: From Mary and St. Francis of Assisi to John XXIII and Mother Teresa.* San Francisco, CA: HarperOne, 2001.

Moon, Susan and Lenore Friedman, eds. *Being Bodies: Buddhist Women On The Paradox Of Embodiment.* Boston, MA: Shambala, 1997.

Pellegrino-Estrich, Robert. *The Miracle Man: The Life Story of Joao de Deus.* Goiania, Goias, Brazil: Grapica Terra, 2002.

Rueckert, Carla L. *A Channeling Handbook,* available from www.llresearch.org/publications/pub_a_channeling_handbook.aspx

Sicardo, Reverend Joseph. *St. Rita of Cascia: Saint of the Impossible.* Rockford, IL: TAN Books, Inc.

Swander, Mary. *The Desert Pilgrim.* New York, NY: Viking Compass, 2003.

Shabkar, Lama Jatang Tsogdruk Rangrol. *Flight of the Garuda.* Translated by Erik Pema Kunsang. Kathmandu, Nepal: Rangjung Yeshe Publications, 1988. Restricted Tibetan publication. Other translations are readily available.

Web Links

Bailey, Marcia, and Julie Wolcott. Breathe Ann Arbor:
    www.breatheannarbor.com
Brodsky, Barbara, and John Orr. Vipassana Healing:
    www.vipassanahealing.com
Coates, Judith. Oakbridge University: www.oakbridge.org
Cumming, Heather. Healing Quests: www.healingquests.com
Deep Spring Center: www.deepspring.org
Friends of the Casa: www.friendsofthecasa.info
João Teixeira de Faria: www.meetjohnofgod.com and
    www.johnofgod.com
James Randi Educational Foundation:
    www.randi.org/jr/021805a.html
Rose, Diana, and Bob Dinga: www.miraclesofjohnofgod.com
Rueckert, Carla. LL Research: www.llresearch.org

Glossary

Aggregates. Buddhist teaching speaks of the five aggregates or *skandhas* (Pali) that comprise our human experience: form, feeling (pleasant, unpleasant, and neutral), thought, perception, and consciousness. These aggregates all arise from conditions and are impermanent and non-self in nature.

Ahimsa. Dynamic compassion.

Astral projection. The temporary projection of the conscious mind out of the physical body and into the subtle plane known as the astral plane.

Astral plane. The subtle plane beyond the physical one.

Bardo. The bardo states are the states between death and birth.

Bodhicitta. The pure, awakened heart that is devoted to the highest good of all beings.

Bodhisattva vow. A vow originated in Mahayana Buddhism to serve all beings and not to take a path of personal full liberation until all beings are free.

Choiceless awareness. Awareness that is able to watch each object as it becomes predominant in our experience, and to let it go when it is no longer predominant.

Current. The word "current" in Portuguese is current, like electrical current, but it also means a chain. So we are really like a chain of light, the creative life force that created us all.

Deva. The term *deva* means deity. There are many genres of devas, both those in some spiritual cosmologies and what we may consider nature devas. In Buddhism, a deva is one of many different types of supernatural, nonhuman beings who are more powerful, more enlightened, and happier than most humans. The term used with nature devas often refers to archetypal spiritual intelligences behind species, what may be considered the group soul of a species, but is also used to designate any elemental or nature spirit, the equivalent of fairies.

Ground of Being. The Essence or core, sometimes thought of as Christ Consciousness or Buddha Nature.

Kaya. This relates to the Buddhist teaching of three kayas or bodies. Dharmakaya is the truth body, the highest level of expression, the expression of our true divine nature. Nirmanakaya is the form body, the relative expressions of physical, mental, and emotional form. Sambhogakaya is the transition body, which holds both dharmakaya and nirmanakaya and knows them as nondual.

> Dharmakaya—truth body
> Nirmanakaya—form body
> Sambhogakaya—wealth or transition body

Metta Sutta. This is the well-known Buddhist teaching on Lovingkindness.[1] In part:

> *Wishing: in gladness and in safety,*
> *May all beings be at ease.*
> *Whatever living beings there may be;*
> *Whether they are weak or strong, omitting none,*
> *The great or the mighty, medium, short or small,*
> *The seen and the unseen,*
> *Those living near and far away,*
> *Those born and to-be-born—*
> *May all beings be at ease!*
> *Let none deceive another,*
> *Or despise any being in any state.*
> *Let none through anger or ill will*
> *Wish harm upon another.*
> *Even as a mother protects with her life*
> *Her child, her only child,*
> *So with a boundless heart*

Should one cherish all living beings;
Radiating kindness over the entire world,
Spreading upward to the skies,
And downwards to the depths;
Outward and unbounded,
Freed from hatred and ill-will.

Mindfulness. Presence in the moment, with whatever arises to mind and physical senses.

Seva. Sanskrit for service.

Sila. Pali for moral awareness; one portion of the Buddhist path; the others are *pañña* (wisdom) and *samadhi* (mindfulness and concentration).

Six sense doors. We perceive the conditioned realm through the six sense doors of eye, ear, nose, tongue, body, and mind. Each sense door contacts an object and results in consciousness as seeing consciousness, hearing consciousness, smelling consciousness, tasting consciousness, touching consciousness, and mental consciousness.

Stream Entry. In the Buddhist tradition, there are four stages of realization. They are:

- stream-enterer (one who has entered the stream of the realization of his/her true nature);
- once-returner (one who is evolving but still has the karma that will draw him/her back into incarnation);
- non-returner (one who has resolved the karma that would draw him/her back into incarnation); and
- Arahant, the fully enlightened being.

Theravada Buddhism. The oldest school of Buddhism, founded in India and practiced today in Burma, Cambodia, Laos, Sri Lanka, and Thailand. The Sanskrit name means "way of the elders."

Notes

INTRODUCTION
[1] Elizabeth Lloyd Mayer, PhD, *Extraordinary Knowing* (New York: Bantam Books, 2007).

CHAPTER 1
[1] See Barbara Brodsky, "No Eye, Ear, Nose ..." in *Being Bodies,* eds. Susan Moon and Lenore Friedman (Boston: Shambhala, 1997), 35–42 for a fuller telling of this first experience of deafness.

[2] Jack Kornfield, Paul Breiter, and Achaan Chah, *A Still Forest Pool: The Insight Meditation of Achaan Chah* (Wheaton, IL: Quest Books, 2008).

[3] Leonard Cohen, "Sisters of Mercy," *Songs of Leonard Cohen* (Sony Music Canada, 1967).

[4] Stephen Levine, *A Gradual Awakening* (New York: Anchor Doubleday Books, 1987).

CHAPTER 2
[1] See Brodsky, "No Eye, Ear, Nose ...".

CHAPTER 4
[1] Ram Dass, *Miracle of Love* (Santa Fe, NM: Hanuman Foundation, 1995), 33.

[2] Kabir, "The Guest is Inside Me, and Also Inside You ...", *The Kabir Book,* trans. Robert Bly (Boston: Beacon Press, 1971).

[3] The Heart Sutra (Sanskrit: *Prajñāpāramitā Hridaya*) is one of the best known Mahayana Buddhist scriptures. In part:

> *Form is no other than emptiness,*
> *emptiness no other than form.*
> *Form is emptiness, emptiness form.*
> *The same is true of feeling, thought, impulse and consciousness.*

CHAPTER 5
[1] T. S. Eliot, "The Waste Land," *The Waste Land* (New York: Boni and Liveright, 1922).

CHAPTER 6

[1] Judith Coates at Oakbridge University's website, www.oakbridge.org.

[2] Heather Cumming's website, www.healingquests.com.

CHAPTER 7

[1] The Findhorn Community, *The Findhorn Garden: Pioneering a New Vision of Man and Nature in Cooperation by the Findhorn Community* (New York: HarperCollins, 1976).

CHAPTER 8

[1] Heather Cumming and Karen Leffler, *John of God: The Brazilian Healer Who's Touched the Lives of Millions* (New York: Atria Books, May, 2007).

[2] John of God informational websites, www.meetjohnofgod.com and www.johnofgod.htm.

[3] Cumming and Leffler, *John of God*.

[4] Spiritism site based on the teachings of Allan Kardec, www.spiritistdoctrine.com.

[5] Emma Bragdon, *Spiritual Alliances: Discovering the Roots of Health at the Casa de Dom Inácio* (Woodstock, VT: Lightening Up Press, February 2002), 16.

[6] Ibid., 18.

[7] Some information on this and other saints was drawn from Richard P. McBrien, *Lives of the Saints: From Mary and St. Francis of Assisi to John XXIII and Mother Teresa* (San Francisco: HarperOne, 2001).

[8] Rev. Joseph Sicardo, *St. Rita of Cascia: Saint of the Impossible* (Rockford, IL: TAN Books, Inc.).

CHAPTER 9

[1] James Randi Educational Foundation, www.randi.org/jr/021805a.html.

CHAPTER 11

[1] As described in Chapter 10.

CHAPTER 12

[1] For the full content of this and other talks from Aaron on karma see www.deepspring.org archives, and insert "karma" as search topic.

INTERVAL III
[1] From Barbara Brodsky and John Orr, taken from retreat instructions.

CHAPTER 13
[1] As partially recounted in Chapter 5.

INTERVAL IV
[1] Many of the terms in this chapter were originated by Ken Wilber and Jean Gebser in their various writings on consciousness.

[2] Deep Spring Center website, http://archives.deepspring.org/Aaron/ EveningwAaron/2004/November172004.php.

[3] Shabkar, Jatang Tsogdruk Rangrol, *Flight of the Garuda,* trans. by Erik Pema Kunsang (Kathmandu, Nepal: Rangjung Yeshe Publications, 1988). Restricted Tibetan publication. Other translations are readily available.

CHAPTER 15
[1] Mary Swander, *The Desert Pilgrim: En Route to Mysticism and Miracles* (New York, NY: Viking Compass, 2003), 270–271.

CHAPTER 16
[1] Emerald Isle Retreat: Tuesday May 2, 2006. See archives.deepspring.org/Aaron/Retreats/2006/May22006.php.

INTERVAL V
[1] A classic book on mediumship is Allan Kardec, *The Mediums' Book,* 1876, reissued as *The Book on Mediums: Guide for Mediums and Invocators* (Newburyport, MA: RedWheel/Weiser, January 2008).

[2] For more about challenging and other aspects of mediumship, see Carla Rueckert, *A Channeling Handbook* (Louisville, KY: L/L Research, 1987).

CHAPTER 17
[1] See entire talk at archives.deepspring.org/Aaron/Retreats/2007/April222007.php.

[2] The Metta Sutta or Sutra on Loving Kindness, in the Buddhist tradition, has these words: "Even as a mother protects with her life her child, her only child. ..."
More of the Sutra is in the glossary.

[3] "All beings, one body. ..." Part of the Bodhisattva vow, the statement of intention to seek liberation for all beings. One version reads:

All beings, one body, I vow to liberate.
Endless blind passions I vow to uproot.
Dharma gates without number I vow to penetrate.
The great way of the Awakened Ones I vow to attain.

CHAPTER 21

[1] Matthew 28: 5–7.

[2] Bob Dinga: for his full story, see his website at www.miraclesofjohnofgod.com/why.htm.

[3] Friends of the Casa de Dom Inacio website: www.friendsofthecasa.info.

[4] This visit the Entities had invited me to become a Casa guide. See the website www.vipassanahealing.com.

[5] Breathe Ann Arbor website: www.breatheannarbor.com.

GLOSSARY

[1] Samyutta Nikaya, "Karaniya Metta Sutta: The Discourse on Loving-Kindness," *Pali Canon,* Sn1:8.

Index